California Evidence

EXAMPLES&EXPLANATIONS

California Evidence

Chris Chambers Goodman
Professor of Law
Pepperdine University School of Law

Wolters Kluwer
Law & Business

AUSTIN   BOSTON   CHICAGO   NEW YORK   THE NETHERLANDS

Aspen Publishers
Attn: Permissions Department
76 Ninth Avenue, 7th Floor
New York, NY 10011-5201

To contact Customer Care, e-mail customer.service@aspenpublishers.com, call 1-800-234-1660, fax 1-800-901-9075, or mail correspondence to:

Aspen Publishers
Attn: Order Department
PO Box 990
Frederick, MD 21705

Printed in the United States of America.

1 2 3 4 5 6 7 8 9 0

ISBN 978-0-7355-8495-2

Library of Congress Cataloging-in-Publication Data

Goodman, Chris Chambers, 1966-
    California evidence : examples & explanations / Chris Chambers Goodman.
        p. cm.
    Includes bibliographical references and index.
    ISBN 978-0-7355-8495-2 (alk. paper)
    1. Evidence (Law) — California. I.   Title.

KFC1030.G66 2010
347.794'06 — dc22

                                                                    2010041174

About Wolters Kluwer Law & Business

Wolters Kluwer Law & Business is a leading provider of research information and workflow solutions in key specialty areas. The strengths of the individual brands of Aspen Publishers, CCH, Kluwer Law International and Loislaw are aligned within Wolters Kluwer Law & Business to provide comprehensive, in-depth solutions and expert-authored content for the legal, professional and education markets.

CCH was founded in 1913 and has served more than four generations of business professionals and their clients. The CCH products in the Wolters Kluwer Law & Business group are highly regarded electronic and print resources for legal, securities, antitrust and trade regulation, government contracting, banking, pension, payroll, employment and labor, and healthcare reimbursement and compliance professionals.

Aspen Publishers is a leading information provider for attorneys, business professionals and law students. Written by preeminent authorities, Aspen products offer analytical and practical information in a range of specialty practice areas from securities law and intellectual property to mergers and acquisitions and pension/benefits. Aspen's trusted legal education resources provide professors and students with high-quality, up-to-date and effective resources for successful instruction and study in all areas of the law.

Kluwer Law International supplies the global business community with comprehensive English-language international legal information. Legal practitioners, corporate counsel and business executives around the world rely on the Kluwer Law International journals, loose-leafs, books and electronic products for authoritative information in many areas of international legal practice.

Loislaw is a premier provider of digitized legal content to small law firm practitioners of various specializations. Loislaw provides attorneys with the ability to quickly and efficiently find the necessary legal information they need, when and where they need it, by facilitating access to primary law as well as state-specific law, records, forms and treatises.

Wolters Kluwer Law & Business, a unit of Wolters Kluwer, is headquartered in New York and Riverwoods, Illinois. Wolters Kluwer is a leading multinational publisher and information services company.

To Marc, Alex, and Max

Summary of Contents

Contents   *xi*

Preface   *xxiii*

Acknowledgments   *xxv*

Chapter 1 Introduction to Evidence, Relevance, and Prejudice   1

Chapter 2 The Character Evidence Exclusion Rules   23

Chapter 3 Other Policy Exclusions for Relevant Evidence   75

Chapter 4 The Hearsay Rule   95

Chapter 5 The Confrontation Clause and Hearsay Exceptions Triggered by Unavailability   119

Chapter 6 Hearsay Exceptions: Party Admissions and Prior Statements of Witnesses   163

Chapter 7 Other Hearsay Exceptions   201

Chapter 8 Witness Testimony Foundations   233

Chapter 9 Opinion Testimony: Lay and Expert   267

Chapter 10 The Burden of Proof, Presumptions, and Judicial Notice   301

Chapter 11 Authentication and the Secondary Evidence Rule   325

Chapter 12 Introduction to Privileges; Professional Relationship Privileges   347

Chapter 13 Personal, Relationship, Counseling, and Other Privileges   383

Appendix of Selected Sections of the California Evidence Code   415

Table of Hearsay Exceptions with Crossover to the Federal Rules of Evidence   461

Index   465

Contents

Preface   *xxiii*
Acknowledgments   *xxv*

Chapter 1   **Introduction to Evidence, Relevance, and
                 Prejudice**   1

The Role of the Lawyers and the Judge   2
Is the Evidence Relevant?   3
When the Answer to the Question of Relevance
  Is "Maybe:" The Doctrine of Conditional Relevance   5
    Establishing Conditional Relevance   6
When Is the Evidence Irrelevant?   7
Objecting to Improper Evidence   8
Objections Overruled and the Doctrine of Limited
  Admissibility   10
After the Relevance Analysis: Other Reasons to Exclude
  Relevant Evidence   10
    Federal Rules of Evidence Compared:
      No Significant Difference   12
      Examples & Explanations   12
The Balancing Test: Probative Value vs. Prejudicial Effect   14
  What Is the Probative Value of the Evidence?   15
  Factors in Evaluating Prejudicial Effect   17
  Balancing the Weight of the Probative Value and
    the Prejudicial Effect   18
  Federal Rules of Evidence Compared: No
    Significant Difference   19
    Examples & Explanations   19

Chapter 2   **The Character Evidence Exclusion Rules**   23

Dangers of Character Evidence   24
Using Character Evidence   25
  The First Purpose: To Prove Character Itself
    When Character Is at Issue   26
  The Second Purpose: Circumstantial Use of Character
    Evidence to Prove Conduct in Conformity   27

Contents

Federal Rules of Evidence Compared: No
    Substantial Differences   28
The Third Purpose: To Prove Something Other
    Than Character or Conduct in Conformity   28
Federal Rules of Evidence Compared: Notable
    Difference   33
The Three Basic Kinds of Character Evidence   34
    Opinion Evidence   34
    Reputation Evidence   34
    Specific Instances of Conduct   35
    Federal Rules of Evidence Compared: No
        Notable Difference   38
Habit Evidence   38
    Federal Rules of Evidence Compared: No
        Notable Differences   39
        Examples & Explanations   39
Exceptions to the Character Evidence Ban   44
    Criminal Defendant's Character to Prove Conduct:
        CEC 1102   45
    Federal Rules of Evidence Compared:
        Notable Differences   48
    Other Sexual Offenses by the Criminal Defendant:
        CEC 1108   48
    Federal Rules of Evidence Compared: Minor
        Differences   51
    Other Crimes of Domestic Violence by the Criminal
        Defendant: CEC 1109   51
    Federal Rules of Evidence Compared: Notable
        Differences   53
        Examples & Explanations   53
    The Character of the Victim Exceptions: CEC 1103   57
    Federal Rules of Evidence Compared: Notable
        Differences   59
    The Victim's Character in Sexual Offenses:
        CEC 1103(c)   61
    Federal Rules of Evidence Compared: Notable
        Differences   62
    The Character of the Victim in Civil Cases Alleging
        Sexual Abuse: CEC 1106   63
    Note on the Truth in Evidence Provision
        (Proposition 8)   64
    Federal Rules of Evidence Compared: Notable
        Differences   64
        Examples & Explanations   65

Chapter 3   Other Policy Exclusions for Relevant Evidence   75

Subsequent Remedial Conduct   76
   Illustrations of Which Measures the Rule Excludes   77
   Federal Rules of Evidence Compared: One
     Notable Difference   77
Offers to Compromise   78
   Humanitarian Offers   79
   What Is Not Protected from Disclosure   80
   Federal Rules of Evidence Compared:
     Notable Differences   81
Offers to Plead Guilty   81
   Federal Rules of Evidence Compared:
     Notable Differences   82
Liability Insurance   83
   Federal Rules of Evidence Compared:
     Notable Difference   84
Expressions of Sympathy and Benevolence   84
   Federal Rules of Evidence Compared: One
     Notable Difference   85
Mediation Provisions   85
Other Less Frequently Used Policy Exclusions   86
   Evidence to Test a Verdict   86
   Records of Medical or Dental Study of
     In-Hospital Staff Committee   86
   Records of Medical and Psychiatric Studies
     of Quality Assurance Committees   87
   Proceeding or Records of Organized Committees
     on Quality of Care   87
   Animal Experimentation in Products Liability Actions   87
     Examples & Explanations   88

Chapter 4   The Hearsay Rule   95

The Rationale for Excluding Hearsay   96
   Illustrating the Decrease in Reliability with Hearsay   98
The Hearsay Analysis   99
   1. Is this a Statement?   99
   2. Was the Statement Made Out of this Court's
     Hearing?   102
   3. What Is the Statement Being Offered to Prove?   103
Options for Admitting Statements that May
  Constitute Hearsay   105

Call the Declarant to Testify in Court 105
Show that the Statement Does Not Meet the
  Three Elements of Hearsay 106
Determine Whether the Statement Satisfies a
  Hearsay Exception 106
Common Non-truth Purposes 107
  To Prove Consciousness 107
  To Prove Notice 107
  To Explain Subsequent Conduct/Effect on Listener 108
  To Prove Further Action Required 108
  To Prove Facts Under Substantive Law 109
  To Prove Relevant Knowledge 110
  To Prove Indirect State of Mind or Emotion 110
  To Impeach a Witness 111
  Limitations on Use for Non-truth Purposes 111
  Federal Rules of Evidence Compared:
    Notable Differences 112
    Examples & Explanations 112

Chapter 5   The Confrontation Clause and Hearsay Exceptions Triggered by Unavailability   119

The Confrontation Clause 120
  When Hearsay Declarants Are Not Physically
    Present at Trial 121
Modern History of Confrontation 122
  Indicia of Reliability 122
  Firmly Rooted Hearsay Exceptions 122
  Particularized Guarantees of Inherent Trustworthiness 123
  The Current Standard: Only Testimonial Statements
    Implicate the Confrontation Clause 123
Determining Whether a Statement Is Testimonial 125
  Statements to Police Officers and Emergency
    Personnel 126
  Statements in Law Enforcement Reports 127
Satisfying the Confrontation Clause When a Statement
  Is Testimonial 128
  Federal Rules of Evidence Compared: No
    Significant Difference 129
Determining Whether a Declarant Is Unavailable 129
  Privilege 131
  Disqualified 131
  Dead or Mentally or Physically Ill 131
  Absent When the Court Is Unable to Compel
    Attendance 132

Absent Despite Reasonable Efforts to Get the
Witness into Court   132
Summary of *Unavailability*   133
Federal Rules of Evidence Compared: No
Significant Difference   134
Hearsay Exceptions that Apply Only When the Declarant
Is Unavailable   134
Declarations Against Interest   134
Federal Rules of Evidence Compared:
Notable Differences   137
Dying Declarations   138
Federal Rules of Evidence Compared:
Notable Differences   140
Previously Existing State of Mind   140
Federal Rules of Evidence Compared:
Notable Differences   141
Declarations Relating to Wills and Estates   142
Federal Rules of Evidence Compared:
Minor Differences   142
Hearsay Exceptions for Former Testimony   143
Federal Rules of Evidence Compared:
Notable Differences   149
Other Limited Exceptions   149
Procurement or Wrongdoing by the Proponent   149
Prior Statements of Deceased Declarant   151
Unavailability Due to Homicide or Kidnapping   151
Statements of Threats   152
Other Limited Exceptions   152
Federal Rules of Evidence Compared:
Notable Differences   153
Forfeiture and the Confrontation Clause   153
Examples & Explanations   153

Chapter 6   Hearsay Exceptions: Party Admissions and Prior Statements of Witnesses   163

Admissions as Exceptions to the Hearsay Rule   164
Any Statement Can Be an Admission   165
Federal Rules of Evidence Compared:
Notable Difference   167
Adoptive Admissions   167
Express, Implied and Tacit Adoption   169
Federal Rules of Evidence Compared: No
Significant Difference   170

Authorized Admissions   170
    Federal Rules of Evidence Compared:
      Notable Differences   172
Co-Conspirators' Admissions   172
    Federal Rules of Evidence Compared:
      Notable Differences   175
Discretion in the Order of Proof   175
    Examples & Explanations   176
Other Exceptions to the Hearsay Rule: Prior Statements
  of Witnesses   183
    Prior Inconsistent Statements   183
    Federal Rules of Evidence Compared:
      Notable Differences   184
    Prior Consistent Statements   185
    Federal Rules of Evidence Compared: No
      Significant Differences   188
    Refreshing Recollection   188
    Past Recollection Recorded   189
    Federal Rules of Evidence Compared: No
      Significant Differences   191
    Statements of Identification   192
    Federal Rules of Evidence Compared:
      Minor Differences   193
      Examples & Explanations   193

Chapter 7   **Other Hearsay Exceptions**   **201**

Spontaneous Statements   202
    The Standards for Determining Whether the
      Elements Are Met   204
    The Rationale for this Exception   204
    Federal Rules of Evidence Compared:
      Notable Differences   205
Contemporaneous Statements   205
    The Standards for Determining Whether the
      Elements Are Met   206
    The Rationale for this Exception   206
    Federal Rules of Evidence Compared:
      Substantive Differences   207
State of Mind Declarations   207
    Indirect State of Mind Is Non-hearsay   207
    Direct State of Mind Requires a Hearsay Exception   208
    Determining Whether the Content of the Statement
      Involves Declarant's State of Mind   209

The Timing Element of the Statement: *Then Existing*   210
Using the Statement to Prove Subsequent Conduct   210
The Trustworthiness Element   211
Federal Rules of Evidence Compared:
    Substantive Differences   211
Multiple Levels of Hearsay   211
Some Less Common Hearsay Exceptions   212
    Examples & Explanations   213
Hearsay Exceptions for Documents   220
Business Records   221
The Elements of the Hearsay Exception for
    Business Records   222
Federal Rules of Evidence Compared:
    Notable Differences   224
The Absence of an Entry   224
Records by a Public Employee   225
Public Employee Records in Criminal Cases   227
    Absence of an Entry in Public Employee Records   228
Federal Rules of Evidence Compared:
    Notable Differences   228
    Examples & Explanations   228

Chapter 8   Witness Testimony Foundations   233

Witness Competency   234
    Truth-Telling   235
    Personal Knowledge   236
    Translators   237
Federal Rules of Evidence Compared:
    Minor Differences   238
Judges as Witnesses   238
Jurors as Witnesses   239
Federal Rules of Evidence Compared:
    Substantive Differences   240
    Examples & Explanations   240
Questioning Witnesses: Direct, Cross-, and Redirect
Examinations   244
    The Types of Witness Examinations   244
    The Order of Witness Examinations   244
    Using Leading Questions in Witness Examinations   245
Federal Rules of Evidence Compared:
    Minor Differences   246
Impeaching and Supporting Credibility   246
    Civil Cases: CEC 786, 787, and 790   251

Criminal Cases: Proposition 8/The Truth in
    Evidence Provision   255
Federal Rules of Evidence Compared: Substantive
    Differences   256
Limitations on Credibility Attacks: Religious Beliefs,
    Sexual History, and Hypnosis   259
    Federal Rules of Evidence Compared: Substantive
        Differences   260
        Examples & Explanations   261

Chapter 9   Opinion Testimony: Lay and Expert   267

Lay Opinions   268
    Opinion Rationally Based on the Witness's Perception   269
    Opinion Helpful to the Trier of Fact   270
Expert Opinions   270
The Basis for the Expert Opinion and the
    Reasonable Reliance Test   272
    Using Hypothetical Questions with Experts   274
    Using Inadmissible Information with Experts   274
    Federal Rules of Evidence Compared:
        Minor Differences   275
Qualifying the Expert   276
Cross-Examining the Expert   277
    Examining the Basis for the Expert Opinion   278
    Examining Bias and Other Interests   279
    Federal Rules of Evidence Compared:
        Some Substantive Differences   279
        Examples & Explanations   280
The Kelly Test for New Scientific Techniques and
    Procedures: General Acceptance   281
    Examples of the Misleading Aura of Infallability   282
    How to Satisfy *Kelly*   283
    Choosing the Right Test: *Kelly* or Reasonable
        Reliance?   284
    Federal Rules of Evidence Compared:
        Substantive Differences   286
Expert Opinions Allowed on Ultimate Factual Issues
    but Not Legal Issues   286
    Federal Rules of Evidence Compared:
        Minor Differences   288
Court-Appointed Experts: CEC 730–733   288
    Federal Rules of Evidence Compared:
        Minor Differences   289

Expert Opinions on Specific Issues: CEC 810–824   289
The Intimate Partner Battering Exception: CEC 1107   290
     Examples & Explanations   291

Chapter 10 **The Burden of Proof, Presumptions, and Judicial Notice**   **301**

The Burden of Proof   302
The Burden of Producing Evidence   304
     Examples & Explanations   307
Presumptions and Inferences   308
     Conclusive Presumptions   309
     Rebuttable Presumptions   310
     Presumptions in Criminal Cases   313
     Federal Rules of Evidence Compared:
       Substantive Differences   314
       Examples & Explanations   314
Judicial Notice: CEC 450–460   319
     Mandatory Judicial Notice   319
     Permissive Judicial Notice   320
     Determining Whether Judicial Notice Is Appropriate   320
     Denying Judicial Notice   321
     Federal Rules of Evidence Compared:
       Substantive Differences   322
       Examples & Explanations   322

Chapter 11 **Authentication and the Secondary Evidence Rule**   **325**

Authentication   326
     What Is a *Writing?*   327
     Methods of Authentication   327
     Federal Rules of Evidence Compared:
       Minor Differences   331
       Examples & Explanations   331
The Secondary Evidence Rule   334
     Types of Secondary Evidence   335
     When the Secondary Evidence Rule
     Does Not Apply   340
     Presumptions for Proving Content   340
Putting It All Together: Meeting the Authentication
and Secondary Evidence Requirements   341
     Federal Rules of Evidence Compared:
       Minor Differences   342

Contents

The Completeness Doctrine 342
    Federal Rules of Evidence Compared: Substantive
    Differences 343
        Examples & Explanations 343

Chapter 12   **Introduction to Privileges; Professional
Relationship Privileges**   **347**

The General Approach to Analyzing Privileges 348
Ruling on Claims of Privilege 350
    Federal Rules of Evidence Compared: No
    Corresponding FRE 352
The Attorney-Client Privilege: CEC 950–962 352
    The Lawyer 352
    The Client 353
    Confidential Communications 354
    Claiming the Privilege 357
    Waiver and Disclosures 357
    Exceptions to the Attorney-Client Privilege:
    CEC 956–962 358
    Federal Rules of Evidence Compared:
    Notable Differences 361
        Examples & Explanations 362
The Physician-Patient Privilege: CEC 990–1007 368
    Exceptions to the Physician-Patient Privilege 369
    Federal Rules of Evidence Compared: No
    Corresponding FRE 370
        Examples & Explanations 370
The Psychotherapist-Patient Privilege: CEC 1010–1027 372
    Exceptions to the Psychotherapist-Patient Privilege 374
    Federal Rules of Evidence Compared:
    No Corresponding FRE 376
        Examples & Explanations 379

Chapter 13   **Personal, Relationship, Counseling, and
Other Privileges**   **383**

Privilege Against Self-Incrimination 384
    Federal Rules of Evidence Compared: No Difference 387
        Examples & Explanations 387
Spousal Testimonial Privileges 389
    Privilege to Decline to Testify Against Your Spouse 389
    Privilege When Your Spouse Is a Party 390
    Waiving the Spousal Testimonial Privileges 391

Contents

Exceptions	393
Federal Rules of Evidence Compared:	
No Corresponding FRE	394
Confidential Marital Communications Privilege	395
A Spouse Whether or Not a Party	395
Has a Privilege During the Marital Relationship and Afterward	396
To Refuse to Disclose and to Prevent Another from Disclosing	396
A Communication Made in Confidence	396
Between One Spouse and the Other Spouse While They Were Husband and Wife	397
Holder and Waiver	397
Exceptions	398
Federal Rules of Evidence Compared:	
No Corresponding FRE	399
Examples & Explanations	399
The Clergy-Penitent Privileges	402
Waiver	403
Examples & Explanations	404
Other Less Common Privileges	406
Sexual Assault Victim-Counselor Privilege	406
Domestic Violence Victim-Counselor Privilege	407
Human Trafficking Caseworker-Victim Privilege	407
Official Information and Identity of Informer Privilege	407
Political Vote Privilege	409
Trade Secrets Privilege	409
Newspaper Immunity Privilege	409
Examples & Explanations	411
Appendix of Selected Sections of the California Evidence Code	415
Table of Hearsay Exceptions with Crossover to the Federal Rules of Evidence	461
Index	465

Preface

In technical classes like evidence, students are understandably looking for some extra assistance with understanding the material. The Federal Rules of Evidence (FRE) are explained in numerous student supplements (including an excellent work in the *Examples and Explanations* series). But until the year I began working on this project, no texts had been written to help students understand the California Evidence Code (CEC). This book, the first comprehensive student supplement focused on the CEC, responds to the increasing number of student requests for this type of guide. It provides an easy-to-read analysis of the various CEC provisions, and then gives examples and explanations to illustrate the practical and theoretical applications of those code provisions.

Evidence is a required course in many law schools, or it becomes a de facto requirement because it is tested on the Multi-State Bar Examination, as well as in the essay portion of the bar examination for numerous states. The law of evidence is the study of what information can and will be presented to the trier of fact to reach decisions at trial. The evidence laws also cover which types of evidence can be used to prove certain types of claims and defenses. For those who want to be litigators in civil or criminal courts, knowledge of evidence law is a critically important tool to competently represent clients' interests in any litigation matter.

Not all law students want to be litigators, of course. But knowing the laws of evidence is useful in other legal practice areas as well. Contract attorneys, for instance, need to know how to draft agreements that will survive an opposing party's objections if the matter ends up in litigation. Those who plan to take a state bar examination will need to understand evidence law for both the multiple choice and essay components of that exam. Even for those who do not plan to practice law, knowing evidence law is useful when friends and family members ask for explanations of high-profile cases in the media.

In 1965, California adopted its own Evidence Code, which was modeled in part after the Uniform Rules from the 1950s. The CEC was designed to provide a more complete, organized, and accurate codification of existing California case law on evidentiary issues. The FRE were adopted and approved by Congress in the early 1970s and took effect a few years later. In many areas, the CEC is similar to the FRE, but there are notable and important distinctions.

Students who wish to practice in the California state courts will need a strong working knowledge of the CEC, but the code is given scant attention in many evidence courses. Now that California evidence is tested on the California bar examination, however, some California law schools have begun offering courses that focus on the CEC, as an alternative or a supplement to existing courses that cover the FRE. Others still offer the standard FRE course because all students will need to know the FRE for the multi-state portion of the bar examination and because some will practice in federal courts.

This book follows the approach of many evidence professors and evidence textbooks, which is to begin with relevance and then consider character evidence (Chapter 2) and other policy reasons for excluding relevant evidence (Chapter 3). Chapters 4 through 7 address the Hearsay Rule and its many exceptions. Chapter 8 explains the foundations of witness testimony and impeachment, and Chapter 9 covers the opinion rules for lay and expert witnesses. Presumptions, burdens of proof, and judicial notice are covered in Chapter 10, and Chapter 11 explains the authentication requirement and the Secondary Evidence Rule. Chapters 12 and 13 conclude the book with a discussion of privileges. Throughout the book, these concepts are reinforced through examples and explanations based on real-world appellate court decisions.

This book also notes important and substantive distinctions between the CEC and the FRE in a separate section at the conclusion of each topic, as well as through the divergent outcomes detailed in the Examples and Explanations sections of each chapter. Minor variations and details of the FRE are beyond the scope of this work given the numerous FRE supplements currently available.

All CEC sections that are discussed at length appear as excerpts in the text; these excerpts appear with an icon so that students can quickly identify them as they skim the text. Other CEC sections mentioned but not discussed in detail are included in the appendix.

This book gives tools to identify objectionable evidence, analyze potential objections, and choose the most appropriate or strongest objections to present to the court. Students should take advantage of opportunities to get hands-on experience making and meeting objections because that is the best way to learn evidence law. Practicing attorneys develop their skills by using the laws of evidence, especially those governing objections. Simply reading about how to make objections is not enough.

This book also teaches students how to anticipate potential objections from opposing parties, how to offer the evidence in ways that are less likely to draw or sustain objections, and thus how to get the evidence they need admitted at trial. Many evidence issues can be argued either way, meaning that clear answers are not always available when it comes to admitting evidence. However, some issues will have a clear answer based on strict application of the evidence rules. Students should keep this in mind as they review.

Acknowledgments

This book is dedicated to my evidence students, who inspired me to write a supplement focusing on the California Evidence Code as a complement to the numerous study aids that cover the Federal Rules of Evidence. I thank my students for their comments on this work in progress, as I tested its explanations and approaches in the classroom laboratory. My former student Chumahan Bowen deserves special mention for creating one of the useful mnemonic devices explained in Chapter 2.

I want to thank the many research assistants who have helped to craft this study aid. The first was John Savage, who did some early research on the character evidence and impeachment materials; then came Sarah Wigdor, who did much of the case research that forms the foundation for many of the chapters; Rachel Rossi performed research and editing on an early draft and helped to create the icons and many flowcharts used in the text; Jen Clark and Linda Echegaray worked on the second and third round of revisions, doing follow-up research and editing. Aaron Moreno did research on the confrontation and privilege chapters and helped to make the draft even more accessible to students.

I also want to express my appreciation for the folks at Aspen Publishers, including Roberta O'Meara, my Aspen representative and the first person to approach me with the idea of writing a California evidence book; Lynn Churchill, who shepherded through the proposal and first draft chapter, and especially to my editor at Aspen, Jessica Barmack, who provided detailed comments, critiques, support, and encouragement at every stage of the process and really helped to fine-tune the manuscript. I thank all of the anonymous reviewers who provided invaluable feedback to the drafts, with particular mention of David Leonard, whose careful reading of the text provided a wealth of useful comments and suggestions with the utmost enthusiasm for a junior colleague in his field. I also wish to express my appreciation to Shoshana Robinson Shine for providing eleventh hour editing assistance on the introductory chapter.

I thank the faculty support personnel at Pepperdine University School of Law, ably led by Supervisor Candace Warren and assisted by Sophia Sipsas, who both provided substantial secretarial support for the various drafts and revisions of this project, and Senior Research and Student Services Librarian Donald Buffaloe, who provided reference and research assistance. The Pepperdine research assistance fund and the Dean's

Acknowledgments

Excellence Fund also provided invaluable financial support to my research assistants.

I could not have completed this project without the support of my friends Jen, Shosh, Suzy, and Maureen, and the patience and understanding of my son Alex and husband Marc.

September 2010

California Evidence

Introduction to Evidence, Relevance, and Prejudice

1

In life as well as in law, unsubstantiated thoughts or opinions do not carry much weight. Just making a point is not effective. To be effective, you need to prove that point.

When a professor asks about the reasoning in an appellate case, a good answer will not just state a reason for the decision but will show *how* the facts of the case apply to the rule and lead to that particular court holding. Similarly, in court, a prosecutor can *tell* the jury "the defendant committed the crime," but unless or until the prosecution provides proof to *show* that the defendant committed the crime, the defendant is innocent.

This is where the rules of evidence come in.

The substantive law tells you *what* you need to prove. Each crime and cause of action has elements that the prosecutor or plaintiff must prove. In criminal law you learned that the crime of first degree murder requires proving the killing of a human being with malice aforethought. In contracts, you learned that a plaintiff must prove the existence of the contract in order to establish its breach. Tort law tells you that to prevail in a negligence case, the plaintiff must prove duty, breach, causation, and damages.

Evidence law governs *how* to prove these substantive elements. The California Evidence Code (CEC) tells you what type of evidence you can use in certain types of cases, whether there are limitations on the format of the evidence, what evidence can be used at certain times in the case, and how much evidence you need to offer. Evidence laws have been developed to promote fairness in the trial process and also to limit the length and scope of trial, which serves the policy interest of "judicial economy."

THE ROLE OF THE LAWYERS AND THE JUDGE

The evidence rules operate in an adversarial system. The party seeking to offer evidence at trial is called the *proponent* of the evidence. The other side is called the *opponent*. The proponent has the burden of producing the evidence and of persuading the court that the evidence is admissible. The opponent has the responsibility to object and to make arguments against the admissibility of the evidence. As an advocate or attorney, your role is to focus on admitting the evidence that helps your client's case and excluding the evidence that harms your client's case.

In our adversarial system, you, the attorney, are charged with the task of proving the case for your client. You are responsible for presenting admissible evidence to prove that case, and you must be vigilant in making sure opposing counsel does not stray from the rules of evidence in her attempts to prove her case or disprove your client's case. If she does, it is your duty to object immediately. By objecting, you call to the judge's attention the transgressions of opposing counsel.

In the courtroom, the judge is not charged with the tasks of objecting on your client's behalf or arguing against the objections of your opposing counsel. That is the attorney's job. The judge's duties are to enforce the rules of evidence, to be fair and impartial, and to minimize time-wasting at trial. The attorney's role is to follow the rules of evidence and to object when opposing counsel fails to follow those rules. The attorney's duty is one of vigorous and competent representation. Take that duty seriously. Learn the rules of evidence. If you fail to follow the rules, opposing counsel will object. If you fail to object when opposing counsel does not follow the rules, no one else will object for your client.

After the lawyers have made their objections, offers of proof, and arguments, the judge will determine whether the evidence is admissible. She will consider the arguments for admitting the evidence as well as the arguments for excluding it, decide whether the objection is well founded, and then rule on admissibility.

If the evidence is admissible, then the judge *overrules* the objection and *admits* the evidence. If the evidence is not admissible, then the judge *sustains* the objection and *excludes* the evidence. Because some evidence is subject to multiple objections, a judge may overrule one objection and sustain another. In other cases, evidence may be objectionable if used for certain purposes, but not objectionable if used for other purposes. In that situation, the judge will find the evidence to be of *limited admissibility* and will prescribe the permissible and impermissible uses of that evidence at trial.

When evaluating evidentiary issues, we begin with the rule of relevance, and we end with whether relevant evidence should nevertheless be excluded because it is unduly prejudicial. In between these two ends of the evidence analysis spectrum, there are numerous other rules and potential objections to consider. Those rules are addressed in the remaining chapters of this book. The California Evidence Code sections are labeled "CEC."

The Text of the California Evidence Code

Whenever you see the icon above, the text of the California Evidence Code section will follow (with the headings supplied). The appendix includes the text of other CEC sections that are not quoted within the text.

IS THE EVIDENCE RELEVANT?

We begin the study of evidence with the basic general rule that evidence must be relevant in order to be admissible. This means that relevance is the very first item on the evidence checklist.

The first inquiry then is to determine what evidence is relevant. The statutory definition is in CEC 210. The general rule is that evidence is relevant if it rationally tends to prove or disprove any fact that matters in the litigation. The CEC favors liberal admissibility of evidence. It is easy to prove that evidence is relevant because the standard for proving relevance is *sufficiency*. This sufficiency standard means that as long as a reasonable juror *could* find the evidence to be useful in deciding the case, the evidence meets the sufficiency standard and is relevant.

CEC §350: Only relevant evidence admissible
No evidence is admissible except relevant evidence.
CEC §210: Relevant evidence defined
"Relevant evidence" means evidence, including evidence relevant to the credibility of a witness or hearsay declarant, having any tendency in reason to prove or disprove any disputed fact that is of consequence to the determination of the action.

"Tendency in reason to prove or disprove." To be relevant, the evidence must be a step along the path to proving a fact that matters in the case. A fact that matters is a fact that relates to an issue that needs to be decided in the case.

Issues that need to be decided are those that support or refute the claims or defenses of the parties in the litigation.

Proving a fact that matters is like building a path out of stepping stones; that path takes you to your destination, to the "fact that matters" in the case. If the path constitutes sufficient proof of the fact that matters in the litigation, you will reach your destination and prove the fact that matters. If a step is missing or if the path is incomplete, you will not be able to reach your destination along that path.

In the case of an auto accident, for instance, the trier of fact will need to determine who was at fault and the amount of damages. The fault determination will require proving such facts as which party had a red light, whether either party was speeding, and whether either party was distracted when the accident occurred. Each of these issues matters in the litigation and each constitutes a "path" to be built in the case. The path is built with evidence, and each item of evidence is a "step" along the path. Some of the steps for paths in an auto accident case would include testimony by an eyewitness about which car had the red light, evidence by the lab technician about the rate of speed to be inferred from the skid marks, and cell phone reports listing the date and time of calls made or received by the drivers near the time of the accident.

Although the definition of relevance states that the fact must be "a disputed fact that is of consequence," California courts are rather lenient in interpreting this phrase. The fact need not be an *ultimate* fact, which is the main issue to be decided (e.g., in this case the ultimate fact would be which driver was at fault). The fact can be something not specifically in dispute (which may occur when the parties admit that there was a collision). The fact simply must be information that helps the jury to make a logical deduction about something that matters in the case (such as a cell phone found on the floor of one of the cars after the collision). As long as the fact can help the jury toward reaching a decision in the case, it will satisfy the "disputed fact that is of consequence" component of the relevance requirement.

Each item of evidence is a "step." A step can be large or small. Some paths will require dozens of steps (using the physics and mathematical principles to establish the rate of speed based on skid marks), and other paths may need only one or two steps (such as the eyewitness who says the light was red) to prove the fact that matters. If the step is a part of a "path," then that step is relevant under the CEC. Every step in a path is relevant.

Some steps of evidence may be irrelevant to one path but relevant to another path. For instance, in the automobile accident case, the parties might not agree as to whether a taxicab was parked on the side of the road near the accident site. One witness will testify that a yellow taxicab was parked on the side of the road, and another witness will testify that it was not. If the taxicab was not involved in the accident and the taxi driver was not a witness to the accident, then whether a taxicab was parked on the side of the road does not matter in terms of deciding which driver is liable for the auto accident.

The taxicab is not a step along the path to proving which driver ran the red traffic light, and the testimony about its presence is irrelevant to liability.

However, knowing whether a taxicab was parked near the accident scene might help the fact finder decide which witness has a more reliable memory of the collision — the witness who saw the taxicab (if indeed there was a taxicab there) or the witness who did not see a taxicab (because there was none). Thus, the taxicab evidence will be a step along the path toward proving which witness's account is more reliable. The path of witness reliability will help the jury to decide the ultimate issue of which driver is liable for the collision.

Credibility is always relevant. Notice that the language of CEC 210 includes a reference to witness credibility. The credibility of witnesses (people who testify at trial, in a deposition, or at a hearing prior to trial) is always relevant. Thus the credibility of a witness's testimony is a path that will be built in every case. Every fact that affects credibility is a step along that path, and thus every credibility fact is relevant. (Chapter 8 discusses witness credibility issues in more detail.)

WHEN THE ANSWER TO THE QUESTION OF RELEVANCE IS "MAYBE:" THE DOCTRINE OF CONDITIONAL RELEVANCE

When asking whether an item of evidence is a step on a particular path, sometimes the answer is "maybe." For instance, if the "path" is whether the brake pads were worn down on one of the cars at the time of the collision, then "steps" used to build that path would include

- evidence about when the brakes were last checked;
- when the brakes were last replaced;
- the number of miles driven since the last brake check or repair; and
- whether the brake warning light was illuminated at or near the time of the collision.

Suppose a mechanic will testify that he checked the brakes on a car. A reasonable juror could find that the mechanic's testimony would be a step along the path because that evidence will help to prove or disprove whether the brakes were faulty. What if instead the mechanic testifies that he examined the brakes on a green Toyota? If the green Toyota that the mechanic examined is one of the cars involved in the collision, then the evidence will be relevant. If however, the collision involved a Honda and a Lincoln, then the mechanic's testimony does not help to build a path that matters in this case.

Because the judge needs to know whether the mechanic examined a car that was involved in the collision before deciding whether the mechanic's testimony is relevant, the mechanic's testimony is conditionally relevant. *Conditional relevance* means that an item of evidence will be found to be relevant only after a condition has been satisfied. In this case, after evidence is presented to show that the mechanic inspected the Toyota that was involved in the collision, then the mechanic's testimony about that inspection will be relevant.

Oftentimes, the attorney can simply ask the witness whether he inspected a car and whether that car was involved in a collision, and then she can ask about the results of that inspection. In many cases, however, the mechanic will not be able to testify about the collision because he did not witness the collision and has no personal knowledge that the collision occurred. (Chapter 8 discusses the personal knowledge requirement.) The attorney needs to find another witness who will testify that a green Toyota with a certain license plate or vehicle identification number was involved in the collision. Then, the mechanic's testimony about examining that green Toyota will be relevant.

Establishing Conditional Relevance

Establishing the relevance of this evidence becomes an issue of whether the mechanic or the witness who saw the green car involved in the collision should testify first. Each has preliminary information to help the judge decide the relevance of the evidence the proponent seeks to offer. For instance, the witness saw the cars at the moment of the collision and can testify about which car braked or failed to brake in time. The mechanic can testify about which car may have had faulty brakes and who brought that car in for service. To prove that the defendant had faulty brakes on the car he was driving and that those faulty brakes led to the collision, the plaintiff will need to show that the defendant was driving the car, that the car had faulty brakes, and that the brakes caused the collision. The witness can testify about who was driving the car, but not about whether the brakes were faulty. The mechanic can testify about who brought the car in for service and whether the brakes were faulty, but he cannot testify about who was driving the car at the time of the collision.

The two people cannot testify simultaneously, and without the doctrine of conditional relevance the witness and the mechanic would have to alternate presenting evidence in court. First, counsel would ask a few questions of the witness to establish the license plate number of the green car that was involved in the collision, and then counsel would call the mechanic to testify that he fixed the brakes on a green car with that license plate number. This testimony would establish that the green car is relevant to the lawsuit. Next, counsel would have to call the witness again to finish describing what occurred during the accident and then call the mechanic to explain how the faulty brakes might account for the witness's description of what occurred leading up to the collision. The calling and re-calling of witnesses wastes court time.

The doctrine of conditional relevance permits the mechanic to testify about the condition of the brakes on the green Toyota before the witness testifies that the green Toyota was involved in the collision. The brakes evidence is conditionally relevant if the brakes belong to one of the cars involved in the collision. Once the witness testifies that the green Toyota was involved in the collision, the condition has been satisfied and the evidence is relevant.

WHEN IS THE EVIDENCE IRRELEVANT?

Examine the issues in the case to determine whether evidence is irrelevant. For instance, in a case about whether the defendant took money from a cash register at the corner market, the color of the store clerk's eyes would be irrelevant information. If one side tries to offer testimony about the color of the clerk's eyes and the opposing party objects, the judge should sustain that objection and exclude the evidence about eye color. The eye color of the clerk would not be considered a step along the path toward identifying the robber. It tells us nothing about who the robber is — it leads us nowhere. On the other hand, information about the eye color of the robber would be relevant because, depending on whether his eye color matches the description, that eye color evidence helps to prove or disprove that the defendant was the robber.

If the evidence is not relevant, then the evidence is not admissible. Allowing irrelevant evidence at trial would waste the court's time and could be unfair to the parties if the jury uses the irrelevant information to reach a decision. For instance, if the mechanic in the auto accident case testified that he fixed the brakes on a red Toyota just after the collision, the jurors might use that information to conclude that because many Toyotas have faulty brakes, the green Toyota in this case must have had faulty brakes as well. If there is no evidence of Toyota brake problems generally, then the information about the brakes on a red Toyota would be irrelevant in this case. It is not a step along a path that needs to be proven in this litigation. The opponent should object on the grounds that the evidence is irrelevant, and the judge should sustain the objection and exclude any and all irrelevant evidence.

When an item of evidence is admitted as conditionally relevant, as discussed in the previous section, the proponent must be sure to offer the supporting evidence to satisfy the condition. For instance, if the witness in the auto accident case never testifies that the green Toyota was involved in the collision, then the condition will not be satisfied. When a condition is not satisfied, the evidence is not relevant. Evidence that is not relevant is not admissible. In this case, however, because the evidence already has been heard by the jury, the opposing party must make a motion to strike, which is discussed in the next section.

OBJECTING TO IMPROPER EVIDENCE

Throughout the trial process, there are opportunities to present and object to the admission of evidence. The attorney has a duty to diligently and competently represent her client by presenting the evidence needed to prove the client's claims or defenses. That duty includes objecting when someone seeks to offer improper evidence in the case.

Decide whether you should object. In deciding whether to make an objection, think about the case from the perspective of the judge who will be ruling on your objection. Is this objection consistent with the evidence rules? Does this objection help to promote fairness? Will this objection help to keep the trial properly focused? Review the grounds for the objection and make your decision. CEC 353 explains why it is important to object to improper evidence.

CEC §353: Erroneous admission of evidence; effect
A verdict or finding shall not be set aside, nor shall the judgment or decision based thereon be reversed, by reason of the erroneous admission of evidence unless:

(a) There appears of record an objection to or a motion to exclude or to strike the evidence that was timely made and so stated as to make clear the specific ground of the objection or motion; and

(b) The court which passes upon the effect of the error or errors is of the opinion that the admitted evidence should have been excluded on the ground stated and that the error or errors complained of resulted in a miscarriage of justice.

Note: CEC 354 applies a similar requirement for an error that prevents proper evidence from being presented to the trier of fact.

State the objection clearly and quickly. Object in a timely manner, such as immediately after the question is asked, not after the witness has answered. Sometimes the witness will answer the question before you can make an objection, for instance, when an attorney asks a question that you do not think will bring out objectionable information. In that case, when you do object, also make a *motion to strike* the answer. If the judge sustains your objection and grants your motion to strike, then that answer will no longer be evidence in the case. When objecting, be sure to make all the arguments that apply because only a timely and proper objection can form that basis for a later appeal. If a ground for objection is missed at trial, it cannot be raised on appeal unless it involves plain error.

Objecting on the grounds of irrelevance. Because the relevance standard is so low and most items of evidence can constitute a "step," judges rarely sustain an objection on the grounds of relevance. If, however, the proponent asks a question and there are no possible circumstances under which the answer to that question could be a step along a path that matters in the litigation, it is appropriate for the opponent to object that the material is irrelevant.

In some cases, the relevance question is a closer call. Imagine that a lawyer asks a witness whether she has a family. Sometimes the lawyer asks this type of question as a form of "small talk," which gives the witness a chance to loosen up before answering the more difficult questions. If increasing the comfort level is the only reason the lawyer is asking the question about a family, then the question is not relevant to proving or disproving a fact that matters in the case. If the opposing party objects that the question seeks irrelevant information, then the judge should sustain that objection.

On the other hand, the existence of a family is relevant when there are family support issues involved in the case or when the case involves a family member's actions. Also, to the extent that the evidence about a family affects a potential bias or motive, then it involves credibility and will be relevant. (Chapter 2 addresses the issue of motive, and Chapter 8 discusses bias issues that impact credibility.) In those cases, the court should overrule an objection on the grounds of irrelevance.

How to respond to the objection: with an offer of proof. The objection provides the proponent with an opportunity to respond by making an offer of proof to the court. After the objecting party has stated the grounds for the objection, the judge may ask the proponent of the evidence to respond. In the alternative, that party can request a response though an offer of proof. An *offer of proof* is when the proponent explains to the judge and opposing counsel why the objection should be overruled. This explanation is done outside of the presence of the jury, usually with both lawyers stepping up to the side of the judge's bench and whispering. This conference is called a *side-bar*.

In the case of a relevance objection, the proponent will tell the judge how and why the expected answer to the question is relevant to the issues in the litigation. In most cases, the proponent should have no trouble making an argument that the evidence is relevant. Sometimes however, lawyers ask irrelevant questions, and in those cases, the opposing counsel will respond to the offer of proof with her own argument about why the evidence is not relevant to the litigation.

The judge makes an evidentiary ruling. The judge's role is to be impartial and to ensure fairness throughout the trial process. After hearing the objections, offers of proof, and arguments from both sides, the judge will rule on each objection. The judge either will sustain the objection (which keeps the evidence out as irrelevant) or overrule the objection. If the judge overrules the objection, then the judge will admit the evidence unless counsel has additional objections. As a general rule, judges rely on the parties to object when appropriate and do not themselves make objections. However, when a missed objection would cause unfairness, the judge can and often will step in and make an evidentiary ruling to exclude the objectionable evidence.

OBJECTIONS OVERRULED AND THE DOCTRINE OF LIMITED ADMISSIBILITY

If an objection is overruled, then the objecting party may want to request a limiting instruction. A limiting instruction tells the jury the appropriate purpose for which the evidence can be considered. It cautions the jurors not to use the evidence for any other (impermissible) purpose. For example, a witness testifies that she has a family and the opponent objects on the grounds of irrelevance. The proponent then makes an offer of proof that the evidence is relevant to help prove the amount of family support that should be awarded as damages in the case. The court overrules the relevance objection and admits the evidence about the witness's family. The opponent may then ask the court for a limiting instruction to remind the jury that the evidence can be used only to help prove the amount of family support and not for some other purpose (such as to garner sympathy for an injured person who has a large family, for instance).

Evidence professors and trial lawyers debate whether limiting instructions are worth stating at all because, for many jurors, a reminder not to think about something engages the brain to actually think about that matter. As some say, one cannot un-ring a bell. If an objection is overruled, carefully consider whether to request a limiting instruction.

AFTER THE RELEVANCE ANALYSIS: OTHER REASONS TO EXCLUDE RELEVANT EVIDENCE

A determination that evidence is irrelevant ends the evidentiary analysis because irrelevant evidence is not admissible. However, the converse is not true. Much relevant evidence will not be admissible after examining other evidence rules. When the answer to the relevance question is "yes," then the next step is to determine whether the evidence should be excluded on other grounds. These other grounds include restrictions in other evidence code sections as well as statutes and even constitutions.

CEC §351: Admissibility of relevant evidence
Except as otherwise provided by statute, all relevant evidence is admissible.

The phrase "as otherwise provided" refers to the rest of the CEC, as well as other state and federal statutes and constitutions. One common ground for excluding relevant evidence is referred to as *undue prejudice*, which is discussed in more detail in the latter half of this chapter. Later chapters also develop additional grounds for excluding evidence. For instance, the next two chapters discuss character evidence and other policy rules as other grounds for excluding relevant evidence. Chapters 4 through 7 address the hearsay rule and its restrictions on relevant evidence. Chapters 8 and 9 provide rules restricting the type of evidence that can be offered against lay and expert witnesses. Other limitations on relevant evidence are covered in Chapters 10 and 11. Privileges also curtail the admissibility of relevant evidence, and those are addressed in Chapters 12 and 13.

Figure 1.1 demonstrates that if the evidence is not relevant, your analysis is complete. If the evidence is relevant or conditionally relevant, then you must consider the other evidentiary rules discussed in the remainder of this book.

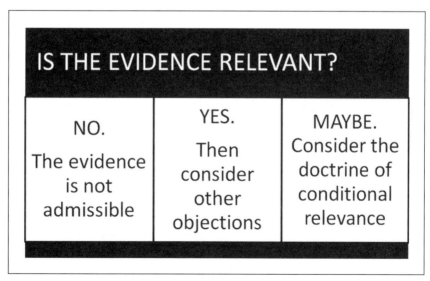

Figure 1.1. Relevance Summary Chart

Federal Rules of Evidence Compared: No Significant Difference

There is no significant difference between the relevance requirements in the CEC and in FRE 401 and 402.

Examples

1. Brad is on trial for fatally stabbing the victim. Brad seeks to introduce evidence that on the night of the murder, the victim was in the company of her friend Carl, in order to show that Carl had the opportunity to kill the victim. The prosecution objects that the evidence of Carl's whereabouts is irrelevant to the issue of Brad's guilt. How should the defense respond, and how should the court rule?

2. Yolanda worked as a nightclub singer. She sued Doctor Zander for committing medical malpractice because he cut her vocal cords while doing a routine tonsillectomy. At trial, Doctor Zander offered evidence that Yolanda had entered the country illegally. Yolanda objected on the grounds of relevance. How should Doctor Zander respond, and how should the court rule?

3. Gail was charged with selling illegal drugs to undercover police officer Herman on June 8. Officer Herman testified about the events leading up to Gail's arrest. In Gail's defense case she testified to facts that were inconsistent with Officer Herman's testimony and suggested that he was being untruthful when he testified. The prosecution then cross-examined Gail and asked, "You're not aware of any bias that Officer Herman has against you, are you?" Gail's attorney objected on the grounds of relevance. How should the prosecution respond, and how should the court rule?

4. Ilene worked for Ken, an unlicensed contractor, and was injured on the job. Ilene sued Ken because his business did not have worker's compensation insurance. At trial, Ilene sought to introduce evidence that other of Ken's workers had been injured on their jobs. Ken objects that the evidence is irrelevant. How should Ilene respond, and how should the court rule?

5. William is on trial for armed robbery. At trial, William sought to offer the testimony of his accountant, who would testify that when he prepared William's tax returns the previous year, William earned enough money to have to pay taxes. The prosecution objected that the accountant's testimony was irrelevant in the armed robbery trial. How should William respond, and how should the court rule?

6. Diane is on trial for homicide. The prosecution alleges that she shot and killed three people in a church. Diane claims that drug dealers did the shooting and seeks to introduce evidence of a white powdery substance inside a small plastic baggie, which was found in one of the pews at the church within an hour after the homicides. The prosecution objects that the presence of the white powdery substance is irrelevant. How should the defense respond, and how should the court rule?

Explanations

1. Brad should respond that the evidence is relevant because it tends to make more likely the proposition that the victim was killed by someone other than Brad. The fact that the victim was with Carl on the night that she was killed is a step on the path of proving that someone other than Brad saw the victim that evening and that someone else had the opportunity to stab her. The prosecution might argue that the fact that Carl was with the victim during part of that evening is not enough, standing alone, to support an inference that Carl killed her without knowing when he saw her compared to the exact time of her death. However, a fact can be relevant without being an ultimate fact (that Carl actually killed the victim or that Brad did not) as long as it is a step on the path of proving some fact that matters in the case. Thus, the court should overrule the relevance objection and admit the evidence.

2. Doctor Zander should respond that the evidence is relevant to her claim for damages, to the extent that she seeks lost wages due to her inability to sing, her former occupation. The court should overrule the objection. Yolanda may wish to ask for a limiting instruction to caution the jury to use the evidence only for the purpose of determining what amount of lost wages she might have earned and not for any other purpose.

3. The prosecution should respond by stating that the credibility of witnesses always is relevant. Officer Herman was a witness, and thus evidence about his credibility is relevant. The court should overrule the objection because the question addresses the motive to fabricate testimony and the existence of any improper bias, and therefore it is relevant.

4. Ilene should respond that the evidence is relevant to show that Ken's contracting business operates under unsafe working conditions, which led to her own injury. Ken will argue that the simple fact that two of his workers were injured, without some connection between the types or causes of the injuries, is not enough to meet even the low sufficiency threshold for relevance in the current trial. The court should overrule the relevance objection.

13

5. William should respond by saying his financial circumstances would give him less of a motive to commit armed robbery, and therefore the testimony of his accountant is relevant in his trial. The court should sustain the objection, however, because whether a person earns enough to pay taxes does not make him more or less likely to commit armed robbery. Paying taxes is not a step on a path that needs to be proven in this criminal case.

6. Diane's defense lawyer should respond that the white powdery substance could be an illegal drug. If it is an illegal drug, then that tends to make more likely the proposition that drugs were involved in the shooting. If drugs are involved in the shooting, then it makes more likely the proposition that drug dealers were involved in the shooting. If the defendant Diane is not a drug dealer, then that inference makes it less likely that she was involved in the shooting. An analysis of these inferences and generalizations shows the weakness of this response. Where drugs are found at a crime scene, the drugs may be the motivation for the crime. Where drugs are the motivations for crimes, the crimes often involve drug dealers. Still, this does not mean that the victim and perpetrator are both drug dealers. Because there are so many other inferences to draw from these facts, this conclusion is not very likely, and the court should sustain the relevance objection unless or until more of a connection is made, such as proving that the substance was an illegal drug. This is a situation where the court may conditionally admit the evidence, leaving open the opportunity for the prosecution to make a motion to strike the evidence about the white powdery substance if defense counsel does not provide evidence of the preliminary facts (that the substance constitutes illegal drugs) to show that the evidence is relevant.

THE BALANCING TEST: PROBATIVE VALUE VS. PREJUDICIAL EFFECT

To begin the analysis of other reasons to exclude relevant evidence, many evidence professors suggest that the next inquiry is to decide whether the evidence should be excluded by any of the policy rules discussed in Chapters 2 and 3. This portion of the chapter focuses on one specific policy reason — *when the probative value of the evidence is substantially outweighed by the prejudicial effect*. It is important to recognize that the best time to engage in this balancing analysis is at the *end*, after completing the analysis of all of the other policy reasons and other evidentiary issues and potential objections discussed in this book. Many professors refer to this as the *balancing test* and teach it early in their evidence courses, which is why the material is presented here in Chapter 1.

CEC §352: Discretion of court to exclude evidence

The court in its discretion may exclude evidence if its probative value is substantially outweighed by the probability that its admission will

(a) necessitate undue consumption of time or

(b) create substantial danger of undue prejudice, of confusing the issues, or of misleading the jury.

The balancing test requires two preliminary determinations: (1) What is the *probative value* of the evidence? (2) What is the *prejudicial effect* of admitting the evidence? The answers to these two questions form the basis for the balancing test analysis. The analysis involves determining how strongly probative the evidence is on the one hand and the likelihood of potential prejudice from admitting the evidence on the other hand. Where the danger of prejudice is substantially greater than the probative value, the court will exclude the evidence.

If one party objects that the relevant evidence is unduly prejudicial and should be excluded based on CEC 352, then the proponent may make an offer of proof about the level of probative value and the level of prejudice. The judge may then hear counterarguments from the objecting party and exercise her discretion in deciding whether the evidence is unduly prejudicial. If the court rules that evidence is unduly prejudicial, then the court will exclude the evidence under CEC 352. Note that because of the inherent discretionary nature of such decisions, CEC 352 rulings will not be disturbed on appeal unless an abuse of discretion is found.

What Is the Probative Value of the Evidence?

The probative value of evidence is measured by how large of a step that item of evidence is on a particular path. If the item of evidence is enough by itself to prove a fact that matters in the litigation, to build the path, then the evidence has an extremely high probative value. For instance, consider evidence that an eyewitness saw one driver run a red light. The fact that matters is whether one driver violated a traffic law just before the collision. If a driver drives through a red light, that driver has broken a traffic law. The eyewitness testimony about a driver running a red light is a large enough "step" to prove that fact. Therefore, the eyewitness testimony will have a *very high probative value* in proving that fact.

Be sure to relate the probative value to a particular fact of consequence before trying to measure it. The probative value can vary depending on which fact is being proven. Consider altering the situation above so that the fact that matters is whether one driver was paying attention to road conditions at the time of the collision. If a driver runs a red light, that does not necessarily mean he is not paying attention to road conditions. He may be paying close attention and note that because there are no other cars approaching the intersection he can rush through. On the other hand, it could mean that the driver looked away from the road for a few seconds and did not see the light change from yellow to red. Other information is needed to fully interpret this eyewitness testimony. Thus, the eyewitness testimony about running the red light has a lower probative value on the issue of whether the driver was paying attention. Other evidence might have a high probative value on this issue, such as right after the collision the driver blurting out, "I wasn't paying attention."

Evaluating the Probative Value of Circumstantial Evidence

To evaluate the probative value, a brief review of methods of proof is in order. Evidence can be circumstantial or direct. *Direct evidence* is evidence that proves the concluding fact without the need for intermediate inferences. For instance, in the running the red light example, the concluding fact is that the driver was not paying attention. Direct evidence is the driver's statement "I was not paying attention." No inference is required to decide whether the driver was paying attention. When the evidence directly proves the fact of consequence, that evidence will be highly probative of the fact at issue.

Circumstantial evidence is evidence that requires an inference or links of inferences to reach the conclusion. For instance, the conclusion is that the driver was not paying attention. The evidence is that an eyewitness saw the driver run the red light. From that evidence, one can infer that the driver was not paying attention because he would not have run the light when it was not safe to do so. The next inference is that it is not safe to run a red light when there is another car approaching the intersection. The next inference is that if he had been paying attention, he would have seen that other car and would have stopped to avoid a collision. The final inference concludes the chain of logic: because the driver did not stop to avoid a collision, he must not have been paying attention. (Note that Chapter 10 discusses inferences in more detail.)

Note that counterinferences can be drawn for each of these steps in the inferential chain. Perhaps the driver runs red lights all the time in his large SUV and has no safety concerns because his car is bigger than most others. Perhaps the driver saw that the other car was moving slowly and thought he could accelerate quickly enough to avoid a collision. Perhaps the driver wanted to get into a collision and was paying close attention to find the perfect opportunity. This circumstantial evidence is subject to multiple inferences, and thus it is less probative of the fact that matters: that the driver was not paying attention at the time of the collision. Standing alone, that step of evidence contributes less to proving something of consequence in the litigation than an item of direct evidence might provide.

Requiring a chain of circumstantial reasoning does not make the evidence less relevant, but it may make the item of relevant evidence less probative. Circumstantial evidence may not be as convincing as direct evidence, depending on the length and strength of the chain of inferences. Thus, the *probative value often is higher with direct evidence than with circumstantial evidence.*

Recall the hypothetical in the beginning of this chapter, about the mechanic checking the brakes on the green Toyota. The probative value of this evidence will vary depending on *when* the mechanic checked the brakes. Was it a week or two before the collision or just after the collision, or a year or two before or after the collision? The probative value of the mechanic's testimony is higher when he inspected the brakes closer to the time of the collision and lower the more time that elapsed between the date of inspection and the date of collision.

All of this analysis will help to classify the evidence as having a high, medium, or low probative value. Once the probative value level is classified, then turn to the other side of the equation to evaluate the level of potential prejudice in admitting the evidence.

Factors in Evaluating Prejudicial Effect

Consider the following four factors in determining whether an item of evidence has an unduly prejudicial effect: (1) undue consumption of time, (2) substantial danger of undue prejudice, (3) substantial danger of confusing the issues, and (4) substantial danger of misleading the jury. If the evidence fits one or more of these factors, next assign a high, medium, or low value to the potential prejudicial effect of the challenged evidence.

1. *Undue consumption of time.* Will admitting this evidence involve an undue consumption of time? For instance, will it require multiple witnesses? Must the court proceedings be halted for days while the witness or evidence is located before it can be presented at trial? Will the evidence be cumulative (involving multiple witnesses testifying to the same evidence)? Will the evidence be very technical and require an extra amount of time to make it understandable to the jurors?

2. *Undue prejudice.* Ask whether there is a substantial danger of undue prejudice. Undue prejudice is a higher standard than mere prejudice.

Where jurors hearing the evidence are more likely to decide the facts on an impermissible basis, such as an emotional or visceral reaction to the evidence that is not based on the facts presented in this particular case, the court will find that the evidence is unduly prejudicial. Mere prejudice is not the standard because all evidence that helps one side has a danger of hurting the other side. Therefore, the CEC limits this restriction to evidence that provides a *substantial* danger that it would unduly prejudice the jury. Actual prejudice is not required.

3. *Confusing the issues.* Sometimes evidence is presented in a "kitchen sink" effort, thrown all in a jumble so that the jury will be confused enough to render a defense verdict in a civil case or reasonable doubt in a criminal case. Either party might choose to object on the grounds of confusing the issues when a barrage of arguably relevant, but less material evidence might overwhelm the jurors. For instance, providing evidence of how many cars have run through a particular red light may confuse the issues when the current litigation involves one car accident caused by one driver running a red light.

4. *Misleading the jury.* When evidence has a misleading appearance of certainty, such as some statistical evidence, the jury may be misled into believing that the evidence is more probative than it actually is. For instance, a statistic that only 1 in 1 million people have a particular genetic marker does not mean that a city of 9 million has 9 people who share that marker. The statistical evidence would be misleading to the jury without additional information. Often this factor plays a role when the proponent offers expert testimony (which is discussed in Chapter 9).

Balancing the Weight of the Probative Value and the Prejudicial Effect

After assigning a probative value and a prejudicial effect value to the evidence, the next step is to determine whether the balance is in favor of admitting or excluding the challenged evidence. The general policy is in favor of the liberal admission of evidence, and in many cases, the evidence will be admitted despite a CEC 352 challenge. Under CEC 352, only where the probative value of the evidence is *substantially outweighed by* the prejudicial effect (time, prejudice, confusing issues, misleading the jury, or some combination of these factors) will the court exclude the evidence.

This language and the relationships are very important to remember because it is easy to get confused and end up applying the wrong standard. Figure 1.2 provides graphical explanations from both the probative value and the prejudicial effect viewpoints.

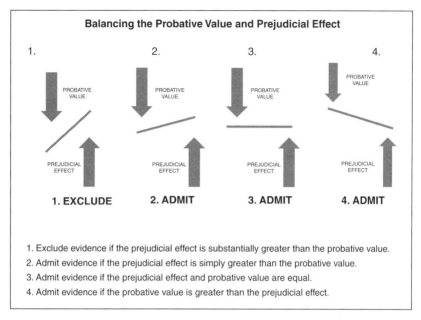

Figure 1.2. Determining Admissibility

Federal Rules of Evidence Compared: No Significant Difference

The only minor differences are in the phrasing, such as where FRE 403 refers to "unfair" prejudice, the CEC refers to "undue" prejudice, and the CEC requires a "substantial danger" whereas the FRE simply requires "danger." However, the case authorities suggest no difference in the way California and the federal courts apply this balancing test. The FRE is somewhat repetitive in stating "undue delay," "waste of time," and "needless presentation of cumulative evidence," though each phrase has slightly different connotations. The CEC includes all of these under the language "necessitate the undue consumption of time" without specifically mentioning cumulative evidence or undue delay.

Examples

1. Larry is charged with several murders as well as the attempted murder of Marty. Marty told his coworkers that Larry had beat him up periodically over the past few months, and the police arrested Larry. When Larry was released on bail, he kidnapped Marty and several other employees at the school where Marty worked. When Larry heard police sirens approaching, he shot all of the employees, wounding Marty and killing the others.

At trial, Larry offers expert testimony of a forensic psychiatrist that he was suffering from a depressive disorder to support his defense that Larry could not form the requisite intent for first degree murder at the time that he pulled the gun's trigger. The prosecution seeks to introduce Marty's testimony about the statement he made to his coworkers that Larry had been attacking him. Larry objects on CEC 352 grounds, arguing that the probative value of the accusation of previous attacks is substantially outweighed by the danger of unfair prejudice. How should the prosecution respond, how should the court rule, and why?

2. Oscar is on trial for robbery and the murder of a young woman named Paula, whom he had met at the gym. Paula's body was found wrapped in a plastic sheet under the bed in Oscar's girlfriend's apartment. Paula's wallet and some jewelry was also found in Oscar's possession. The prosecution seeks to introduce evidence about the various ways Oscar had tried to obtain money and property from other women he had met at the same gym, such as offering to work as their personal trainers in exchange for cash, "borrowing" their credit cards and their cars, asking them to loan him money and never repaying it, and stealing cash, jewelry, and checkbooks. Oscar objects that the probative value of the evidence of his attempts to gain money and property from other women is substantially outweighed by the substantial danger of unfair prejudice. How should the prosecution respond, how should the court rule, and why?

3. Quinn is charged with six counts of bank robbery, and the identity of the robber is the main issue. Quinn seeks to have the charges tried separately on the grounds he will be unfairly prejudiced if the jury hears about all of the bank robberies in one trial. The prosecution argues that because the bank robberies have a distinctive pattern, they should all be tried together. The similarities include that the robber entered the bank in the late afternoon, stood in line and handed the teller a note with almost the exact same message each time: "I have a gun; give me all of your large bills," and that the tellers were warned to refrain from triggering the alarm. The robberies were done in the course of a ten-week period, and all of the banks were within a two-mile radius. In addition, the physical description of the robber in each case matched that of Quinn. How should the court rule, and why?

4. Roger is charged with murdering his estranged wife, Sarah, and her mother, Tina. Roger married Sarah while he was in prison serving a sentence for killing his previous wife Uma. When Roger was released on parole, he came home to Sarah, and she told him that things were over. A few months later, Sarah and Tina's bodies were discovered in the home that they had shared. Several clues led police to Roger, who was

arrested a few days later. Police found a tape recording in Roger's car, with Roger's voice describing in chronological and gruesome detail his plan to revenge what he thought was disloyal behavior and how he had committed the murders of Tina and Sarah. Roger claims that he is not competent to stand trial. The prosecution seeks to admit the tape recording in a competency hearing, which is held in front of a judge, not a jury, to determine whether Roger is mentally competent to stand trial. Roger objects on CEC 352 grounds. How should the prosecution respond, how should the court rule, and why?

5. Nurse Victor is charged with molesting two women in a mental health live-in facility. Victor had been arrested for robbery with infliction of great bodily harm 20 years previously, when he broke into a stranger's home and assaulted an elderly woman who was asleep in her bed. The prosecution seeks to offer evidence of Victor's prior arrest, and Victor objects on the grounds of CEC 352. How should the court rule?

Explanations

1. The prosecution should explain that the accusation of previous assaults is highly probative because it provides a motive for Larry's shooting of Marty and his coworkers. This argument is based on the generalization that people who are accused of violent crimes often react with violence against their accusers, thus making it much more likely that Larry intended to hurt or kill Marty. The defense would respond that the evidence will inflame the jury and cause them to decide the case based on their passion against a bully who assaulted Marty, which is not the crime for which he is being tried. The danger of unfair prejudice can be minimized by a limiting instruction that the jury is not to consider the statement as substantive evidence that Larry is someone who commits violent assaults, but rather as evidence of intent and motive for the crime. Based on these arguments, the court should overrule the CEC 352 objection and admit the evidence with the limiting instructions described above.

2. The prosecution should respond that the evidence of Oscar's prior acts of seeking and obtaining money and property from women he met at the gym is highly probative of a common plan or scheme to steal from women for his own financial gain. The fact that Paula's wallet and some of her jewelry were found in Oscar's possession makes it more likely that he planned to steal from Paula and provides context for the killing. The danger of unfair prejudice is low because the misconduct with other women is not particularly inflammatory when compared to the circumstances of the murder. Thus, the court should overrule the CEC 352 objection and admit the evidence of Oscar's financial misdeeds.

3. This case will be a close call. The probative value of a number of bank robberies with similar circumstances will be high, but only to the extent that at least one of those bank robberies is linked to the defendant Quinn. If Quinn had been convicted of one of the bank robberies already, the probative value of evidence of other bank robberies committed under similar circumstances would be quite high, especially because the acts occurred within a short ten-week time period. The evidence of other robberies is highly probative of Quinn's plan to rob banks, and the prejudicial effect is not unduly high because no robbery is more inflammatory than the others. Applying the factors described above, the evidence of the other robberies should be admitted and the CEC 352 objection should be overruled.

4. The prosecution should respond that the tape is relevant to show that the defendant was coherent and competent at the time of or shortly after he allegedly committed the murders. The recording is highly probative of the defendant's mental functioning as he graphically, in great detail, and in sequential order described the events surrounding the murders. This detail supports an inference that Roger is feigning mental instability to avoid punishment for his crimes, and thus is highly probative of his competence to stand trial. The court should rule that there is no undue prejudice and the tape recording should be admissible for the purpose of determining Roger's competency.

5. Victor should argue that the probative value of the prior arrest is slight, given the long time frame in between and given the different nature of the current sexual assault allegation of women under his care, compared to the robbery and assault of a stranger in the previous incident. In addition, Victor should state that the danger of unfair prejudice is high because although he was not convicted of sexual assault in the prior case, the jurors might infer some sort of sexual assault given that the victim was elderly, like the current victims; the victim was asleep or incapacitated, like the current victims; and the assault occurred in the bedroom, as with the current victims. The infliction of great bodily harm in the prior incident may be significantly more violent than the molestation alleged in the current incident, and that would increase its prejudicial effect. The court should sustain Victor's objection and decline to admit the evidence.

The Character Evidence Exclusion Rules

Character is the essential quality or nature of a person and is often used to refer to specific traits or attributes. A person can have character as to many different aspects of behavior. For instance, one may have a character for honesty or dishonesty, carefulness or carelessness, peacefulness or violence. Being punctual or chronically tardy is also a character trait.

In everyday life, people frequently consider information about the character of others because that information is useful and important in determining how to treat people and how much to trust them. For instance, if a good friend wants to borrow your favorite sweater, you will consider her character for carefulness. If she is the kind of person who is careful, then you will expect her to take good care of your sweater. On the other hand, if she has a character for being messy, sloppy, or simply careless with her own things, then you may decide not to loan her your favorite sweater.

Similarly, litigants may wish to use evidence of a person's character at trial. Recall from Chapter 1 that evidence is admissible only if it is relevant. Character evidence is no exception to that rule. Character evidence is relevant when it makes it more or less likely that a fact of consequence in the litigation will be proven. For instance, Elizabeth is accused of committing a violent assault on another person who jumped ahead of her in line. Information about Elizabeth's character for violence or peacefulness would be useful character evidence to help the jury decide whether she had a violent angry fit that resulted in the charged assault.

If Elizabeth's friends know she is prone to violent angry fits whenever she does not get her way, their testimony makes it more likely that Elizabeth committed this assault. The prosecution would want to introduce this evidence of Elizabeth's character for violence. On the other hand, if Elizabeth is known as a very peaceful and patient person, testimony about that makes it less likely that Elizabeth committed the assault. She would want to introduce that evidence in her defense. In either case, evidence of Elizabeth's character for violence is relevant.

DANGERS OF CHARACTER EVIDENCE

Despite the relevance of character information, its use in California trials is severely limited because of the danger that juries will find liability based on evidence of what kind of person someone is rather than on the facts of the case. While character evidence is useful information to have, it does not necessarily indicate how a particular person acted on a particular occasion. Unrestricted admission of character evidence would be harmful to our foundational presumption of innocence and would damage other interests that the legislature has determined are more important than admitting all relevant evidence. The concern about judging people based on what is proven, rather than on how they have behaved in the past, acknowledges that the probative value of character evidence is not always high.

If the trial judge allows evidence of what the defendant has done to others in the past to become an issue in the trial, then the evidence multiplies to include the two sides of the story for each of the past instances. With the violent angry fit example above, the court would have to consider evidence about each of the past alleged fits, including the triggering circumstances and the resulting assault or injury. This evidence would need to be offered for all of the past instances in addition to the evidence for the instance at issue in the current litigation. The jurors may be confused by the additional evidence of multiple situations, and that additional evidence would extend the time of the trial three- or fourfold.

Expanding the volume of issues and evidence in trials increases the danger of the undue consumption of time and resources. This expansion may confuse the jury, as well as raise the risk of unfair prejudice because the jurors may give undue weight to the character evidence and find someone guilty of the pending charge simply because the jurors believe that the past instances occurred. With a lower probative value and a high prejudicial effect, character evidence could be excluded based on CEC 352 (discussed in Chapter 1). Notwithstanding CEC 352, there is a general rule that excludes character evidence in many circumstances, which are discussed in the next section.

USING CHARACTER EVIDENCE

Despite these reasons for excluding character evidence, the common law and statutes recognize the critical role that character evidence can play. Therefore, the CEC and FRE provide several ways in which character evidence can be used at trial. First, it can be useful to prove one's actual character or disposition when that character or disposition is at issue in the litigation. Second, it can be useful as circumstantial evidence to help prove one's conduct in conformity with that character on a particular occasion. However, it will be admissible to prove conduct in conformity only if an exception applies. This second purpose is often referred to as the *propensity* or *conduct in conformity* purpose. Third, it can be useful to prove something other than the person's essential character or conduct, such as the motive for his conduct. In those situations, the character evidence will be admissible only for that limited purpose. (Recall the doctrine of limited admissibility discussed in Chapter 1.) When evaluating a potential character evidence objection, it is important to first identify the purpose for which the evidence is being offered.

Figure 2.1 shows the process of analyzing character evidence admissibility. Initially, determine whether the evidence is character evidence. Next, ask whether the evidence is being offered to prove what happened on a particular occasion or to prove a person's quality or trait. If being offered to describe the events of a specific occasion, then the evidence is not character evidence, and it can be admitted if relevant and not unduly prejudicial under CEC 352. If the evidence is being offered to prove a trait or essential quality of a person, however, it is character evidence, and it is admissible in only three situations:

1. to prove that trait or quality, but only when that trait is at issue;
2. to prove that a person acted in a certain way on a certain occasion, in keeping with that person's character — but this is allowed only when a character exception applies; and

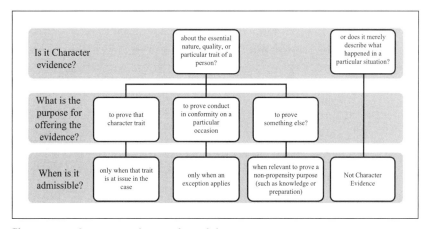

Figure 2.1. Character Evidence Admissibility

3. to prove something else, a non-propensity purpose, as long as it is relevant.

When the evidence is about a person's essence, nature, quality, or a particular trait, it transcends an individual circumstance. Evidence that a person was late to one meeting would be merely describing what happened in a particular situation. Evidence that a person is always late to meetings is describing that person's trait for tardiness and thus can constitute character evidence.

The First Purpose: To Prove Character Itself
When Character Is at Issue

When character evidence is offered to prove the first purpose — to prove a person's actual quality or attribute — it is admissible only when that character trait is at issue in the litigation under CEC 1100.

CEC §1100: Manner of proof of character

Except as otherwise provided by statute, any otherwise admissible evidence (including evidence in the form of an opinion, evidence of reputation, and evidence of specific instances of such person's conduct) is admissible to prove a person's character or a trait of his character.

Character is *at issue* in a case when a character trait is an element of a claim or defense in the litigation. In other words, where the existence or nonexistence of a particular character trait matters under the substantive governing law, then character is "at issue" in that litigation. The evidence is not being used to prove conduct in conformity with a person's character, but rather to prove the underlying character trait. For instance, in a negligent entrustment case, the plaintiff must prove that the defendant was negligent in loaning his vehicle to a person who is an unsafe driver. An essential element of the cause of action is that the driver is an unsafe driver. Thus, the driver's character for being an unsafe driver is at issue in the litigation. If the driver is not an unsafe driver, then the defense will prevail. If the driver is an unsafe driver, then the plaintiff has a case. The litigants on both sides can use character evidence to prove that character. Because the driver's character is *at issue*, it is permissible to use the evidence to prove that he has the character of being an unsafe driver, and no additional inference is required to establish the relevance of the evidence.

The Second Purpose: Circumstantial Use of Character Evidence to Prove Conduct in Conformity

When character evidence is offered for the second purpose, it is generally inadmissible. This means that the court will sustain an objection when the evidence is being used to prove that the person acted in conformity with her character, unless an exception applies. (Most of the exceptions are discussed in this chapter. The character for honesty of witnesses is discussed in Chapter 8). If a litigant tries to use evidence about a person's essential quality of being punctual to prove that the particular person was punctual on a particular occasion, she would be using character evidence to prove conduct in conformity with that character on that particular occasion. In that case, the evidence of the person's character for punctuality is being used circumstantially to prove that she was punctual on a particular occasion. This circumstantial use, or conduct in conformity purpose, for character evidence is generally prohibited because we prefer that juries decide matters based on the facts presented to them and not on the essential nature, quality, or attributes of particular persons involved in the litigation.

CEC §1101(a): Evidence of character to prove conduct

Except as provided in this section and in Sections 1102, 1103, 1108, and 1109, evidence of a person's character or a trait of his or her character (whether in the form of an opinion, evidence of reputation, or evidence of specific instances of his or her conduct) is inadmissible when offered to prove his or her conduct on a specified occasion.

Note: CEC 1104 specifically prohibits evidence of character for care or skill, except under CEC 1102 and 1103.

For instance, the prosecutor in a homicide case would like to offer evidence that the defendant had killed two people in the past under circumstances that began as a bar room brawl. The current case involves evidence that the defendant and the victim were hitting each other during a bar fight before the victim fell down and eventually died from head trauma. No one saw the defendant strike the fatal blow, although witnesses did see the defendant and victim fighting before the victim died. The evidence the prosecution wishes to offer is that the defendant has killed people twice before when he fought with fellow bar patrons. The inference the jury should draw from this evidence is that because the defendant has killed people when he was in fights in the past, it is likely that he struck the fatal blow that killed the victim in this case as well. The prosecution is relying on the generalization that people who have killed people in bar fights before are likely to kill people in subsequent bar fights too.

The conclusion is that because the defendant has killed people in bar fights before, he acted in conformity with his homicidal character by killing the person in this particular case also. Thus, when offered to prove this conclusion, the evidence is being used for a conduct in conformity purpose — to show that the defendant has a predisposition to kill people when he fights with them, based on past specific instances of killing people when he has fought with them. Using the evidence of past killings to prove conduct in conformity is using the evidence for the prohibited character purpose and thus is not admissible.

Note that the CEC also specifically prohibits using the character traits for care or skill to prove the quality of one's conduct on a specified occasion. Some commentators suggest that this provision in CEC 1104 is unnecessary because those two character traits are covered by the general character prohibition of 1101(a). However, to the extent that care or skill was pertinent to a case involving CEC 1108 (sex crimes) or CEC 1109 (domestic violence crimes), it could have been admitted in the absence of CEC 1104. These additional exceptions are discussed below.

Federal Rules of Evidence Compared: No Substantial Differences

This general prohibition under the CEC is virtually the same as the FRE 404(a), which prohibits character evidence "to prove action in conformity therewith on a particular occasion." Like the CEC, the FRE includes a number of exceptions to this general prohibition. However, unlike the CEC, the FRE does not have a separate rule that specifically prohibits evidence of character for care or skill. Those character traits fall under the general rule of FRE 404(a).

The Third Purpose: To Prove Something Other Than Character or Conduct in Conformity

Using character evidence for a purpose other than when character is at issue or to prove conduct in conformity is not prohibited by CEC 1101. In addition, CEC 1101(b) provides that when evidence that would otherwise be character evidence is offered for a non-conduct in conformity purpose — a purpose other than to show a predisposition to engage in that sort of behavior — then it can be admissible. Some commentators say that

CEC 1101(b) is not necessary because subsection (a) prohibits such evidence only when offered to prove conduct in conformity, and thus under the technical application of subsection (a), the same evidence would not be prohibited if offered for non-conduct in conformity purposes.

CEC §1101(b): Evidence of character to prove conduct

Other acts. Nothing in this section prohibits the admission of evidence that a person committed a crime, civil wrong, or other act when relevant to prove some fact (such as motive, opportunity, intent, preparation, plan, knowledge, identity, absence of mistake or accident, or whether a defendant in a prosecution for an unlawful sexual act or attempted unlawful sexual act did not reasonably and in good faith believe that the victim consented) other than his or her disposition to commit such an act.

Section 1101(b) allows evidence about crimes, civil wrongs, and other specific acts a person engaged in, as long as the evidence is not used to prove the nature or essential quality of that person. The evidence is not admissible to prove that a person is predisposed to act in a particular way or is the "kind of person" who engages in these types of acts. For instance, the fact that a person committed an armed robbery in the past can be used to prove that the person has access to a weapon. It cannot be used to prove that because he committed an armed robbery before, he is the kind of person who commits armed robberies.

This type of evidence often is referred to as the *prior bad acts doctrine.* The fact that a person engaged in prior bad acts or committed other crimes may be useful to show something other than what kind of person he is. The list of other permissible purposes includes, but is not limited to, motive, opportunity, intent, preparation, plan, knowledge, identity, and absence of mistake or accident. The parenthetical phrase "such as" in CEC 1101(b) means that this is not an exhaustive list, and thus, other non-conduct in conformity purposes can be permissible also.

With all of this prior bad acts evidence, it is crucial to analyze the purpose for which the evidence is being offered. Is the evidence being offered to prove character or conduct in conformity on a particular occasion? If so, then it is inadmissible under CEC 1101(a) unless it falls within an exception discussed in the next few sections of this chapter. If the evidence is being offered to prove something else, perhaps from the list in CEC 1101(b), then the evidence should be admissible.

The main challenge is in telling the difference between these two situations. For instance, some evidence can be used to prove character or conduct in conformity, but can also be used to prove a non-character purpose such as motive or identity. In those cases, you must make the arguments as to how the evidence is most probative (reviewing the techniques from Chapter 1) and how the evidence is most likely to be used by the jurors — either for an impermissible character purpose or for a permissible non-conduct in conformity purpose.

One useful mnemonic device, offered by one of my evidence students a few years ago, is I-PIMP-O-MACK (*identity preparation, intent, motive, plan, opportunity, [absence of] mistake/accident, consent, and knowledge*).

Proving Identity

On the issue of *identity*, non-conduct in conformity evidence can be used to prove that other crimes the accused did commit are *earmarked* with the criminal signature of the accused. For instance, evidence that the defendant wore a Robin Hood costume, spoke with a British accent, and threatened the bank tellers with a bow and arrow during three prior bank robberies would be relevant to show that the person who committed the present bank robbery in a Robin Hood costume while speaking in a British accent and threatening the bank tellers with a bow and arrow is likely to be the defendant.

This evidence about the robber's appearance helps to prove the identity of the perpetrator of the crime and is not being offered to show that because the accused has committed this crime before, he is likely to have committed the crime again. Rather, it is used to show that because of the peculiar nature of the costume, accent, and weapon used in the past crimes, the person who committed the prior crimes is likely to be the same person who committed the present crime.

When used to prove identity or earmark, the California courts require a very high degree of similarity between the prior crime or bad act and the current charged crime. The method of the crime must be so unusual or unique as to be the equivalent of a calling card or criminal signature. Here, the Robin Hood costume, accent, and weapon would meet that requirement.

Proving Preparation

To prove *preparation*, consider how the evidence can be used to show that the person engaged in certain acts that are precursors to the criminal conduct at issue in the current trial. For instance, if a defendant is accused of bank robbery, information that he called the bank to find out its hours, went to the bank to find the emergency exit doors, and tried out four different escape routes supports the notion that he was preparing to rob the bank. When using the evidence of preparation for a non-conduct in conformity purpose, the prosecutor will argue that these activities are circumstantial evidence that he did rob the bank. Do not argue that he robbed the bank because people who try out escape routes are the kind of people who rob banks. That would be a propensity use of the evidence. Though that may be a fair characterization, the evidence will not be admissible for this conduct in conformity purpose unless an exception applies.

Establishing Intent

Prior bad act evidence can also help establish intent. For instance, in a homicide prosecution, to prove whether the accused pulled the trigger intending to kill or only accidentally, the prosecution might wish to offer evidence that the defendant had been involved in a hit and run accident (a prior bad act) and that the victim threatened to report him to the police if he did not pay blackmail. California courts recognize that the same motive can manifest itself in different ways (for instance, a motive to silence someone can be manifested by threats, physical assault, attempted kidnapping, and even homicide), and therefore a low level of similarity between the prior bad act and the charged crime can be sufficient to establish motive or intent. Another example, cited in *People v. Williams*, would be using evidence of prior drug convictions to prove that a defendant's current possession of drugs was for the purpose of sale and not for personal use.[1]

Establishing Motive

Motive is another permissible purpose. There are many different kinds of motives for criminal behavior, so one must ask about the motive for this crime and what evidence connects to the motive. Consider motives like loyalty, marital fidelity, disrespect, money, greed, power, fear, racial animus, religious animus, and revenge. Evidence of having poor financial resources is usually not admissible to establish motive for robbery or theft because so many people have less money than they want or need.

Demonstrating a Common Plan

Where there is evidence of a series of crimes, only one of which is currently being tried, there might be other evidence that suggests that the crimes are interrelated. This *common plan or scheme* evidence can be useful proof of the charged crime, and may also help prove *motive*, *identity*, and sometimes *intent*.

---

1. People v. Williams, 170 Cal. App. 4th 587, 88 Cal. Rptr. 3d 401 (2009); holding that evidence of prior drug convictions of defendant gang member was admissible under CEC 1101(b) to prove that defendant possessed drugs (under the current charge) for sale and not for personal use.

For example, evidence about a scheme to provide laundered money to a foreign government would be relevant to an embezzlement charge.

However, admitting evidence of numerous bad acts through the common plan or scheme factor can result in some unfairness for criminal defendants, and the California Supreme Court has thus provided some safeguards for the use of this evidence. In discussing the differing levels of similarities required between uncharged misdeeds and the charged crime, the court determined that an intermediate level of similarity is required to prove a common plan or scheme. The two misdeeds must be sufficiently similar for one to infer that they are "manifestations of a common design or plan." The evidence must do more than merely prove that the charged and uncharged misdeeds produced similar results. Spontaneous and unconnected misdeeds will not be found to be the product of a plan.

Establishing Opportunity

Opportunity includes being at the right place at the right time, as well as possessing the skills or abilities needed to take advantage of a particular situation. For example, evidence that a person has dismantled burglar alarms in the past would be useful to help prove that the person robbed a bank. Because the person possesses the skills to dismantle an alarm system, he has a greater opportunity and knowledge to rob the bank. In addition, evidence that the person was seen walking into the bank earlier in the day is used to show his proximity to the crime. His location and the timing of his bank visit are not being used to show he is the kind of person who robs banks, but rather that he had the opportunity to rob the bank because he was nearby when the robbery occurred.

Demonstrating the Absence of Mistake or Accident

The *absence of mistake* factor often arises when a person has engaged in some wrongful conduct multiple times. The previous instances provide circumstantial evidence that the present conduct was not a mistake. For instance, Mark starts building a fence around his yard. One neighbor comes by to tell Mark that he has put the fence in the wrong spot because it lies on some of the neighbor's land. Mark apologizes and moves the fence. The next week, while Mark is building the fence on the other side of his property, a second neighbor comes over to tell Mark the fence is encroaching, and Mark moves the fence. The following weekend, Mark begins building the fence at the back of his property. That back neighbor does not come over to complain. Instead, he waits until the fence is finished and then sues Mark. If Mark claims that his encroachment was a mistake, then evidence of these past encroachments and complaints would be useful for the non-conduct in conformity purpose of showing that Mark did not make three mistakes when measuring the fence line.

Accident is closely related to the absence of mistake factor. The more times I step on your foot as I walk past your seat to the aisle of the theater, the more likely that I am doing so on purpose, rather than by accident. Evidence of the other times I stepped on your foot will be circumstantial evidence that this latest time was not an accident. The purpose is not for conduct in conformity. Rather, my repeated act of stepping on your foot is circumstantial evidence that when I stepped on your foot the last time, it was not an accident.

Establishing Consent

The *consent* factor applies when past acts suggest that the current act was not unwanted. For instance, if Suzanne always asks the masseuse to give her "a really deep tissue massage, even if it hurts" that would be circumstantial evidence that Suzanne consented to the massage that left her bruised.

Demonstrating Specialized Knowledge

The existence of specialized *knowledge* can be also determined from the prior bad acts. This non-conduct in conformity purpose presents some challenges. If a defendant in the present case denies having specialized knowledge of how to hot-wire a car and yet has hot-wired cars in the past, the jury is more likely to disbelieve the defendant based on the assumption that once a person has obtained specialized knowledge, it is fair to assume that the person retains that specialized knowledge. On the other hand, merely general knowledge of past criminal behavior or of facts to support a particular mental state, such as the nature of illegal drugs sold in the past, may involve a propensity inference — that because the defendant knowingly sold illegal drugs before, she has acted in conformity with her character for selling illegal drugs and therefore she knew the substance she sold in the present case was illegal drugs. The more general the knowledge, the easier it is to make the argument that it is probative based mostly on propensity reasoning, and therefore should be inadmissible under CEC 1101(a).

Federal Rules of Evidence Compared: Notable Difference

FRE 404(b) has a non-exhaustive list that is almost identical to that of the CEC, but the FRE omits the consent issue from the list. The main difference is that the FRE provides an opportunity for the accused in a criminal case to request advance notice as to the "general nature" of any 404(b) evidence that the prosecution plans to use at trial.

THE THREE BASIC KINDS OF CHARACTER EVIDENCE

Now that we have examined the three different *purposes* for offering the evidence of character or a character trait, we must also consider the three different *methods* of proving character. The three basic ways to prove character are with opinion evidence, reputation evidence, and specific instances of conduct evidence. All three types of character evidence are admissible to prove character or trait of character under CEC 1100, unless prohibited by another statute. One major limiting statute is CEC 1101(a), which specifically prohibits the use of the three types of character evidence to prove conduct in conformity (unless an exception applies, as discussed in the sections below).

Opinion Evidence

Opinion character evidence is when a witness testifies that in his opinion, someone is a particular kind of person or is the kind of person who behaves in a particular way. For instance, Snow White is on trial for breaking and entering into Cinderella's castle, and Grumpy the Dwarf is called as a prosecution witness. Grumpy the Dwarf testifies: "I am well acquainted with Snow White. In my opinion, she is the kind of person who breaks into homes." This is not direct evidence of whether Snow White broke into Cinderella's castle, but it is circumstantial evidence and thus would require an inference to reach the conclusion that Snow White is guilty. What is the inference that the prosecution wants the jury to draw? The inference is that Grumpy's opinion of Snow White's character tends to make more likely the proposition that Snow White is guilty of the current breaking and entering charge. It is relying on the prohibited conduct in conformity purpose that Snow White is the kind of person who breaks into homes and therefore she likely acted in conformity with that character by breaking into Cinderella's castle also.

Reputation Evidence

Reputation evidence is the second type of character evidence. This evidence is like an aggregate of opinions and is offered when a witness familiar with the person's reputation in the community as to a particular character trait testifies about that reputation. Depending on the character trait, the relevant community for reputation purposes can include a social, a professional, an educational, or a business community. For example, among the business community, a person may have a reputation for "not taking no for an answer" when putting together business deals. In an educational community, a person may have a reputation for studying at all hours or for cheating on tests. The reputation testimony is an aggregate of opinions because witnesses must be able to testify that they know the reputation of the individual at issue based on observations, conversations, and other interactions within the relevant community.

Imagine that in Snow White's trial, the prosecution calls the Evil Witch as a reputation witness. The Evil Witch testifies: "I am out in the Forest every day, and I know what is going on with all the people and animals in the Forest. In fact, I use my magic mirror to keep an eye on everyone and everything. I disguise myself and walk among the people, so I am well informed about the Forest, and I hear a lot of things. Whenever anyone talks about Snow White, it is about breaking and entering. She has a reputation in the Forest community for breaking into people's homes."

As with the opinion evidence of Grumpy the Dwarf, this evidence is relevant only to prove that Snow White is the kind of person who breaks into homes. Snow White's reputation in the community is as someone who breaks and enters into people's homes. Therefore, she is more likely to be guilty of the current breaking and entering charge because she is the kind of person who breaks into homes.

Specific Instances of Conduct

Evidence of specific instances of conduct shows how a person actually has behaved in the past. For instance, in an assault and battery case, the prosecution asks the victim of the assault, "What happened next?" and the victim responds, "The defendant raised his fist and struck me in the face." The victim's statement is specific instance evidence of the defendant's character for violence. However, the issue to decide is whether the specific instance evidence is being used to prove what actually happened in this case, or as circumstantial evidence of conduct in conformity with the character trait exhibited in that specific instance. In the battery case, the victim's statement merely describes what happened, and although it is evidence of how the defendant behaved on a specific occasion in the past, it is, more importantly, direct evidence of what occurred in this particular altercation. This type of evidence of a specific instance will be admissible to prove what happened in this case because it is not being used as circumstantial evidence to prove his conduct in conformity with that violent character.

The problem arises when litigants seek to use examples of a person's past behavior to prove that the person acted in a particular way on another occasion. When using the specific instances of past behavior in this way, then the evidence is relevant based on the conduct in conformity purpose, and inadmissible under CEC 1101(a).

Illustrations of Impermissible Uses of Specific Instance Evidence

For example, in a lawsuit alleging a fraudulent misrepresentation as to the value of a used car, the plaintiff may wish to offer evidence that on three prior occasions, the defendant misrepresented the value of a used car to a prospective buyer. When analyzing this offer of evidence, first ask how the evidence is relevant. Knowing that the defendant misrepresented the value of cars on three prior occasions, one can infer that the defendant is a dishonest car dealer who misrepresents the value of used cars. From that inference, a juror may conclude that it is more likely that the defendant misrepresented the value of the used car on the present occasion. Thus, the specific instance evidence of the defendant's past misrepresentations tends to make more likely the fact of consequence that the defendant misrepresented the value of the most recent used car as well and therefore is relevant.

This inferential chain is logical, in part because it conforms to common sense. If you had a friend who repeatedly overpriced used goods he sold to you in the past, you would not be surprised if he inflated the price for used goods in the future. You would not be surprised because, based on your past specific experiences with that friend, you have applied the generalization that he is a person who misrepresents values, at least when trying to sell you used goods. Your generalization is reasonable, and without knowing any additional facts, it is a fair characterization of your friend. For that reason, it is specific instance evidence being used to prove conduct in conformity. You are using the specific instance character evidence to help prove that because he did this before, it is likely that he is guilty in this instance as well, simply because he is the kind of person who does this sort of thing.

Illustrations of Permissible Uses of Specific Instance Evidence

On the other hand, if the evidence of past misrepresentations was offered not to prove the current misrepresentation, but rather to prove the defendant's poor knowledge of the value of the used goods, then that would be a non-character and non-conduct in conformity purpose, and the evidence would not violate the character evidence prohibition. It would be relevant for one of the I-PIMP-O-MACK factors, such as knowledge or absence of mistake or accident.

Similarly, evidence that a defendant rear-ended four automobiles in a one-year period would not be admissible for the purpose of proving that he is the kind of person who causes car accidents (his character for carelessness) or that because he has caused car accidents in the past, he likely caused this car accident as well (conduct in conformity with that character trait of carelessness). However, the evidence of the prior rear-endings will be admissible to prove an absence of mistake (such as that by now the defendant should have figured out how to properly use his brakes in such a way as to avoid rear-ending other cars). Using the evidence to prove that he should have known he had faulty brakes or needed remedial driving lessons is permissible, and is very different from allowing the jury to infer that because the defendant was in four other car accidents, he is the kind of person who caused the present car accident.

Why Specific Instance Evidence Is Impermissible Generally for Conduct in Conformity Purposes

Finally, imagine that in the Snow White trial from above, the prosecution would like to ask the following questions during cross-examination: "You have broken into homes before, haven't you?" "In fact, you broke into the home of the Seven Dwarves just last year, isn't that right?" What is the inference that this prosecutor wants the jury to draw? Two potential inferences are relevant to the issues in this case. The first is that Snow White's character or essential nature is that she is the kind of person who trespasses into other people's homes, which is the character inference. The second inference is that because she has broken into homes before, she is predisposed to break into homes and is more likely to have broken into this home, which is the circumstantial or non-conduct in conformity purpose.

The conclusion of both of these inferences is that Snow White probably broke into Cinderella's home, just like she did to the home of the Dwarves. This judgment would be based on the character of Snow White or an assumption about her predisposition to act in a particular way. It is based solely on her past behavior and not on any evidence that links her to this specific breaking and entering charge. Because jurors must decide cases based on what the defendant actually did, rather than on the content of the defendant's character, CEC 1101(a) generally prohibits the use of specific instance evidence (unless an exception applies).

Character evidence can be very prejudicial to a criminal defendant because his life or liberty may be at stake on conviction. Jurors who think that people who have done bad things in the past are likely to do bad things in the future may be more ready to convict, even if the evidence does not quite amount to proof beyond a reasonable doubt. For this reason, courts are particularly careful when an exception permits admitting specific instance character evidence to prove conduct in conformity.

Federal Rules of Evidence Compared: No Notable Difference

The Federal Rules recognize the same three types of character evidence.

HABIT EVIDENCE

Where there is evidence of numerous specific instances, one can try to establish a habit. Unlike opinion, reputation, and specific instance evidence, habit evidence is admissible to show conduct in conformity. Thus, if one can prove that a person has a habit of behaving in a particular way based on a large number of specific instances, those specific instances can be used to prove that the person acted in conformity with that habit. Similarly, when a business has a particular custom that is repeated, evidence of that custom can be used to prove that the business acted in conformity with that custom on a specific occasion. The evidence is not considered to be character evidence because it does not rely on the character or essential nature of the person or business, but rather on how the person or business habitually or customarily responds to a particular situation.

CEC §1105: Habit or custom to prove specific behavior
Any otherwise admissible evidence of habit or custom is admissible to prove conduct on a specified occasion in conformity with the habit or custom.

To prove a habit of a person or a custom of a business, the party will need to provide evidence of a *regular, repeated response to a specific stimulus.* For instance, each time a soldier is tapped on the shoulder, he wheels around and crouches into a fighting stance, and every time a payment is received from a customer, the business sends out an updated invoice that same day. When a person is exposed to the same stimulus on multiple occasions and responds the same way each time, that will help prove that the response is a habit. The same applies to businesses.

If a habit or custom is established, then evidence of specific instances of that habit can be admitted to prove that the person or business acted as the habit would predict. This use of habit evidence is not as character evidence to prove that the soldier has a character for getting into a fighting stance after being tapped on the shoulder, but rather as substantive evidence that he actually did get into a fighting stance because that is how he always reacts to a tap on the shoulder.

Federal Rules of Evidence Compared: No Notable Differences

FRE 406 also permits evidence of a habit or routine practice to prove conduct in conformity with that habit.

Examples

1. Prometheus is on trial for an armed bank robbery where stacks of $20 and $50 bills were stolen. In its case in chief, the prosecution offers evidence that Prometheus had consecutively numbered $20 and $50 bills on his person when he was arrested two days after the crime. Prometheus objects that the evidence is impermissible character evidence offered to show that he is the type of person who carries stolen bills. The prosecution responds that the money is not being offered to show that he has a propensity to rob banks or to carry stolen bills, but rather as substantive circumstantial evidence that he is the person who stole the stacks of money from this particular bank. How should the court rule, and why?

2. Nestor is on trial for the homicide of Odysseus. In its case in chief, the prosecution seeks to offer evidence that at a party five days before Odysseus was killed, Nestor and his friends got into a fist fight with Odysseus and his friends. Odysseus's friends won the fight, and Nestor and his friends departed the party, embarrassed. Nestor objects that the evidence is an impermissible specific instance of character evidence. How should the prosecution respond, and how should the court rule? How would the arguments and ruling differ in federal court?

3. Sergio is suing his former employer Kurt Law School for breach of an employment contract. During his case in chief, Sergio provides witness testimony that he fulfilled all the requirements of his job duties as a law professor: faithfully teaching his classes, holding office hours regularly, and providing prompt feedback to students on their exams and papers. Sergio alleges that Kurt Law School breached the contract by firing him after only one month of a nine-month teaching contract. During the defense case in chief, Kurt Law School seeks to offer the testimony of Professor Perez, who will testify that she had the office right next door to Sergio, and she often saw lines of students waiting to speak to him

because he had forgotten to show up for office hours. At other times, students came knocking on his door, yelling, "Aren't you coming down to class, Professor?" to no avail. Further, she will testify that she reviewed a draft of Sergio's examination and found numerous typos, missing text, and more questions than could be answered within the allotted time limitations. Sergio objects to this testimony as impermissible character evidence. How should the court rule, and why?

4. Fergie and Georgie are brothers who are on trial for attempted murder resulting from shooting three people with a shotgun. All three of the victims were relatives of Georgie's estranged wife Helen. In its case in chief, the prosecution seeks to offer evidence that (a) Georgie made threats to Helen and her family, (b) cars belonging to Helen and several of her family members were set on fire, and (c) Fergie threatened Helen's neighbor with a shotgun one afternoon. Fergie and Georgie object that the evidence is impermissible specific instance evidence offered to prove character or conduct in conformity. How should the prosecution respond, how should court rule, and why?

5. Dionysius is on trial for the murder of three people. Each victim was strangled and then placed in the bedroom closet with a necklace around the neck. Relatives of each victim said that they did not recognize the necklace found around their loved one's neck. Investigators determined that the necklaces found on the three victims in the present case belonged to victims of strangulation in three prior unsolved homicide cases. The prosecution seeks to offer evidence of those three prior unsolved murders in which all the victims were also strangled and left in their closets. Dionysius objects on the grounds of relevance and impermissible character evidence. How should the prosecution respond, and how should the court rule?

6. Justine is a reporter for the *Beach Gazette*, a local weekly newspaper. She has written numerous stories, including one printed in January about a robber who has been breaking into residents' homes while they are present, threatening them with a gun, and forcing them to help him gather up their valuables. Justine's story states that each witness has said the robber wore a neoprene yellow face mask. Mannie is the editor-in-chief of the *Beach Gazette*, and he has learned that Justine has been fabricating many of her stories. Some were based on truth but had no sources to back up all of the specifics; other stories are completely untrue. The robber-in-neoprene story was completely false. In February, the *Beach Gazette* issued a retraction as to all of Justine's stories for the past two months. Unfortunately, on January 31, Larry (who teaches self-defense classes and is not a robber) went jogging in the early morning fog and decided to wear his neoprene yellow face mask. As Larry was returning from his run, he cut

through an alley in his neighborhood. His neighbor Maggie saw the man in the neoprene mask run by her kitchen window and grabbed her husband's gun from the kitchen drawer. Maggie shot Larry in the back as he was running by, and the police arrived and arrested Larry for attempted robbery. After his arrest, Larry lost most of his individual clients, and the gym that employed him to teach group self-defense classes fired him. Larry sued the *Beach Gazette* for defamation (which requires a false statement of fact that damages a person's reputation) and money damages to make up for his injuries and loss of reputation in the community when he was labeled as a robber. The *Beach Gazette* seeks to offer the following evidence in its defense case in chief: a coworker's testimony that Larry has a reputation as an alcoholic and a drug addict, and Larry's employer's testimony that he never trusted Larry with cash or valuables lying around his office, and even locked such items in his safe if Larry was there working alone. How should the judge rule on each item of evidence, and why?

7. Kayla was charged with first degree murder, robbery, and burglary of Joan and David, a married couple who managed an apartment building. The authorities found their bodies on the floor of their apartment, next to two empty baby food jars labeled in crayon with the phrase "spending money." To prove that a robbery occurred, the prosecution seeks to offer the testimony of Joan's mother that Joan had a habit of storing money in empty baby food jars. Joan's mother had regularly visited Joan in the six months before the crime and saw Joan put money in the jars whenever she returned from the bank, and every time Joan's mother was in her daughter's apartment, she noticed that the jars contained money. The defense objects that this is an impermissible use of specific instances of conduct. How should the prosecution respond, how should the court rule, and why?

Explanations

1. The court should overrule Prometheus's objection on the grounds that the evidence is not being offered for an impermissible propensity purpose, but rather as substantive evidence that he was found with consecutively numbered bills stolen from this particular bank. While this may seem like evidence of a specific instance of conduct, it is conduct that constitutes the underlying facts to support the charge in the current trial. The evidence that the defendant was found in possession of stolen money is not being used to show his propensity to carry stolen money, nor is it being used to show that he acted in conformity with that propensity on this occasion. Rather, it is direct evidence that Prometheus carried consecutively numbered stolen bills on this particular occasion. Because the

evidence is not used to show that Prometheus conducted himself in conformity with a character for carrying consecutive bills, it is not character evidence and therefore will be admissible. The court would reach a different result if the evidence was that Prometheus had been found carrying stolen money on a prior occasion. Then, the only relevance of that prior occasion would be to prove that Prometheus likely conducted himself in conformity with that character of being a thief.

2. The prosecution should respond that the evidence is not being offered for an impermissible character purpose because it is not being offered to show that Nestor is the kind of person who fights or that Nestor has a violent character and likely acted in conformity with that character by killing Odysseus. Rather, the prosecution is offering the evidence to prove a non-conduct in conformity purpose, specifically that Nestor had a *motive* for killing Odysseus — revenge for the humiliating defeat at the party five days earlier. Nestor might respond that the evidence will be used to show his violent character and thus may result in unfair prejudice to him because the jury will be more likely to convict him based on his prior violent acts, rather than based on what is currently proven in court. Nevertheless, the judge should overrule the objection and admit the evidence of the prior fight for the purpose of proving motive. *In federal court*, the argument for the use of non-conduct in conformity motive evidence will be the same. However, there is an additional federal requirement of advance notice to the accused. If Nestor requested advance notice of the use of any FRE 404(b) evidence and the prosecution did not comply, then the judge should sustain the objection and the evidence would not be admitted, even for the non-conduct in conformity purpose.

3. The first question is whether this evidence is character evidence. Sergio seeks to testify on his own behalf about how he fulfilled his job functions. This is not character evidence offered to show conduct in conformity with his character for being a good worker, but rather is evidence of what he actually did while employed. Thus, it is substantive evidence of his actual performance of his job duties. Therefore, Sergio's testimony is admissible. The testimony of Professor Perez likewise is admissible because it is not character evidence. It is evidence of the underlying facts to support the law school's claim that Sergio did a poor job as a professor. The court should overrule Sergio's objection.

4. The prosecution should respond that the evidence is being offered for a non-character and non-conduct in conformity purpose — to show that the defendants had a *motive* to kill the victims (to follow through on their threats), that the defendants had an *opportunity* to kill the victims (just like they had an opportunity to torch their cars), and that the defendants can

be *identified* as the people who killed the victims (because they had a shotgun, with which they threatened a neighbor). If the court is satisfied that the threats actually were made by Georgie, then the court should rule that the evidence of threats should be admissible to prove motive. The court likely will expect more evidence to connect the torching of the cars to the defendants because the facts state only that the cars were burned and not who was responsible for those fires. For that evidence to be admissible as prior bad acts of the defendants to show opportunity, a closer connection would have to be made to the defendants. As for the threat with the shotgun, because the courts require a high degree of similarity between the prior bad act and the current charge to prove identity, the mere possession of a shotgun likely will not be considered so unusual as to be unique, and therefore would not be admissible for this non-conduct in conformity purpose. However, if there was something special about this type of shotgun, then the court may admit the evidence.

5. The prosecution should respond that the evidence of the prior homicides is relevant to prove that the six murders likely were all committed by the same person as part of a *common plan or scheme*. The defendant planned to kill people, steal a necklace from each victim, and then place that necklace on a subsequent victim. This is more than unconnected misdeeds and shows a deliberate pattern of action. The defendant will respond that there is no evidence of a connection between the defendant and the prior victims, but the prosecution will reply that the necklaces establish that connection. The court should overrule the defendant's relevance and character objections. The defendant may then want to object under CEC 352 on the grounds of unfair prejudice. It is likely that the court will find the probative value to be quite high because the necklaces suggest an earmark or signature as well as a long-term plan to engage in multiple murders. The court may find that the danger of unfair prejudice is high as well, given that the jury may be led to decide the case based on passions and prejudices against serial killers, rather than on the facts of the case. However, unless the high probative value is substantially outweighed by the high prejudicial effect, the evidence of the prior homicides will not be excluded by CEC 352.

6. This is a civil action alleging defamation, and therefore the plaintiff's reputation for being an alcoholic or drug addict is at issue in the litigation. To assess the damages to Larry's reputation, the court will have to decide whether Larry actually is a drug addict or an alcoholic because truth is a defense. All three types of character evidence will be admissible, as this situation is not covered within the general character ban of CEC 1101(a). The evidence of Larry's reputation as an alcoholic and a drug addict is admissible under CEC 1100 as reputation evidence. One may

argue that Larry's reputation as to substance abuse is not very probative of his reputation as a potential robber, but because he has alleged damage to his reputation generally, the evidence will be admissible. Larry may assert that the evidence has a low probative value and is unfairly prejudicial, and thus should be excluded by CEC 352, but this argument is not likely to prevail because the evidence is highly probative on the issue of damages and the value of Larry's reputation. Larry's employer's testimony involves his opinion about Larry's character for being a thief and stealing valuable items. The opinion is admissible under CEC 1100.

7. The prosecution should respond that the testimony by Joan's mother is sufficient to establish that Joan had a habit of putting money in the baby food jars. The testimony that she saw her daughter put money in the jars every time she returned from the bank and that the jars always contained money should be enough to meet the sufficiency test to establish the existence of Joan's habit for putting money in those baby food jars. With a sufficient foundation established, the court should overrule the defense objection and admit evidence of conduct in conformity with that habit as relevant to prove an element of the robbery charge.

EXCEPTIONS TO THE CHARACTER EVIDENCE BAN

There are several exceptions to the general character evidence ban of CEC 1101(a). These exceptions permit the use of character evidence to prove conduct in conformity under certain limited situations. These situations arise in criminal cases, in cases involving misconduct of a sexual or an intimate nature, and when witnesses testify at trial. In determining whether an exception might apply, it is important to ask three questions.

- *First*, is the case criminal or civil? Certain exceptions apply only in criminal cases.
- *Second*, does the case involve intimate abuse (such as a sex crime, domestic violence, or abuse of dependent children or elders)? Some exceptions apply only in intimate abuse cases.
- *Third*, what type of character evidence does the exception permit? Some exceptions permit all three types (opinion, reputation, and specific instances) of character evidence, and others are more limited.

The exceptions that apply to criminal cases are found in CEC 1102, 1103, 1108, and 1109. CEC 1106 contains an exception for the sexual character of the plaintiff in certain civil cases. Each of these exceptions is explained more fully in the subsections below. CEC 787-790 contain additional rules that apply when the evidence relates to the character of a witness who testifies in the case. (Those rules are discussed in Chapter 8.)

Criminal Defendant's Character to Prove Conduct: CEC 1102

CEC 1102 permits the defendant to throw himself on the mercy of the court by offering character evidence that will assist in his defense. But when the defendant chooses to take advantage of what some refer to as the *mercy rule* by offering evidence about his (good) character for a particular relevant character trait, he also opens the door to the prosecution's use of character evidence on that particular character trait. Once the defendant offers his own character evidence at trial, he activates a fairness provision, which allows the prosecution to respond by offering evidence of the defendant's (bad) character *for that same character trait only.*

CEC §1102: Opinion and reputation evidence of character of criminal defendant to prove conduct

In a criminal action, evidence of the defendant's character or trait of his character in the form of an opinion or evidence of his reputation is not made inadmissible by Section 1101 if such evidence is:

    (a) Offered by the defendant to prove his conduct in conformity with such character or trait of character.

    (b) Offered by the prosecution to rebut evidence adduced by the defendant under subdivision (a).

For example, the defendant in a homicide prosecution decides that he would like his mother to testify that (1) in her opinion, her son is a peace-loving person. She will testify that (2) in fact, everyone in the community feels the same way about her son, and (3) he is often asked to babysit for small children, (4) to escort the elderly to doctors' appointments, and (5) to play with puppies and kittens. The prosecution would like to offer evidence that (6) several of the puppies and kittens died under suspicious circumstances shortly after they were left under the defendant's care, that (7) some of the elderly people that he escorted home returned with unexplained bruises, and (8) that several of the small children ended up in the emergency room within hours after the defendant finished watching them. Use Figure 2.2 to determine which evidence in this hypothetical will be admissible.

45

2. The Character Evidence Exclusion Rules

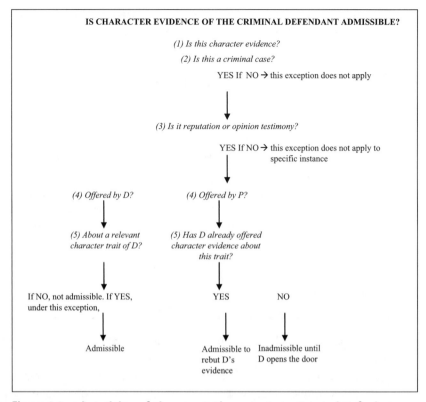

IS CHARACTER EVIDENCE OF THE CRIMINAL DEFENDANT ADMISSIBLE?

(1) Is this character evidence?

(2) Is this a criminal case?

YES If NO → this exception does not apply

(3) Is it reputation or opinion testimony?

YES If NO → this exception does not apply to specific instance

(4) Offered by D?   *(4) Offered by P?*

(5) About a relevant character trait of D?   *(5) Has D already offered character evidence about this trait?*

If NO, not admissible. If YES, under this exception,   YES   NO

Admissible   Admissible to rebut D's evidence   Inadmissible until D opens the door

Figure 2.2. Admissibility of Character Evidence Against a Criminal Defendant

Using Figure 2.2, first ask, *is the evidence character evidence?* If offered to prove that the defendant is a peace-loving and caring person who would never harm a fly, then yes, all of the evidence is character evidence.

Second, is this a criminal case? Yes, because it is a prosecution (brought by a district attorney) for homicide (a crime). *If so, is the evidence in the form of reputation or opinion testimony?*

- Item (1) is opinion testimony because it reflects another person's opinion about the character of the defendant.
- Item (2) is reputation testimony because it explains how the community views the defendant's character on this particular trait.
- Items (3)-(8) are neither reputation nor opinion, but rather are specific instances of conduct.
- Items (3)-(5) refer to past acts that the defendant has engaged in.
- Items (6)-(8) refer to the results of past conduct the defendant had engaged in (watching pets, adults, and children who later ended up hurt). Because this character exception permits evidence only in the form of reputation and opinion, items (3)-(8) are not admissible under this character evidence exception.

For items (1) and (2), the next step is to ask: *Is the evidence being offered by the criminal defendant? If so, then ask whether the character evidence is about a relevant character trait of the defendant?* Recall from Chapter 1 that only relevant evidence is admissible. If the character evidence about the defendant does not relate to a pertinent character trait — one that makes more or less likely some fact of consequence in the trial — then the evidence would not be admissible under the relevance rules. For instance, a general character for peace-loving is not relevant to fraud charges but may be relevant to assault charges. In the example above, the evidence is about the defendant's character for being peace-loving, which is relevant to a homicide charge. Items (1) and (2) are being offered by the defendant and therefore are admissible. Item (3) also is relevant, but because it is evidence of a specific instance of conduct, it is not admissible under this exception.

If the evidence is being offered by the prosecution, has the criminal defendant already offered character evidence about this trait? Items (6)–(8) are being offered by the prosecution. If they are being offered after the defendant has successfully offered items (1) and (2), then the defendant has opened the door to the use of character evidence by the prosecution on that particular character trait. However, the evidence must be in the form of reputation or opinion. Items (6)–(8) are specific instance evidence, and therefore are not admissible under this exception. Once the defendant has opened the door, the prosecution has the opportunity to walk through that door by using opinion or reputation character evidence but not specific instance character evidence.

The prosecution can offer another person's opinion that the defendant is not peace-loving or that he has a reputation for provoking conflicts to rebut the defendant's evidence. For instance, the prosecution might wish to offer the testimony of one of the elderly men who will give his opinion that the defendant is a violent person.

Inquiring about rather than proving specific instances. Returning to items (1) and (2), on cross-examination of the defendant's mother, the prosecution may ask questions about the character witness's knowledge of specific instances. The prosecution may wish to test whether the character witness actually knows what goes on in the community enough to testify competently about the defendant's reputation within that community. For example, the prosecution may ask the defendant's mother whether she has heard about the injuries to the pets, elderly people, and children left in the defendant's care. Either the mother heard about those instances and disregarded them in describing the defendant's great reputation, or she had not heard about the instances, which calls into question her personal knowledge and competency to testify about the defendant's reputation in the community. In addition, the prosecution may ask whether she knew about these instances because if she did know about them, it raises a question about how she maintains an opinion that his character is peace-loving. If she did *not* know about them, then she is ill-informed, and her opinion of his character for peace-loving is less reliable. All of these questions are designed to test the character witness's basis for her opinion or for her testimony about the defendant's reputation.

To protect against wild and unfounded accusations that may prejudice the jury, the prosecution must have a good faith basis for asking about the specific instances. It is an ethical violation for a prosecutor to manufacture false accusations. Because the questions are not evidence, the prosecutor does not violate the character evidence rules by asking these questions. These inquiries are permitted because the question is not using character evidence to prove action in conformity with the character, but rather to undermine the credibility of the character witness. In addition, the prosecution is not permitted to prove the specific instances if the witness denies knowing about them. If the prosecutor wanted to offer evidence in the form of answers to these specific instance questions, then the character objection would be correct. (Undermining witness credibility is addressed in more detail in Chapter 8.)

Federal Rules of Evidence Compared: Notable Differences

FRE 404(a)(1) also has a fairness provision, but it has broader application than that of the CEC because it allows two ways for the defendant to open the door to his character. The first way is identical to that of the CEC — by offering character evidence about himself. The second way is that when the defendant offers evidence of a character trait of the victim under FRE 404(a)(2) (discussed in the "Character of the Victim" section below), he also opens the door for the prosecution to offer evidence on that same trait of the defendant's character.

Other Sexual Offenses by the Criminal Defendant: CEC 1108

CEC 1108 lifts the general ban on conduct in conformity character evidence when the defendant is charged with a sexual offense in a criminal case and evidence exists that the defendant has committed other sexual offenses. In such cases, the prosecution can offer evidence of the defendant's commission of other sexual offenses without waiting for the defendant to open the door to his own character on that trait. The type of evidence that is usually offered under this section is evidence of prior bad acts — and other specific instances of misconduct.

CEC §1108(a): Evidence of another sexual offense by defendant

In a criminal action, in which the defendant is accused of a sexual offense, evidence of the defendant's commission of another sexual offense or offenses is not made inadmissible by Section 1101, if the evidence is not inadmissible pursuant to Section 352.

Much of this evidence could be offered under CEC 1101(b) for a non-propensity purpose. But CEC 1108 permits the use of evidence of prior sexual misconduct and permits its use for the propensity purpose in sexual offense prosecutions. For instance, if the defendant is on trial for rape, this section allows the prosecution to offer evidence of other rapes the defendant has committed to prove that the defendant is the kind of person who commits rapes. However, evidence of a prior act of indecent exposure is not admissible to show propensity for sexual assault without the assistance of some expert opinion evidence showing how indecent exposures helps to prove a propensity toward sexual assault. (Expert testimony is addressed in Chapter 9.)

The prosecution is required to give advance notice to the accused, including a witness statement or summary of the witness's testimony that the prosecution expects to offer into evidence. CEC 1108(b) describes the procedure for notice and disclosure to defendant. Once the prosecution gives notice that it will offer evidence under CEC 1108 to prove the criminal defendant's propensity to commit sexual misdeeds, the prosecution may then offer evidence of specific instances. The statutory language refers to the "commission" of other sexual offenses, which allows the prosecution to use specific instances of prior bad acts. On rebuttal, however, the defendant is not limited to specific instance evidence and can rebut using all three types of character evidence under CEC 1100.

CEC 1108(c) explains that it should not be "construed to limit the admission or consideration of evidence under any other section of this code." Subsection (d) defines sexual offenses to include rape; non-consensual contact with genitals, anus, or other body parts; sexual battery; deriving sexual gratification from the infliction of pain or death on another; possessing pornographic materials depicting minors; distributing obscene material to minors; and any attempt or conspiracy to engage in such conduct. It is crucial to remember that the defendant *need not have been convicted of* these prior sexual offenses and *need not even have been charged with any offense.* This is consistent with the scope of permissible evidence under CEC 1101(b) as well, which is discussed in the section on circumstantial use of character evidence above.

2. The Character Evidence Exclusion Rules

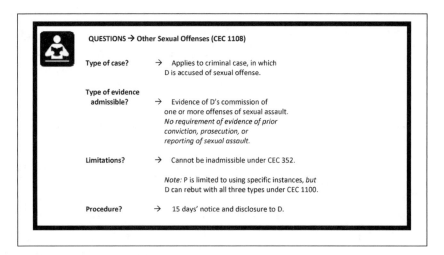

QUESTIONS → Other Sexual Offenses (CEC 1108)

Type of case?	→ Applies to criminal case, in which D is accused of sexual offense.
Type of evidence admissible?	→ Evidence of D's commission of one or more offenses of sexual assault. *No requirement of evidence of prior conviction, prosecution, or reporting of sexual assault.*
Limitations?	→ Cannot be inadmissible under CEC 352. *Note:* P is limited to using specific instances, *but* D can rebut with all three types under CEC 1100.
Procedure?	→ 15 days' notice and disclosure to D.

Figure 2.3. Determining When Other Sexual Offenses Can Be Admitted as Character Evidence

Figure 2.3 shows the basic analysis for whether specific instances of prior sexual offenses can be admitted as evidence against the defendant. First, the case must be a criminal one in which the defendant is *accused of a sexual offense*. Next, the evidence must be *a prior act that is a sexual offense*, regardless of whether the act was charged or defendant was convicted. Third, the evidence must satisfy the balancing test of CEC 352. Fourth, the prosecution must give 15 days' notice and disclosure to defendant. The defendant can rebut with all three types of character evidence.

If the defendant was *never charged* with the prior offense, however, the CEC 352 balancing test may provide a mechanism for keeping the evidence out. For instance, in a criminal case in which the defendant is charged with forcible sodomy, the prosecution may seek to offer evidence of a witness who will testify that the defendant committed forcible sodomy on someone else, but that the victim refused to cooperate with the authorities and thus the defendant was never prosecuted for or even charged with that crime. The principal factor affecting probative value is the similarity of the previous uncharged act with the current charge of sexual assault. However, the probative value of the evidence is lower if the defendant was never charged with the crime because there may have been insufficient evidence to bring charges against the defendant. The insufficient evidence could be as to whether the crime was committed at all (attacking the credibility of that first victim) or as to whether the defendant was the person who committed that first crime. The more uncertainty about whether the defendant committed the prior crime, or whether a prior crime occurred, the less probative is the evidence of that prior crime.

Moreover, the prejudicial effect of the evidence is likely to be high given the prevalence of recidivism in sexual offenders. The California judge must explicitly engage in the balancing test to determine whether the probative value of the prior sexual offense evidence is substantially outweighed by the danger of unfair prejudice. By enacting the statute, the legislature recognized that the mere fact that the evidence involves prior sexual misconduct is not enough to constitute undue prejudice. Thus, many California judges regularly admit CEC 1108 evidence in criminal trials.

Federal Rules of Evidence Compared: Minor Differences

The language of FRE 413 is very similar to CEC 1108. The FRE does not explicitly include the probative value/prejudicial effect balancing test. In addition, the scope of crimes that trigger the FRE sexual assault exception is a bit narrower.

Other Crimes of Domestic Violence by the Criminal Defendant: CEC 1109

In criminal prosecutions for domestic violence, CEC 1109 lifts the character evidence ban by permitting evidence of other acts of domestic violence committed by the accused. Those acts can be used to show proof of her propensity to commit such acts. Under California's definition, domestic violence includes elder abuse and abuse of other dependents. For example, if a defendant is charged with child abuse, the prosecution may seek to offer evidence that the defendant has committed child abuse in the past. If the defendant is charged with abusing an elderly relative in her care, evidence that she abused other elderly relatives in her care will be admissible. If the defendant is charged with beating her current husband, prior instances of beating her current husband or a previous husband will be admissible under this exception.

CEC §1109(a)(1): Evidence of defendant's other acts of domestic violence

(1) Except as provided in subdivision (e) or (f), in a criminal action in which the defendant is accused of an offense involving domestic violence, evidence of the defendant's commission of other domestic violence is not made inadmissible by Section 1101 if the evidence is not inadmissible pursuant to Section 352.

2. The Character Evidence Exclusion Rules

Note: The similarly worded subsections (a)(2) and (a)(3) apply to defendants accused of elder and dependent abuse and child abuse, to permit evidence of the defendant's commission of those other crimes under the same terms.

This provision also contains a time limitation, so that evidence of acts occurring more than ten years before the current charged offense is inadmissible unless the interests of justice require admission. Evidence of findings of administrative agencies regarding health facilities also is not admissible under this section. CEC 1109 also explicitly provides that the CEC 352 balancing test must be met before the evidence will be admitted. Advance notice to the defendant is required when the prosecution seeks to offer such evidence.

Figure 2.4 summarizes the process of determining whether prior acts of domestic violence (or elder/dependent or child abuse) are admissible. First, the case must be a criminal case in which the defendant is charged with a crime involving domestic violence (or elder/dependent or child abuse). Second, the evidence of the prior abuse must pass the CEC 352 balancing test. Third, the acts must have occurred within the prior ten years (unless an extension of this time limit is in the interests of justice). Finally, the prosecution must give notice and disclosure of the prior acts to the defendant.

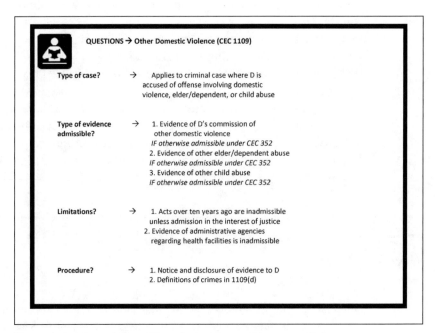

Figure 2.4. Admissibility of Specific Instances of Domestic Violence

Federal Rules of Evidence Compared: Notable Differences

FRE 414 permits evidence of similar crimes to be admitted when the defendant is accused of child molestation. It is much narrower than CEC 1109 because it does not apply to intimate abuse, elder abuse, or other types of child abuse.

Examples

1. Andrew was charged with assaulting Justin but claimed that he acted in self-defense because Justin hit him first. In its case in chief, the prosecution sought to introduce Kris's testimony that Kris knew about Andrew's reputation and that Andrew had a reputation for being out of control and provoking fist fights. In Andrew's case in chief, he offered testimony of his boss, Kendall, who said that Andrew had a reputation for being a peaceful and non-violent person. The prosecutor asks Kendall, on cross-examination, whether she knows that Andrew has been in a number of fights in the past few years. Which of the preceding evidence is admissible and for what purposes?

2. Sandra the Shoplifter has been watching the cosmetics counter at the department store in the mall, looking for an opportunity to steal some products while the sales clerk is involved with another customer. When she saw her chance, Sandra grabbed a handful of lipstick and mascara, dropped the makeup into her handbag, and slowly moved over to the shoe department. After trying on several pairs of shoes, Sandra decided to leave the store. As she walked through the outer door, Glenn the Security Guard grabbed her wrist and said, "Come with me, dear. Let's go check out whether you have a receipt for those cosmetics in your purse." Sandra tried to get away, but Glenn's grip was tight. Glenn then took her into a small windowless room in the interior of the department store. Glenn offered to refrain from calling the police if Sandra would remove her clothing. Sandra reluctantly agreed. Glenn then sexually assaulted Sandra. Sandra fought back but was overcome by Glenn. Sandra went to the police after Glenn released her, and Glenn is now being prosecuted for sexual assault. The prosecution seeks to offer a witness Cynthia, who will testify that Glenn sexually assaulted her two years ago when he caught her shoplifting from the lingerie department of that same department store. Cynthia did not report the crime at the time, but she came forward when she saw a news report about Glenn's current trial. Should the court admit Cynthia's testimony in Glenn's trial?

3. Devon is on trial for assault and false imprisonment of an elderly person. The prosecution seeks to admit evidence that Devon assaulted other elderly people on two prior occasions. Each time, the elderly person had taken a parking spot that Devon was patiently waiting for. Devon objects that the evidence is inadmissible character evidence. The prosecution responds that the evidence is admissible under CEC 1109 because Devon is on trial for a crime involving elder abuse, and the past attacks also involved elder abuse. Devon responds that the person he assaulted was not his dependent or an elderly person living with him under his care and therefore it did not constitute elder abuse. How should the court respond?

4. Morton is being prosecuted for spousal abuse. His wife Deidre finally sought police help on Friday night when Morton broke both her nose and her arm in one evening of battering. When they were at the emergency room that night, a nurse called Morton away to sign some forms, and a police detective was able to speak to Deidre alone for several minutes. During that time, Deidre tearfully related how Morton had struck their nine-year-old daughter Ashley that evening, and when Deidre stepped in between them, he began to beat her severely. Deidre told the police that Morton also abuses his elderly parents who live in an apartment over the garage on their property. Deidre explained to the officers that the abuse is always physical and psychological, but never sexual. Over an anticipated character evidence objection, can the prosecution offer this evidence about Morton in its case in chief? How would the analysis and outcome differ under the FRE?

5. Petunia and Victor dated for several years. When Victor met someone else on the Internet, he broke up with Petunia. Two days after the breakup, Petunia went to Victor's house and rang the doorbell. When Victor answered the door with flowers in his hand and said, "Oh, it's you. I was expecting someone else," Petunia pulled a gun from behind her back and shot Victor in the chest. Victor survived the wound, and Petunia was prosecuted for attempted murder of an intimate. The prosecution seeks to offer evidence that five years previously, Petunia dated Igor, and when he broke up with her, she stalked him and threatened him with a gun. Petunia objects, arguing the evidence is irrelevant and impermissible character evidence. How should the court rule, and why?

6. Bartholomew is on trial for killing Cassandra, a small child whom he was babysitting. Bartholomew claims that Cassandra fell down some steps when he turned his back for a minute and that her death was an unfortunate accident. The prosecution seeks to offer the testimony of Abigail, Cassandra's older sister, who will say that Bartholomew left Cassandra in the house alone for hours at a time while he went out to

party with his friends. Abigail also will testify that several months before, when Bartholomew had left Cassandra alone, she had fallen down the stairs and had gotten several bruises but no broken bones. Bartholomew objects. How should the court rule?

Explanations

1. Going through the approach outlined in this chapter for the mercy rule and fairness provisions, we must first determine whether this is a civil or criminal case. The words *charge* and *prosecution* indicate that this is a criminal case. The first piece of evidence under review is given in the prosecution's case in chief. In a criminal case, the prosecution is permitted to offer character evidence only when character is at issue, when intimate crimes are involved, or when the defendant has opened the door to the use of character evidence. Character is not at issue in this assault case, and there is no intimate crime involved. During the prosecution's case in chief, the defendant has not yet presented any evidence, so he cannot have opened the door. Therefore, the judge should rule that Kris's testimony is not admissible because it is improper for the prosecution to attack defendant Andrew's character in its case in chief. The second item of evidence occurs during the defendant's case in chief. Recall that the defendant is permitted to offer character evidence of his own under CEC 1102, as long as it is limited to reputation and opinion evidence. Kendall's testimony that Andrew is a peaceful, non-violent person is in the form of reputation evidence, and it is admissible if offered by the defendant. Now the defendant has opened the door to the use of the character evidence, and so the prosecution may use character evidence when the prosecution cross-examines Kendall. The CEC is interpreted to permit inquiry into the basis for the reputation or opinion witness's testimony for purposes of impeachment. Therefore, the prosecution can inquire about the past fist fights to test the thoroughness of the character witness's knowledge about the defendant's reputation.

2. This is a criminal case involving a sexual offense, and thus CEC 1108 governs the analysis. CEC 1108 provides an exception to the general ban on character evidence in CEC 1101(a) and allows evidence of the defendant's commission of other acts of sexual offenses to be offered at trial as long as the evidence passes the CEC 352 balancing test. Here, Cynthia's testimony is about another sexual offense that the defendant Glenn committed in the past. The CEC does not require proof that criminal charges were filed based on that prior commission of a sexual assault. Cynthia's testimony has a high probative value because her situation and Sandra's were very similar — both were caught shoplifting and then were sexually

assaulted by the same security guard (Glenn) at the same department store. The prejudicial effect of Cynthia's testimony may not rise to the level of undue or unfair prejudice because the similar situation is not likely to lead the jurors to convict on an improper basis. If the conditions of the other sexual assault were much more egregious than the current assault, then an issue of unfair prejudice may exist. In this case, however, the jurors will use the evidence that Glenn has done this sort of sexual assault before for the purpose that CEC 1108 allows — to show Glenn's propensity for committing sexual assaults on suspected shoplifters. Thus, any objection likely will be overruled.

3. The court should overrule Devon's objection because the statute does not require that the elder be a dependent. There is a separate provision for the abuse of dependents, regardless of whether they are elderly.

4. Morton is being prosecuted for spousal abuse. Therefore, this is a domestic violence case and is governed by CEC 1109. CEC 1109(a) permits evidence of other specific instances of domestic violence to be admitted against a criminal defendant currently on trial for a domestic violence assault. CEC 1109(b) permits evidence of other elder or dependent abuse instances to be admitted against a criminal defendant currently on trial for an elder or a dependent abuse crime. Because spousal abuse is a form of domestic violence, the other instances of Morton's spousal abuse will be admissible under CEC 1109(a). Because the evidence of elder and dependent abuse also relates to abuse in the home, it can fall within the definition of domestic violence, and thus the evidence will be admissible as well. However, if the elder abuse involved people outside of Morton's family or living situation, then that evidence would not be admissible in this case because that abuse would not be acts of domestic violence. If Morton were also being charged with elder or dependent abuse in this case, the instances of his prior abuse of elders or dependents also would be admissible under CEC 1109(b). Under the FRE, the prior instances of elder or dependent abuse will not be admissible to prove conduct in conformity. FRE 413 applies to sexual crimes only, and FRE 414 applies to child molestation only. The FRE does not provide an exception for domestic violence, elder, or dependent abuse.

5. The court should overrule both objections. Petunia is being charged with a crime against an intimate — a former boyfriend — and her previous crime against an intimate makes it more likely that she also committed this current crime against an intimate. In addition, the evidence in both cases constitutes a crime of domestic violence under CEC 1109. Thus, her prior commission of other acts of domestic violence is not excluded by the character evidence rules. The attack on her former boyfriend Igor also constitutes a prior commission of an act of domestic violence. The court

must apply the CEC 352 balancing test, and if it decides that the probative value is not outweighed by the danger of unfair prejudice, then the evidence will be admissible. In addition, the ten-year limitation is not implicated here because the first offense occurred five years previously.

6. The court should admit the evidence of the prior incident involving Cassandra to help prove the non-character purpose of absence of mistake or accident. Because Bartholomew had left Cassandra alone before, and because she suffered an injury similar to the injury that proved fatal this time, he was on notice that she could get hurt when he left her alone. Therefore, he acted with knowledge or recklessness (rather than with mere negligence) in leaving Cassandra alone on the occasion of her death.

The Character of the Victim Exceptions: CEC 1103

CEC 1103 permits the *accused* in a criminal case to offer evidence of *the victim's character* to prove that the victim engaged in behavior that under the substantive criminal law excuses or justifies the conduct of the accused. For instance, the accused can offer evidence of the victim's propensity for violence to prove that the victim was the provoker in an attack. The victim character exception is analogous to the mercy rule for the defendant's character in CEC 1102. It permits the defendant to offer relevant character evidence about the victim in a criminal case to prove the victim's conduct in conformity with that character. Note, however, that the victim's character will be relevant less often than the criminal defendant's.

CEC §1103(a): Character of crime victim to prove conduct offered by defendant, or by prosecution to rebut

(a) In a criminal action, evidence of the character or a trait of character (in the form of an opinion, evidence of reputation, or evidence of specific instances of conduct) of the victim of the crime for which the defendant is being prosecuted is not made inadmissible by Section 1101 if the evidence is:

(1) Offered by the defendant to prove conduct of the victim in conformity with the character or trait of character

(2) Offered by the prosecution to rebut evidence adduced by the defendant under paragraph (1).

For instance, the defendant in a criminal case may wish to offer evidence of the victim's character for a quick temper to prove that the victim acted in conformity with that character and provoked a confrontation with the defendant in the altercation that led to the present assault charge. When the defendant offers this evidence, he opens the door on this character trait. The prosecution can walk through that door and offer evidence to rebut the defendant's evidence about the victim on that particular character trait. For example, the prosecution may offer evidence that the victim has a reputation for being slow to anger and difficult to provoke.

CEC 1103(b) adds a further nuance to this rule. When the defendant opens the door by bringing in character evidence about the victim's character for violence, or a predisposition or tendency toward violence, *two doors are opened*. The prosecution is permitted to offer evidence about the victim's good character for non-violence (peacefulness) *as well as* the defendant's character for violence.

CEC §1103(b): Evidence of defendant's violent character after evidence of victim's violent character

In a criminal action, evidence of the defendant's character for violence or trait of character for violence (in the form of an opinion, evidence of reputation, or evidence of specific instances of conduct) is not made inadmissible by Section 1101 if the evidence is offered by the prosecution to prove conduct of the defendant in conformity with the character or trait of character and is offered after evidence that the victim had a character for violence or a trait of character tending to show violence has been adduced by the defendant under paragraph (1) of subdivision (a).

Figure 2.5 explains that when the criminal defendant offers evidence of the victim's character for violence, he is opening a door for evidence of his own character for violence even if he has not offered any character evidence specifically about himself. Thus, if the accused offers evidence of his good character for peacefulness under the mercy rule of CEC 1102(a) or evidence of the victim's bad character for violence under CEC 1103(a), he opens the door for the prosecution to offer evidence of his own bad character for violence.

Note that when the evidence involves the character of the victim or the defendant's character for violence after he has offered evidence of the victim's character for violence, all three types of character evidence may be used in a California court. This is in contrast to the mercy rule and fairness provision of CEC 1102, which permit only the use of reputation and opinion character evidence.

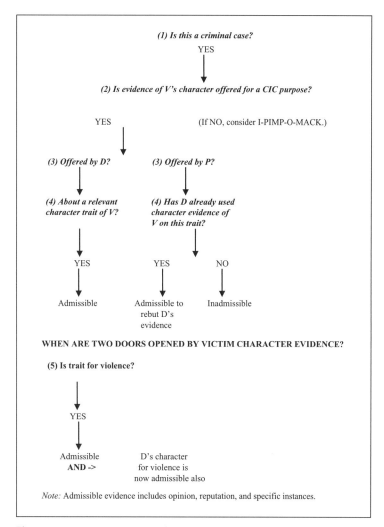

Figure 2.5. What Character of Crime Victim Evidence Is Admissible?

Federal Rules of Evidence Compared: Notable Differences

There are several important differences between CEC 1103(a) and FRE 404(a)(2). The primary distinction is that under the FRE, a party cannot offer specific instance character evidence to prove the conduct of the victim or the conduct of the defendant during the direct examination of a witness. For example, in a federal prosecution of an assault case where John is charged with assaulting victim Dan, the defense cannot ask defense witness Dennis whether victim Dan had ever assaulted someone to prove that Dan is the type of person who provokes attacks on himself. In contrast, in California, the defense can ask its own witness Dennis whether Dan has provoked attacks in the past.

Under the FRE, the only way to ask about those specific instances is on cross-examination, which means that the question can be asked only of the other side's witness. For example, under the FRE, if the defendant offers evidence that victim Dan was an aggressive bully through the testimony of defense witness Dennis, the defendant will be limited to offering Dennis's opinion or knowledge of Dan's reputation for being an aggressive bully. Under the FRE, Dennis cannot testify on direct examination about any specific instances that illustrate Dan's aggression. This is unlike the CEC, which allows the defense counsel to ask Dennis about specific instances of Dan's aggressive behavior on direct examination, and thus to use specific instance character evidence to help prove Dan's conduct in conformity.

A second difference is that when the defendant offers character evidence about the victim on any trait, the fairness provision is triggered in a much broader way than under the CEC. Under the FRE, two doors are opened for the prosecution to respond:

1. with evidence of the victim's good character on that trait, and
2. with evidence of the defendant's bad character on that trait.

For example, if the defendant offers evidence of the victim's character for defrauding investors in federal court, then he opens two doors. The first door is for the prosecution to rebut with evidence of the victim's good character on fraudulent conduct, which is the same as under the CEC. In contrast under the FRE, the defendant also will have opened the door for the prosecution to offer evidence of the *defendant's* character for defrauding investors, even if the defendant has not offered any character evidence about himself. While the CEC opens both doors only on issues of violence and non-violence, the FRE opens both doors on any character trait that the defendant raises about the victim.

The third major difference between the CEC and the FRE applies in the limited circumstance of a homicide prosecution in which the defendant offers *any* evidence that the victim of that charged homicide was the first aggressor. If the defendant offers any type of evidence in federal court, including testimony that the victim struck him first (which would not be character evidence because it is not offered to show conduct in conformity but rather to show exactly what actually happened on the particular occasion at issue), the prosecution may offer evidence of the victim's character or trait for peacefulness to rebut that first aggressor evidence. Thus, in a federal homicide prosecution, the defendant also can open the door to the victim's character for peacefulness *without offering any character evidence first*. Merely providing testimony that the victim struck first permits the prosecution in federal court to offer evidence about the victim's character for peacefulness. In California state courts, the prosecution can offer such evidence only if the accused has first offered character evidence showing that the victim was violent or non-peaceful.

The Victim's Character in Sexual Offenses: CEC 1103(c)

The CEC provides specific code sections to address sexual offenses; these are often referred to as the *rape shield laws*. Sexual offenses include sexual harassment, sexual assault, rape, and sexual battery. In a criminal case involving a sexual offense, a question arises as to whether the general victim exception of CEC 1103(a) should apply because with many rape and sexual assault cases, the primary issue is whether there was consent to the sexual act — no "crime" has occurred unless there is a lack of consent. If there is no crime, then there is no "victim." In these cases, courts instead use the term *complaining witness* to identify the alleged victim of a rape or sexual assault. In such cases, CEC 1103(c) applies instead of 1103(a), and it prevents the defendant from offering evidence of the complaining witness's character to prove her consent, except for specific instances of sexual conduct with the particular defendant.

 CEC §1103(c): complaining witness' sexual conduct and manner of dress

(1) Notwithstanding any other provision of this code to the contrary, and except as provided in this subdivision, in any prosecution [for sex crimes] . . . , opinion evidence, reputation evidence, and evidence of specific instances of the complaining witness' sexual conduct, or any of that evidence, is not admissible by the defendant in order to prove consent by the complaining witness.

(2) Notwithstanding paragraph (3), evidence of the manner in which the victim was dressed at the time of the commission of the offense shall not be admissible when offered by either party on the issue of consent in any prosecution for an offense specified in paragraph (1), unless the evidence is determined by the court to be relevant and admissible in the interests of justice. . . .

(3) Paragraph (1) shall not be applicable to evidence of the complaining witness' sexual conduct with the defendant.

(4) If the prosecutor introduces evidence, including testimony of a witness, or the complaining witness as a witness gives testimony, and that evidence or testimony relates to the complaining witness' sexual conduct, the defendant may cross-examine the witness who gives the testimony and offer relevant

evidence limited specifically to the rebuttal of the evidence introduced by the prosecutor or given by the complaining witness.

(5) Nothing in this subdivision shall be construed to make inadmissible any evidence offered to attack the credibility of the complaining witness as provided in Section 782.

Thus, despite the broad permission to use all three types of character evidence to prove the character of the victim in CEC 1103(a), if the alleged victim is in a case involving a sexual assault, then the defendant may not use any character evidence of her sexual relations with others to prove her consent. CEC 1103(c) also prohibits proving consent with evidence of the alleged victim's manner of dress at the time of the assault, unless the court finds that it is relevant and in the interests of justice to admit that evidence. Evidence as to the condition of the clothing, before, during, or after the offense is not precluded by this rule.

While evidence of the alleged victim's sexual conduct with others is prohibited by CEC 1103(c), the defendant is permitted to offer character evidence as it relates to the alleged victim's sexual conduct with the defendant himself. Moreover, if the prosecution offers testimony that relates to the complaining witness's sexual conduct, then the defendant in fairness may cross-examine those witnesses on that evidence, specifically limited to undermining the evidence introduced by the prosecution. This section does not limit evidence offered to attack the credibility of a witness, such as evidence that directly contradicts the witness's own testimony about her behavior.

Federal Rules of Evidence Compared: Notable Differences

The federal rule that corresponds to CEC 1103(c) is FRE 412, which specifically addresses the alleged victim's past sexual behavior or predisposition. The FRE generally prohibits evidence of other sexual behavior and sexual predisposition, but provides three exceptions that permit the criminal defendant to offer specific instances of the victim's sexual behavior if offered (1) to prove that someone other than the accused was the source of fluids, injury, or other physical evidence; (2) to prove past sexual relations with the defendant to demonstrate consent; or (3) where exclusion would violate the constitutional rights of the accused. This third exclusion applies in California cases as well because the federal constitution trumps any CEC provisions. In addition, the prosecution can offer evidence of past sexual relations with the defendant. Any offer of evidence under these exceptions must be subjected to an evidentiary hearing according to FRE 412(c).

The Character of the Victim in Civil Cases Alleging Sexual Abuse: CEC 1106

When sexual offenses are the subject of civil litigation instead of criminal charges, the uses of character evidence are more strictly proscribed, with a stronger emphasis on which party is offering the evidence. If the defendant in the civil action seeks to provide character evidence about the plaintiff's sexual conduct, he can do so for evidence about her sexual conduct with him under CEC 1106(b). Since the admissibility of character evidence then would fall under CEC 1100 (otherwise admissible evidence), all three types of evidence are available.

CEC §1106: Sexual harassment, sexual assault, or sexual battery cases; opinion or reputation evidence of plaintiff's sexual conduct
(a) In any civil action alleging conduct which constitutes sexual harassment, sexual assault, or sexual battery, opinion evidence, reputation evidence, and evidence of specific instances of plaintiff's sexual conduct, or any of such evidence, is not admissible by the defendant in order to prove consent by the plaintiff or the absence of injury to the plaintiff, unless the injury alleged by the plaintiff is in the nature of loss of consortium. (b) Subdivision (a) shall not be applicable to evidence of the plaintiff's sexual conduct with the alleged perpetrator.

For instance, imagine a civil action where the plaintiff claims that the defendant is liable for sexual harassment because he compelled her to submit to sexual intercourse when they traveled on business trips by booking only one hotel room for the two of them. The defendant may offer evidence that the plaintiff had a consensual sexual relationship with the defendant during the time period that included two of those business trips.

When the character evidence about the plaintiff's sexual conduct does not involve conduct with the defendant, then the defendant cannot use that evidence to establish consent or absence of injury under CEC 1106(a). If, for example, the defendant sought to admit evidence that the plaintiff had shared a hotel room and had consensual sexual relations on business trips with her previous supervisor, CEC 1106 would prevent the defendant from offering this evidence. However, if the plaintiff claims loss of consortium (physical intimate relations with a spouse or partner) as part of her damages, then the defendant could offer evidence of the plaintiff's current sexual conduct with others to prove an absence of injury to her.

As with CEC 1108, if the plaintiff opens the door to evidence of her character by testifying or putting another witness on the stand who testifies about the plaintiff's sexual conduct, then under CEC 1106 the defendant can cross-examine that witness and offer relevant evidence to rebut the plaintiff's evidence about her sexual conduct. All three types of character evidence are permitted under CEC 1100. For example, the plaintiff brings her former supervisor to the witness stand, who testifies that they had a prior relationship and that they participated in consensual sexual relations during business trips. He also testifies that when their relationship ended, they stopped sharing hotel rooms and never resumed sexual relations. Because the plaintiff has opened the door, the defendant can then cross-examine the supervisor about any subsequent resumption of sexual relations in an effort to prove that the plaintiff continued her sexual relationship or to prove that the plaintiff lied about her past sexual conduct.

Note on the Truth in Evidence Provision (Proposition 8)

In 1982, the California passed Proposition 8 as an amendment to the California Constitution. Also known as the Victim's Bill of Rights and the Right to Truth in Evidence provision, this amendment made some major changes in how the rules of evidence apply in California criminal proceedings. It does not apply to civil cases. The Right to Truth in Evidence provision of Proposition 8 gave parties to criminal proceedings the constitutional right to admit all relevant evidence and jeopardized the character evidence restrictions described in this chapter.

However, the *Ewoldt* decision of the California Supreme Court in 1994 found that the character evidence provisions discussed above have been restored based on their amendment and/or reenactment subsequent to the passage of Proposition 8.[2] The only effect that Proposition 8 still has is on the character of witnesses (whether they are victims or defendants or otherwise). (This issue is addressed in Chapter 8 on the character for truthfulness of witnesses at trial.)

Federal Rules of Evidence Compared: Notable Differences

FRE 412 covers both criminal and civil cases, and the part of that rule that corresponds to CEC 1103(c) is discussed in the "Character of the Victim"

---

2. People v. Ewoldt, 7 Cal. 4th 380, 867 P.2d 757 (1994).

FRE comparison section above. FRE 412 also applies to civil cases alleging sexual misconduct in the following way: evidence to prove the sexual behavior or predisposition of the alleged victim is not admissible unless it is "otherwise admissible" under these rules and the probative value substantially outweighs the danger of harm to the victim and of unfair prejudice to either party. Note that this is a higher standard for admissibility than that of FRE 403 (which states that the evidence is admissible unless its probative value is substantially outweighed by the danger of unfair prejudice). Reputation evidence is admissible under this rule only if placed at issue by the alleged victim.

The federal rules also contain an explicit notice requirement, which provides that the party seeking to offer such evidence must give the opposing party 14 days' written notice of her intent to offer such evidence and the purpose for which that evidence is being offered. FRE 415 also applies in civil cases involving claims of sexual assault and/or child abuse and permits evidence of the party's commission of other acts of sexual assault or child molestation as long as advance notice (15 days) of the disclosure is provided. There is no analogue to the Truth in Evidence provision under federal law.

Examples

1. Mercedes is on trial for resisting arrest and committing battery on a police officer. After the prosecution's case in chief, Mercedes offers evidence that the police officer was belligerent and yelled at her for no reason. Then the prosecution seeks to admit evidence that Mercedes has committed violent assaults on people in the past and that Mercedes has a reputation for being violent. Mercedes objects to this evidence as impermissible character evidence. The prosecution responds that Mercedes has opened the door to her own character for violence because she offered character evidence about the victim police officer's character for violence. How should the court rule, and why?

2. Jimmy and his codefendants are charged with attempted murder and conspiracy to commit first degree murder, arising from a fight with the victim, Luke. Jimmy and his buddies went to collect money that Luke owed them. Luke denied owing the money, and they started arguing. At trial, Jimmy testified that he struck Luke with a fire extinguisher in self-defense after Luke had started hitting him with a baseball bat. Luke was still hospitalized at the time of trial. The prosecution seeks to offer the testimony of Luke's mother that in her opinion, Luke is a peace-loving guy, and his reputation in the community is as a generous and kind person who always pays more than his fair share of expenses. Jimmy

objects as impermissible character evidence. How should the prosecution respond, and how should the court rule? Assume now that Luke dies, and Jimmy is prosecuted for murder instead of attempted murder. Would this fact change the analysis and outcome if the case were tried in federal court?

3. Leah is an associate at a small law firm, Pheelum, L.L.C. She sued the senior partner Harry, the office manager Butch, and the law corporation for sexual harassment and creation of a hostile work environment. Leah had dated Harry several years ago, but their relationship had been over for more than two years when she joined the law firm. Leah claims that Harry put his arms around her waist in violation of the firm's "no touching" policy, and that he made frequent sexual jokes, innuendos, and derogatory remarks about her sexuality and appearance. The defendants sought to admit evidence that Leah had engaged in sexual horseplay in the office and made statements to her coworkers and to Harry about her own past sexual exploits, as well as her planned future conquests. The defendants also sought to admit evidence that Leah had rubbed Harry's back, pinched his rear end, and caressed his chest on numerous occasions in the workplace — and that he did the same to her. Plaintiff Leah objects to this evidence as impermissible character evidence under CEC 1106. How should the defense respond, how should the court rule, and why? How would the outcome differ if this case were tried in federal court?

4. Carolyn has sued Ron for sexual harassment in civil court. Carolyn alleges that while she worked at the local coffee shop, Ron, the owner, subjected her to repeated harassment by using sexually explicit descriptions about movies, her uniform, and various customers of the coffee shop. Ron claims that he and Carolyn were just joking around and that there was no way she could be offended by his comments because they used to have these same types of conversations in bed when they were lovers the year before she began working in the coffee shop. Analyze the following transcript and determine which objections and rulings are appropriate, and whether additional objections should be made.

Cross-examination of Carolyn:

a. **Defense Counsel:** Isn't it true that you had sexual relations with Ron last year?
b. **Plaintiff's Counsel:** Objection. Impermissible character evidence.
c. **Defense Counsel:** The evidence is offered to show consent, Your Honor.
d. **Judge:** Objection sustained.

e. **Defense Counsel:** Isn't it true that you enjoyed Ron's sexually explicit conversations?

f. **Carolyn:** No, I did not enjoy them. His comments were gross.

g. **Defense Counsel:** But you had listened to his comments before, right?

h. **Plaintiff's Counsel:** Objection, Your Honor. Impermissible character evidence.

i. **Defense Counsel:** Yes, Your Honor. If I may make an offer of proof: if allowed to finish this line of questioning, the evidence will prove the absence of injury.

j. **Judge:** I'll allow you some leeway, Counsel. Objection overruled for now. The witness is directed to answer the question.

k. **Carolyn:** Yes.

l. **Defense Counsel:** Just last year, right?

m. **Carolyn:** Yes.

n. **Defense Counsel:** And last year you did not call them "gross," right?

o. **Carolyn:** That's correct.

p. **Defense Counsel:** In fact, you listened to those comments willingly, last year, isn't that right?

q. **Carolyn:** Yes.

r. **Defense Counsel:** So the comments really didn't bother you, did they?

s. **Carolyn:** Not last year, when we were sexually involved. This year, they did.

t. **Defense Counsel:** Isn't it true that his comments were about sexual activities that you and Ron had engaged in while dating?

u. **Plaintiff's Counsel:** Objection. Impermissible character evidence.

v. **Judge:** Overruled. She has opened the door.

w. **Carolyn:** Yes, they were.

x. **Defense Counsel:** Isn't it also true that you use sexual innuendos and sexually explicit language when talking to men other than the defendant in the workplace?

y. **Plaintiff's Counsel:** Objection, Your Honor. This evidence about the victim's character is totally inappropriate.

z. **Judge:** Overruled.

5. Tommy is being prosecuted for assault and battery of James. Witnesses saw James walk up to Tommy and slap Tommy in the face. Tommy then hit James in the stomach and then hit James's back, knocking him down. As James tried to get up from the floor, Tommy began to stomp on James's head and back, causing severe injuries and pain. Analyze the following transcript of the defense's case in chief to determine which objections are appropriate and whether additional

objections should be made. How would the objections and rulings differ under the FRE?

Direct examination of Witness One:

a. **Defense Counsel:** What did you see after James approached Tommy?

b. **Witness One:** James slapped Tommy in the face.

c. **Defense Counsel:** Had Tommy hit James?

d. **Witness One:** No. Tommy had not done anything. He was just minding his own business when James walked up and started slapping him.

e. **Defense Counsel:** In your opinion, is Tommy the kind of person who gets into a fist fight with others for no apparent reason?

f. **Witness One:** No, he is not. He is an easygoing person.

g. **Defense Counsel:** Thank you. No further questions.

Cross-examination of Witness One:

h. **Prosecution Counsel:** You saw the defendant strike James, didn't you?

i. **Witness One:** Yes, I did. I like ice cream.

j. **Prosecution Counsel:** Objection. Relevance. Move to strike everything after the first sentence as irrelevant, Your Honor.

k. **Judge:** Objection sustained. The second sentence is stricken.

l. **Prosecution Counsel:** In fact, you have seen the defendant hit James before, haven't you?

m. **Defense Counsel:** Objection. Impermissible character evidence.

n. **Judge:** Counsel, would you like to be heard?

o. **Prosecution Counsel:** Your Honor, the evidence is admissible because the defendant has raised the issue and presented evidence that the victim was the first aggressor.

p. **Judge:** Objection sustained.

q. **Prosecution Counsel:** You have seen the defendant hit other people before, haven't you?

r. **Witness One:** No, I have not.

s. **Prosecution Counsel (with sarcasm):** Your opinion is that the defendant is peaceful, right?

t. **Defense Counsel:** Objection. Impermissible character evidence.

u. **Judge:** Objection overruled.

v. **Witness One:** I do think he is a peaceful person.

w. **Prosecution Counsel:** Isn't it true that the defendant once attacked you when you failed to say "good morning" while walking by him one day?

x. **Witness One:** Yes, that's true.

y. **Defense Counsel:** Objection, Your Honor. Impermissible character evidence. Move to strike the witness's last answer.

z. **Judge:** Objection overruled and motion denied.

6. Frieda is on trial for homicide, and she claims that the victim, her husband George, came toward her with a knife after a series of beatings over the course of the previous week. George had never been violent toward Frieda before, and in its case in chief, the prosecution seeks to offer the testimony of Holly, who will testify to the following: that George was a peace-loving person who would never hurt a fly, that George loved Frieda dearly, and that George brought roses to Frieda every week. Frieda objects to Holly's testimony as impermissible character evidence. The prosecution responds that Frieda has opened the door to character by claiming self-defense.
   a. How should the court rule on this objection, and why?
   b. Assume for purposes of this subpart that the court sustains the defense's objection to Holly's testimony. Then in her case in chief, Frieda seeks to offer the testimony of Ignacio, who will testify that George often got into fights when he was out drinking at bars, and that in Ignacio's opinion, George was a mean, violent guy who hid his temper from his wife until he finally snapped the week before she killed him. Is the testimony of Ignacio admissible?
   c. Assume for purposes of this subpart that Ignacio's testimony is admitted. The prosecution then seeks to offer Holly's testimony above in its rebuttal case. Frieda renews her objection. How should the court rule, and why?
   d. How would the rulings in each of the subparts above change, if at all, if Frieda were prosecuted in a federal district court instead of a California state court?

Explanations

1. The court should sustain the objection. Mercedes has not opened the door to character evidence because she has not offered any character evidence about the victim police officer. Rather, she offered evidence of the events that occurred on the specific day in question to prove what happened. There is no character purpose — that the officer is a violent kind of person — nor is there any conduct in conformity purpose that the officer acted in conformity with a violent character. Therefore the character of the victim exception does not apply, and the evidence should not be admitted.

2. The prosecution may respond that Jimmy opened the door to the character of the victim Luke under CEC 1103(a) by testifying that Luke was the first aggressor in this situation. If Jimmy has opened the door, then the prosecution would be entitled to respond with evidence of Luke's good character for that relevant trait. However, the court should sustain the objection because Jimmy's testimony is not character

evidence about Luke (that he is the kind of person who fights or that he acted in conformity with his fighting nature). Rather, Jimmy's testimony is evidence about what happened on that particular day and is not for a character or conduct in conformity purpose. Thus, Jimmy has not opened the door to the character of the victim, and therefore the prosecution cannot use the fairness provision to respond with character evidence of Luke's peaceable nature.

If Luke had died and this was a homicide prosecution in federal court, there would be two notable differences. First, Jimmy's evidence that Luke struck first would trigger the special first aggressor exception under FRE 404(a)(2), which permits the prosecution to offer evidence of the peacefulness of the victim in a homicide prosecution in which the defendant offers any evidence (not necessarily character evidence) that the victim was the first aggressor. With this door open, the prosecution is entitled to bring in the reputation and opinion evidence through Luke's mother. Second, her statement that he "always pays more than his fair share" would remain inadmissible because it is specific instance evidence, which can be presented in federal court only as an inquiry on cross-examination or when character is at issue. Neither situation applies here.

3. The defense should argue that under CEC 1106(b), the general prohibition against offering evidence of the plaintiff's past sexual conduct is not applicable to plaintiff's sexual conduct with the alleged perpetrator. That evidence is relevant to prove whether a hostile work environment existed as well as whether the touching was "unwelcome." Therefore, the court should admit this evidence on the issue of consent or to prove an absence of injury. Evidence of Leah's sexual conduct with non-perpetrators or conduct that occurred outside the workplace (her future sexual exploits) are not carved out of the general prohibition and therefore would not be admissible under CEC 1106(a).

   If the case were tried in federal court, the court would have to analyze whether the probative value of the evidence of her sexual innuendos and contact in the workplace substantially outweighs the danger of harm to Leah and the unfair prejudice to any party. Here, the probative value of the evidence is quite high because these instances make it significantly more probable that Leah did not suffer from unwelcome sexual advances and that she did not find the work environment to be a sexually hostile one. The danger of harm to Leah is minimal because she made the information about her sexual past and future public by speaking to her coworkers in the office (not in private) and by engaging in touching and rubbing in the public spaces of the office. Therefore, a federal judge likely will find that the workplace evidence is admissible under FRE 412. The evidence of events occurring outside of the workplace is much less probative, though similarly less prejudicial, and therefore might be excluded by the court.

4. This is a civil case alleging sexual harassment and therefore will be governed by CEC 1106. CEC 1106(a) prohibits the defendant from admitting evidence of the plaintiff's sexual conduct to prove consent or an absence of injury (except for loss of consortium, which is not indicated by this fact situation). However, CEC 1106(a) does not apply to the plaintiff's sexual conduct with the alleged perpetrator, who is the defendant in this case. Thus, if the defendant is trying to prove consent, as his attorney asserts in line c, the judge should have overruled the objection in line d.

    When defense counsel explains that he is trying to show an absence of injury in line i, the objection also should be overruled as the judge did in line j. The objection at line u is properly overruled in line v because the evidence relates to the plaintiff's past sexual conduct with the defendant. When the defense counsel seeks to offer evidence about the plaintiff's own use of sexual innuendos with other men, the evidence relates to the plaintiff's sexual conduct with others and therefore is included within the general prohibition of CEC 1106(a). Thus the court erred and should have sustained the objection at line z.

    The defense counsel may try to argue that under CEC 1106(c) the plaintiff has introduced evidence of her own past sexual behavior, and thus the door is opened for the defendant to cross-examine her on this point to offer rebuttal evidence. However, this evidence was introduced by the defense because the only testimony that has been offered in this transcript was in response to the defense cross-examination, and therefore the court will not find that the plaintiff has opened this door under CEC 1106(c).

5. Tommy is being prosecuted in criminal court, and the case involves an assault of a non-sexual nature. The transcript is from the defense case in chief. CEC 1102 governs the use of evidence of the defendant's character, and CEC 1103 governs the use of the victim's character. The evidence testified to by the defense witness in line f is admissible opinion testimony because the defendant is permitted to offer opinion and reputation character evidence about himself in a criminal case under CEC 1102.

    The objection in line j is appropriate because the witness's second sentence had no tendency to prove or disprove a fact of consequence in the case, and thus the court's ruling in line k is correct. In line l, the prosecution seeks evidence that Tommy has hit the victim before. This evidence could be considered specific instances of Tommy's violent character. While the defendant has opened the door to his own violent character by offering evidence of his easygoing nature, the prosecution is permitted to respond only with reputation or opinion evidence about the defendant's own character.

The defendant has not opened the door to the victim's character for violence under CEC 1103 because the defendant's witness merely described what happened on this occasion and did not offer any propensity or conduct in conformity evidence. Thus, the evidence of specific past instances of violence would not be admissible under CEC 1102 or CEC 1103. However, the prosecution may argue that the question in line l is merely to test the basis of the character witness's opinion, and if so, it would be permissible to ask the question.

The prosecution also may argue that the evidence is not character evidence, but rather is offered to show past animosity between the defendant and the victim and thus would be admissible under CEC 1101(b). In *federal court*, specific instances may be inquired into on cross-examination, and thus, once the defendant has opened the door to his character, the prosecution could ask about specific acts of violence and the objection in line p would be overruled. The judge improperly sustained the objection in line m because the first aggressor situation applies only in federal court, and then only in homicide prosecutions under FRE 404(a)(2). The objection in line t is properly overruled because now that the character door is opened, the prosecution may inquire into reputation and opinion of the defendant's character. The objection in line y is timely and also involves using a specific instance to test the basis for the witness's opinion.

6. a. The first objection to Holly's testimony should be sustained during the prosecution's case in chief. Frieda has not opened the door to the use of character evidence by simply asserting that she acted in self-defense. Also, because the prosecution presents its case in chief first, she has not yet offered any evidence. Therefore, she did not yet open the door to character evidence in this trial.

   b. When Frieda seeks to offer the testimony of Ignacio in her defense case in chief, she is permitted to offer this evidence as to George's character under the victim exception of CEC 1103. Frieda is permitted to offer all three types of character evidence about the victim.

   c. Once Frieda offers character evidence about the victim, then she has opened the door to permit the prosecution to offer evidence about George's character to rebut Frieda's evidence. Therefore, the prosecution can now offer Holly's testimony about George's peaceful nature after Frieda has offered evidence about George's violent nature.

   d. In federal court, the analysis would be a bit different, but the outcome would be the same for most of the evidence. Because in (a) Frieda is claiming that George attacked her first, and this is a homicide prosecution, the special clause of FRE 404(a)(1) would permit the prosecution to offer evidence about George's character for peacefulness after Frieda has offered any evidence (character or non-character) that George was the first aggressor. At this stage of the prosecution case in chief, Frieda has not yet had the opportunity to offer any evidence, and therefore, the character door is not open yet.

The testimony of Ignacio in (b) would be permitted under FRE 404(a)(2), which permits the defendant to offer reputation or opinion evidence of a pertinent character trait of the victim. The evidence of the specific instances of flowers will not be admissible under the FRE. The victim's character for violence and bar fights would be admissible, except that under the federal rules, only reputation and opinion evidence would be admissible during a direct examination. Thus, the objection to Ignacio's opinion about George being violent will be overruled and that evidence will be admissible. However, the objection will be sustained as to the specific instances of George's getting into bar fights. In (c), after Ignacio's testimony, the door will be opened for the prosecution to rebut with good character evidence about the victim, and thus Holly's testimony will be admissible in the prosecution's rebuttal case.

CHAPTER 3

Other Policy Exclusions for Relevant Evidence

The previous chapters in this book have addressed specific rules for excluding evidence: relevance and prejudicial effect (Chapter 1) and character (Chapter 2). This chapter addresses some additional limitations on relevant evidence based on the subject matter of the evidence and the context in which it is being used. These additional limitations are based on public policy concerns that override the parties' desire to admit all relevant evidence in litigation. For instance, under certain circumstances, evidence about efforts to fix a problem like a fence that is leaning over and about to fall onto the sidewalk cannot be used to show liability for harm caused when that leaning fence eventually topples over and hits someone on the sidewalk. The policy rationale for this exclusion is to encourage people to fix problems once they become aware of them.

Similarly, there are policy concerns that preclude using evidence of offers to settle cases, offers to plead guilty, and offers of sympathy and benevolent assistance to establish liability. These exclusions rely on public policies that encourage people to try to resolve disputes, engage in plea bargaining, and apologize when they harm another person. If those efforts at resolution and benevolent gestures could be used as substantive evidence of liability for the harm, then fewer people would try to settle cases and fewer people would express sympathy for harms.

It is important to note that evidence that is not made inadmissible by the rules in this chapter still will be subject to the other evidence rules discussed in subsequent chapters.

SUBSEQUENT REMEDIAL CONDUCT

When a person is injured or an accident occurs, people and businesses sometimes take *remedial* action. An example would be adding a mirror to a driveway with a blind turn after an auto collision. While the mirror does not help the first person who already has been injured, it may help prevent future collisions at that location. In litigation brought by the first person who was injured, the plaintiff might want to offer evidence that the defendant installed a mirror after the accident.

Remedial measures might be considered an admission of wrongdoing, and this evidence raises the question of why the mirror was not already in place before the accident. When the jurors ask themselves that question, they may be more likely to assume that the defendant *should* have installed a mirror prior to the accident and is likely at fault for the plaintiff's accident and the injury it caused. Recognizing the risk of jurors using this reasoning, some people and businesses would forgo fixing a problem by installing a mirror if they knew that the remedial action could be used as evidence of their liability for the harm.

Taking action to help prevent future injuries is good public policy, and therefore the California legislature wants to encourage people to fix things, to make dangerous conditions safer, and to take other remedial actions when someone is harmed. For this reason, CEC 1151 excludes evidence of these remedial measures when they are offered to prove negligence (that the defendant should have known of the risks of the dangerous condition) or to prove culpable conduct (that the defendant acted wrongfully in a way that resulted in the injury or harm).

CEC §1151: Subsequent remedial conduct
When, after the occurrence of an event, remedial or precautionary measures are taken, which, if taken previously, would have tended to make the event less likely to occur, evidence of such subsequent measures is inadmissible to prove negligence or culpable conduct in connection with the event.

This evidence is excluded because potential defendants would be less likely to fix problems and to correct the defects if their corrective efforts could be used against them to prove their responsibility in subsequent litigation. The evidence can be offered to prove some other purpose, but not to prove culpability or negligence.

To be protected under CEC 1151, the remedial measures must have been taken *after* an injury or accident has occurred. Repairs made *prior* to any accident or injury do not implicate the policy concerns because the subsequent harm cannot be the motivating factor for making *prior* repairs. Harm motivates any *subsequent* repairs, and that motivation is relevant to the issue of whether the defendant was responsible for that harm. Therefore, that harm must be the subject of the current lawsuit.

Illustrations of Which Measures the Rule Excludes

What kinds of remedial measures are excluded by CEC 1151? Replacing a sewer line, installing guardrails or handrails, sending warning notices, and even terminating problem employees are examples of remedial measures. Any action can be considered a remedial measure, as long as if taken previously, that action would have made the injury or accident less likely to have occurred.

What kinds of remedial measures are *not* excluded by CEC 1151? Evidence of remedial measures undertaken by third parties independent of the defendant is not barred by the subsequent remedial conduct doctrine. The policy limitations are not implicated because liability is not sought against the person who made the repair, and thus there is not the same chilling effect on people repairing their own dangerous conditions.

In addition, California courts have determined that evidence of the *failure* to take remedial measures after an injury or accident is not excluded by CEC 1151 and thus can be admissible. For instance, the evidence of a failure to make repairs to an unsafe amusement park ride despite injuries to several children will be admissible to establish the basis for punitive damages in a torts lawsuit by a child injured later.

While the remedial evidence is not admissible to prove negligence or culpable conduct, it will be admissible to prove some other relevant matter. For instance, where fault is not at issue, such as in a *strict liability* case, relevant evidence of subsequent remedial measures will be admissible.

Similarly, the evidence can be admissible for impeachment purposes. When using the evidence for impeachment, the impeaching party must show that the evidence is relevant by showing that the witness to be impeached authorized, recommended, approved, directed, or supervised the repair or change. If the witness did not have this connection to the remedial measure, then the evidence will not be admissible for impeachment.

Federal Rules of Evidence Compared: One Notable Difference

FRE 407 contains a similar prohibition, but extends it to also exclude evidence of subsequent remedial action in strict liability litigation and failure to warn cases in federal courts. In addition, the FRE provides a non-exhaustive list of permissible purposes, which includes proving ownership, control, and impeachment. The FRE further permits the use of the evidence to prove the feasibility of precautionary measures, but only when feasibility is disputed by the other side. If, for instance, the defendant testifies that he would have made the product safer but it was prohibitively expensive to do so, then the plaintiff can offer evidence that after the plaintiff suffered her injury, the defendant actually did find a way to make the product safer, and thus it was not "prohibitively" expensive.

OFFERS TO COMPROMISE

To promote the policy of encouraging settlements in civil cases, CEC 1152 prevents the use of settlement offers and statements made in the course of settlement negotiations to prove liability on a civil claim. This code section allows parties to feel free to make settlement offers because the offer cannot be used against them if the other party declines the offer and the case proceeds to trial. This protection is not limited to litigation situations and attaches to efforts to resolve disputes before any litigation has been filed with the courts.

CEC 1154 protects the non-offering party by preventing admission of *offers to accept* a compromise and *agreements to accept* a compromise. CEC 1154 bans the use of this settlement information to prove the *invalidity* of a claim and thus prevents the defendant from using evidence that the plaintiff was willing to settle for much less than she is asking for at trial to prove that the plaintiff has a weak case. It is important to examine both CEC sections when determining which statements will be excluded at trial.

CEC §1152: Offers to compromise and the like
Evidence that a person has, in compromise or from humanitarian motives, furnished or offered or promised to furnish money or any other thing, act, or service to another who has sustained or will sustain or claims that he or she has sustained or will sustain loss or damage, as well as any conduct or statements made in negotiation thereof, is inadmissible to prove his or her liability for the loss or damage or any part of it.

Subsection (b) provides a specific exception in actions for breach of the covenant of good faith and fair dealing and in certain cases under the Insurance Code.

3. Other Policy Exclusions for Relevant Evidence

Subsection (c) contains two additional exceptions for evidence of

1. a partial satisfaction without questioning its validity, when offered to prove its validity, and
2. a debtor's payment or promise to pay all or part of the debt when such evidence is offered to show a new duty or revival of existing duty to pay.

CEC §1154: Offer to discount a claim

Evidence that a person has accepted or offered or promised to accept a sum of money or any other thing, act, or service in satisfaction of a claim, as well as any conduct or statements made in negotiation thereof, is inadmissible to prove the invalidity of the claim or any part of it.

To use the protection of CEC 1152, the statement must have been made either in an effort to compromise an actual dispute over the validity or amount of a claim or for a humanitarian purpose. The dispute does not need to be one already in existence — an offer to compromise under CEC 1152 can also include an offer to compromise a *future* dispute. A dispute over the validity of a claim can occur when the plaintiff seeks to collect an overdue payment on an invoice, and the defendant says that the invoice already has been paid. A dispute over the amount of the claim would occur if the plaintiff seeks payment plus a late fee and the defendant states that he made the payment on time and therefore no late fee is due. In the second scenario, the defendant is not disputing that he owes the money, just the amount of the debt.

Any offer to compromise on the amount of the claim (such as when the defendant offers to pay half of the late fee amount to maintain a good relationship with the plaintiff) or on the validity (such as when the defendant says that he already made the payment but is willing to let the plaintiff charge him more for the next order to help the plaintiff make up the difference) will be protected under CEC 1152. If the plaintiff accepts or offers to accept this compromise, then CEC 1154 protects the plaintiff's offer to accept or acceptance.

Humanitarian Offers

An example of a humanitarian purpose would be when the defendant says, "I know your business is slow right now, and I do not want you to go under, so even though I paid the bill in full already, I am going to pay you that same amount again to help you keep the doors of your business open." This defendant is not trying to compromise because he believes that nothing is owed; he is simply trying to be a good person and his altruistic offer will be protected under CEC 1152. If the plaintiff accepts this compromise, that acceptance is protected under CEC 1154.

If the plaintiff accepts the defendant's offer of a partial payment, that acceptance would be *inadmissible* under CEC 1154 if the defendant later tries to prove at the trial that he does not owe the plaintiff the full amount because she was willing to accept only $2000.

When the settlement negotiation is comprised of multiple statements, the courts will determine whether each specific statement is connected to, or independent from, any settlement negotiation. Connected statements are protected; independent statements are not. *Connected statements* include explanations of how numbers were calculated and information about surrounding circumstances that may influence the settlement (such as a pending surgery in a personal injury case).

What Is Not Protected from Disclosure

If the defendant does not dispute the amount of the claim or its validity and is not acting from humanitarian motives, then any offer to make a partial payment is not protected from admission at trial. For instance, if instead our defendant had said, "I know I did not make the payment (or did not make it on time), and I owe you the entire amount. I am just a little short right now and can pay you only $2000 this month, but I will pay a little bit each month until the debt is fully repaid," then the defendant is not disputing the amount or validity and merely is working out a repayment plan. This situation is an example of when the exception in CEC 1152(c) applies to permit evidence of a partial payment, when there is no reservation of rights or assertion of an ongoing dispute, to be admitted into evidence if the defendant later defaults on his agreement to make partial payments.

Independent statements, such as information about the current strength of the stock market or where the party plans to go on vacation after the settlement is concluded, will not be protected. In making the determination as to whether a statement is connected or independent, the courts rely on the strong public policy in favor of promoting candor during settlement negotiations as guidance, and they err on the side of providing greater protection.

If the evidence is protected under CEC 1152 or 1154, the evidence will not be admissible to prove liability or invalidity of a civil claim. However, the evidence still can be admitted for some other purpose, such as for impeachment purposes if the defendant presents contrary evidence, or to show bias or some other relevant issue. Admissibility in these situations is subject to the CEC 352 balancing test (discussed in Chapter 1) and will be excluded if the probative value of the offer to compromise is substantially outweighed by the prejudicial effect of that evidence. The courts generally exclude the statements offered for impeachment purposes in order to promote settlements under the CEC 352 balancing test, rather than under the specific limitations of CEC 1152 and 1154.

Federal Rules of Evidence Compared: Notable Differences

The FRE combines offers to compromise and offers to accept a compromise into FRE 408 and prohibits the offers and statements made in compromise negotiations from being admitted in order to prove liability, or amount or invalidity of the claim. In addition, the FRE prohibits using the statements to impeach as prior inconsistent statements or to impeach by contradiction, and although this use is not excluded by the CEC, California courts generally reach the same result using the balancing test of CEC 352. (Chapter 8 provides a more detailed discussion of impeachment.) The FRE also contains an exception for negotiations with public offices or agencies when the evidence is sought to be used in certain criminal cases. A non-exhaustive list of permitted purposes for such statements is explicitly stated in the FRE, while such purposes are implicit in the CEC.

OFFERS TO PLEAD GUILTY

In criminal cases, a similar provision applies to prevent the defendant's offer to plead guilty from being used against her later whether that case goes to trial or the offer becomes relevant in any subsequent case, hearing, or other proceeding of any type. This code section applies whenever the defendant offers to plead guilty and that offer is not accepted, as well as when she actually pleads guilty and later changes her mind and withdraws that guilty plea. In either situation, the evidence of the guilty plea or offer is inadmissible in that criminal case as well as in any subsequent proceeding.

CEC §1153: Offer to plead guilty or withdrawn plea of guilty by criminal defendant

Evidence of a plea of guilty, later withdrawn, or of an offer to plead guilty to the crime charged or to any other crime, made by the defendant in a criminal action is inadmissible in any action or in any proceeding of any nature, including proceedings before agencies, commissions, boards, and tribunals.

3. Other Policy Exclusions for Relevant Evidence

CEC 1153 supports the public policy of encouraging criminal defendants to plead guilty because if they later withdraw their guilty plea (for instance, when newly discovered exculpatory evidence becomes available or when they decide that the prosecutor's offer of less jail time is not low enough), the original guilty plea also is inadmissible at the subsequent trial.

California courts have interpreted this ban to cover statements made in the course of plea negotiations as well, so that prosecutors do not circumvent the policy behind CEC 1153. The statements must be made in the course of bona fide plea negotiations. Plea negotiations are bona fide when there is a good faith effort made to plea bargain the case. Factors the courts consider in determining good faith are the parties to the negotiation (was the defendant talking to a desk clerk at the police station, to the prosecutor, or to the detectives assigned to the case?); the statements made during the negotiation ("I'd like to cut a deal" or "We have no authority to negotiate with you"); as well as conduct of the parties (for instance, waiting for the attorney to arrive to finalize the deal or choosing to remain silent instead of continuing a negotiation).

The ban is not absolute, however. It does not apply to pleas of nolo contendere or to statements made in the course of the plea negotiations when used for impeachment purposes. A plea of *nolo contendere* means that the defendant will not contest the charges, although he is not technically admitting or denying the charges either. The fact that a defendant pleaded nolo contendere is not covered by this code section, but the California Penal Code prohibits the use of a nolo plea in a later civil case.

Case law has determined that if the defendant testifies and says things that are inconsistent with statements he made in the plea negotiations, then the prosecution can use those plea negotiation statements for the limited purpose of impeaching the defendant, but not as a party admission for the truth of the matter asserted.

When the crime is a property crime, such as theft, and the defendant offers to resolve the matter through the civil system rather than the criminal justice system (for instance, by offering to return the stolen property or to repay the value to the owner), evidence of that offer is excluded by CEC 1153.5.

Federal Rules of Evidence Compared: Notable Differences

Unlike the CEC, FRE 410 also protects pleas of nolo contendere and statements made in certain criminal procedure proceedings, but it limits statements in the course of plea negotiations to those with *an attorney for the prosecuting authority*, which is usually the assistant U.S. attorney. Thus it will not apply to negotiations with police officers and other law enforcement personnel unless it can be established that they are acting as agents of the prosecutor in that situation. The FRE contains an exception when other statements made in the course of the same negotiations already have been admitted, and another exception for criminal perjury proceedings.

LIABILITY INSURANCE

The CEC prohibits offering evidence of liability insurance to prove negligence or other wrongdoing. The rationale is that having insurance should be encouraged and should not be used as evidence that a party knew a harm was likely to occur.

CEC §1155: Liability insurance
Evidence that a person was, at the time a harm was suffered by another, insured wholly or partially against loss arising from liability for that harm is inadmissible to prove negligence or other wrongdoing.

The rationale for this policy exclusion is not as strong as it once was. Because liability insurance is increasingly common, evidence of insurance does not have the same potentially negative connotation that it used to have when fewer people purchased liability insurance policies. Currently, in the state of California all drivers are required to have automobile liability insurance, and many people have a variety of insurance policies covering liability for accidents at their homes or malpractice in their professions. Thus, the mere fact that someone has insurance is not likely to convince jurors that the person acted wrongfully. Nevertheless, CEC 1155 remains in effect, preventing offering evidence that a person was insured for loss when used to prove negligence or other wrongdoing.

If the evidence of insurance is offered to prove something other than liability, it may be admissible. Evidence of insurance can be admitted to prove ownership and control when it is relevant to the issues in the litigation or to the credibility of witnesses. For example, if the defendant testifies that he did not own the car that hit the plaintiff, the plaintiff can offer evidence that the defendant was the named insured on the insurance policy covering the car to prove that the defendant did indeed own the car.

Note that evidence of the *lack of insurance* is not included within the prohibitions of the CEC 1155. If the lack of insurance is relevant, then it will not be excluded by this rule, even if offered to prove negligence or other wrongdoing. However, when a party seeks to admit evidence of another party's lack of insurance, the other party should object on relevance grounds — the lack of insurance is rarely relevant to substantive issues. If the lack of insurance is indeed relevant, object under CEC 352 and argue that the prejudicial effect of admitting the evidence would substantially outweigh the low probative value of the lack of insurance.

Federal Rules of Evidence Compared: Notable Difference

FRE 411 prevents admission of evidence that a person was insured, and also that he was *not* insured for purposes of proving negligence or wrongful conduct. In addition, the FRE provides a non-exhaustive list of permissible purposes, such as agency, ownership, control, bias, and prejudice.

EXPRESSIONS OF SYMPATHY AND BENEVOLENCE

When accidents occur, people sometimes express their sympathy. If that sympathy is expressed by someone who is potentially at fault in the accident, it could be relevant evidence in any subsequent litigation. For that reason, those who might be at fault would be discouraged from expressing sympathy because it might be used against them to prove fault. However, some studies show that people who receive apologies are less likely to sue and settle for lower amounts when they do sue. To avoid discouraging such humane expressions that help to lessen civil litigation costs, CEC 1160 makes inadmissible any expressions of sympathy or benevolence regarding pain, death, or suffering of a person involved in an accident.

CEC §1160: Admissibility of expressions of sympathy or benevolence; definitions
(a) The portion of statements, writings, or benevolent gestures expressing sympathy or a general sense of benevolence relating to the pain, suffering, or death of a person involved in an accident and made to that person or to the family of that person shall be inadmissible as evidence of an admission of liability in a civil action. A statement of fault, however, which is part of, or in addition to, any of the above shall not be inadmissible pursuant to this section.

3. Other Policy Exclusions for Relevant Evidence

Subsection (b) defines the terms "accident," "benevolent gestures," and "family."

This prohibition applies when the statements are made to that person or her family and where such expressions are offered to prove an admission of liability in a civil action. This limitation does not apply in criminal cases. Expressions of sympathy that are excluded under CEC 1160 include statements like "I am sorry," "I am sorry you were injured," "I am sorry our cars met on the same part of the road," and "Sorry that your car was totaled."

A statement of fault, however, is not covered by this policy exclusion. Statements of fault include "I wasn't looking where I was going when I hit you" and "I was using my cell phone while driving, and that's why we crashed." When the expression contains both an expression of sympathy and a statement of fault, the court will redact (cut out a portion of) the statement and admit the statement of fault but exclude the statement of sympathy or benevolence. So, when one driver says to the other driver, "I am sorry your car was totaled. I was talking on the phone and dropped my Bluetooth headset," the first sentence will be excluded by CEC 1160 because it conveys only sympathy, and the second sentence will be admissible because it does not convey sympathy or benevolence and merely expresses fault.

Federal Rules of Evidence Compared: One Notable Difference

FRE 409 excludes evidence that a person offered or actually furnished medical, hospital, or similar expenses to prove liability for the injury, but it does not address mere expressions of sorrow, sympathy or benevolence. If such an expression is connected to compromise negotiations, then it may be protected under FRE 408.

MEDIATION PROVISIONS

The increasing use of mediation and other non-litigation dispute resolution mechanisms prompted the California legislature to provide some protections for disclosures occurring in the course of mediations. These protections are found in CEC 1115 through 1128. Mediation is defined in CEC 1115(a) as "a process in which a neutral person or persons facilitate communication between the disputants to assist them in reaching a mutually acceptable agreement." These sections do not apply to certain Family Code proceedings or to settlement conferences in civil litigation. CEC 1119 provides the general limitation that all admissions and other matters, including writings, that are disclosed in the course of mediation are inadmissible in any non-criminal proceeding. Additionally, all communications, negotiations, and settlement discussions remain confidential. Mediator reports are excluded under CEC 1121 unless all parties agree to disclosure. CEC 1126 continues to protect the information after the mediation has concluded.

The parties to the mediation can decline the protection of these provisions and agree to disclose and offer into evidence communications and writings, including their oral and written settlement agreements. Such information also can be admitted in certain cases when used to prove fraud, duress, or illegality under CEC 1123 and CEC 1124. Otherwise, references to mediation in a subsequent non-criminal trial are inappropriate and, under CEC 1128, could result in vacating or modifying a decision or granting a new hearing or trial if substantial rights of a party are materially affected by the reference.

OTHER LESS FREQUENTLY USED POLICY EXCLUSIONS

Evidence to Test a Verdict

Sometimes litigants challenge the validity of a jury's verdict after a decision has been rendered. In those situations, a hearing will be held and evidence of statements, conduct, conditions, or events will be admitted to prove whether there was an improper influence on the jury's verdict. However, CEC 1150 specifically excludes any evidence to show the *effects* of any such statement, conduct, condition, or event on a juror. For instance, a juror can testify at the hearing about the substance of a statement, such as a verbal threat received, or about an event, such as another juror having a heart attack during the deliberations, but cannot testify about how that threat or heart attack may have impacted the jury deliberations. (This CEC section is discussed in more detail in Chapter 8 in the section on jurors as witnesses.)

Records of Medical or Dental Study of In-Hospital Staff Committee

To encourage research into reducing deaths at hospitals, CEC 1156 excludes any records, interviews, reports, statements, or memoranda created by in-house hospital committees that conduct studies to reduce deaths in hospitals. However, CEC 1156(d) makes an exception for this type of evidence in criminal trials when it is relevant.

Records of Medical and Psychiatric Studies of Quality Assurance Committees

A similar provision in CEC 1156.1 applies to quality assurance committees established in compliance with certain California Welfare and Institutions Code provisions.

Proceeding or Records of Organized Committees on Quality of Care

CEC 1157 and 1158 apply more broadly to medical, dental, podiatric, dietitian, psychological, marriage and family therapists, licensed clinical social workers, and others (including veterinary staff) to prevent compelling any person who participated in a meeting of a quality of care committee from testifying in any action. There are several exceptions: when the person whose testimony is sought is a party to the action, when that person is requesting hospital staff privileges, when the action involves insurance bad faith settlement, and when the quality care committee is made up of more than 10 percent of the relevant medical society.

Other CEC sections extend similar protection to non-profit medical foundations (CEC 1157.5); county health facilities (CEC 1157.6); and to proceedings and records of committees established by local government to monitor, evaluate, and report on health services (CEC 1157.7). A related code section, CEC 1158, is not really a policy limitation, but rather provides the procedure, penalties, and reimbursement rate for the copying of medical records by attorneys or their representatives when a written authorization is presented to the medical staff.

Animal Experimentation in Products Liability Actions

CEC 1159 applies only to products liability actions involving motor vehicles, and prevents the admission of evidence of any live animal experimentation, including but not limited to experiments about injury or impact.

Examples

1. In March, Donald tripped over a crack in a sidewalk, fell, and broke his hip. The sidewalk was adjacent to a condominium complex owned by Elmore. One week after Donald's accident, Elmore hired a company to fix the sidewalk bumps. Donald sued Elmore and sought to introduce evidence about the bumps being fixed as well as evidence of the minutes from a February condominium association meeting where one of the agenda items was entitled "Bumps in the Sidewalk: Upcoming Repair." Elmore objected to both items of evidence. How should Donald respond, how should the court rule, and why?

2. Pantages and Schubert were a married couple who were involved in a car accident with two other vehicles — one driven by an insured motorist named Tony and the other driven by a presumably uninsured motorist who fled the scene. Pantages and Schubert's insurance policy with Union Insurance Company had a mandatory arbitration provision for uninsured motorist claims. When Pantages and Schubert sued Tony, they sought to consolidate the uninsured motorist claim with Union with the lawsuit against Tony. Union objected that the consolidation of cases was improper in part because it would require disclosure of the fact of insurance in violation of CEC 1155. How should Pantages and Schubert respond, how should the court rule, and why? Would the analysis and ruling differ if the case were tried in federal court?

3. Alisa had to undergo a colonoscopy, and her doctor, Bradford, explained that Alisa needed to remain alert during the procedure. Thus, she would be given just enough anesthesia to relieve the pain, but not enough to reduce her to unconsciousness. During the procedure, Alisa complained about still feeling the pain and asked Dr. Bradford to stop. When he did not, she started crying and screaming. Dr. Bradford yelled, "Stop being a baby!" and told the anesthesiologist Dr. Carter to give Alisa more anesthesia, which rendered her unconscious and allowed them to complete the procedure. Subsequently, Alisa suffered emotional distress, developed a fear of medical personnel, and sued Dr. Bradford. At trial Alisa seeks to offer evidence that Dr. Carter was reprimanded by the hospital, placed on suspension, and ordered to take additional training courses in the proper dosing of anesthesia, and that the hospital ordered Dr. Bradford to attend anger management classes, which he did not attend. Dr. Bradford objects that the evidence is inadmissible. How should Alisa respond, how should the court rule, and why?

4. Frank and Hilda are minority shareholders in Gogreen, a closely held corporation. Their father Ivan also was a minority shareholder before his death the previous year, and their uncle Jeremy is the majority

shareholder in Gogreen. Jeremy claimed that shortly before his death, Ivan had transferred 5000 shares of preferred stock to Jeremy. Frank and Hilda responded that Ivan was incompetent in the weeks before his death and therefore was unable to effectively transfer the shares to Jeremy. A few days later, Frank sent an email to Hilda and to Jeremy in which he suggested that they try to buy back 5000 shares from Kayla, another minority shareholder, and retire those shares. A few months after that email was sent, Frank and Hilda sued Jeremy for wrongful conversion of corporate assets for personal use. During the civil trial, Jeremy sought to admit the email message between Frank and Hilda, and they objected on the grounds that it was protected as an offer to compromise. Jeremy responded that the statement is admissible because there was no dispute regarding Kayla's shares, and therefore the statement was not made in an offer to compromise. How should the court rule, and why?

5. Leonard was charged with two counts of murder in the deaths of a convenience store clerk and a customer. Prior to the trial date, the court conducted a hearing on Leonard's motion in limine to exclude the media from the courtroom. During the hearing, Leonard raised one finger, and the judge said, "Let's take a short break. Defendant has his finger up." Immediately after the judge's comment, Leonard said, "I am guilty." The judge did not accept Leonard's attempted guilty plea at that hearing. At trial, Leonard made a motion to preclude the prosecution from using that statement on the grounds that it was an offer to plead guilty and therefore is protected by CEC 1153. How should the prosecution respond, and how should the court rule?

6. Melvin was injured when a company car driven by Nelson crashed into the back of Melvin's car while he was stopped at a red light. Melvin had several surgeries as a result of that accident, and he sued Nelson and Nelson's insurance carrier. Nine months later, while Melvin was still experiencing neck and back pain as result of the accident, Olga slammed into the back of Melvin's car and exacerbated his existing neck and back pain. Melvin wrote a letter to Olga's insurance carrier explaining how Olga had aggravated his injuries from a prior accident; requesting payment for neck and back pain, chiropractic visits, and another anticipated surgery; and asking the carrier not to involve Nelson's insurance company in this deal. Olga's insurance carrier passed Melvin's letter along to Nelson's insurance carrier. When Nelson attempted to offer the letter into evidence in his trial against Melvin, Melvin objected on the grounds that it was protected as a settlement negotiation. Nelson argued that the letter was an attempt to settle a different claim, not the claim against Nelson, and therefore should be admitted in this case. How should the court rule, and why? Would the analysis and ruling

be different if Olga tried to use the letter in a subsequent lawsuit brought against her by Melvin?

7. Uncle was driving his company car with the radio blaring when his cell phone rang. He reached for his Bluetooth headset and realized that the battery was dead. Knowing that it was illegal to drive while holding the cell phone, he pushed the speaker button and answered the call. Unbeknownst to Uncle, the caller was the driver in the car behind him, Victim. Victim was reading a bumper sticker on the back of Uncle's car that said, "How am I driving? Call 1-310-NOPHONE." Victim started yelling at Uncle for cutting her off, and Uncle responded, "I am sorry I cut you off. But I had my blinker on and you kept speeding up and slowing down, so I finally just had to cut in. If you weren't such a bad driver, you wouldn't get cut off." Victim yelled back, "That was not my fault. You idiot! I'll show you who is a bad driver." Then Victim changed lanes, sped up, cut back into Uncle's lane just barely ahead of Uncle's car, and slammed on her brakes. Uncle's car crashed into Victim's car and both were injured. Uncle said, "I can't believe you did that! I said I was sorry," and Victim responded, "Sorry didn't do it, you did." Victim sued Uncle and seeks to admit Uncle's statements. Uncle objects. How should the court rule, and why?

8. Wolfgang and Yvette were in a dispute about a contract and decided to pursue their claims through mediation rather than civil litigation. During the course of the mediation, Wolfgang admitted that when he realized that Yvette had forgotten to sign the last page of their contract, he had forged Yvette's signature on the contract. Wolfgang showed the mediator a piece of paper on which he had practiced copying Yvette's signature. Yvette was so distraught by this news that she withdrew from the mediation despite Wolfgang's apology (he stated, "I am so sorry I forged your name") and sued Wolfgang in civil court for breach of contract. Yvette also notified the fraud squad of the local police department, and the assistant district attorney filed fraud charges against Wolfgang in criminal court. Yvette seeks to testify that Wolfgang admitted forging her signature on the contract and that he apologized for doing so. Wolfgang objects that his admission is protected by CEC 1119. How should the court rule, and why?

9. Xavier is a magician, and during his show one evening he used magic to set a bouquet of roses on fire. Unfortunately, the audience volunteer who had been holding the flowers was severely burned. As the victim was being carried to the ambulance, Xavier wrote a note, which he handed to the victim. The note said, "I am so sorry. I will pay for all your medical expenses and give you a free show every month for a year." The next evening, Xavier handed oven mitts to his audience volunteer, and no one

was injured. Two days later, Xavier went to visit the victim in the hospital, and she said that she was going to sue him. Xavier asked her why she was suing him, given his apology and his offer. She responded, "What offer? And you didn't even apologize." Xavier asked her to reread the note, and she said that it was blank. Realizing his mistake in using invisible ink, Xavier performed his magic to reveal the writing. The victim said that it was too late because her lawyer had already filed the papers. At trial, the victim seeks to offer into evidence the note and Xavier's use of oven mitts the night after her accident. Xavier objects. How should the court rule, and why? How would the analysis and ruling change if the case were tried in federal court?

Explanations

1. Donald should respond that the evidence of the minutes from the condominium association meeting does not meet the requirements for exclusion under the subsequent remedial measures doctrine because the minutes were created in February, which was prior to the accident that occurred in March. Thus the minutes fail the "subsequent" element of the exclusion. The actual fixing of the sidewalk satisfies that element because it was fixed one week after the accident. Therefore, the repair is not admissible to prove liability. Donald's best argument would be to offer the evidence for some purpose other than to prove negligence or wrongdoing, such as to prove ownership or control of the sidewalk.

2. Pantages and Schubert should remind Union's counsel that the evidence of insurance is inadmissible to prove negligence or other wrongdoing. Therefore it is admissible for other purposes, such as to show that Union Insurance has a duty to resolve the uninsured motorist claim. In federal court, the only difference is that evidence of a lack of insurance also is inadmissible for that purpose, but because Pantages and Schubert will offer the evidence for another purpose, FRE 411 will not render it inadmissible.

3. While the evidence of Dr. Carter's reprimand and additional training is relevant to show that he might have acted in violation of the hospital's policies, it may also constitute evidence of a subsequent remedial measure, which would be inadmissible under CEC 1151. Both actions were taken after the plaintiff's incident and thus meet the timing element. The next element to consider is whether the reprimand is a "remedial or precautionary measure," which, if taken prior to the incident with Alisa, may have made that incident less likely to occur. Courts might find that the simple act of chastising Dr. Carter, without any other tangible ramifications, does not constitute an action that would have made the incident less likely to occur. The additional training is more likely to be considered

evidence of actions that would have made the incident less likely to occur. The next question is to ask whether that action was taken by the defendant or whether the defendant authorized, controlled, or participated in the decision to engage in the remedial measure. Here, the defendant is Dr. Bradford, not the hospital, and so unless Dr. Bradford had input into the decision about the actions taken against Dr. Carter, this would not satisfy the subsequent remedial measure doctrine, and thus the evidence about Dr. Carter will be admissible in the liability trial against Dr. Bradford. The evidence about Dr. Bradford and anger management classes, while connected to the defendant, is not a subsequent remedial measure because he did not attend the classes. If Dr. Bradford had attended the classes, that action would meet the definition of a subsequent remedial measure and would be excluded by CEC 1151.

4. The facts indicate the presence of a dispute over the proper allocation of stock and ownership of certain stock, and therefore there is a dispute involved. Even if the dispute did not specifically involve the 5000 shares of preferred stock owned by Kayla, it involved the ownership of 5000 shares of stock, and thus the email message is sufficiently connected to the settlement efforts to meet the statutory language of "conduct or statements in negotiation" thereof. Moreover, the email was sent to Jeremy as well and thus could be interpreted as an effort to engage in settlement negotiations. As an offer to compromise an existing dispute, the email message is inadmissible to prove liability under CEC 1152.

5. The prosecution should respond that Leonard's statement was not an actual guilty plea because he did not make the statement at a time when he was asked "How do you plead?," and the statement is not an offer to plead guilty because the defendant did not say that he would plead guilty, just that he was guilty. Thus the statement was not made in the course of any negotiations over a plea. It was an unsolicited admission of guilt, and the policy to encourage the resolving of criminal cases would not be furthered by excluding this statement. Therefore Leonard's objection should be overruled, and his statement is not made inadmissible by CEC 1153.

6. Nelson is offering the letter to show the partial invalidity of Melvin's claim against Olga, and thus we must consider CEC 1154. The letter admits that some of Melvin's injuries were preexisting at the time of the accident with Olga, and it offers to accept a settlement for the injuries suffered — thus it is a settlement negotiation between Melvin and Olga. Even though there is no litigation pending between them at the time the letter was sent, there is a dispute over how much of Melvin's medical expenses should be paid by Olga's insurance carrier, and so the letter would be inadmissible under CEC 1154 to prove the invalidity of

Melvin's claim against Olga. However, the current case does not involve Melvin's claim against Olga but rather his claim against Nelson, and CEC 1154 limits the exclusion to evidence that proves "the *invalidity of the claim* or any part of it." The phrase "the claim" refers to the claim that is the subject of the litigation, and here the letter is about Melvin's claim against Olga. Thus, CEC 1154 does not apply to bar the letter about the Melvin/Olga claim in Melvin's case against Nelson. If Olga tried to bring the statement into her case against Melvin, then CEC 1154 would apply and the letter would be inadmissible to prove the invalidity of all or part of Melvin's claim against Olga.

7. Uncle should object to the statements about being sorry on the grounds that these are statements of benevolence and cannot be used to prove culpability under CEC 1160. The statement about "cutting in" is a statement of fault, and it will not be excluded by CEC 1160. The admissible statements will still need to satisfy a hearsay exception if offered to prove the truth of the matter asserted. (Hearsay exceptions are discussed in Chapters 5, 6, and 7.)

8. It depends on the court proceeding in which Yvette seeks to testify. If she is testifying in her civil case against Wolfgang, then the objection should be sustained because CEC 1119 makes inadmissible evidence of admissions obtained during the course of mediations. Wolfgang's statement about forging her signature and his apology were both obtained during the course of the mediation, and evidence of them will be inadmissible. However, the limitation of CEC 1119 does not apply to criminal cases, and thus the objection will be overruled as to Wolfgang's admission of forging if Yvette seeks to testify in the criminal fraud case against Wolfgang. Wolfgang's apology also will be admissible because the limitation for expressions of sympathy under CEC 1160 does not apply when the evidence is offered in a criminal case.

9. The court should sustain the objection to the note if it is offered to prove Xavier's liability. The first sentence is an expression of sorrow and thus is inadmissible to prove liability under CEC 1160. The victim might argue that the second sentence was not a compromise offer because Xavier did not say he would make these payments in exchange for anything (like refraining from suing him or reporting it to the insurance company). However, CEC 1152 also applies to humanitarian offers when no compromise is involved. The second sentence is a humanitarian offer to pay medical expenses and to pay for her entertainment for the year and thus will be excluded under CEC 1152 if offered to prove liability. In federal court, FRE 409 also protects the offer to pay medical and related expenses, but would not apply to the offer for entertainment expenses. Under the FRE, the apology standing alone is not protected;

3. Other Policy Exclusions for Relevant Evidence

it must be connected to a settlement negotiation. There would be no difference in federal court, applying FRE 407. The objection to the use of oven mitts should be sustained on the grounds that it constitutes a subsequent remedial measure and therefore would be inadmissible to prove negligence or culpable conduct.

The Hearsay Rule

The Hearsay Rule, along with its numerous exceptions, is a significant portion of the evidence rules you will be studying. Hearsay is evidence that meets the following three requirements:

1. it is a statement
2. made outside of this court's hearing
3. that is offered to prove what the statement asserts is true.

For instance, suppose someone in the hallway outside the courtroom says, "The judge's chambers are freezing." If you use that statement as evidence in the courtroom that the judge's chambers are below 32 degrees, then you are using the statement to prove that what it asserts ("the judge's chambers are freezing") is true (that the temperature in the judge's chambers is actually freezing). (This analysis is more fully discussed later in the chapter.)

Essentially, you must answer three questions: what, where, and why:

1. *What* is the form of the evidence? It must be a statement as defined under CEC 225.
2. *Where* was the statement originally made? If it occurred anywhere other than in the current proceeding, it could be hearsay.
3. Finally, *why* is the evidence being offered? If the reason is to prove that its content is true, then the statement can be hearsay.

It is crucially important to determine whether evidence meets the criteria described above — after all, the Hearsay Rule is not implicated if the evidence is not hearsay in the first place. The rule in CEC 1200(b) simply states that hearsay is not admissible unless an exception applies.

This chapter also explains the rationale behind the Hearsay Rule. Knowing the reason for the rule makes applying it (and its exceptions) much easier to understand. Basically, statements that fit the hearsay definition are not as reliable as live testimony (statements made in person, under oath, in a court of law). As you undoubtedly know from everyday life, information gets less and less reliable as it passes from person to person.

Finally, this chapter introduces methods of admitting evidence that seem to meet the definition of hearsay. Those methods include

- *showing* that the evidence really does *not* fit the definition and is *not* hearsay;
- *changing* the way the evidence is offered so that it no longer meets the hearsay definition;
- or *finding* an exception to the Hearsay Rule that will apply.

The CEC provides over 60 exceptions to the Hearsay Rule. (These and other hearsay issues are discussed in later chapters of this book.)

THE RATIONALE FOR EXCLUDING HEARSAY

Recall that the rules of evidence govern conduct in courtrooms. Hearsay is a statement that was not made in the *current court proceeding*. Furthermore, the hearsay statement is being introduced as evidence that the words of the statement are true. It is important to understand the rationale for the Hearsay Rule — it may help distinguish between what is and is not hearsay in a particular circumstance.

The CEC excludes hearsay for several reasons. The primary reason is that it is difficult to determine the reliability of a hearsay statement, which is made outside of court without an oath and then repeated secondhand in court, often by someone else. When a statement is made in court under oath, it is easier for the jury to examine the reliability of that statement.

Judges and juries evaluate the reliability or quality of witness testimony using four main components:

1. perception
2. memory
3. narration, and
4. sincerity.

The *perception* component is what a witness knows based on her sense of sight, hearing, touch, taste, and smell. What did the witness see, hear, feel, taste, or smell? When the witness testifies from her own perceptions, the opposing counsel can effectively cross-examine the witness about her senses and her perceptions to uncover inconsistencies and outright falsehoods. Conversely, if a witness testifies from secondhand knowledge and did not perceive the information herself, she will not be able to provide answers to all of the questions needed to evaluate the credibility of her testimony. Thus courts prefer to get the testimony directly from the person with firsthand knowledge. (The personal knowledge requirement and competency issues are discussed in more detail in Chapter 8.)

The memory component is closely related to perception. This factor asks whether the witness accurately remembers what happened — what he saw, heard, felt, tasted, or smelled. However, with secondhand information, the witness has a memory only of getting the information from someone who perceived the events, not a memory of his own perceptions. Courts prefer that the actual declarant — the person who made the original statement — be a witness at trial so that the opposing party may cross-examine the declarant about how she remembers the actual course of events.

The narration component is based on the witness's ability to tell the story without making errors in the recitation. Consider whether the words being spoken convey the message that the speaker intended to convey. For instance, some people have trouble repeating a story; they may mix up the names or characters in the story or describe events out of order. Suppose a person says, "This guy ran into a bank. Then he pulled out his gun and started shooting. Oh and the police were already there." You may wonder whether the man was a police officer and whether the shooting was part of a robbery or part of law enforcement efforts. These narration errors impact the reliability of the story. The jurors would need more information to understand what actually happened at the bank, and thus this witness would have a low score on the narration component.

Finally, the sincerity component is based on the witness's oath to tell the truth, the ability to examine the demeanor of the witness, and the use of cross-examination. Hearsay statements usually are not made under oath. When a witness on the stand repeats what the declarant said outside of court, that hearsay statement was not originally made under an oath to tell the truth (with the threat of perjury). If a witness is in court, under oath, and facing the judge, jury, and parties, courts have more confidence in the reliability of the witness's testimony. In addition, the judge and jury can examine the witness's demeanor to see how she acts and looks when answering questions, which provides some additional evidence of the witness's credibility (discussed in Chapter 8). A witness who looks furtively around and hesitates before answering a question appears less credible than one who answers forthrightly, making eye contact with the lawyer as she responds.

Cross-examination is an important way to test the strength of these four components of testimony reliability. If the hearsay declarant does not appear in court as a witness, then there is no opportunity to cross-examine the hearsay declarant to test his perception, memory, recollection, and sincerity.

Illustrating the Decrease in Reliability with Hearsay

The following example illustrates the decrease in reliability between hearsay and non-hearsay statements:

Pat is on trial for shooting someone. Neal is a witness for the prosecution, and he will give proof that Pat pulled the trigger. But Neal did not actually *see* Pat pull the trigger — he just heard April say that Pat did it. April is the declarant, and Neal is the witness at trial. Neal testifies, then, that "I heard April say 'Pat is the person who pulled the trigger.'" Do you see the problems with that? When Neal is cross-examined by the defense attorney, all that Neal can say is that he accurately heard April and that he remembers what she told him. Even if he is completely sincere and took the oath to tell the truth, all he can really tell the court is what he heard April say.

To get reliable evidence about whether Pat pulled the trigger, the court prefers testimony from April. April needs to be in court to testify about what made her tell Neal that Pat is the shooter. Did she see Pat's finger pull the trigger? If so, was her vision impaired in any way? Or did April hear from someone else that Pat shot the gun? Did Pat himself admit to April that he pulled the trigger? Or does April dislike Pat or want to frame him? Neal may not know anything about any of these questions, which is why courts prefer to have the original declarant on the witness stand. That person is the best person to answer counsel's cross-examination questions to test the reliability of the statement.

As seen by the questions above, even April's non-hearsay testimony may not be reliable for a wide variety of reasons under perception, memory, narration, and sincerity. Using Neal to testify about April's hearsay statement instead of having April herself testify amplifies the questions of reliability that much more. This extra layer of inquiry decreases the reliability of hearsay testimony.

Another benefit if April appears as a witness is that her testimony may now escape the definition of hearsay and thus will not implicate the Hearsay Rule. If April says "I saw Pat pull the trigger" instead of "I said to Neal, 'I saw Pat pull the trigger,'" then her statement in court is not hearsay at all. For these reasons, the CEC prefers in-court testimony by the original declarant whenever possible. Thus CEC 1200(b) bans hearsay evidence from trials unless the evidence fits an exception. The exceptions usually involve situations in which the evidence tends to be reliable even when it is technically hearsay.

THE HEARSAY ANALYSIS

There are three questions to ask when analyzing a potential hearsay issue: what, where, and why. First, *what* type of evidence is it? Is it a *statement*? Second, *where* was the statement made? Was it outside of the hearing conducted by this court? Third, *why* is the statement being offered? What is it supposed to prove?

CEC §1200(a): The hearsay Rule.
(a) "Hearsay evidence" is evidence of a statement that was made other than by a witness while testifying at the hearing and that is offered to prove the truth of the matter asserted.

1. Is this a Statement?

The usual definition of a *statement* is the use of words to convey information. The CEC recognizes that spoken or written words constitute statements. Spoken words can be repeated by another person, and written expressions can be brought to court contained in notes, documents, books, reports, and even computer screens and text messaging devices.

CEC §225: "Statement" means
    (a) oral or written verbal expression or
    (b) nonverbal conduct of a person intended by him as a substitute for oral or written verbal expression.

Questions generally seek rather than convey information, and seeking information does not constitute an expression. However, leading questions do make assertions and therefore can be considered statements. For instance, the question "Sam robbed the bank, didn't he?" could be hearsay if offered to prove that Sam robbed the bank. Similarly, questions that contain implicit assertions can also be hearsay. The question "What did you do after Sam robbed the bank?" implies that Sam robbed the bank, and if offered to prove that Sam robbed the bank, that portion of the question would be hearsay as well.

99

The Declarant Under CEC 135

As noted above, the person making the statement is called the *declarant* under CEC 135. It follows that the declarant of a hearsay statement has to be a "person." This seems pretty straightforward. Did a person speak or write the words that one side is trying to use as evidence? A written assertion printed by a machine meets the definition as long as a person was responsible for the input of information that was printed in the written document. For instance, department store receipts are considered to have been made by a person because a person inputs the sales information into the register, which then prints a receipt. The statements contained in the store receipt constitute expressions, such as the name of the buyer and descriptions of the purchased items.

Animals Are Not Declarants

Statements made by animals are not made by a "person" and thus are not hearsay. What kinds of statements or assertions might be made by an animal? Imagine a drug-sniffing dog that always barks twice when his officer handler asks "Is he carrying drugs?" and he smells drug residue on a detained person. The officer stops a suspect, allows the dog to sniff him, and asks the dog "Is he carrying drugs?" The dog barks twice, which the officer interprets to mean "Yes, this guy is carrying drugs!" If the officer testifies in court that the dog expressed that the suspect had drugs, the officer's testimony will not be excluded by the Hearsay Rule, even though it is offered to prove that the dog confirmed that the suspect was carrying drugs. On the other hand, if the officer tried to testify that his human partner searched the suspect and then the partner panted and said, "Yes, this suspect is carrying drugs," the partner's statement could constitute hearsay if offered to prove that the suspect was carrying drugs. However, the statement still may be admissible if an exception applies (exceptions are discussed in Chapters 5 through 7).

Verbal Statements

Statements can be oral or written verbal expressions or non-verbal conduct intended to act as words (CEC 225). *Verbal* means using words. A declarant can make an oral or a written verbal expression by either speaking or writing his statement using words. For instance, when a professor takes class attendance, Student A says out loud, "I am here." Student B writes "I am here" along with her signature on the attendance sheet. Have both students made a statement? Yes. Student A has made an oral statement, and Student B has made a written statement.

Conduct: Assertive and Non-assertive

Nonverbal conduct does not use words, but it can be *assertive* or *non-assertive*. Assertive conduct can relate an expression by doing some act intended to substitute for words. For example, Student C raises his hand in class when the professor takes attendance. Like Student A and Student B, he has made a statement, even without using words. The act of raising his hand was meant to substitute for the words "Yes, I am here."

Non-assertive conduct, on the other hand, is not intended to substitute for words at all. For example, Student D runs out of the room when the professor asks for a volunteer to a question about a hypothetical legal scenario. Student D did not intend to convey a verbal message by running out — she did not run out of the classroom to say "No. I will not answer your question." The act of running has a primary purpose that is not communicative — it is to escape that place or to get to another place quickly (or to get some exercise). The act of running has independent significance that does not relate to communication. Maybe Student D forgot her book, or felt sick, or realized she was in the wrong class! If the conduct has a primary purpose that is not communicative, it is non-assertive conduct — not a statement, and thus not hearsay.

Assertive and non-assertive conduct exists along a spectrum of conduct. Conduct that is clearly assertive is at one end. These actions are clearly intended to substitute for words. For example, if a person asks willing volunteers for hypnosis to stand up, the act of standing up in that context would clearly be meant as a substitute for the words "I volunteer to be hypnotized." Pure conduct is at the other end of the spectrum. Pure conduct, given particular circumstances, is conduct that clearly does not substitute for words, such as running away from a burning building. In the middle of that spectrum, the inquiry becomes whether the person engaging in that non-verbal conduct *intended* it to be an assertion or whether the act has independent significance.

Determining the Actor's Intent

The best way to determine the actor's intent is to ask. Student C above could have raised his hand for a reason other than to answer the professor's question; he might have wanted to ask his own question, for instance. Asking Student C would readily establish whether his conduct was meant to substitute for words. When there is no opportunity to ask the declarant about his intent, then common sense is the next inquiry. We can expect that Student C knows that raising his hand conveys the message that he will answer the professor's question. We can argue that by raising his hand, Student C meant the act as a substitute for saying "I will." Thus, raising his hand constitutes a statement under the CEC.

The Intent that Matters

The intent that matters is the *intent of the person who acted*. For instance, a neighbor stands on the sidewalk engaged in a heated conversation with the mail carrier. The neighbor is shifting his weight from one foot to the other, back and forth, back and forth. The neighbor seems to be either (1) impatient with the conversation or (2) urgently in need of a bathroom. His conduct may be a substitute for the assertion, "Finish talking; I'm bored," or "Hurry up, I need to go!" It may also be pure conduct — simply a shifting of his weight. Observers may have their own interpretation of his body language, but what matters is what the neighbor himself intended with his conduct. If he intended the movements to substitute for an assertion, then those movements are assertive conduct implicating the Hearsay Rule. If the neighbor did not intend for his movements to constitute assertions, then those movements are non-assertive conduct and do not implicate the Hearsay Rule.

In close cases, examine the factual circumstances to see whether there is an argument that a person intended her conduct to substitute for an assertion. Some factors to consider include whether the conduct was voluntary or involuntary, whether the conduct is commonly associated with a particular message (such as nodding one's head or raising one's hand), or whether the conduct itself accomplishes something (such as walking to a destination, in contrast to wiggling one's fingers). For instance, shivering could be an involuntary reaction to being very cold, whereas pretending to shiver and making your teeth clatter would be voluntary acts. The involuntary acts are not intended as expressions because the actor did not intend to engage in those acts. Voluntary acts may or may not be intended as assertions. The party making the hearsay objection has the burden to show that the conduct was intended as an assertion.

Silence as Hearsay

Consider also the issue of silence. In general, silence is not interpreted to substitute for an assertion. However, if directly asked to "speak up if everything is not perfect," for example, silence could be interpreted as non-verbal conduct intended to substitute for the assertion that everything is perfect. The surrounding circumstances are useful to help determine whether silence can or should constitute an assertion, but the general rule is that silence, standing alone, will not constitute an assertion in a particular situation.

2. Was the Statement Made Out of this Court's Hearing?

In determining the second element of the hearsay definition, consider whether the statement was first made in court, at the current hearing, or if it is being repeated from an earlier time outside of court. We have much less confidence in the credibility of witness statements made outside of court. Whatever answer is given outside of court is tainted because it is not under oath. Therefore, the safer bet in the search for the truth is not to allow those hearsay statements in (unless there is an appropriate exception to the Hearsay Rule) and to rely instead on the evidence obtained on the witness stand, under oath.

The language from CEC 1200(a) — "other than a witness while testifying at the hearing" — is important to flesh out. The statement could be from a witness's testimony in a previous hearing in the same case. If the witness is being asked to repeat that statement at a subsequent hearing in the case and says, "What I said at the last hearing was . . ." and then repeats the statement from the last hearing, then that repetition will be hearsay. This is because even though the actual statement was originally made at *a* hearing, it was not made at *this* hearing (but an exception could still get this statement into evidence).

In addition, a witness can make a statement that is hearsay even while that witness is currently on the stand. For example, the witness on the stand is asked, "What did you say to him then?" and answers, "I told him 'Pat did it.'" The portion of the witness's statement in single quotation marks is hearsay because it is an oral statement that was made other than while testifying in the current trial or hearing. However, it is very easy to make this statement not hearsay by simply asking the question in a different form. How to rephrase the question is discussed below in the section describing methods for admitting hearsay evidence.

3. What Is the Statement Being Offered to Prove?

The third step in the hearsay analysis is to determine why the statement is being offered into evidence. What is the statement being used to prove in the case? If the statement is being used to prove that its message is true, then this third element is established and the statement is hearsay evidence subject to exclusion under CEC 1200(b). In determining whether a statement is being used to prove that its message is true, you first need to understand what message the statement is intended to convey.

Direct and Indirect Assertions

Statements can convey information directly as well as indirectly or implicitly. When a statement conveys a message directly, it is called a direct assertion. When a statement conveys a message indirectly or implicitly, it is called an indirect assertion or an implied assertion.

A *direct assertion* is explicitly stated. For example, if a person says, "I am talking on the phone right now," it directly conveys the message that the person is talking on the phone right now. The statement asserts what it explicitly states.

On the other hand, an *indirect or implicit assertion* has an implicit and intended meaning that is not explicitly stated. Both direct and indirect assertions can exist in one statement. For instance, if a person says, "I am putting on my jacket before I go outside," the direct assertion is that she is putting on a jacket. The indirect assertion is that it is cold enough outside to need a jacket. Sarcastic comments, such as "Great work, Sherlock!" always have indirect assertions. When someone makes a sarcastic comment, the person does not mean to convey the direct assertion of that statement. Rather she intends the opposite: the work is not great, and the person she is speaking to is not the famous detective.

Proving the Direct or Indirect Assertion

After you have deciphered the direct and any indirect or implicit assertion in the statement, ask whether the statement is being offered to prove the truth of those direct or indirect assertions. For example, the statement "I am talking on the phone right now," from above, is being used to prove the truth of the matter asserted (TOMA) if its purpose in evidence is to prove that the witness was on the phone. The evidence might be used in a criminal trial to prove that the person was indeed on the phone when making the statement. That purpose would be to prove the TOMA, and thus the statement would constitute hearsay. Similarly, if the statement is offered to prove that the person was busy, then there is a good argument that it is being offered to prove the indirect assertion (that the person cannot talk to anyone else at the moment because she is already talking on the phone) and therefore would also be for the TOMA (indirectly). But, if the statement is offered to prove that the person speaks English, for instance, then the assertion is not being offered to prove the truth of the matter of any assertion, whether direct or implicit. All that matters is whether the statement was in the English language. If the statement is not offered to prove the TOMA, it would not be hearsay.

Proving Something Other than the Direct or Indirect Assertion

Even when a statement could be useful for proving the TOMA, if the statement does not meet a hearsay exception, then the next best approach is to characterize the statement's purpose as not for the TOMA. For instance, suppose a witness testifies that she overheard the victim say that the victim was worried that the defendant would harm her if she left him. The prosecution wants to offer this statement against the defendant for TOMA purposes — to prove that the victim was worried that the defendant would harm her. If no exceptions allow this statement into evidence, then in the alternative the prosecution could use the evidence to prove that the victim was afraid of the defendant. In that case, the statement would not be hearsay because it is not being used for the TOMA. (Other non-truth purposes are discussed in the section entitled "Common Non-truth Purposes" below.)

When this strategy is used, the opposing party should consider asking for a limiting instruction (as discussed in Chapter 1) that will remind the jury that the statement is not to be considered by them for its truth, but rather as circumstantial evidence of some other non-truth purpose, such as proving state of mind.

In summary, here are the key questions for hearsay analysis:

1. Is it a statement?
2. Was the statement made outside of this court hearing?
3. What is the statement offered to prove?

OPTIONS FOR ADMITTING STATEMENTS THAT MAY CONSTITUTE HEARSAY

Sometimes hearsay statements might be the only or the best evidence that the litigants have to prove a particular point. There are three basic options for admitting statements that may constitute hearsay:

1. reevaluate the evidence and show that it does not actually fit the three requirements for hearsay (usually by using the statement for a non-truth purpose)
2. change the way the evidence is introduced in court so that it is no longer hearsay, or
3. find an exception to the Hearsay Rule.

Call the Declarant to Testify in Court

For the first option, *simply call the declarant to testify*. Recall the earlier example in which April made an out-of-court statement to Neal that Pat pulled the trigger, and Neal later tried to testify about April's statement. In that case, the prosecutor should simply call April as a witness at trial. This enables April to explain firsthand — in court, under oath, and subject to cross-examination — what she saw or heard. Phrase the question in a way that asks April to explain what she actually observed, not what she said about what she observed. In some cases, however, the witness may be unwilling or unable to testify, and this first option is not possible.

Show that the Statement Does Not Meet the Three Elements of Hearsay

For the second option, *analyze the three elements of hearsay to determine whether there is a plausible argument that the particular statement does not meet the hearsay definition.* Remember, hearsay is (1) a statement (2) made outside of the court's hearing (3) that is offered to prove what the statement asserts is true.

For instance, for the first element, ask whether the statement was made by an animal, whether it is a question rather than an assertion, or whether it is non-verbal conduct that was not intended as assertive conduct. If any of these answers are "yes," then the first element is not met: the evidence is not a statement and thus is not hearsay.

For the second element, ask if the witness is repeating quotations from a conversation that was originally held outside of court. If yes, this element is met. If the witness is merely relaying the general substance of such a conversation without verbatim quotations, then the second element is not met, and the statement is not hearsay.

For the third element, ask what the statement is being used to prove. To answer this question, first think about what the statement is relevant to prove. As discussed in Chapter 1, information can be relevant to more than one proposition, so analyze all potential lines of relevance (all potential paths that the statement could be a step in building). Figure out the direct and any indirect assertions contained in the statement and ask whether the statement is relevant to prove anything other than the truth of those assertions. If the statement can be a step on the path toward proving something relevant that is not the TOMA, then the statement does not meet the third element of the hearsay definition. (The next section explains common non-truth purposes.)

Determine Whether the Statement Satisfies a Hearsay Exception

Finally, if the statement meets the requirements for an exception, the statement will not be excluded based on the Hearsay Rule. (Hearsay exceptions are discussed in Chapters 5 through 7.) Other CEC sections may provide grounds for excluding the statement, however. In addition, the California and U.S. Constitutions provide further grounds for excluding hearsay evidence in criminal cases, even when the requirements of a hearsay exception have been established. For example, if admitting the evidence will infringe on a criminal defendant's constitutional right to confront witnesses against him, the hearsay evidence can be excluded on that basis. These rights are contained in the Confrontation Clause of the Sixth Amendment to the U.S. Constitution and are explained in Chapter 5.

COMMON NON-TRUTH PURPOSES

A number of non-truth purposes defeat the third element. Evidence professors and textbooks tend to focus on some or all of the eight identified below. Those eight common non-truth purposes are those that have independent significance aside from communication:

1. To prove that the declarant was conscious or alive
2. To prove notice was given
3. To explain subsequent conduct or the effect on the listener
4. To prove that further action should have been taken
5. To prove there was a verbal act under the substantive law or a legally operative act
6. To prove knowledge
7. To prove indirect state of mind
8. To impeach the credibility of the witness

To Prove Consciousness

One non-truth purpose is to prove the declarant was *conscious or alive*. The statement "I'm still alive" would technically constitute hearsay if said by a person outside of court and offered to prove that person was alive when making the statement. However, if the statement is used to prove that the declarant was conscious or alive (because only people who are alive can talk), then the statement is not being offered to prove the truth of its assertion. In this situation, the content of the statement is completely irrelevant. If the person had said, "I am a dog" or "My name is Mudd," it would not matter. The mere fact that the person spoke means that she is alive. When the substance of the matter asserted is not important for the proof, the statement can be offered for a non-truth purpose and will be admissible as non-hearsay.

To Prove Notice

A second non-truth purpose that often is tested by evidence professors is to prove that *notice was given*. For instance, a warning statement about a dangerous condition can prove that the listener was on notice of the dangerous condition. "Watch out! I broke a glass on the floor and there are shards everywhere," is a warning statement about broken glass. It would be hearsay if the statement were used to prove that the declarant broke the glass or that there were shards everywhere. Instead, however, a party may want to use that statement to prove that it was the plaintiff's fault that she sliced her bare foot on broken glass. The argument is that if the plaintiff heard the warning that there was broken glass on the floor but walked barefoot through the broken glass anyway, then she caused her own injury.

Where the substance of the warning is not offered to prove the existence of the condition warned about, but rather to prove that the warning was given, it will be allowed as non-hearsay. This is a situation where the opposing party should be sure to ask for a limiting instruction. The instruction should ask that the jurors limit their use of the statement to prove that there was a warning, and not to prove who broke the glass or that there were glass shards all over.

To Explain Subsequent Conduct/Effect on Listener

A third common non-truth purpose is to explain *subsequent conduct or the effect on the listener*. An assertion can be offered into evidence to show that the person who heard the out-of-court statement reacted in a certain way to that statement. For instance, if a student tells her roommate "it is raining very hard outside," that roommate may refuse to leave the apartment until she can find her raincoat and umbrella. If a party needed to prove that the roommate left the apartment later than usual, she can offer the student's statement as circumstantial evidence of why it took her roommate so long to leave the apartment.

Another common example of this non-truth purpose is when highway patrol officers explain why they decided to stop and search a particular car. If the officer received a radio report to "be on the lookout for a white Mercedes with a suspected car thief driving," then that assertion would provide circumstantial evidence of why the officer subsequently detained and searched a white Mercedes and its driver. If the officer's motive for detaining the Mercedes is relevant to the litigation, then the truth of the actual radio dispatch does not matter. What matters is that because the police officer heard that statement, he engaged in the particular subsequent conduct of pulling over and searching the white Mercedes.

To Prove Further Action Required

A fourth and fairly common non-truth purpose that arises in litigation is to prove that *further action should have been taken*. For instance, in the suspected car thief example above, imagine that the officer calls in the license plate number of the white Mercedes and is told "it matches the plate for a Mercedes reported stolen just an hour ago," but the officer does not pull the Mercedes over. In a later case where the officer is being reprimanded for not acting, the statement that the plates matched could be non-hearsay if used to prove that the officer had a reason to take further action. If, however, the statement was offered to prove that the license plates actually did match, the purpose would be to prove the TOMA, and it would be hearsay.

To Prove Facts Under Substantive Law

A fifth purpose that also commonly arises is to prove *a verbal act that is material under the substantive law or a legally operative fact*. Some professors refer to this as proving *verbal acts*. *Verbal acts* are words that have *independent legal* meaning under the substantive law (e.g., tort, contract, or criminal law). Verbal acts include statements that are an element of a cause of action or criminal charge. This doctrine comes up in contract cases, defamation cases, illegal betting or gambling cases, solicitation and conspiracy cases, extortion cases, and others.

For instance, in a breach of contract case, an element of the cause of action is proving the existence of the contract. When the defendant said, "I accept your contract terms," the defendant engaged into a verbal act that is material under substantive contract law. At trial, the plaintiff may want to testify that this is what the defendant said outside of court. The verbal act is not being offered to prove that when the defendant *said* that she accepted the contract offer she was speaking truthfully, but rather to show that her words constituted the act of accepting the contract offer.

Similarly, in a criminal trial for conspiracy, an element of the conspiracy is to prove that the parties agree to do an illegal act or a legal act in an illegal manner. When the defendant said, "I agree to help you rob the bank," the defendant engaged in a verbal act that is legally operative under the substantive criminal law. If the prosecution witness repeats the defendant's out-of-court statement, it can be offered for a non-truth purpose — to prove that he engaged in the verbal act of agreeing to join a conspiracy. The verbal act is not offered to prove the truth of the assertion, but rather to prove the conduct that satisfies the element of the cause of action or affirmative defense under the substantive law.

This use also arises in disputes over gifts. If a stranger says, "I am giving you this Bentley. Here are the keys. Enjoy it and drive safely," but later sues for non-payment of the purchase price of the Bentley, then that stranger's statement that it was a gift is relevant as substantive proof that nothing is owed on the car because it was a gift. The substantive law does not care about the exact words of the stranger's statement, just whether words of gifting were expressed. If so, the item is a gift, and the purchase price need not be paid under the substantive law.

To Prove Relevant Knowledge

A sixth and relatively common non-truth purpose is to prove *relevant knowledge*. This non-truth purpose is useful to prove that the declarant knew something, but not to prove whether that something is accurately true. For example, consider a statement by the declarant that "the bank has three emergency exits that trigger the silent alarm and one exit from the teller booth that triggers a sound alarm." This statement proves the declarant's knowledge of the layout of the bank and the alarm triggers, and it can be used as circumstantial evidence that he was planning to rob the bank. It does not matter whether the bank truly had three emergency exits and one, two, or three silent or sound alarms. Simply using the statement as circumstantial evidence of the declarant's alleged knowledge of a condition, without proving the truth of that condition, does not violate the Hearsay Rule. It may turn out that the assertion is false, which will be circumstantial evidence that the declarant was only bluffing and did not really plan on robbing the bank because he never did any reconnaissance. Nevertheless, this assertion will be non-hearsay if offered for the purpose of proving the declarant's knowledge.

To Prove Indirect State of Mind or Emotion

The seventh non-truth purpose is a bit more complicated than the others. It is to prove the declarant's *state of mind*. One can prove state of mind with direct evidence of that person testifying as to her state of mind, or by circumstantial evidence and inferences based on what that person says, does, or refrains from saying or doing. When evidence of state of mind is used to directly prove the statement asserted, it is referred to as *direct state of mind*. This book refers to the circumstantial use of state of mind evidence as *indirect state of mind*. The state of mind issue comes up in criminal cases often, as well as in competency hearings. (Because the Hearsay Rule has two specific state of mind exceptions, this category is discussed in more detail in Chapters 5 and 7.)

Circumstantial evidence of one's state of mind is not hearsay because it is not offered to prove the truth of the assertion but rather as an interpretation of what that assertion means about the declarant's state of mind. With *indirect state of mind evidence*, there is no need to consider the direct state of mind hearsay exception because that use of the evidence will not constitute hearsay. For instance, if the declarant says, "The defendant told me, 'I will kill you if you try to run away,'" that statement would be hearsay if offered to prove that the defendant would kill her (but admissible as a party admission exception discussed in Chapter 6). But, if offered to prove that the declarant's state of mind was one of fear toward the defendant, it is indirect state of mind evidence and therefore not hearsay. It is not being offered to prove he would kill her but rather as circumstantial evidence to prove that she had reason to fear him.

To Impeach a Witness

The eighth and final non-truth purpose that you are likely to encounter is to *impeach a witness* by disputing the previous assertions offered as testimony by that witness. Under the impeachment category, out-of-court statements can be offered to show inconsistencies with in-court testimony as long as the out of court statement is not offered to prove the TOMA in that statement. The statement will be non-hearsay if offered to prove simply that the declarant told one version of the story at one time and now on the witness stand is telling a different version of the story. To prove that the out of court statement is the true one, the proponent will need to fit the requirements of one of the hearsay exceptions. (This category is developed in more detail in the Chapter 6 discussion of prior statements of witnesses, as well as in Chapter 8 addressing the credibility of witnesses.)

Limitations on Use for Non-truth Purposes

Remember that when offering evidence for a non-hearsay purpose, its use will be limited to that non-truth purpose. If you need the evidence to prove an element of a claim or defense in the litigation, then it would be more advantageous to use the second or third options. Either change the form of the evidence so that it no longer meets the definition of hearsay or look for a hearsay exception.

Hearsay exceptions can often be confused with non-truth purposes, but it is important to distinguish the two. *Non-truth purpose* means that the statement is not being offered to prove the truth of the content of the actual statement — which means that the statement is *not hearsay*. The Hearsay Rule is not implicated at all because you changed the purpose of introducing the statement. Other evidentiary rules still may prevent the statement from being admissible, however, such as the character and other policy exclusion code sections discussed in Chapters 2 and 3, as well as others explained in the remainder of this book.

In contrast, exceptions to the Hearsay Rule acknowledge that a statement *is still hearsay* (being offered for the TOMA), but it will be admissible as an exception to the rule as long as the elements of the exception are met and no other evidentiary rules bar the use of the statement. (The exceptions are listed in the Hearsay Exceptions Chart in the appendix and are discussed in Chapters 5, 6, and 7.)

Federal Rules of Evidence Compared: Notable Differences

There are two major differences between the FRE and the CEC on the definition of hearsay. FRE 801 specifically excludes from its hearsay definition certain prior statements of witnesses and certain admissions by or related to a party to the litigation. The rationale behind this federal exclusion is that the declarant is testifying at trial, so the opportunity for cross-examination is there, or the declarant is a party to the litigation, and thus has the opportunity to testify on his own behalf if he wants to. In California, those same categories are considered hearsay but are admissible as exceptions to the Hearsay Rule.

Examples

1. Mike is on trial for kidnapping and murdering Nancy. Mike claims that Nancy asked to come along with him on a hike, so she was not taken against her will. He also claims that she slipped while hiking and that when he reached out to grab her, she pushed his hand away and fell to her death. The prosecution seeks to admit a statement made by Nancy shortly before her death in which she stated "I am really afraid of Mike because of his violent temper." Mike's defense counsel objects to the admission of Nancy's statement on the grounds of hearsay. How should the prosecution respond, how should the court rule, and why?

2. Andy is on trial for the murder of his next-door neighbors Clara and David. A purse, wallet, and some rare coins were missing from the victims' home after the homicide. The district attorney has filed a notice of intent to seek the death penalty based on a special circumstance of murder for financial gain and murder occurring during a robbery. At the time he was arrested, Andy had some rare coins in his pockets. The prosecutor seeks to prove that Andy killed the victims during a robbery and intended to gain financially by selling the rare coins. During the trial, the prosecutor asked the victims' daughter Beth whether her mother had mentioned anything about having her purse or wallet stolen at some time *before* the night of the murder to prove that Andy stole the purse when he killed the victims. Before Andy's attorney can object, Beth testifies, "My mother did not mention her purse or wallet being stolen

when I talked to her earlier on the day that she was found dead." Andy's attorney objects on the grounds of hearsay and moves to strike Beth's answer. How should the court rule?

3. Evan is on trial for the murder of Frank. A few days before the murder, Frank told his wife Georgia, "Evan has been blackmailing me." Georgia took Frank to the police station to file a report about the blackmail. Later that evening, Georgia saw Evan and told him, "The police are going to stop you from blackmailing Frank." At trial, the prosecution seeks to offer Georgia's testimony that Frank told Georgia that Evan was black-mailing him. Evan's defense attorney objects on the grounds of hearsay. What arguments should the prosecution make in response, how should the court rule, and why?

4. Henrietta is on trial for murder and conspiracy to commit murder. She had been plotting with several other female friends including Irene to kill a local drug dealer. Irene called Henrietta several times to discuss the potential homicide. Kim overheard Irene's side of the conversations about the murder plot. The prosecution sought to admit Kim's testimony regarding two out-of-court statements by Irene. In the first statement, Irene said, "Can you get me a gun to take care of a problem?" In the second statement, Irene said, "I no longer need that gun that I asked you for. We took care of the problem, and we dumped the body at Balboa Park." Henrietta's defense attorney objects to the admission of both of these out-of-court statements on the grounds of hearsay. How should the prosecution respond, how should the court rule, and why?

5. Quentin and Robert are on trial for burglary and felony murder. The defendants attempted to steal drugs from the home of one dealer, but Robert was shot as they tried to escape. They hid at Quentin's house for a few hours while Quentin's wife dressed Robert's wound. During that time, Quentin accused Robert of "getting weak." Robert responded that "I am not getting weak," and said, "If you have something else for us to do, I'll show you that I'm not weak." Quentin then told Robert that he had another dealer in mind. They went to the home of the second drug dealer and shot him before he could reach his weapon. The prosecution sought to offer the testimony of Quentin's wife that she overheard these statements. Robert objected to these statements as inadmissible hearsay. How should the prosecution respond, and how should the court rule?

6. Samantha was a police officer in the Tetris City Police Department and was promoted to the rank of detective. Her new supervisor gave her bad performance reviews that Samantha felt were unwarranted. Eventually, Samantha was demoted back to the rank of patrol officer. Samantha then began to receive numerous hang-up phone calls at home with a caller identification notification stating "Tetris Police Department." These calls

caused her great stress, and she began to suffer from anxiety attacks. Eventually Samantha left work on disability, and then she sued the police department for gender discrimination. At trial, Samantha sought to admit statements made by the now-deceased Sergeant Ugo to a Department of Justice investigator, which stated that "Samantha was demoted because she is a woman." Defense counsel for the Tetris Police Department objected to the admission of Ugo's statement as hearsay. How should Samantha respond, how should the court rule, and why?

7. Yasmine was a teenage mother who put her baby up for adoption. The baby's father Zeke later challenged the adoption, stating that he was not informed of the pregnancy and adoption in time to properly exercise his parental rights. The adoption agency claimed that Zeke had not shown any evidence of parental responsibility or commitment, and therefore the adoption could go through without his consent. Zeke seeks to admit the following evidence: (a) his own testimony that Yasmine told him that abortion was the only option; (b) his own testimony that he refrained from contacting Yasmine on the advice of his counsel; and (c) a letter from Zeke's attorney to Yasmine's parents offering to provide financial support for the baby. The adoption agency objects to each item of evidence as inadmissible hearsay. How should Zeke respond, how should the court rule, and why?

8. Victoria sued her employer, Wuma Bank, for sexual harassment and sought to admit her own statements from a signed and sworn affidavit, attesting to the following harassing statements allegedly made to her by her supervisor, Xavier: "Xavier told me, 'Your hair is beautiful,'" "Xavier asked me, 'Please accompany me for a drive,'" and "Xavier asked me, 'Would you like to come with me to my hotel room?'" Wuma's defense counsel argued that the statements were inadmissible hearsay. How should Victoria respond, and how should the court rule?

Explanations

1. Nancy's statement that she was afraid of Mike because of his violent temper is a statement of her state of mind. If the prosecution is offering the statement to prove that Nancy had a fear of Mike, then it is direct evidence of Nancy's state of mind and would be hearsay. On the other hand, the prosecution may choose to offer the evidence as circumstantial evidence that Nancy would not voluntarily go on a hike with Mike and thus her presence with him was likely involuntary. If offered for that purpose, then the statement would be admissible as non-hearsay because it would not be offered for the TOMA. The court should admit the statement as non-hearsay because it is being offered for a non-truth

purpose — as circumstantial, indirect evidence of Nancy's state of mind regarding going places alone with Mike.

2. This question involves the issue of whether silence can constitute an assertion. Clara never said anything to her daughter about being robbed. Beth's testimony is hearsay if Clara's silence is considered a statement. The prosecution's theory is that since Clara never mentioned that the purse had been stolen prior to her murder, then the purse was not stolen prior to the murder. The defense will argue that if Clara's purse had been stolen she would be likely to tell her daughter Beth about it. The prosecution will respond that the failure to make a statement cannot constitute an assertion unless that failure is in response to a direct question involving a situation where one ordinarily would respond if the answer were not in the affirmative. An example of this situation would be if Beth had specifically asked Clara to tell her if she had been robbed recently or if she had had anything taken from her lately. If Beth had asked such a question and Clara responded with silence, then there would be a stronger argument that Clara's silence constitutes an assertion that the purse had not been stolen. However, the court should rule that the failure to speak was not hearsay because there was no statement made and there was no evidence that a failure to speak was a substitute for an assertion.

3. The prosecution should respond that Frank's out-of-court statement is not being offered for the TOMA (to establish that Evan actually did blackmail him), but rather to show the fact that the accusation was made and thus provided a *motive* for Evan to kill Frank. Evan's defense attorney might respond that the statement is useful only to prove its truth because if Evan was not a blackmailer, then the false accusation would not give him a motive to kill his accuser. Thus the statement is relevant to explain Evan's conduct only if it is considered to be true. The court should overrule the hearsay objection and admit the statement because it does not matter whether the statement is true. The mere fact that the statement was made provides a motive for the murder and demonstrates why Evan would be angry and perhaps resort to violence. The statement should be admitted as non-hearsay because it is offered for a non-truth purpose. Evan should ask for a limiting instruction to make sure that the jury considers the statement only for its non-truth purpose.

4. The prosecution should respond that the request for a gun in the first statement was not an assertion. It was a question, which does not implicate the Hearsay Rule. In addition, the prosecution can argue that the information conveyed by "to take care of a problem" is not offered for the TOMA but rather to explain subsequent conduct or to provide a rationale or motive for needing the gun. The second statement that

"I no longer need" what was asked for because "we took care of the problem" and "dumped the body" fits the definition of hearsay because these statements are only relevant to prove the truth. Unless the co-conspirator hearsay exception applies (which is addressed in Chapter 6), this second statement would be inadmissible hearsay.

5. The prosecution should respond by arguing that the statement Quentin's wife overheard about "getting weak" is not being offered for the TOMA but rather to show a motive for the later robbery and murder. The statement was not offered to show that Robert actually was getting weak but merely that he had a motive to participate in yet another criminal offense to prove his manhood. The court should overrule the hearsay objection and admit the statement as non-hearsay.

6. Samantha should argue the statement of Sergeant Ugo is not being offered to show the TOMA — that Samantha was demoted because she was a woman — but rather as circumstantial evidence of the hostile work environment in which she found herself. If a fellow officer thought she was demoted because of her gender, then it is more likely that gender discrimination was going on. This statement helps to prove the climate of gender discrimination circumstantially. Thus, it is not necessary to use the statement for its truth. The defendant should respond that the statement is really only relevant when offered to prove its truth, that Samantha was demoted because she is a woman. Also, the defendant should argue that it is unlikely that a jury would be able to abide by a limiting instruction (discussed in Chapter 1) to consider that statement only for its non-truth purpose. Therefore, the court should sustain the hearsay objection and decline to admit the statement (unless there is an applicable exception) because its most probative, and most likely, use is to prove the TOMA.

7. Zeke should respond that the statements are not being offered for the TOMA. Statement (a) is not offered to show that abortion was the only option, but rather to explain why Zeke did not contact Yasmine after she made that statement. It is circumstantial evidence of his belief that there no longer was a child to try to support. The behavior in (b) is not an assertion; rather it is his testimony about his conduct of failing to contact the mother, with an explanation for that conduct. There is no out-of-court statement involved; thus statement (b) is not even hearsay. Statement (c) is an out-of-court statement with an assertion, but it is not offered to prove the TOMA — that he will pay financial support. Instead, the letter can be offered to show that he said he would pay financial support (not that he actually would). Saying that he would provide financial support is evidence of intent to show some parental responsibility and commitment, which is at issue in the litigation. The court

should overrule all three objections because the statements are non-hearsay: (a) and (c) are offered for non-truth purposes, and (b) is not an out-of-court statement.

8. The affidavit involves two levels of hearsay: Victoria's out-of-court written statement and the quotation of the statements made by Xavier. The best way to address both levels of hearsay is option one: to call Victoria as a witness and simply ask her what made her uncomfortable with her supervisor. Because Victoria is the plaintiff in the case, it is likely that she is available to testify. Phrasing the questions in a way that does not require her to repeat Xavier's actual statements would eliminate the hearsay issue and make the evidence more reliable. If for some reason Victoria is not available to testify about these statements (for example, if she has a loss of memory or is too ill to appear at trial), then the next best option would be to use Xavier's statements in the affidavit for non-truth purposes. Victoria's counsel should explain that the first statement is not offered for the TOMA, that Victoria's hair is beautiful, but rather is circumstantial evidence of how Xavier treated her.

   In addition, the statements could be considered verbal acts that demonstrate the inappropriate nature of his attentions and constitute the actual harassment. The second and third quotes were actually questions, or requests, rather than statements, and they made no assertions (other than the implicit assertion in the third question that he had a hotel room). Thus, Xavier's quotations do not meet the requirements of the hearsay definition. The trial court should overrule the hearsay objection as to all three quotations on the following grounds: the first can be offered for a non-truth purpose, and the second and third are not assertions or statements. In addressing the second layer of hearsay, that the statements were contained in an affidavit, the court will sustain that hearsay objection. The affidavit is an out-of-court statement, and if offered for the truth of the matters it asserts, such as that Victoria said that Xavier told her certain things and asked her certain questions, then the affidavit is hearsay. Unless a hearsay exception applies (discussed in Chapters 5 through 7), the affidavit will be inadmissible hearsay.

The Confrontation Clause and Hearsay Exceptions Triggered by Unavailability

When a witness testifies at trial against a criminal defendant, the defendant has an opportunity to confront that witness. However, when a witness repeats a hearsay statement made by someone else, like the statements described in Chapter 4, the parties do not always call the declarant to the witness stand. In addition, some declarants are unable or unwilling to come to court. When the hearsay declarant does not appear on the witness stand, then the criminal defendant is not able to confront one of the people who provided evidence against him.

However, the Sixth Amendment of the U.S. Constitution guarantees criminal defendants the right to confront people who give evidence against them. The language of the amendment is referred to as the *Confrontation Clause*. Over the past few decades, the courts have been modifying the extent of the criminal defendant's confrontation rights. This chapter begins with an explanation of the court's evolving interpretation of the requirements of the Confrontation Clause and then describes the most recent holdings in this area.

The second half of this chapter addresses the hearsay exceptions that are accessible only when the hearsay declarant is unavailable to appear at court. *Unavailable* has a precise meaning under the California Evidence Code, which is explained in detail below. All of the CEC exceptions requiring unavailability are discussed together in this chapter. When the declarant is unavailable in a criminal case, the criminal defendant will not be able to confront him. This chapter also addresses the circumstances under which the unavailability of a hearsay declarant will violate the defendant's confrontation rights.

Note on the FRE: It is important to understand that some exceptions that require unavailability under the CEC do not require unavailability under the

FRE and vice versa. The FRE divides its hearsay exceptions into those that require unavailability (FRE 804 exceptions) and those for which availability is immaterial (FRE 803 exceptions). Thus, many evidence professors address the CEC provisions in that order, even though the availability requirement for a particular exception may be different under the CEC and the FRE. To help you to compare and contrast the availability requirements under the CEC and the FRE, the appendix contains a Table of Hearsay Exceptions with Crossover to the Federal Rules. That table indicates when the unavailability requirement differs between them. The table will help you determine which chapter of this book contains the CEC sections that correspond to the FRE sections you are studying.

THE CONFRONTATION CLAUSE

The Confrontation Clause of the Sixth Amendment includes three confrontation rights:

1. to have prosecution witnesses present at the trial
2. to cross-examine prosecution witnesses, and
3. to be present at one's own trial.

Because this is a federal constitutional right, its requirements trump state laws (such as the CEC) and federal statutes (such as the FRE). This constitutional right applies in *all criminal cases* regardless of whether the trial is in state or federal court.

What is the rationale for the Confrontation Clause? Its primary purpose is to ensure reliability by subjecting the evidence to rigorous cross-examination in an adversarial proceeding. The absence of confrontation reduces public confidence in the integrity of the fact-finding process. Courts want to be especially careful when admitting evidence against criminal defendants, if that evidence has not been tested or challenged in the adversarial system.

The physical presence of prosecution witnesses is important because it permits the jury to evaluate the body language and demeanor of the witnesses, which aids in the jurors' consideration of credibility. Also, having the witness stand face to face with the defendant as well as with the jury can heighten awareness of the duty to tell the truth and reduce the motivation to lie.

In addition, the Confrontation Clause reflects the purpose of cross-examination discussed in Chapter 4 — to evaluate the credibility of the witness and to test his or her perception, memory, narration, and sincerity.

When Hearsay Declarants Are Not Physically Present at Trial

Admitting hearsay evidence at trial implicates the first and second components of the right to confrontation — to have prosecution witnesses present
at trial and to actually cross-examine those prosecution witnesses. When a
witness is repeating an out-of-court statement made by a declarant, then
both the witness and the declarant are "prosecution witnesses." The witness
who is repeating the statement in court is a prosecution witness present at
trial and subject to cross-examination. The declarant becomes a "witness for
the prosecution" when the declarant's own out-of-court statement is offered
through the mouth of the in-court witness.

The graphic below illustrates this point:

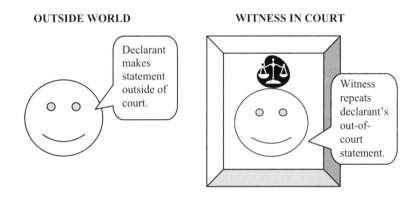

OUTSIDE WORLD   WITNESS IN COURT

Declarant makes statement outside of court.

Witness repeats declarant's out-of-court statement.

While CEC 1203 allows a party to call a hearsay declarant to the witness
stand to cross-examine him about his out-of-court statement, in many cases,
the parties do not call the hearsay declarant to the witness stand. Having
every declarant appear as a witness would expend too much court time and
substantially lessen the utility of the Hearsay Rule. Moreover, if every declarant came to court, then the attorneys could ask many questions in a way that
would not implicate the Hearsay Rule (as discussed in Chapter 4). When the
hearsay declarant does not also testify in court, the criminal defendant
misses out on his rights to have prosecution witnesses present and to
cross-examine prosecution witnesses. The courts have decided that the
inability to cross-examine a hearsay declarant violates the Confrontation
Clause only when the hearsay statement is *testimonial*. (This standard is
explained below in the section entitled "Determining Whether a Statement
Is Testimonial.")

MODERN HISTORY OF CONFRONTATION

The confrontation doctrine has changed dramatically in recent years, and this section gives you a brief history of those changes. Be sure to check with your evidence professor for more recent cases in this active area of law. Initially, the Confrontation Clause required all witnesses and hearsay declarants to be present for cross-examination. Slowly, the courts began to relax this rigid rule and apply a more flexible standard.

Indicia of Reliability

In determining whether admitting a hearsay statement violated the Confrontation Clause, courts were looking for *indicia of reliability*. That means, if the circumstances suggested that the hearsay statement was reliable enough, then the court could admit the statement as evidence in a criminal case without requiring the declarant to testify. For example, when a person makes a statement that is against his interest, such as confessing to a crime, the courts find the statement to be reliable if it is the kind of statement that a person would not make unless he believed it to be true. Most people would not confess to a crime unless they really committed the crime, and so that confession has indicia of reliability. Those indications of reliability allow the court to admit the hearsay statement without having to satisfy the Confrontation Clause.

Firmly Rooted Hearsay Exceptions

The U.S. Supreme Court relaxed the rule even further in *Ohio v. Roberts*,[1] stating that if the hearsay testimony is admitted under a well-established hearsay exception, then it would not violate the Confrontation Clause — even if the declarant is not present and not available for cross-examination. The Court called these exceptions *firmly rooted*, which simply meant that the hearsay exception had been in existence for a long time in case law or in statutes. The rationale was that these long-standing hearsay exceptions were created because the circumstances of the statements contain adequate indicia of reliability as under the earlier standard.

One example of a firmly rooted exception is the eception for former testimony. When a person testifies in a trial, a court reporter makes a transcript of the witness's testimony. If a party wants to quote from that

---

1. 448 U.S. 56 (1980).

transcript in another trial, the statements in that transcript would be out-of-court statements as discussed in Chapter 4. If those statements are offered to prove the truth of the first trial testimony, then those statements are hearsay when offered in the second trial. The former testimony hearsay exception provides a way to offer those statements in the second trial. (The elements of this exception are explained in the second half of this chapter.) This exception was considered firmly rooted because it was well established and recognized by all courts. Because the statement satisfies the requirements of a firmly rooted hearsay exception, the statement was reliable enough to satisfy the constitutional concerns.

Other firmly rooted exceptions include dying declarations (addressed later in this chapter), state of mind, excited utterances, and business records (all addressed in Chapter 7).

Particularized Guarantees of Inherent Trustworthiness

The Supreme Court continued to relax the standard for determining whether admitting a hearsay statement violated the Confrontation Clause. In *Idaho v. Wright*,[2] the Court decided that a firmly rooted hearsay exception was no longer necessary, as long as other circumstances existed to show that the hearsay statement was reliable. This new standard called for *particularized guarantees of trustworthiness*, which required analyzing the circumstances under which the statement was made and the declarant's motivation to be truthful under those conditions. For instance, statements made under duress would not have particular guarantees of trustworthiness because people have a motive to lie when lying may lessen the stress they are experiencing. On the other hand, a patient making a statement about his drug allergies to an emergency room doctor about to operate would have sufficient guarantees of trustworthiness because the patient is not likely to want to lie under these circumstances. As you can see, this standard was very fact-specific.

The Current Standard: Only Testimonial Statements Implicate the Confrontation Clause

The U.S. Supreme Court doctrine on confrontation has evolved even more in the past few years. Continuing to refine the scope of which hearsay statements implicate the right to confrontation, the Supreme Court in *Crawford v. Washington*[3] determined that in the context of hearsay, the Confrontation

---

2. 497 U.S. 805 (1990).
3. 541 U.S. 36 (2004).

Clause applies solely to testimonial statements. A *testimonial statement* is one that has *governmental involvement* and the *solemnity of testimony at trial*. This means that some governmental representative had some role in the making of the out-of-court hearsay statement and that it is the kind of statement that a reasonable person would expect to be used at trial. A testimonial statement often is given under somewhat formal circumstances, as in a police department interrogation room, and a government representative such as a law enforcement officer, or an officer of the court, is present when the statement is being made.

For instance, when a victim goes to the police station and fills out a detailed statement describing what happened when her car was stolen, there is government involvement in making that statement. That police report is the type of statement that a reasonable person would expect to be used at trial if the car thief is apprehended.

As that doctrine stands at the time of this writing, the Confrontation Clause is limited to situations where the hearsay evidence a party seeks to admit is categorized as a *testimonial* statement. If the statement is *non-testimonial*, then the Confrontation Clause no longer bars admission of the hearsay statement. In *Davis v. Washington*,[4] the Court clarified that the Confrontation Clause *does not apply when the hearsay evidence is a non-testimonial statement.* If the statement is non-testimonial, there is no need to address confrontation issues.

For instance, when a car thief tells his friend that he stole the victim's car, the car thief does not expect his statement to be used at trial, and there is no government involvement (because if he knew his friend worked for law enforcement, he would not make the statement in front of him). The car thief's confession to his friend is *not testimonial*, and therefore the friend can testify about that out-of-court statement without violating the Confrontation Clause. The party will simply analyze whether the statement fits a *hearsay exception* in order for the statement to be admissible. (Hearsay exceptions are discussed in the later portion of this chapter, as well as Chapters 6 and 7.)

Thus, the state of the law as of this writing is that when applying the Confrontation Clause to hearsay declarations in a criminal case, you must evaluate whether there is (1) an out-of-court statement, (2) offered for the truth of the matter asserted, (3) by the prosecution, (4) against the accused, (5) that is testimonial.

Answering "yes" to all of the questions presented in Figure 5.1 triggers the Confrontation Clause. If "no" is the answer to any one of these questions, the Confrontation Clause does not apply. For instance, if the statement

---

4. 547 U.S. 813 (2006).

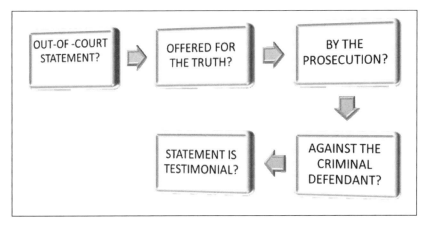

Figure 5.1. Is The Confrontation Clause Implicated?

is offered for a non-truth purpose (as discussed in Chapter 4), then there is no confrontation issue. If the defendant seeks to bring in a hearsay statement, the Confrontation Clause does not apply.

Once triggered, the prosecution must satisfy the confrontation requirement by doing one of the following: either (1) producing the hearsay declarant as a witness at trial, or (2) establishing by a preponderance of the evidence both that the hearsay declarant is unavailable for trial, and that the criminal defendant had an opportunity, at some point in the past, to cross-examine the declarant about the statement. (These two prosecution options are discussed after the section below on satisfying the Confrontation Clause.)

DETERMINING WHETHER A STATEMENT IS TESTIMONIAL

How does one determine whether a statement is testimonial or non-testimonial? *Testimonial* statements are those made under circumstances that indicate solemnity and formality similar to that for testimony. In *Crawford*, the U.S. Supreme Court provided a non-exhaustive list of statements that are testimonial: "the term [*testimonial*] . . . applies at a minimum to prior testimony at a preliminary hearing, before a grand jury, or at a former trial; and to police interrogations."[5] Statements made at court hearings or under oath or in any formal situation tend to be more reliable than

---

5. 541 U.S. at 68.

everyday conversations. Responses to questions posed by law enforcement officials (in non-emergency situations) have sufficient solemnity and formality to be testimonial.

Subsequent cases have provided more substance to the definition of *testimonial*. When the declarant makes the statement under circumstances that would lead a reasonable person to believe that it would be used at trial, then that statement is testimonial. Statements *in furtherance of a conspiracy* are not considered to be testimonial because co-conspirators do not make statements to one another when the government is involved, nor do they do so with a reasonable belief that their statements will be used at trial.

Statements to Police Officers and Emergency Personnel

If the declarant makes a statement to police officers, whether in an interview or an interrogation, then the purpose of the statement will determine whether it is testimonial. The statement will be considered testimonial if *the primary purpose of the communication with the police is to establish or prove past events that are potentially relevant to a later criminal prosecution.* Thus, a statement aimed at helping the police to locate a suspect is categorized as testimonial. Statements that assist the police with investigating a crime are testimonial.

On the other hand, *statements primarily made to aid with a contemporaneous emergency are not testimonial.* In *Davis v. Washington*, the U.S. Supreme Court further refined the rule in addressing 911 calls. The statements made for the purpose of obtaining immediate help for an emergency are not testimonial. If a caller says, "My husband just stabbed me, and I'm bleeding all over. Please send help right away to my location," that statement is not testimonial. If the prosecution offers this hearsay statement into evidence against the husband in his criminal trial, that offer does not implicate the Confrontation Clause.

Contrast that call with another 911 call where the caller says, "This is the third time my husband has attacked me with a knife. This time he only nicked my skin, so I'm fine. But I want you to arrest him. He just left the house in a black SUV and is heading to the beach. Let me give you his license plate number." This caller is not seeking emergency help, and the primary purpose of the call is to get the police to arrest her husband. Statements that are aimed at assisting with apprehending the suspect or investigating the crime are testimonial. Thus, this second caller's statements are testimonial. Offering these statements into evidence implicates the Confrontation Clause. Once the testimonial trigger has been activated, the prosecution must exercise one of the two options listed above to avoid a confrontation violation.

What begins as a response to an emergency can evolve into a testimonial statement as the police questioning continues. While the first response may not be testimonial, subsequent responses to police questioning can become testimonial as more time passes from the actual emergency. In one case, the lapse of an hour between statements was sufficient to define the later statement as testimonial when the earlier statement was not.

In *Hammon v. Indiana*,[6] the Court addressed a situation in which the victim of a domestic battery was interviewed by the police at the scene twice and then completed an affidavit. The court determined that the statements obtained during the second questioning and those made in the affidavit were testimonial because they were not made to find out what was happening in the present, but rather what had happened (to prove a past fact).

In *People v. Cage*,[7] the California Supreme Court applied this rule and determined that a victim's statements to a deputy while she was in the hospital emergency room were testimonial where the "primary purpose, objectively considered, was not to deal with an ongoing emergency, but to investigate the circumstances of a crime [to prove a past fact]."[8]

Statements in Law Enforcement Reports

The California Supreme Court held that forensic reports were not testimonial in *People v. Geier*[9]. The court's rationale was that the report was a "contemporaneous recordation of observable events" because the analyst was running tests and *as the results came in* he was documenting those results. The court did not consider the reports to be past facts related to criminal activity.

However, the U.S. Supreme Court disagreed in *Melendez-Diaz v. Massachusetts*[10], holding that affidavits from the analysts were testimonial statements and that the analysts were "witnesses" for confrontation purposes. The affidavits were prepared by government personnel for the express purpose of providing evidence against the accused at trial. The *Melendez-Diaz* dissenters argued that the affidavits were "near-contemporaneous observations of the test" and therefore should not be considered testimonial,[11] but the majority rejected this argument because the affidavits were completed more than a week after the tests were performed.[12]

---

6. This case was consolidated with Davis v. Washington at 547 U.S. 813 (2006).
7. 40 Cal. 4th 954, 155 P.3d 205 (2007).
8. *Id.* at 985, 155 P.3d at 218.
9. 41 Cal. 4th 555, 161 P.3d 104 (2007).
10. 557 U.S. — , 129 S.Ct. 2527 (2009).
11. *Id.* at 2551-52.
12. *Id.* at 2535

The decision was a narrow 5-4 and therefore may be subject to further refinement as the Court roster changes.

A subsequent California Court of Appeal held in *People v. Guiterrez*[13] that contemporaneous notes in lab reports regarding the tests performed and observations made during the technician's visual examination of a victim were not testimonial. However, where the background narrative portion of the report recorded past events and was made under circumstances that would lead an objective witness reasonably to believe that the statement would be available for use at trial, the narrative portion is testimonial. This case is on review by the California Supreme Court at the time of this writing.

What do you do if the statement is non-testimonial? Under current U.S. Supreme Court doctrine, the Confrontation Clause does not apply when the evidence is a non-testimonial statement. Simply find a hearsay exception (from those to be discussed in Chapters 5 through 7) to offer the out-of-court statement for the truth of the matter asserted. The next section discusses how to satisfy the Confrontation Clause when the statement is testimonial.

SATISFYING THE CONFRONTATION CLAUSE WHEN A STATEMENT IS TESTIMONIAL

If the statement is testimonial, then the prosecution in a criminal case must satisfy the Confrontation Clause requirements for the court to admit the statement. There are two different ways to satisfy the requirements. The first is to bring the declarant who made the testimonial statement outside of court to testify in court. The declarant thus will be present in court and will satisfy the first component of the confrontation right. The defendant can then cross-examine the declarant about the hearsay statement under oath, which satisfies the second component.

However, if the statement is testimonial and the declarant is not present at trial, then the prosecution must use the second option. Under this option, the prosecution must prove two things, as mentioned above: (1) the declarant is unavailable to testify in court under CEC 240 (which is addressed in the next section of this chapter), and (2) the accused had a prior opportunity to cross-examine that declarant about that statement. If the prosecution cannot meet these two additional elements, admitting the hearsay statement to prove the truth of the matter asserted violates the criminal defendant's confrontation rights. Because the constitutional right trumps the CEC, the hearsay statement will not be admissible.

---

13. 177 Cal. App. 4th 654 (2009) rev. granted 102 Cal. Rptr. 3d 281.

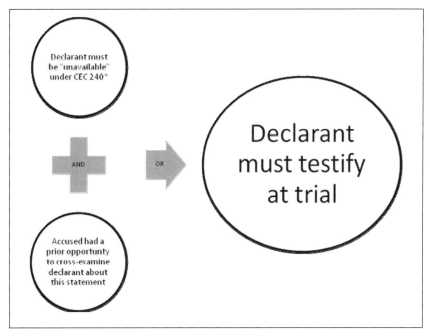

Figure 5.2. Satisfying the Confrontation Clause When a Statement Is Testimonial

Figure 5.2 shows the two options for ensuring that testimonial statements do not violate the Confrontation Clause. Either (1) the declarant must be unavailable *and* the defendant must have had an earlier chance to cross-examine that declarant, or (2) the declarant must testify at the trial.

The next section explains how to prove that a declarant is unavailable. If a declarant is unavailable under CEC 240, she is unavailable for confrontation purposes also.

Federal Rules of Evidence Compared: No Significant Difference

Because the Confrontation Clause is based on the U.S. Constitution, the holdings of the U.S. Supreme Court take precedence over any California Supreme Court cases as well as the CEC on this issue.

DETERMINING WHETHER A DECLARANT IS UNAVAILABLE

Recall that the best way to get hearsay evidence admitted is to make it not hearsay by bringing the declarant to the witness stand and asking the question anew, as discussed in Chapter 4. For instance, instead of asking "What did you tell the police officer about who robbed the bank?," ask "Who robbed the bank?" If amending the question in this way is not possible, then you need to consider potential hearsay exceptions (many of which are discussed in Chapters 6 and 7). When the hearsay declarant is unable or unwilling to testify at the trial, then you should analyze whether the court should classify the declarant "unavailable as a witness," and then consider the exceptions discussed in the second half of this chapter.

There are three basic types of unavailability, which this book calls *physical, constructive,* and *fake.* Physical and constructive unavailability are adequate to trigger the exceptions in this chapter. Fake unavailability, if proven as fake, will defeat a party's attempt to use these unavailability exceptions.

Physical unavailability is when the witness is not physically present to testify, for reasons including but not limited to death, illness, or logistical difficulties. *Constructive* unavailability is when the witness is not testifying because of a privilege, a failure of recollection, or a simple refusal to testify despite being in court. *Fake* unavailability is when the witness is faking an improper privilege claim, a mental or physical condition, or lack of memory to prevent testifying.

CEC §240: "Unavailable as a witness"

(a) Except as otherwise provided in subdivision (b), "unavailable as a witness" means that the declarant is any of the following:

(1) Exempted or precluded on the ground of privilege from testifying concerning the matter to which his or her statement is relevant.

(2) Disqualified from testifying to the matter.

(3) Dead or unable to attend or to testify at the hearing because of then existing physical or mental illness or infirmity.

(4) Absent from the hearing and the court is unable to compel his or her attendance by its process.

(5) Absent from the hearing and the proponent of his or her statement has exercised reasonable diligence but has been unable to procure his or her attendance by the court's process.

(b) A declarant is not unavailable as a witness if the exemption, preclusion, disqualification, death, inability, or absence of the declarant was brought about by the procurement or wrongdoing of the proponent of his or her statement for the purpose of preventing the declarant from attending or testifying.

Subsection c addresses expert testimony to establish unavailability.

A brief explanation of each category follows.

Privilege

Privileges provide an opportunity for a witness to decline to answer a question at trial. The witness must establish that the elements of the privilege apply, and then he can decline to testify on the grounds of privilege. For instance, the attorney-client privilege protects statements about legal issues made between clients and their attorneys. If a client is called to the witness stand and asked about what she told her attorney, her attorney will object and the client can refuse to answer the question based on the attorney-client privilege. If the elements of the privilege are established, then the client will be deemed unavailable to testify on that matter. (Privileges are addressed more fully in Chapters 12 and 13.)

The refusal to testify, despite being physically present in court, means that the witness is constructively unavailable. Counsel therefore cannot "make it not hearsay" and will need to find a hearsay exception to get the statement admitted. This unavailability means that counsel can also consider using one of the hearsay exceptions discussed in this chapter. The privilege against self-incrimination is another example. A witness cannot be forced to testify in a way that incriminates herself. If asked incriminating questions, that witness can object on privilege grounds and decline to testify. The witness will then be constructively unavailable to testify on these points.

Disqualified

A disqualified declarant is one who is no longer able to give testimony, often because she has been deemed incompetent or unable to tell the truth. The declarant who has been disqualified is constructively unavailable.

Dead or Mentally or Physically Ill

A deceased person is physically unavailable to testify. A mentally or physically ill person also may be physically incapable of appearing in court. Others will be constructively unavailable to testify. California cases have determined that someone who refuses to testify out of fear is unavailable under the "mental infirmity" language. Mere inconvenience, stress, or some additional anguish is not enough to be considered unavailable. However, the suffering of substantial additional mental trauma can be sufficient if an expert will testify as to that harm, usually in a separate hearing on the issue. In addition, California cases have determined that a person who persists in a refusal to testify, despite a court order and being physically present in court, is considered unavailable. Moreover, a witness who testifies to a lack of memory can be found unavailable.

Absent When the Court Is Unable to Compel Attendance

This absence usually happens when the declarant is not subject to the jurisdiction of the court. The declarant is physically unavailable, and the court cannot issue a subpoena or body attachment order to get the declarant brought into court. If the declarant lives in another jurisdiction or a certain distance away from the courthouse, the court has no power to compel attendance. Still, the party seeking to use the declarant's hearsay statement must show efforts to obtain attendance using the court process in that other state or any existing agreements between the two states to compel attendance.

Absent Despite Reasonable Efforts to Get the Witness into Court

This situation arises when the witness does not show up for court. The party seeking to establish the unavailability of a witness must show good faith efforts to secure that witness's attendance, including using the court process of another state or treaties with another nation where the witness resides. This good faith effort may also include offering a modest sum to cover travel expenses to the place of the trial.

The courts have equated the terms *reasonable diligence* with *due diligence*. There is no mechanical definition of what steps must be taken to satisfy this standard. To evaluate *due diligence*, courts will review the totality of the efforts made. Some factors the courts consider include (1) whether the party seeking to use the witness's testimony reasonably believed that the witness would appear willingly and did not need a subpoena, (2) how quickly that party began looking for the witness when it seemed the witness might not appear at trial, and (3) whether it would have made any difference if that party had been more diligent earlier in time.

As a general rule, the prosecution has to take additional special precautions to try to prevent a witness from disappearing if the testimony is vital to the prosecution. Where the prosecution has reason to expect that the witness might flee, the prosecution must take "adequate preventative measures" to ensure that the witness will not flee, such as "timely, reasonably extensive" efforts carried out over a reasonable period of time. While prosecutors need not "keep periodic tabs" on every material witness in a criminal case, the prosecution's failure to use due diligence to prevent that flight will mean that the judge will not find the witness to be unavailable under CEC 240.

Other factors the courts have considered include

1. the seriousness of the criminal charges;
2. the importance of the witness's testimony;
3. the length of the proposed detention;
4. evidence relevant to whether the witness will appear, including employment, residence, and other community ties;
5. the age and maturity of the witness;
6. the harm to the witness's family from taking the witness into custody;
7. the witness's financial resources;
8. the likelihood of continuances that will prolong the prosecution; and
9. whether steps short of taking the witness into custody are feasible.[14]

Courts are reluctant to find a lack of due diligence, but when they do, it is because the attorney's efforts have been negligent or perfunctory. Efforts that likely would be considered negligent or perfunctory include making only one phone call to find a witness, declining to consider known aliases for a witness who is frequently incarcerated, or waiting until the day of trial to contact a witness who was a known flight risk.

Summary of *Unavailability*

In summary, for unavailability, the witness must be

1. exempt or precluded from testifying on grounds of privilege,
2. disqualified from testifying,
3. dead or unable to testify because of mental or physical health,
4. absent and beyond the court's process, or
5. absent despite reasonable efforts to compel attendance.

Recall that if the declarant is determined to be unavailable under CEC 240, then that declarant is also deemed unavailable for confrontation purposes.

The proponent of the hearsay evidence has the burden of persuading the judge of the unavailability by a preponderance of the evidence. For instance, in the case of *Joan v. Brad*, if Joan wanted to offer Maggie's out-of-court hearsay statement under one of the exceptions in this chapter, then Joan would have the burden to prove that Maggie was unavailable under CEC 240 to establish the foundation for using one of the unavailability hearsay exceptions.

---

14. *See, e.g.*, In re Francisco M., 86 Cal. App. 4th 1061, 1076-1078 (2001).

Federal Rules of Evidence Compared: No Significant Difference

The only differences between the FRE and the CEC on unavailability are semantic. First, the FRE explicitly recognizes the contumacious witness — the one who refuses to testify despite a court order — as unavailable. The CEC does not make this recognition explicit, but the cases interpreting the CEC consider such a person to be unavailable as long as the witness has rejected reasonable inducements to testify. Second, the FRE explicitly provides that someone who cannot testify because she no longer recalls what happened is also considered unavailable. California cases also recognize this circumstance as unavailable, though the CEC does not list it explicitly.

HEARSAY EXCEPTIONS THAT APPLY ONLY WHEN THE DECLARANT IS UNAVAILABLE

For certain types of hearsay, the legislature has decided that a heightened level of analysis should be involved, to make sure that a party uses a hearsay exception only when it is virtually impossible to have the declarant testify about the statement on the witness stand. In these cases, the party trying to offer hearsay evidence must first show that the declarant is unavailable to testify in court, as discussed in the section above. Once the party establishes unavailability, then she must show that the other requirements for the particular hearsay exception are met. *Unavailability is the trigger to using the hearsay exceptions discussed in the remainder of this chapter.* The exceptions in subsequent chapters do not require unavailability.

Declarations Against Interest

When the declarant makes a statement that is contrary to her self-interest, the courts consider that statement to be particularly reliable. The rationale is that a person would not say something that goes against her self-interest unless she believed that statement to be true. This exception can be used only when the declarant is unavailable because the court would prefer to have the declarant take the witness stand and testify to the statement that she made outside of court. When the declarant is unavailable, then a party may use the declaration against interest exception to offer the statement into evidence.

CEC §1230: Declaration against interest

Evidence of a statement by a declarant having sufficient knowledge of the subject is not made inadmissible by the hearsay rule if the declarant is unavailable as a witness and the statement, when made, was so far contrary to the declarant's pecuniary or propriety interest, or so far subjected him to the risk of civil or criminal liability, or so far tended to render invalid a claim by him against another, or created such a risk of making him an object of hatred, ridicule or social disgrace in the community, that a reasonable man in his position would not have made the statement unless he believed it to be true.

For a statement to come in as a statement against interest, first look at whether the declarant is unavailable as a witness. Once unavailability has been established, look at whether the statement, when made, (1) was so far contrary to the declarant's pecuniary or proprietary interests; (2) subjected him to the risk of civil or criminal liability; (3) tended to render invalid a claim by him against another; or (4) created such a risk of making him an object of hatred, scorn, ridicule, or social disgrace that a reasonable person in that position would not have made the statement unless s/he believed it to be true. If these elements are met, then the statement is admissible under CEC 1230.

Unavailable means the declarant must be unavailable according to CEC 240, as discussed at the beginning of this chapter.

The element of *statement, when made* ensures the reliability by limiting the statements to those that were against the declarant's interest at the time that the words were spoken or written. If a statement is not against one's interest, then the reliability is diminished because people are more likely to stretch the truth in ways that they expect will help them, and less likely to do so in ways that hurt them at the time that they are speaking. If the statement was not against the interest at the time the statement was made, then the rationale that no reasonable person would make the statement unless true does not apply, and the statement should not be admitted pursuant to this hearsay exception.

The language *was so far contrary to . . .* requires the statement be more than just a little bit against the speaker's interest. This exception is reserved for important matters and statements that are noticeably against self-interest. For instance, saying "I was completely at fault the last four times I was involved in a car accident" is much more serious than saying "I drove a mile over the speed limit."

A *pecuniary* interest is a financial interest. A *proprietary* interest is an interest in property, whether real or personal property, and can include issues of title as well as issues of theft.

When a statement contains both *self-serving and disserving parts*, the disserving parts can be admitted if they meet these requirements and if they can be severed (redacted) from the self-serving parts of the statement. When one cannot easily separate the appropriate portions of the statements, then the judge will base her ruling on the overall interpretation of the entire statement, admitting it if the statement is predominantly disserving or excluding the statement if it is predominantly self-serving or neutral.

These statements are distinguishable from party admissions (which are discussed in Chapter 6) because the party admission need not be against the interest when made, as long as it is being offered against the party in the present trial.

Next, *a reasonable person would not have made* the statement. The standard is an objective one, requiring a consideration of what the reasonable person would say or refrain from saying in that circumstance. A subjective standard would be difficult to administer simply because the declarant is not available to testify on the witness stand, and the hearsay statement may be the only evidence that can be presented on that issue. If a reasonable person would not make such a statement unless it was a true reflection of her belief at that time, then the statement fulfills this element. For instance, one would not say, "I am the person who broke the coffee maker in the lounge," unless it were true. When the statement involves information that is commonly the subject of jokes (such as "I was practically thrown out of that bar last night"), hyperbole ("I must have been driving a hundred miles an hour to get here on time"), or understatement ("I only rarely exceed the speed limit"), then the reasonable person test is not met, and this element is not satisfied.

Or the statement can *tend to subject the declarant to civil and criminal liability*, or to *render a claim invalid. Tending to* means that the statement increases the chance of subjecting the declarant to liability. It does not mean that the declarant certainly will be subject to liability if the statement is heard by the wrong person, but rather that it might help to support such an argument. "I was partially at fault in the auto accident" can subject the declarant to civil liability, as "I helped him pull off the robbery" can subject one to criminal liability. Saying "he doesn't really owe me that money" would tend to render the claim invalid or would be against a pecuniary interest. "That land never belonged to me" would be against one's proprietary interest.

Finally, the statement could make the declarant the *object of hatred, ridicule, or social disgrace*. Whether this factor is met will be based on the relevant community standards, so the attorney must make an argument in close cases. Embarrassing statements or those showing low moral character or poor ethical judgment will satisfy this component, such as "I only slept with him because his wife had a nicer car than mine" or "I was so wasted when I worked on that brief for the client, I can't believe he didn't sue me for malpractice."

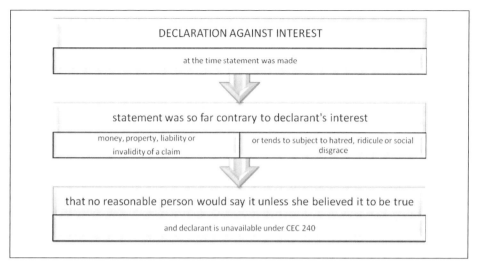

Figure 5.3. Determining Whether a Statement Can Be Admitted as a Declaration Against Interest

Figure 5.3 shows the process for determining whether a statement meets the requirements to satisfy the declarations against interest exception to the Hearsay Rule. First, ask whether the statement was against the declarant's interest at the time it was made. If so, then ask whether the statement was so far against the declarant's interest — either in money, property, etc., or because the statement subjects the declarant to negative social responses — that no reasonable person would say it unless it was true. Then, if the declarant is also unavailable, the requirements of CEC 1230 are met.

The court will examine the timing of the statement to ensure that the statement was against the declarant's interest at the time it was made. The court will also evaluate whether the statement goes against one of the interests noted in the CEC. Then the court will determine whether a reasonable person would make the statement only if she believed it to be true. Do not forget that this exception applies only when the declarant is unavailable. If the prosecution seeks to offer the statement in a criminal case, be sure to determine whether admitting the statement implicates the Confrontation Clause.

Federal Rules of Evidence Compared: Notable Differences

There are two important differences. First, FRE 804(b)(3) does not include "hatred, ridicule or social disgrace" within the list of areas against one's interest, and thus some statements that will be included within the CEC will not satisfy the requirements under the FRE. Second, the FRE contains an additional requirement applying in limited circumstances in criminal cases. When a statement tends to expose the declarant to criminal liability and also is offered in an attempt to exculpate the accused, the FRE requires that it be "supported by corroborating circumstances that clearly indicate the trustworthiness, if it is offered in a criminal case as one that tends to expose the declarant to criminal liability."

Dying Declarations

When a person believes he is dying, his out-of-court statement about how and why he is dying can be admitted under the dying declarations exception. The rationale for this exception is that reliability is increased because no one wants to die with a lie on his lips. Even for those without a religious belief in an afterlife, the motive to ensure that your killer is caught and punished can be a strong one. For the statement to be a dying declaration, it must be (1) a statement made by a dying person (2) about the cause and circumstances of death, (3) if made upon personal knowledge and (4) under a belief of impending death.

CEC §1242: Dying declaration

Evidence of a statement made by a dying person respecting the cause and circumstances of his death is not made inadmissible by the hearsay rule if the statement was made upon his personal knowledge and under a sense of immediately impending death.

The first requirement is *a dying person*. To qualify for this hearsay exception, the declarant must actually have been seriously injured or very ill in a way that raises the possibility of death from those injuries or from that illness. The judge will use the *sufficiency* standard to determine whether the person made the statement. Then, the judge will use the *preponderance* test to determine whether the person was dying. While the CEC does not specifically state that the declarant must have died, case law provides that this exception is available *only when the declarant dies from his injuries or illness*.

Second, the statement must be made about the *cause or circumstances of impending death*. The statement does not have to specifically say "Justin killed me." It can be more general, such as "We were arguing an hour ago, and

I had no idea that Justin had a knife." This statement addresses the circumstances of the impending death, who was there, when it happened, and how the declarant might have been mortally injured. The judge also decides this element using the preponderance standard.

The crucial point of the *personal knowledge* requirement is that the declarant has some basis for making the statement about the cause or circumstances of the impending death. "I looked in Justin's eyes as he stabbed me in the chest" would satisfy the personal knowledge requirement because presumably the dying person could see who was stabbing her in the chest. However, the statement "I bet it was Justin who stabbed me in the back because that's the kind of guy he is" is not based on personal knowledge but rather on speculation; it therefore would not satisfy this element of the dying declaration exception. The personal knowledge element is easier to establish because the sufficiency test applies to personal knowledge.

Finally, there must be *belief of impending death*. The declarant needs to believe that she is dying, and dying immediately. This is a subjective standard, and there must be some evidence other than the declarant's own belief to show that the declarant thought she was dying. Having a slowly debilitating condition is not enough, but a terminally ill person who feels she has only a few hours or days can fit this element. One way to establish this belief is through statements made *to* the declarant, such as "You're losing a lot of blood, and we're not sure we can get you to the hospital in time. Tell us who did this to you." Because telling a person she is dying is not the kind of "bedside manner" most health care professionals practice, few examples of this explicit type of notice of impending death may exist. The more likely scenario involves an EMT worker who tells the victim, "You're going to be fine. Just keep your eyes open and listen to me." In such a situation, the victim may believe the EMT, and thus the "belief in impending death" element of this hearsay exception would not be met. Without a belief of impending death, the rationale for the reliability of these types of out-of-court statements disappears.

Procedurally, the judge must decide whether there is sufficient evidence so that a reasonable fact finder could determine that the declarant made the statement and made it based on personal knowledge. In addition, the judge must decide whether the declarant was dying, whether she had the requisite belief of impending death, and whether the declaration addresses the cause or circumstances of the death. In making those determinations, the judge uses the preponderance test. The judge can also weigh the proponent and opponent's evidence and take credibility into consideration. If the judge decides that these elements are established by a preponderance, then she can admit the evidence.

Federal Rules of Evidence Compared: Notable Differences

FRE 804(b)(2) has two notable differences. First, the declarant must be unavailable under the definition of FRE 804(a) (though it is generally used only when the unavailability is due to death). Second, the statement can be admitted in all civil cases, but the only type of criminal case in which it can be admitted is a homicide case. In contrast, under the CEC these dying declarations can be used in any civil or criminal case.

Previously Existing State of Mind

Continuing down the list of exceptions that are triggered by unavailability, CEC 1251 provides an exception to admit some statements that described the declarant's *previously existing* state of mind, emotion, or physical sensation. We use the shorthand reference *state of mind* to refer not only to physical and emotional feelings, but also to plans, motives, and intentions. The term *previously existing* refers to how the declarant was feeling, etc., at some time prior to the moment that she made the statement about those feelings. For example, if the declarant says, "I was so depressed yesterday," she is talking about her previously existing state of mind — how she felt yesterday. CEC 1251 applies when the previous mental state is an issue in the litigation, and it permits evidence of memory or belief of a past mental or physical state to be used to prove that prior mental or physical state. (Chapter 7 explains another exception for statements a declarant makes about her current state of mind under CEC 1250.)

CEC §1251: Statement of declarant's previously existing mental or physical state
Subject to section 1252, evidence of a statement of the declarant's state of mind, emotion, or physical sensation (including a statement of intent, plan, motive, design, mental feeling, pain or bodily health) at a time prior to the statement is not made inadmissible by the hearsay rule if:
    (a) The declarant is unavailable as a witness; and
    (b) The evidence is offered to prove such prior state of mind, emotion or physical sensation when it is itself an issue in the action and the evidence is not offered to prove any fact other than such state of mind, emotion, or physical sensation.

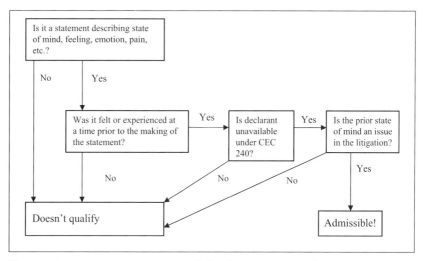

Figure 5.4. Does the Statement Qualify for the Exception Under CEC 1251?

For example, if litigation involved the amount due on a life insurance policy and the issue of whether the decedent took her own life, then her state of mind as to depression and thoughts of suicide might be an issue. In that case, the decedent's own statements about her depression would be admissible under this exception, as long as the trustworthiness element was satisfied. The unavailability requirement means that this evidence will be admitted only when the declarant is unable to come to court to testify under oath about the statement or feeling, emotion, or pain.

Figure 5.4 shows how to determine whether a statement satisfies the requirements of CEC 1251 and can be admitted under the previously existing state of mind hearsay exception. The statement must describe an earlier state of mind, felt at the time of making the statement, and the declarant must be unavailable. Furthermore, the declarant's prior state of mind must be an issue in the litigation. Also note that CEC 1252 renders such a statement "inadmissible if made under circumstances such as to indicate its lack of trustworthiness."

Federal Rules of Evidence Compared: Notable Differences

There is no FRE directly corresponding with CEC 1251. FRE 803(4) contains some overlap in terms of pains and symptoms under the medical diagnosis exception (which is discussed in Chapter 7).

Declarations Relating to Wills and Estates

Once the declarant has died, the only evidence the potential heirs have is what the declarant said or wrote before she died, and so *necessity* and *expediency* are the main reasons for permitting hearsay statements about past acts in will contests. CEC 1260 allows for such statements to be admitted if they relate to the execution, revocation, identification, or terms of the declarant's own will. CEC 1261 applies to statements offered in lawsuits arising from a claim or demand against the estate of the declarant. This exception permits hearsay statements of the decedent to be admitted, as long as they were based on personal knowledge, while her recollection was clear, about matters recently perceived by her.

CEC §1260(a): Statements concerning declarant's will

Evidence of a statement made by a declarant who is unavailable as a witness that he has or has not made a will, or has or has not revoked his will, or that identifies his will, is not made inadmissible by the hearsay rule.

CEC §1261(a): Statement of decedent offered in action against his estate

Evidence of statement is not made inadmissible by the hearsay rule when offered in an action upon a claim or demand against the estate of the declarant if the statement was made upon the personal knowledge of the declarant at a time when the matter had been recently perceived by him and while his recollection was clear.

Note: Subsection (b) of both CEC 1260 and CEC 1261 explicitly permits the court to exclude the statement if the circumstances indicate a lack of trustworthiness.

CEC 1260 applies only when the declarant is unavailable, whether alive or dead, and CEC 1261 applies only when the litigation involves a will or an action against the estate of a *deceased* declarant who is therefore unavailable.

Federal Rules of Evidence Compared: Minor Differences

The difference between the FRE and CEC 1260 is that the FRE exception for wills is contained in the last clause of the general state of mind exception. FRE 803(3) adds "but not including a statement of memory or belief to prove the fact remembered or believed unless it relates to the execution, revocation, identification or terms of the declarant's will."

Hearsay Exceptions for Former Testimony

When parties try to admit statements of witnesses that were made outside of the present court proceedings, the concern about reliability is increased. But when those statements were made in another court proceeding, under oath, reliability concerns diminish. While the concern may diminish, it does not disappear because the oath is not the only factor that increases the reliability of testimony. In fact, the access of the opposing counsel to cross-examine the witness under oath is perhaps the most important factor for evaluating the reliability of witness testimony. When a witness under oath has been subjected to a rigorous cross-examination and tells a consistent story, then the fact finder is likely to be more convinced that her perception, memory, and narration skills are sufficient and that the witness is telling the truth. For this reason the CEC contains a hearsay exception for former testimony.

CEC §1290: Former Testimony

As used in this article, "former testimony" means testimony given under oath in:
    (a) Another action or in a former hearing or trial of the same action;
    (b) A proceeding to determine a controversy conducted by or under the supervision of an agency that has the power to determine such a controversy and is an agency of the United States or a public entity in the United States;
    (c) A deposition taken in compliance with law in another action; or
    (d) An arbitration proceeding if the evidence of such former testimony is a verbatim transcript thereof.

What is former testimony? The CEC contains a precise definition of what fits the definition of former testimony to trigger the use of this particular hearsay exception. Former testimony is testimony given under oath in this case or in some other proceeding, including depositions (but only in other proceedings) and arbitrations (when a verbatim transcript was made).

What is not former testimony? The defendant's testimony at a motion to suppress cannot be used as substantive evidence against that defendant by the prosecution at trial. Probation revocation hearing testimony may not be offered at a subsequent trial of the charges arising from that same transaction. In addition, depositions taken in the action in which they are offered are not considered former testimony (though they will be admissible under provisions of the CCP).

Former Testimony Exception for Parties to the Former Proceeding

Former testimony is admissible against a party to the current case, as an exception to the hearsay rule, under either one of the following situations: (1) the declarant is unavailable as a witness, *and* (2) the former testimony is offered against a person who offered it on his own behalf before, or the successor in interest of such person; *or* (1) the party against whom the former testimony is offered was a party to the action or proceeding in which the testimony was given *and* (2) had the right and opportunity to cross-examine the declarant (3) with an interest and a motive similar to that which he has at the hearing.

CEC §1291 Former testimony offered against party to former proceeding

(a) Evidence of former testimony is not made inadmissible by the hearsay rule if the declarant is unavailable as a witness, and:

(1) The former testimony is offered against a person who offered it in evidence in his own behalf on the former occasion or against the successor in interest of such person; or

(2) The party against whom the former testimony is offered was a party to the action or proceeding in which the testimony was given and had the right and opportunity to cross-examine the declarant with an interest and motive similar to that which he has at thehearing.

(b) The admissibility of former testimony under this section is subject to the same limitations and objections as though the declarant were testifying at the hearing, except that former testimony offered under this section is not subject to:

(1) Objections as to the form of the questions which were not made at the time of the former testimony was given,

(2) Objections based on competency or privilege which did not exist at the time the former testimony was given.

The statement is subject to the same limitations and objections as though the declarant were testifying, except objections as to the form not made at the time and objections based on competency or privilege that did not exist.

The types of parties against whom the former testimony can be offered include a person who offered that testimony on her own behalf in the former case; a successor in interest to that person who offered it on her own behalf; or someone who was a party when the former testimony was given and who also had a right and opportunity to develop and explore the testimony of the declarant with an interest and a motive similar to those which the party in the present case now has. When the testimony is elicited by the opposing side during cross-examination, then an opportunity to develop the testimony on redirect examination satisfies this element as well. An example of a successor in interest would be when a person assigns her rights under a contract to her agent. The agent stands in the shoes of the person and can collect the money due under the contract. That agent is the *successor in interest* to the person who originally signed the contract.

In determining the similarity of interest and motive, one must analyze the facts surrounding the taking of the former testimony, how it was being used, and its purposes. The similar interest and motive relies on the relative importance of the testimony to the case or issue in each case. If the issue was a major factor in the first case, then the party likely had an adequate opportunity to develop the evidence, as well as to challenge it through rigorous cross-examination. On the other hand, if the first case was less significant than the second one, then the motive to develop and cross-examine about that testimony might not have been a strong one in the first case. If the evidence is much more important in the second case, then the similar interest and motive element for this hearsay exception will not be met.

In looking whether there is similar interest and motive, consider whether the same major issues were involved in the two litigations. Ask whether the party who might object to the admission of the former testimony was on the same side of the litigation (plaintiff/prosecution or defendant) that he is on now. If a party is on a different side now, then that party might have a different motive to develop the testimony, and also would have a different burden of proof.

Even when the party did not switch sides, *the burden of proof is a factor* because criminal proceedings have a higher burden on the prosecution than civil proceedings. (Burdens of proof are discussed in Chapter 10.) For criminal defendants, the burden of persuasion at trial is simply one juror to avoid a unanimous jury verdict. For civil defendants, a jury majority of three-fourths may be adequate for liability, and so the civil defendant will have to persuade just over one-fourth of the jurors to prevail. At a preliminary hearing, the defendant may have a less strong motive for cross-examining a witness, particularly if the prosecution already has presented sufficient evidence for the defendant to be bound over for trial. Similarly, in a civil case, there might be a lower incentive to aggressively cross-examine the witness in a deposition than there might be at trial. A somewhat lesser motive in the first case may be similar enough to satisfy this element, but if the difference is substantial, then this element will not be satisfied.

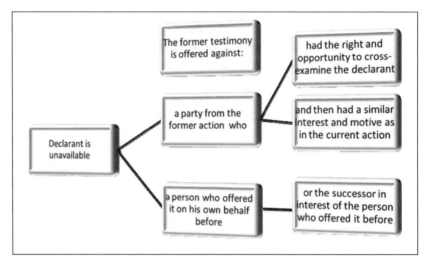

Figure 5.5. Former Testimony Exception for Parties to Former Proceeding

Criminal cases may involve a higher motivation to rigorously cross-examine than a civil case, but if the same issues are involved, then some courts will find that the motive is similar enough, even if the punishment is higher in the criminal case. For instance, in a civil case against the insurer for nonpayment after a house was destroyed by fire, the owner would have a similar motive to prove that he did not purposefully burn down the house as he would if he were in a criminal trial for arson of the same house.

Figure 5.5 shows the two circumstances that permit a party to use the former testimony hearsay exception against another party in the case. When former testimony is admitted under this hearsay exception, it is still subject to evidentiary objections, such as those based on relevance and character. However, several objections are not available for former testimony. The first is objections to the form of the question, if those objections were not made at the time the question was asked in the former proceeding. The second is objections that did not exist at the time of the former proceeding, if they are based on competency or privilege.

Former Testimony Exception for Non-parties to the Former Proceeding

If the litigant seeks to offer the testimony against someone who neither (1) offered the statement in her favor in the prior litigation, nor (2) was a party to the prior action, nor (3) is a successor in the interest to someone who was a party to that prior action, then the testimony will not be admissible under CEC 1291, and the proponent of the statement should consider CEC 1292.

CEC §1292: Former testimony offered against person not a party to former proceeding

(a) Evidence of former testimony is not made inadmissible by the hearsay rule if:

(1) The declarant is unavailable as a witness;

(2) The former testimony is offered in a civil action; and

(3) The issue is such that the party to the action or proceeding in which the former testimony was given had the right and opportunity to cross-examine the declarant with an interest and motive similar to that which the party against whom the testimony is offered has at the hearing.

(b) The admissibility of former testimony under this section is subject to the same limitations and objections as though the declarant were testifying at the hearing, except that former testimony offered under this section is not subject to objections based on competency or privilege which did not exist at the time the former testimony was given.

The CEC 1292 exception is available to admit testimony only in civil cases. This means that the second or subsequent case must be a civil case. The first case in which the former testimony was actually given can be either civil or criminal. Like the CEC 1291 exception, the current case must involve an issue for which there was a similar interest and motive to cross-examine the declarant in the former case. If similar interests and motives exist in the two cases, the declarant is unavailable, and the current case is civil, then the elements of this non-party former testimony hearsay exception will be met.

This exception permits all objections, except those based on competency or privilege if they did not exist at the time of the former proceeding. Note that there is no limitation on the form of the question. The rationale for the distinction from CEC 1291 is that under CEC 1291, the person was a party to the former proceeding and could have made all objections to the form of the question and fixed the problem at the time that the declarant gave her oral testimony. In contrast, CEC 1292 addresses non-parties and non-successors in interest (those who do not stand in the shoes of someone who was involved in the first case), who had no such opportunity to make all appropriate and necessary objections at the time.

Figure 5.6 applies only when the party in the current proceeding was not a party to the original case in which the former testimony was given under oath. All objections may be made, except those that did not exist at the time relating to privileges or competency.

Remember, for evidence to be admissible under the former testimony hearsay exception,

1. the declarant must be unavailable as a witness;

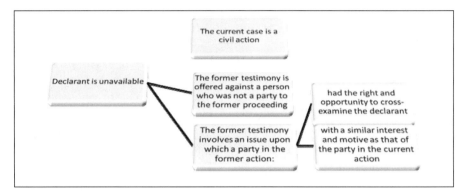

Figure 5.6. Former Testimony Offered Against a Non-party to the Former Proceeding

2. the former testimony must be offered in a civil action; and
3. the issue must be such that the party in the former action had the right and opportunity to cross-examine the declarant;
4. with an interest and a motive similar to that which the party against whom the testimony is offered currently has at the hearing;
5. not subject to objections as to competency or privileges not then existing.

Figure 5.7 compares CEC 1291 and 1292.

Prior case	CEC 1291 (party)	CEC 1292 (non-party)
Current case	Offered against a party to prior and current cases	Offered against a non-party to prior case; party in current case
Declarant unavailable	Required	Required
Type of current case	Criminal or civil	Civil only
Issue in current case	Party either offered this evidence on his own behalf in prior case or had right and opportunity to cross-examine on this issue in the prior case	A party in prior case had right and opportunity to cross-examine on this issue
Motive in current case	Similar for party in prior case and current case	Similar for party in prior case with party in current case

Figure 5.7. Former Testimony Exceptions Comparison Chart

Focused Former Testimony Exceptions

The CEC contains several more focused exceptions for particular types of former testimony. CEC 1293 applies to minor children and CEC 1294 applies to statements made in preliminary hearings or prior proceedings. (The text of those sections is included in the appendix of this book for further reference.)

Federal Rules of Evidence Compared: Notable Differences

First, the former testimony exception in FRE 804(b)(1) does not list specific waivers of objections.

Second, the FRE permits the use of depositions in the action in which they are taken, whereas in California this is not governed by the CEC, but rather the Code of Civil Procedure.

Third, under the FRE the only way to offer former testimony against someone who was not a party in the former case is to offer it against the successor in interest of a party in a subsequent civil action. Thus, unlike the CEC, having a similar interest and motive as a party to the former proceeding will not be adequate to meet the requirements for this hearsay exception.

The fourth distinction does not have a practical impact: the FRE notes that direct, cross, and redirect are all ways to develop the testimony to satisfy this exception. The CEC lists only cross-examination, but courts have interpreted the CEC as consistent with what is explicitly stated in the FRE.

OTHER LIMITED EXCEPTIONS

Several other CEC exceptions are worth mentioning, but only apply to very limited circumstances. Those sections are briefly outlined below.

Procurement or Wrongdoing by the Proponent

A party who ensures that a declarant is unavailable to testify will not get the benefit of access to these hearsay exceptions that require unavailability. For instance, if you offer the witness an all-expenses-paid trip to Europe for the summer while the trial is being heard, you cannot claim that because the witness is *unavailable* you can use a hearsay exception that *requires unavailability*. The CEC specifically states that a declarant will not be deemed to be unavailable if the proponent of the evidence purposefully made the declarant unavailable to prevent the declarant from testifying at trial. This situation is referred to as *forfeiture*.

CEC §240(b): Unavailable as a witness

(b) A declarant is not unavailable as a witness if the exemption, preclusion, disqualification, death, inability, or absence of the declarant was brought about by the procurement or wrongdoing of the proponent of his or her statement for the purpose of preventing the declarant from attending or testifying.

A party can procure the unavailability of a witness in a benign or in a malignant way. For instance, one can encourage the declarant to stay away from the trial by offering him a paid vacation or by killing him. Whether the inducement is welcomed or unwelcomed by the declarant, the party engaging in that conduct loses access to this category of hearsay exceptions if the other side can prove that the party procured the unavailability of the declarant.

If it is alleged that the proponent made the witness unavailable to prevent him from testifying, then the opponent has the burden to prove by a preponderance of the evidence that the proponent's improper conduct is the reason for the declarant's failure to attend the trial. For example, in the case of *Joan v. Brad* described above, if Brad asserted that the reason Maggie was unavailable was because Joan made her unavailable, perhaps by threatening or intimidating Maggie into leaving town, then Brad would have the burden to prove, by a preponderance of the evidence, that Joan's wrongful conduct is the reason Maggie is unavailable. If Brad satisfied his burden, then Joan would be denied the benefit of using any hearsay exception that required unavailability.

The court will not let a party use a hearsay exception requiring unavailability when the party purposefully made the declarant unavailable to testify. In a situation where the party accidentally made the declarant unavailable, then there is no prohibition. For instance, suppose a party negligently drives his car into a parking attendant while exiting a garage. The parking attendant shouts, "I should have looked both ways before I walked across the garage!" and then dies. When the driver is sued by the attendant's family for wrongful death, the driver then seeks to admit the attendant's statement for the truth of the matter asserted as a declaration against interest. Recall that a declaration against interest requires unavailability. This forfeiture provision would not apply in this situation because the party did not intentionally or purposefully engage in wrongdoing to make the witness unavailable.

Prior Statements of Deceased Declarant

CEC 1231 provides another hearsay exception that applies in the narrow circumstance where the declarant is dead and the statement relates to criminal street gang activities. This exception applies when the party seeking to offer the statement establishes each of the following elements: (1) the statement relates to criminal acts involving street gangs; (2) a verbatim transcript, copy, or record exists; (3) the statement is based on personal knowledge; (4) the statement was made under oath or under penalty of perjury; (5) the declarant's death was not due to natural causes; and (6) the surrounding circumstances indicate the trustworthiness of the statement.

This exception generally applies when a former gang member testifies in a grand jury proceeding or swears out an affidavit in the prosecutor's office, and then is killed before being able to testify at trial. If the prosecution could prove that the defendant played a role in either killing or kidnapping the declarant such that the declarant was made unavailable to testify, then the statement would be admissible under CEC 1350 (which is discussed in the next section). CEC 1231 opens that door a bit wider in that it covers situations where the connection to the defendant cannot be directly established, as long as some gang activity is involved.

Unavailability Due to Homicide or Kidnapping

In another narrow circumstance, where the declarant was the victim of either homicide or kidnapping and thereby becomes unavailable to testify, the hearsay statement can be admitted against a criminal defendant charged with a serious felony if there is "clear and convincing evidence" that that defendant played a role in the killing or kidnapping of the declarant.

CEC 1350 provides an exception with the following detailed list of elements:

1. only in cases charging a serious felony,
2. declarant is unavailable,
3. there is no evidence that the proponent had something to do with that unavailability,
4. there is clear and convincing evidence,
5. that the declarant's unavailability was "knowingly caused by, aided by, or solicited by,"
6. the party against whom the statement is offered,
7. for the purpose of preventing the arrest or prosecution of that party. In addition,
8. the unavailability is due to death or kidnapping of the declarant, and

151

9. the statement has been memorialized on tape made by a law enforcement official, or paper by a law enforcement official, signed and notarized,
10. the statement was made under circumstances indicating trustworthiness,
11. it is relevant,
12. it has been corroborated by other evidence, and
13. the notice requirement of 10 days has been met.

Statements of Threats

California has another specially tailored exception to apply to *statements about threats or the infliction of physical harm*. Some of these statements involve state of mind (for instance, fear of an abusive spouse) and can be admitted under the previously existing state of mind exception, but others will not meet the requirements of that exception because the victim's state of mind is not an issue.

For this reason, the legislature crafted another specific hearsay exception: CEC 1370, threat or infliction of injury. In this exception, a victim's hearsay statement is admissible for the truth of the matter asserted when

1. the victim is unavailable to testify;
2. the statement purports to narrate, describe, or explain the infliction of or threat of physical injury upon that victim;
3. the statement was made at or near the time of the infliction or threat;
4. in writing, recorded or made to medical or law enforcement officials;
5. was made under circumstances indicating its trustworthiness;
6. the proponent gives advance notice of that statement to the other side; and
7. the statement is less than five years old.

In evaluating *trustworthiness*, the courts consider three factors: whether the statement was made in anticipation of litigation, whether the declarant has a bias or motive to fabricate (weighing against admissibility), and whether the statement is corroborated by other evidence that weighs in favor of admitting the statement under this exception.

Other Limited Exceptions

CEC 1360 is another exception specifically tailored to statements about child abuse (who may testify or be unavailable), and CEC 1380 provides a similarly focused exception for statements about elder abuse in cases involving elder abuse charges.

Federal Rules of Evidence Compared: Notable Differences

The FRE does not contain specific provisions that correspond to the specific CEC sections referenced in the sections above. Instead, FRE 804(b)(6) prevents the exclusion of evidence on hearsay grounds where the declarant is unavailable due to the other party's engaging in, or acquiescing in, some type of wrongdoing directed at securing the unavailability of the declarant as a witness, similar to CEC 240(b).

Forfeiture and the Confrontation Clause

With all of these forfeiture exceptions, you must consider the Confrontation Clause if the statement is *testimonial*. If the prosecution persuades the judge by a preponderance of the evidence that the accused engaged in some intentional criminal act that made the declarant unavailable, the accused's confrontation right will be forfeited. That means he cannot object on confrontation grounds to the use of hearsay statements by that witness who is no longer available to testify. In *Giles v. California*[15], the U.S. Supreme Court noted that this forfeiture of rights applies only when the defendant's conduct was done *in order to* prevent the witness from giving evidence against him. Thus, while this requirement is not explicitly stated in the CEC sections, parties must now satisfy the court regarding the defendant's purposeful involvement in order to admit the declarant's testimonial statement when using the exceptions in this chapter.

Examples

1. Paul is on trial for the second time on charges of murder with special circumstances. In the first trial, Randy testified that Paul asked him to kill Paul's wife. After a mistrial was declared, a retrial was scheduled. One month before the scheduled trial date, Randy was arrested pursuant to a warrant issued in a nearby state. The court required him to post a $10,000 bond to be released, with a promise that he would check in with the prosecutor every week until trial. Randy checked in the first two weeks. He did not check in on the third week, and he did not show

---

15. 128 S.Ct. 2678.

up for trial a week after that. At trial, the prosecution argued that Randy was unavailable. The defense objected. What arguments should the defense make, how should the court rule, and why?

2. May is on trial for robbing a convenience store. The store had a video-taping system, and the tape was played on local news shows the day after the robbery. Sally, one of May's neighbors, is an avid television watcher, and when she saw the videotape, she called the police and told them that she recognized her neighbor May. Sally refused to come to court to testify at the trial because her psychiatrist explained that she has a severe panic disorder called agoraphobia. Sally experiences extreme fear, dizziness, and shortness of breath when in open spaces and par-ticularly when around strangers, such that she is in danger of passing out. The prosecution sought to admit Sally's statements to the police identifying May, and the defense objected. How should the court rule?

3. John and Carol lived together for several years in the early 1990s. During that time, John executed a holographic will, leaving everything to Carol. In 1993, John and Carol were married. In 2000, John and Carol separated, but they still saw each other frequently and dated each other occasionally. When they were out to dinner one night, John said, "Even though we are separated, I think of you every day. If something were to happen to me before I could win you back, I want you to know that when I wrote that will, I meant it and what is mine is yours." John died in a tragic car accident in 2010 without ever fully reconciling with Carol. In the action dividing up John's estate, Carol sought to introduce John's statement that "what is mine is yours." The executor of John's estate objected that the statement was inadmissible hearsay. How should the court rule, and why?

4. Joe held a joint bank account with Edward, an elderly man for whom Joe worked as a paid companion and helper. Kerry, Edward's nephew, was named as Edward's only heir and was set to inherit all of Edward's property. When Edward died, there was litigation over the distribution of the estate. Joe testified that Edward had intended for Joe to inherit their joint bank account, and he explained that Edward had told a teller one day, "I want to put this boy's name on my bank account because pretty soon I am going to die, and I want him to have the money as an extra thank you for the years of service and companionship that he has provided." Kerry objected as inadmissible hearsay. How should the court rule, and why?

5. Lori was a clerk in a drugstore and was shot in the chest one night when the store was robbed. The bullet went through her chest. She was bleeding, in severe pain, and curled up into a fetal position when the police arrived. She managed to gasp to the police, "The person who shot

me was a short man with light skin and blonde hair." Lori was rushed to the hospital where she spent ten nights in intensive care. She never spoke again and died on the eleventh day. Using the surveillance camera, the police were able to find and arrest Mitchell while Lori was in intensive care. Mitchell is now on trial for felony murder, and the prosecution seeks to offer the police officer's statement about Lori's description of the robber and shooter. Mitchell's defense counsel objects. How should the prosecution respond, and how should the court rule? Would your answer and analysis change in federal court?

6. George was visiting with his son, Junior, and they decided to lure drivers into a back alley to rob them. Their first victim did not have much cash, so after taking his money, George beat the victim with a tire iron, and then both George and Junior stuffed the victim into the trunk of their car, drove away, and rolled the victim's body over a cliff a few miles away. Junior testified at a preliminary hearing, explaining what his father, George, had done. At trial, Junior refused to testify. The prosecution seeks to admit Junior's preliminary hearing testimony about George's involvement in the crime. George objects on two grounds: first, that it is inadmissible hearsay; and second, that its use would violate the Confrontation Clause. How should the prosecution respond, how should court rule, and why?

7. Kimber and Jillian were making dinner when someone rang the doorbell to their apartment. Kimber opened the door, and Igor shot him several times. Jillian hid in the kitchen until the shooting stopped and she heard footsteps running away from the apartment. When Jillian came over to the front door, Kimber said, "Why did you let Igor shoot me?" Jillian called 911, but Kimber died before help arrived. At Igor's trial, the prosecution sought to offer Kimber's out-of-court statement through Jillian. The defense objected as inadmissible hearsay. The prosecution responded that it is a dying declaration. How should the court rule, and why?

8. One Tuesday morning, Sarah told her mother Nancy that she was afraid of Steven, the photographer who was assigned to shoot pictures for her upcoming article in the *Hockey Mom's Monthly* magazine. A few days later, on Friday after a photo shoot, Sarah went hunting moose and was never seen again. Her body was not found until the spring thaw months later, and the gunshot wound to her abdomen was perfectly preserved. Barry was prosecuted in California state court for killing Sarah, and he sought to introduce the testimony of Nancy that Sarah had been afraid of Steven, not Barry, in the days prior to her disappearance. The prosecution objected on hearsay grounds. How should Barry respond, and how should the court rule?

9. Arnold and Maria were clerks in a convenience store, and Davis came into the store and started yelling at and insulting them. Arnold asked Davis to step outside and went out with Davis to try to calm him down. Davis struck Arnold in the face, and they started fighting. Maria came out of the store to help Arnold, and Davis shot Maria. Maria died from the gunshot wound. Arnold testified against Davis at a preliminary hearing. Davis's attorney did not cross-examine Arnold about the shooting. By the time the trial date arrived, Arnold had fled to Canada and refused to come back to California to testify in Davis's trial. The prosecution sought to admit Arnold's preliminary hearing testimony, and Davis objected that it violated the Hearsay Rule and the Confrontation Clause. How should the court rule?

10. Karl was a witness when Alberto tortured and killed a rival gang member, and he testified against Alberto at the preliminary hearing. When the trial date approached, the prosecution noticed that Karl was no longer living at the address he had given to them previously. Prosecution investigators were unable to find Karl, despite visiting his friends and family, checking with the Department of Motor Vehicles, and looking through court records. At trial, the prosecution sought to admit Karl's preliminary hearing testimony, and Alberto objected on the grounds that Karl was not proven to be unavailable. How should the court rule?

11. Laura asked her friend, Ken, to find someone who would kill her husband, Dick. Ken contacted Colin, who agreed to kill Dick in exchange for some stock options. After Colin killed Dick, Ken got nervous and told his girlfriend Condi, "I helped Laura find someone to kill Dick. I am feeling really bad about it, and I think I might go to the police." Condi told Ken to think about it before he made a confession. A few days later, Ken was found dead. Condi told the police about Ken's statement, and Laura and Colin were charged with murder for hire. At trial, the prosecution sought to have Condi testify about Ken's statement. The defendants objected as inadmissible hearsay and a violation of the Confrontation Clause. How should the court rule?

12. D.J. was prosecuted for the murder of his ex-wife and her friend. During the criminal trial, the prosecution offered the testimony of Detective Mark, and when counsel for D.J. cross-examined Detective Mark, inconsistencies in his testimony gave rise to the inference that he might have planted some of the evidence against D.J., such as a bloody glove and a black sock. D.J. was acquitted of the murder charges. D.J. was sued in civil court by the parents of his ex-wife. In the meantime, Detective Mark was criminally prosecuted and rendered unavailable to testify in the civil trial. Defendant D.J. sought to admit Detective Mark's prior

testimony from D.J.'s criminal case, and the plaintiffs objected. What is the proper basis for the plaintiffs' objection, and how should the court rule?

13. Edward suspected that Mitt had been leaving anonymous messages on Edward's home phone about the affair that he was having, so Edward went to Mitt's house and beat him to death. Edward then confessed to his coworker Willy and asked Willy to provide him with an alibi. Willy initially agreed, but when the police contacted Willy a few days later, Willy gave a tape-recorded statement to the police, explaining Edward's confession to the crime. Edward was charged with the murder of Mitt. While out on bail, Edward heard about Willy's conversation with the police and Edward killed Willy. At trial, the court sought to admit Willy's recorded statement to the police, and Edward objected on hearsay and confrontation grounds. How should the court rule, and why?

14. Bill threw his wife Hilary to the ground, severely twisting her neck, and threatened to kill her. Hilary began having neck and back pain, and went to see her doctor a week later. She did not tell her doctor about Bill throwing her or hurting her neck, but simply said, "My back is hurting a lot." Two months later, as Hilary's condition worsened, she finally told her doctor that "a few months ago, Bill twisted my neck severely, and I have been in excruciating pain since then." Her doctor phoned the police, who came to the office, and Hilary repeated the statement to them. The doctor began treating her neck condition, but too much time had passed. Within a few weeks Hilary was completely paralyzed and rendered comatose. She died a few weeks later. Bill is on trial for the murder of Hilary, and the prosecution seeks to admit Hilary's second statement that she made to her doctor and police. Bill objects as inadmissible hearsay. How should the court rule, and why?

Explanations

1. The defense should object on the grounds that the prosecution did not exercise reasonable diligence to make sure that Randy showed up for trial. Given that Randy did not show up for his appointment in week three, the prosecution should have engaged in additional efforts to try to locate Randy. After Randy was arrested, he should not have been released on bond if the prosecution suspected that he might not show up given the arrest warrant he had pending in another state. The court should find that the prosecution did not make reasonably diligent efforts to make sure that Randy appeared at trial, and therefore Randy is not unavailable for purposes of CEC 240.

2. The court should overrule the objection. Because testifying would cause the witness severe physical discomfort and risk her health, she is deemed unavailable to testify. However, because Sally's statements were made to law enforcement officials with an expectation that they would be used at trial, they are testimonial and implicate the Confrontation Clause. Unless May had a prior opportunity to cross-examine Sally about the statements, admitting the statements against May for the truth of the matter asserted would violate the Confrontation Clause in a California court.

3. The court should admit the statement. While statements about memory or belief are not admissible, those pertaining to the execution or revocation of the declarant's will are admissible under CEC 1260. If the statement is relevant, as it would be in a will contest litigation, then the Hearsay Rule would not bar admission of the statement.

4. The court should admit the statement as long as there is evidence to show that Edward made the statement based on his personal knowledge, about a recently perceived event, on which his recollection is clear, under CEC 1261. Here, Edward is talking about a matter within his personal knowledge (the help and companionship that Joe had provided), and Joe is providing the help and companionship on the day that the statement was made (helping Edward at the bank), so it was a recently perceived event that likely was fresh in Edward's recollection at the time he made the statement to the teller.

5. The prosecution should respond that Lori's statement meets the dying declaration exception. Blood loss and severe pain from a gunshot in the chest is sufficient evidence that the victim may have a belief of impending death. In addition, the statement is about the cause and circumstances of her death — namely, a description of the person who shot her. Therefore the statement will be admissible as a dying declaration. If the case were tried in federal court, the statement of impending death exception would still apply because Lori is dead and therefore unavailable and because this is a criminal homicide case.

6. The prosecution should respond that the preliminary hearing testimony meets the requirements of the former testimony hearsay exception of CEC 1291, and the Confrontation Clause has been satisfied by the prior opportunity to cross-examine Junior about his testimony. The former testimony exception defines former testimony to include testimony in a former hearing of the same action, which the preliminary hearing is in this case. The exception also requires that the witness be unavailable, and here Junior is *constructively* unavailable because his privilege gives him the option to decline to testify.

In addition, the exception applies when the party to the first action (the preliminary hearing) was a party to the second action (the trial), and George was the defendant in both the hearing and the trial. Also, George had a right and an opportunity to cross-examine Junior with a similar motive and interest at the preliminary hearing as he does now at trial. Therefore the requirements for the former testimony exception are met.

As for the Confrontation Clause, it is implicated where the hearsay statement is testimonial and is being offered against a criminal defendant. Preliminary hearing testimony clearly is testimonial. Where the declarant is unavailable to testify at trial, the defendant must have had a prior opportunity to cross-examine the declarant about the statements. The defense attorney might argue that her actual motive was not to cross-examine at the preliminary hearing to avoid tipping her hand, given that she expected her client to be bound over for trial. Nevertheless, the court likely will find that there was a similar motive in the hearing as at trial. George had the prior opportunity at the preliminary hearing to cross-examine Junior, and therefore the requirements for satisfying the Confrontation Clause are met. The court should overrule the objection and admit Junior's preliminary hearing testimony.

7. The first issue is whether Kimber's question can be considered a statement for hearsay purposes. If not, then there is no need for a hearsay exception because the Hearsay Rule would not bar admission of the question (for instance, if there was no truth to be asserted in an inquiry). This question makes an indirect assertion because it also conveys information, namely the identity of the shooter, and therefore the Hearsay Rule is implicated. If Kimber had merely said "Who shot me?" then that would be a pure question simply seeking information and would not implicate the Hearsay Rule because it is not an assertion. However, Kimber's question here includes the assertion that Igor shot him and therefore fits the definition of a statement for hearsay purposes, with an applicable exception. The court should admit Kimber's remark as a dying declaration because a person who has been shot multiple times is likely to believe that his own death is imminent, and Kimber did die from his injuries. Furthermore, the remark concerns the cause of death (being shot by Igor), and it is based on personal knowledge (Kimber stood facing Igor as he pulled the trigger multiple times).

8. Barry should respond that he is not offering Sarah's out-of-court statement for its truth, and therefore is not implicating the Hearsay Rule. Rather, Barry is offering Sarah's statement for the non-hearsay purpose of circumstantial evidence that someone other than Barry might have

been making Sarah fearful and might have had a motive or opportunity to kill Sarah. The prosecution likely will respond that the statement is being offered for the truth of the matter asserted, to prove that Sarah feared Steven, not Barry, and therefore that Steven is more likely to be the person who killed Sarah. The statement is relevant only to prove its truth — which man Sarah feared. Barry might counter that the statement should be admissible under the exception for previously existing state of mind, but Sarah's state of mind is not an issue in the trial of her alleged murderer, and therefore this argument will be unsuccessful. The court should sustain the objection and exclude Nancy's statement about Sarah's fears.

9. The court should overrule the objection and admit Arnold's preliminary hearing testimony under CEC 1291. It was in a preliminary hearing in the same case, against the same criminal defendant. Moreover, Davis had an opportunity to cross-examine Arnold at the preliminary hearing, with an interest and a motive similar to the interest and motive that he has now at trial. The fact that Davis's attorney did not cross-examine Arnold does not matter because the crucial requirement is that Davis had an opportunity to cross-examine Arnold, not whether Davis actually used that opportunity. For this reason, the former testimony exception is met and the Confrontation Clause is satisfied.

10. The court should admit Karl's preliminary hearing testimony because he meets the requirements for the former testimony exception of CEC 1291. He is *physically* unavailable, given that he is absent despite due diligence in the efforts to compel his attendance. In addition, the same party is involved in both the preliminary hearing and the trial, so the interest, motive, and opportunity to cross elements are all present. Asking friends and family and following up with the DMV and court records all constitute reasonable efforts to find Karl. If the prosecution had reason to believe that Karl might flee, however, then the prosecution should have taken additional precautions to ensure his attendance. If these additional precautions were required and the prosecution failed to implement them, then the prosecution would not be entitled to use the benefit of the unavailability exception, and the objection would be sustained. The gang exception of CEC 1231 is not available without more facts to show that Karl is dead.

11. The court should admit the first sentence of Ken's statement as a statement against interest because it was against his penal interest to admit to being an accomplice to a contract killing, and because Ken is unavailable as a witness due to his death. The statement does not violate the Confrontation Clause because it was not testimonial, given that there is no governmental involvement in Ken's making the statement to Condi.

Laura's defense lawyer may argue that the portion of the statement about "helping Laura" was not against Ken's interest and should be redacted. However, because helping with a crime subjects a person to criminal liability as an accomplice, the court should find that the entire first sentence was against Ken's interest. The portion of the second sentence about confessing also meets the against interest requirement. But the portion of the sentence about feeling remorse is not against Ken's interest, and therefore the reliability factor is not met. For this reason, the court should sustain the objection as to that portion of the statement and redact that portion if requested to do so by defense counsel. (You may also wish to consider the co-conspirator admission exception, which is discussed in Chapter 6, and the state of mind exception discussed in Chapter 7.)

12. The plaintiffs should object that Detective Mark's prior testimony is not admissible under either CEC 1291 or 1292. CEC 1291 applies when the party against whom the evidence is being offered (here the plaintiffs) was a party to the prior litigation or is a successor in interest to a party in that prior litigation. Detective Mark's direct testimony was offered against Defendant D.J., and his cross-examination testimony arguably helped Defendant D.J. in his criminal case. The ex-wife's parents were not parties to that criminal case, nor were they successors in interest to either party, D.J. or the prosecution. Therefore, even though Detective Mark is unavailable, CEC 1291 will not apply.

Under CEC 1292, which permits the introduction of evidence against those who were neither parties nor successors in interest to parties in the prior litigation, the second case must be civil, as is this one. Unavailability is required, and the facts state that Detective Mark is unavailable. In addition, to use CEC 1292, the party in the former action must have had the right and opportunity to cross-examine the declarant in that former action, with an interest and a motive similar to the party in the current case. The prosecution had no right or opportunity to cross-examine its own witness in the criminal case, but did have a chance to conduct a redirect examination, which can serve the same purpose. Therefore, all of the elements are met. Thus, the court should overrule the hearsay objection and admit the prior testimony of Detective Mark.

13. The court should admit Edward's confession as a party admission and then admit Willy's recorded statement about Edward's confession under CEC 1350. Edward is charged with a serious felony, there is no evidence that the prosecution had anything to do with Willy's unavailability, and there is evidence that Edward, by killing him, is responsible for Willy's unavailability. Willy's statement was made to the police and memorialized on tape under circumstances indicating

trustworthiness. As long as the court finds that there is "clear and convincing" evidence that Edward is responsible for Willy's death, the court should overrule the objection and admit the tape. If Edward made Willy unavailable by participating in killing him, then it does not violate Edward's confrontation rights to admit Willy's hearsay statement against Edward. CEC 1370 would provide another option for admitting any portions of the recorded statement that included a threat against Willy.

14. The court should sustain the objection to the second statement Hilary made to her doctor and the police. Her second statement is hearsay and does not meet the requirement for state of mind because it is a statement of memory or belief (about the cause of her pain) offered to prove that memory or belief (that Bill attacked her). If her state of mind were an issue in the litigation, then CEC 1251 would provide a way to admit the portion of the second statement that deals with her pain. However, her state of mind is not an issue in this murder trial. In addition, the second statement does not meet the requirement for the CEC 1370 exception because it was not made at or near the time of the injury or threat. Hilary did not tell the doctor and police until two months later, which dramatically diminishes the reliability of her statements. Therefore the court should sustain the objection to the second statement.

CHAPTER 6

Hearsay Exceptions: Party Admissions and Prior Statements of Witnesses

This chapter addresses two more categories of hearsay exceptions that depend on the *identity* or *status* of the hearsay declarant. The first is *admissions by parties and their representatives*, and the second is *prior statements of witnesses testifying at the trial*. The first group applies only when the declarant is identified with a party in the case. The second group applies only when the declarant's status is as a witness at the trial. (Chapter 7 addresses the final category of hearsay exceptions that are based on the *content* of the out-of-court statement.)

The first category in this chapter is referred to as *party admissions*. This category provides hearsay exceptions when a party at the current trial has made an out-of-court statement or when a party has a particular connection to the declarant who made an out-of-court statement. Certain connections between the declarant and a party in the current case permit the court to treat the declarant's statements as though the party made those statements. These exceptions apply when a party (1) makes a statement herself, (2) agrees with a statement made by the declarant, (3) authorizes the declarant to make a statement on that party's behalf, or (4) conspires with the declarant who makes statements in furtherance of the conspiracy. This chapter discusses the elements of each of these hearsay exceptions.

The second category of hearsay exceptions explained in this chapter are *prior statements made by witnesses at trial*. These exceptions include (1) prior inconsistent statements, (2) prior consistent statements, (3) prior statements of identification, and (4) past recollection recorded. For each of these exceptions, the declarant must also be a witness who is present and available to testify at trial. When the declarant is not a witness at trial or is unavailable (as discussed in Chapter 5), the parties may not use these prior statements of witness exceptions.

ADMISSIONS AS EXCEPTIONS TO THE HEARSAY RULE

What is an admission? Generally people think of an admission as similar to a confession. For instance, in response to Alma's question, "Did you break the antique grandfather clock?" Bert might respond, "Yes, I broke the clock." Bert's response is a confession, admitting that he broke the clock. If Alma sued Bert for the value of the antique clock, it would be helpful to Alma's case to use Bert's out-of-court statement ("Yes, I broke the clock.") to help prove that Bert broke the clock. Alma would be testifying to Bert's hearsay statement. If Bert is a party to the litigation, as would be the case if Alma sued Bert for the value of the antique clock, then the party admission exception applies. In that case, Bert's out-of-court statement that he broke the clock can be admitted for the truth of the matter asserted (TOMA), to help prove that Bert broke the clock.

CEC §1220: Admission of party

Evidence of a statement is not made inadmissible by the hearsay rule when offered against the declarant in an action to which he is a party in either his individual or representative capacity, regardless of whether the statement was made in his individual or representative capacity.

What if Bert had said something other than confessing to breaking the antique clock? For instance, if Bert had responded, "That clock was too old," he is not admitting or confessing to anything. Nevertheless, Alma may want to use that statement for the TOMA to prove that the clock was old. Proving the age of the clock could be relevant to show that Bert was less likely to be careful with an old clock and therefore might have broken it.

If Alma sued Bert for the value of the clock, she can offer into evidence both of these hearsay statements because the party admission exception applies. She can offer Bert's out-of-court statement that he broke the clock for the TOMA, to help prove that Bert broke the clock. Alma can offer Bert's out-of-court statement that the clock was old to show that the clock was old (and therefore valuable). The second statement could also be offered for the non-truth purpose of explaining Bert's subsequent conduct (for instance, that he broke the clock because he thought it was worthless).

Any Statement Can Be an Admission

If Bert had responded to Alma's question by saying something like "That was an ugly clock" or "You don't need to know what time it is," Bert's response would be admission for purposes of this exception. These statements do not actually confess to anything, but the definition of an admission in the evidence context is broader than in the normal course of conversation. The words need not actually be admitting anything and can be mere commentary, such as "I don't need to know what time it is." If Bert, as the declarant who made that statement out of court, is a party to the litigation (or is connected to a party to the litigation in the ways that are discussed below), then that statement could meet the party admission exception to the Hearsay Rule.

The main limitation on admissions is relevance. As long as the statement meets the low relevance threshold that is explained in Chapter 1, was made by a party (or connected to a party in the ways discussed below), and is offered into evidence against that party, then the admission will meet this exception to the Hearsay Rule. Even if the substantive statement itself would be inadmissible on other grounds, the court may admit it under this group of exceptions. For example, the personal knowledge requirement and the opinion rule do not apply to admissions. If a party admits that his brakes must have failed, without any basis for that admission, the admission will come in as a party admission, even though it is not based on personal knowledge and would not be competent testimony. The party admission exception applies broadly, regardless of *what* the declarant said, regardless of *to whom* the declarant was speaking at the time, and regardless of *why* the declarant made the statement. Other rules of evidence such as those relating to privileges still might render the statement inadmissible, but the Hearsay Rule will not be an obstacle.

What is the rationale for the party admissions hearsay exception? Even before the Hearsay Rule was developed, admissions by a party opponent were historically admissible. After the Hearsay Rule evolved, such statements remained admissible as exceptions to, or exclusions from, the rule, in part because these statements do not implicate the "no opportunity for cross- examination" criticism that can apply to hearsay in general. Because the out-of-court declarant also is a party to the litigation, she cannot complain that she did not get the chance to cross- examine herself. She can cross-examine the witness who delivers the party's hearsay statement, and the party can take the stand herself to present her side of the story. Of course, criminal defendants are not compelled to take the witness stand, and many will make the strategic decision not to testify, thus leaving their own hearsay statements unchallenged. If the criminal defendant's admission was obtained in violation of his constitutional rights, however, it will not be admissible because constitutional rights trump the CEC.

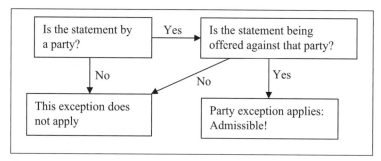

Figure 6.1. Is the Statement Admissible?

Figure 6.1 illustrates how to determine whether a statement is admissible. The first question is "Who said it?" Is that person a party to the litigation? If the name is in the title to the case, then that person is a party. In civil cases, look to see who is suing whom and be sure to identify all listed plaintiffs and defendants. As long as the person who made the statement is listed on one side of the case, that statement satisfies the first item on the party admissions checklist. In criminal cases, the prosecution side is the state, or common-wealth, or the people, and therefore the only individual "party" for pur-poses of this hearsay exception will be the criminal defendant or defendants in the case. The prosecutor, or assistant district attorney, is not considered a party on the prosecution side because the attorney is merely a representative of the people of the state of California. Victims of the crimes, police officers, and investigators are not considered parties either.

Being a party in a representative capacity for purposes of the CEC includes situations where one is litigating in a particular capacity, such as the guardian of a minor child, the conservator of a mentally incapacitated adult, or the executrix of a will.

The second question looks at which party is trying to offer the out-of-court statement into evidence. If the party whose statement is being offered (the declar-ant) is on the other side of the "v." in the title of the case from the party who is trying to offer the statement into evidence, then the answer is "yes," and the party admission exception applies to render the admission admissible. For example, in the case of *Alma v. Bert*, in which Alma seeks to offer Bert's out-of-court statement that he broke the clock, the admission exception would apply.

It is important to note that the exception permits the hearsay statement to be admitted only against the party who made the statement. If there are multiple defendants in a case, the party admission exception permits only a party's own statement to be used against him. Statements by other parties (even if they are both on the same side of the case) cannot be used against everyone on that side of the case. For instance, if Alma sued both Bert and Sam, Bert's statement that he broke the clock could be admissible under the party admission exception as evidence against Bert, but it would not be admissible under this exception as evidence against Sam. In such a case, consider the co-conspirator admissions exception described below

If Bert had instead said, "Sam and I broke the clock," another issue would arise. Bert's statement would be admissible against him as a party admission, but it would not be admissible against Sam on those grounds. If Bert and Sam were tried as co-defendants in the same trial, then the court would have to redact, or delete, the portion of Bert's statement that implicates Sam or find another hearsay exception that permits the court to admit the remainder of the statement.

Note that this exception will not help admit the statement on the same side of the "v." Sometimes tricky lawyers will try to use this hearsay exception to admit statements on the same side of the "v." For instance, if in response to Alma's question Bert had said, "I would never break such a valuable treasure," Bert might want that statement to be admitted into evidence. Bert's lawyer may then ask Bert, "What else, if anything, did you say to Alma?" Alma's counsel should make a hearsay objection because Bert's answer would be hearsay if offered for the TOMA. The party admission exception would not apply because Bert's attorney and Bert the declarant are both on the same side of the "v." — that is, on the defense side of the case.

Federal Rules of Evidence Compared: Notable Difference

In federal litigation, under FRE 801(d)(2)(a) admissions by a party-opponent are not considered to be hearsay as it is defined, and thus no exception is needed to allow those statements into evidence. This category includes adopted, authorized, agency, and co-conspirator admissions as well. The rationale for the FRE exclusion is that parties should have to live with their own statements. Moreover, a party has an opportunity to testify on his own behalf and thus has no need to cross-examine himself.

In contrast, under the CEC, these admissions are not excluded from the definition of hearsay, but are considered an exception to the Hearsay Rule under the circumstances described above. Be careful to recognize that a statement might be *non-hearsay* if applying the FRE and *admissible hearsay* or *hearsay admissible based on an exception*, if applying the CEC.

ADOPTIVE ADMISSIONS

Another category of party admissions is adoptive admissions, which occur when the party does not make the statement herself, but uses words or deeds to suggest that she agrees with a statement that someone else has made. In those cases, the statement will be admissible against the party as an adoptive admission.

CEC §1221: Adoptive admissions

Evidence of a statement offered against a party is not made inadmissible by the hearsay rule if the statement is one of which the party, with knowledge of the content thereof, has by words or other conduct manifested his adoption or his belief in its truth.

Why not just use the party admission exception discussed in the section above? That exception will allow admission of the words that the party actually spoke, which may prove nothing when out of context. For instance, a police officer says: "This looks like the accident was your fault entirely," and the party responds, "Yes, Officer, you're right." The party admission exception would permit the other side to offer into evidence the hearsay statement "Yes, Officer, you're right," but would not admit the officer's statement about fault. The party's statement by itself is not helpful, and so the concept of adoptive admissions provides the context so that the party admission has some meaning in the litigation.

Figure 6.2 illustrates how to determine whether a statement qualifies for the adoptive admission exception. The first question is easy to address: if the declarant is the party that the statement is being offered against, then this element is satisfied.

The second question is whether the party has *knowledge of the content* of the statement. Did the party hear the statement, understand what was being said, and know the subject matter? If so, then this question can be answered

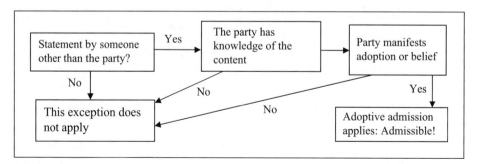

Figure 6.2. Does a Statement Satisfy the Exception for an Adoptive Admission?

"yes." For instance, Cordelia walks over to Dennis and Erin, who are in the middle of the conversation. Dennis says to Erin, ". . . and then we beat them," and Erin responds, "I'm sure they deserved it." Cordelia then says, "That was the fun part." Cordelia heard the statement about beating them, but she really does not know the context of the statement because she does not know who *them* refers to. Is it a football team or a group of senior citizens? While Cordelia may agree that it is "fun" to beat the opposing football team, she may not mean to agree that it is "fun" to beat older members of society. If the senior citizens sued Dennis and sought to admit Dennis's and Cordelia's statements, it would be difficult to prove this second element without more information.

The third question is whether the party has somehow *adopted* the statement. The jurors should be instructed to disregard the statement unless they first find that the party did adopt it. The standard is sufficiency: is there sufficient evidence from which a reasonable fact finder could find that the statement was adopted by a party? In the example above, has Cordelia adopted Dennis's statement about beating them? Saying "that was the fun part" are words that suggest Cordelia was present and perhaps even participated in the "fun" beating, and thus that she has adopted the statement as her own. If she has no understanding of the context, however, then the second element is not met.

Express, Implied and Tacit Adoption

Adoptive admissions can be express, implied, or sometimes even silent. *Express adoption* is straightforward. It can occur with words that indicate agreement or approval. Using the example above, when a police officer says, "This looks like the accident was your fault entirely," and the party responds, "Yes, Officer, you're right," the party has expressly adopted the officer's statement, and thus both statements are admissible against the party through the adoptive admission hearsay exception.

Implied or tacit adoption is not as straightforward when the party has engaged in some conduct that is subject to interpretation as to whether it manifests an adoption or a belief in the truth of the statement. Gestures are one type of conduct that can be interpreted to be an adoption or a manifestation of a belief in the truth of another's assertion. For instance, in the example above, if instead of speaking, Cordelia had raised her hand for a high-five, her conduct would suggest an adoption of the statement about "beating them."

Finally, on rare occasions *silence* may be considered an adoptive admission. Under the CEC, silence is not enough unless the judge determines that a juror could reasonably find that it was the party's intention to adopt the statement as his own. When there is silence, ask each one of these questions:

1. Did the party *hear* the statement?
2. Did the party *understand* the statement?
3. Did the party *know* what the declarant was talking about?
4. Is this the type of accusation or assertion that *most people would respond* to, under these circumstances, if it were untrue?

Consider who was making the statement, whether the declarant is someone the party would be expected to respond to, and whether circumstances might prevent or hinder the party's response (for instance, was the party bleeding or going into shock from injuries sustained?).

In criminal cases, additional issues arise because the accused has the right to remain silent. Silence can be interpreted either as exercising that right or as an adoption of an admission. California cases have found that pre-*Miranda* silence is not considered to be exercising that right, and it can be construed as an adoptive admission. Post-*Miranda* silence is not deemed to be an admission because it is an exercise of the right to remain silent.

Tacit adoption can also occur through conduct like using or relying on the statements. For instance, some employers may use an employee handbook at their training seminars for new employees. If the employer becomes a defendant in litigation about employment policies, then an argument can be made that by using the handbook at the training session the defendant adopted the statements contained in it. If so, then those statements could be considered admissions if offered against the employers at trial.

Federal Rules of Evidence Compared: No Significant Difference

For adopted admissions, the only difference is a semantic one — that the CEC is more explicit about how one manifests "adoption or belief in truth," by requiring knowledge of content and words or other conduct.

AUTHORIZED ADMISSIONS

When the party neither makes nor adopts the admission, it can still fit within the admissions exception if the party authorized the declarant to make the out-of-court statement. There are several different ways in which such authorization can be found, including express authorization (CEC 1222), implied authorization as a co-conspirator (CEC 1223), and implied authorization based on a relationship of common liability (CEC 1224) or predecessor/successor in interest (CEC 1225). The broadest category is CEC 1222, which we now address. (CEC 1224 and 1225 are included in the appendix but are not discussed in this chapter.)

CEC §1222: Authorized admission

Evidence of a statement offered against a party is not made inadmissible by the hearsay rule if:

(a) The statement was made by a person authorized by the party to make a statement or statements for him concerning the subject matter of the statement; and

(b) The evidence is offered either after admission of evidence sufficient to sustain a finding of such authority or, in the court's discretion as to the order of proof, subject to the admission of such evidence.

Many courts require *express* authorization to admit a statement under this hearsay exception, although the occasional argument based on implicit authorization is successful. *Express authorization* is when Frank, the boss, tells his accountant Ginger that she can give the employees a summary of their recent conversation about the financial situation of the firm. *Implied authorization* would be where employees asked Ginger about the firm's financial condition, and Ginger responded to them, without any explicit directions from Frank about the parameters of the conversation but within her capacity as accountant.

Ginger is speaking "for" Frank when she discusses the firm's financial condition with the other employees, and thus her statements are considered authorized by Frank. Therefore, the court can impute her statements about financial matters to Frank as admissions if the financial condition becomes relevant in some later litigation.

When is there an authorized admission? When there is a

1. statement made,
2. by a person authorized by the party to make the statement for him,
3. concerning the subject matter of the statement,
4. after (or subject to) sufficient evidence offered to show such authority.

The phrase "for him" in the CEC is particularly important because California courts have determined that statements *made by an authorized person to the party himself* are not covered by this hearsay exception. Thus, if Ginger were speaking *to* Frank about the financial situation and Herman overheard that conversation, Ginger's out-of-court statements would not be admissible against Frank under this authorized admission exception because they were made *to*, not *for or on behalf of*, Frank.

Evidence law does not determine whether an agency relationship exists. Instead, the substantive law of agency provides the rules for ascertaining whether an authorization exists. Remember that where the evidence shows that the declarant was authorized to speak on matters covered by the admission, such as the financial situation of the firm spoken about by the firm's accountant, then the courts will find *sufficient evidence*. When there is an employee-employer relationship, such a declaration can amount to an admission by an agent made about a topic that is within the scope of his employment duties.

Federal Rules of Evidence Compared: Notable Differences

The FRE has a higher threshold for determining whether an admission was authorized, requiring a preponderance of the evidence. The FRE's preponderance of the evidence standard means more than 50 percent of the evidence suggests that the foundational facts are likely to exist. The judge makes the initial determination as to whether the preponderance standard has been met before permitting the jurors to hear the evidence.

In contrast, under the CEC, a sufficiency standard applies. This means that viewing the facts in the light most favorable to the proponent of the evidence, a reasonable fact finder could find the existence of the foundational facts. If the judge finds that this lower threshold is met, she will permit the jurors to hear the evidence and then decide whether they think there is sufficient evidence of authorization to impute the statement to the party.

Another important distinction between the CEC and the FRE is that the FRE does not contain the "for him" language, and thus statements made to the party can be admitted under this exception. The FRE has a specific exception for employment and agency admissions.

CO-CONSPIRATORS' ADMISSIONS

Several specific types of implicitly authorized admissions have their own CEC sections, and the most important of those is co-conspirator admissions. The co-conspirator admission exception is based on necessity because without admitting the hearsay statements of co-conspirators, it would be exceedingly difficult to prove conspiracies. A second justification is based on the notion that those involved in conspiracies implicitly authorize the others involved in the conspiracy to speak for them about anything that furthers the goals or objectives of that conspiracy. In reality, the implicit authorization is a fiction. It is more likely that the legislatures followed the trend in criminal law of expanding liability for co-conspirators and crafted the evidence code to aid in that effort.

CEC §1223: Admission of co-conspirator

Evidence of a statement offered against a party is not made inadmissible by the hearsay rule if:

(a) The statement was made by the declarant while participating in a conspiracy to commit a crime or civil wrong and in furtherance of the objective of that conspiracy;

(b) The statement was made prior to or during the time that the party was participating in that conspiracy; and

(c) The evidence is offered either after admission of evidence sufficient to sustain a finding of facts specified in subdivision (a) or (b) or, in the court's discretion as to the order of proof, subject to the admission of such evidence.

This hearsay exception allows the statements of one of the defendant's co-conspirators to be admitted into evidence as substantive evidence against that defendant. The rationale for this CEC exception is necessity, given how difficult it is otherwise to prove conspiracies and to stop them before their goals are successfully achieved. There are four elements of this exception:

1. Statement made by declarant while participating in the conspiracy
2. Made prior to or during the time that the party participated in the conspiracy
3. In furtherance of a conspiracy
4. Offered after sufficient evidence to find participation in the conspiracy, or in the judge's discretion as to the order of proof.

The timeline of events shown in Figure 6.3 is important to an analysis of the applicability of this hearsay exception. First, note when the declarant joined the conspiracy and whether she made the statement after she joined but before she left the conspiracy. Second, determine when the party joined the conspiracy as well as when she left the conspiracy to ascertain whether the statement was made before or during the time the party was involved

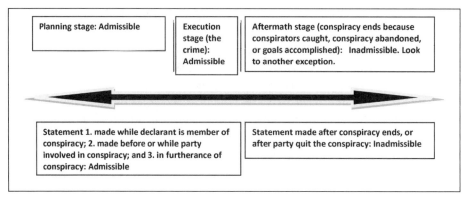

Figure 6.3. Timeline of the Co-conspirator Declaration Exception Timeline

in the conspiracy. The statement must have been made while the declarant was a member of the conspiracy. If the declarant was a member before the party joined the conspiracy, the declarant's statement made before the party joined will satisfy this element. Recognize that statements made by co-conspirators before the party joined the conspiracy still can be used against that party as admissions under this exception.

Third, to determine whether a statement was made in furtherance of the conspiracy requires an analysis of whether the statement helps the conspirators to plan or execute their unlawful conspiracy. Statements that provide for a division of labor and responsibilities or that address contingencies and other anticipated problems or obstacles are all in furtherance of the conspiracy.

Statements made after the end of the conspiracy — after its objectives have been achieved but while the participants are trying to avoid getting caught — are not admissible under this code section. Prosecutors try to define the objectives of the conspiracy broadly to allow a long time period for additional statements to be covered by this exception. Conversely, defense attorneys will try to narrow the scope and duration of the conspiracy so that fewer statements will be admissible.

The fourth element sets forth the foundation requirement, or the minimum that must be proven for the judge to permit the parties to benefit from this hearsay exception. The test is one of sufficiency, as it is for the other exceptions discussed above. Recall that the sufficiency test means that as long as there is sufficient evidence from which a reasonable juror could find the existence of these foundational facts, the judge can allow the hearsay evidence in as an exception to the Hearsay Rule. The foundational facts that must be established are (1) the existence of a conspiracy, (2) the declarant was a member of the conspiracy at the time the statement was made, and (3) the party was a member of that same conspiracy during or after the time that statement was made.

If the judge permits a party to use this hearsay exception, the opposing counsel should request that the jury be instructed to disregard the co-conspirator statement if the jury finds that one or more of these foundational facts have not been established to the jury's satisfaction.

The Confrontation Clause, which gives the accused the right to have witnesses against him appear in court (discussed in Chapter 5), will not bar admission of co-conspirator declarations because such declarations are not testimonial. Recall that a testimonial statement has governmental involvement and is one that a reasonable person would expect to be used later at trial. If a statement is in furtherance of the conspiracy, it is not intended to be used at trial. Moreover, such statements usually do not include any governmental involvement.

Federal Rules of Evidence Compared: Notable Differences

One difference is the *type* of evidence that can be used to establish the foundational facts. The CEC permits the consideration of admissible evidence only, and one cannot offer the hearsay declaration as the proof of the foundational fact of the existence and participation in the conspiracy. In contrast, the FRE 801(d)(2)(D) allows a party to use the hearsay declaration to help establish the existence of the foundational facts. The federal judge recognizes that the statement alone will not be adequate support to establish the conspiracy because the conspiracy must be proven by a preponderance of the evidence. The judge must also consider the circumstances surrounding the statement, including the identity of the speaker, the context, and any corroborating evidence offered.

Where the judge determines that the declaration is admissible because the preponderance standard has been met, the jury merely determines the weight of the co-conspirator's admission because the judge has made the decision on the issue of admissibility. If the judge determines that the preponderance standard has not been met, then the jury does not hear the hearsay statement. On the Confrontation Clause issue, under the FRE co-conspirator declarations are excluded from the definition of hearsay. As non-hearsay, they do not implicate the Confrontation Clause. Also, they are not testimonial under the more recent Supreme Court cases discussed in Chapter 5.

DISCRETION IN THE ORDER OF PROOF

The order in which the parties present evidence at trial can vary. Judges have discretion to permit a party to introduce some evidence out of order. The authorized admission and co-conspirator exceptions provide some flexibility in the order of proof, which helps to ease the burden on witnesses and attorneys, permitting information to be presented out of order when doing so serves the interests of judicial economy

For example, in a wrongful termination case filed by employee Herman against his former boss Frank, Herman may wish to testify about Ginger's out-of-court statement about the financial condition of the firm. If Herman offers Ginger's statement for the TOMA, then Frank's attorneys will object on the grounds of inadmissible hearsay. Herman's attorneys will respond that Ginger's out-of-court statement is an authorized admission and therefore can be admitted against Frank. Frank's lawyers will respond that there is no evidence of authorization, and therefore the statement is inadmissible.

If Herman does not have personal knowledge about whether Ginger was authorized to speak on financial matters, then Herman's lawyers would have to call another witness to the stand to testify about any authorization. Calling another witness would interrupt Herman's testimony and take more time. Thus, the CEC permits the court to admit Herman's rendition of Ginger's hearsay statement, and then give Frank the opportunity to move to strike the testimony as hearsay if the authorization is not established by sufficient evidence through a subsequent witness. This discretion in the order of proof is similar to the concept of conditional relevance discussed in Chapter 1.

As a practical matter, trial counsel should consider asking for a limiting instruction to let the jurors know that they cannot consider the hearsay statement unless or until they find that the foundation fact of the existence of the authorization has been established. For instance, with the co-conspirator exception, jurors should be instructed to disregard the statement if they find that there was no conspiracy, or that the declarant and party were not members of the same conspiracy during the relevant time periods.

Examples

1. Plaintiff sues the defendant for damages resulting from an automobile collision. At trial, a witness for the plaintiff testifies that she saw the defendant at a bar a few hours after the accident. To prove that the defendant fell asleep at the wheel, plaintiff's counsel asks the witness what the defendant said to her at the bar. The witness responds, "The defendant said, 'I think I fell asleep when I was driving earlier today.'" The defendant objects on the grounds of hearsay. How should the court rule, and why?

2. In the same case, another witness for the plaintiff testifies that she over-heard the defendant's mechanic respond to the defendant's question, "So my car is in tip-top shape?" The witness testifies that she heard the mechanic say to the defendant, "Next time you come in, we really need to check your brakes." The witness then testifies that the defendant

responded to the mechanic by saying, "Let's pray that everything works fine until I get back here next week." The defendant objects to the mechanic's statement and to the defendant's response on hearsay grounds. How should the court rule?

3. In a criminal prosecution against three defendants — D1, D2, and D3 — for robbery, conspiracy, and assault in California court, a prosecution witness testifies that she overheard the defendants speaking to each other just before they robbed the store. Which of the following statements are admissible at trial? Would your answers change in federal court?
   a. D1 said to D2, "You take the people on the left side and I'll take those on the right."
   b. D2 responded, "Sounds good. Breaking the law. Breaking the law. It's so fun when I've got good backup like you guys."
   c. D1 then said to D3, "Are you ready to help out with your first big score?"
   d. D3 responded with a smile and said, "What are you talking about?"

4. Ibrahim met with Jacob to discuss buying Jacob's motor home. During that meeting, Jacob's wife overheard Ibrahim say to Jacob, "You look familiar. Do you have a younger brother?" When they met a few days later to finalize the sale, Ibrahim shot Jacob and drove off with the motor home. Ibrahim was caught by the police when he tried to sell the motor home to someone else. Ibrahim is now on trial for the murder of Jacob, and the prosecution seeks to have the wife testify about Ibrahim's out-of-court statement about looking familiar to prove the identity of Jacob's killer. Jacob's younger brother came to visit Ibrahim's cell mate when Ibrahim was jailed on a prior assault offense. What objection should the defense make, how should the prosecution respond, and how should the court rule?

5. Kaleb attempted suicide, but his girlfriend Lucy found him and called 911. Police officers and an ambulance reported to the scene and saved Kaleb's life. While searching the scene, the police officers confiscated several guns hidden in Kaleb's home. Kaleb was then detained in a mental hospital for a 72-hour hold to be watched and to ensure that he was not a danger to himself or others. Immediately after he was released from the mental hospital, Kaleb tried to get the police to return his weapons on the grounds that he was no longer a danger to himself. At the trial on the gun charges, the police officers seek to testify that when Kaleb came to try to pick up his guns from the station, he claimed, "I am so depressed about all of this." The prosecution wants this testimony to prove that Kaleb was not mentally competent to have weapons in his possession. Kaleb objects that this police officer statement is inadmissible hearsay. How should the prosecution respond, and how should the court rule?

6. Liam asked his coworker Moira if she would give him and his girlfriend, Nuala, a ride to a campsite to party with some friends. Moira agreed and when they got to the campsite, Liam choked Moira while Nuala beat Moira. Moira died within a few hours from her injuries. Driving around in Moira's car and stopping to try to cash some of Moira's checks, Liam and Nuala were apprehended by the police. They waived their *Miranda* rights and confessed. The confession was videotaped. During the confession, Nuala explained that Liam had come up with the idea, that Liam had first strangled Moira, and that Nuala started beating Moira only after Moira had passed out from the strangulation. Liam was in the room when Nuala made these statements and did not contradict her. The prosecution seeks to offer Nuala's statements against Liam in his murder trial. Liam's attorneys object that the statements are inadmissible hearsay. The prosecution responds that Nuala's statements are adoptive admissions by Liam and are therefore admissible under that exception. How should the court rule, and why? Suppose that when Nuala finished her part of the confession, Liam had said, "it could have happened that way, but I don't really remember who started it." Would that change the court's ruling?

7. Omar was being chased by the police after he attempted a car-jacking in front of the local Starbucks. A canine unit responded, and the dog chased Omar and cornered him underneath a parked car. The dog tried to crawl under the car, grabbed Omar's leg in his mouth, and then tried pulling Omar out from beneath the car. As the dog pulled Omar out, Omar began hitting the dog with his fists, and the officers yelled at him to stop. When Omar continued to hit the dog (who had a firm grip on Omar's leg), one police officer hit Omar on the head with a flashlight. A county investigator prepared a report that stated that "the police used excessive force by beating Omar over the head after Omar had been apprehended by the canine who was chewing on his leg." Omar sued the police department for excessive use of force and sought to admit the county investigator's report. The police department lawyer objected that the report was inadmissible hearsay. How should Omar's lawyers respond, how should the court rule, and why?

8. Petra filed an internal grievance against her employer, University of Rachmon, and was laid off for "budgetary reasons" the following year. Petra was given deferential rehiring rights to other positions that she was qualified for at the university. The university's human resources personnel advised Petra as to which positions she would qualify for, and she applied for each of those positions. Petra was turned down for each of the 30 open positions that she applied for in the course of the next year. Petra then filed a lawsuit accusing the University of Rachmon of hiring discrimination. Petra sought to admit statements from various employees of the university's human resources department, which said that "it was pointless for Petra to keep applying for jobs

because she had filed a grievance and will not get re-hired." The University of Rachmon objected to these statements as hearsay, and Petra countered that the statements were authorized admissions. How should the court rule, and why?

9. Shinto and Ugo cornered Victor in a deserted parking lot. Ugo took out a knife and told Victor to hand over his purse, cell phone, and laptop computer. Victor yelled, "It's a man bag, not a purse!" and swung the laptop at Ugo's head. As Ugo was falling down, he saw Shinto pull out a gun and shoot Victor. Later the night, Ugo told his friend William, "Shinto and I only planned to rob that man. I didn't know Shinto would use his gun." At Shinto's trial, the prosecution calls William to the witness stand, to testify about Ugo's statement. Shinto's lawyers object on the grounds of inadmissible hearsay. The prosecution responds that the statement is admissible as a co-conspirator admission. How should the court rule, and why? Would the ruling and analysis differ in federal court?

10. Yolanda and Zuniga were pulled over by police when they drove away from a suspected methamphetamine laboratory located on a ranch outside of town. When questioned by the officers, Yolanda and Zuniga gave inconsistent answers. For instance, Yolanda said that she had known Zuniga for a few weeks, whereas Zuniga said she had known Yolanda for 15 years. Yolanda said they had gone to the ranch to ride horses, and Zuniga said they had gone to the ranch to drink beer and visit her cousin. When the police searched Yolanda's person, they found a receipt listing items necessary to make methamphetamine. Zuniga's fingerprints were later found at the ranch on a can of denatured alcohol, which is an essential ingredient of methamphetamine and also one of the items on the receipt. Yolanda and Zuniga were both charged with conspiracy to manufacture methamphetamine. Zuniga is seeking to exclude the contradictory statements made by Yolanda during questioning. How should the court rule as to Yolanda's statements?

Explanations

1. The court should overrule the hearsay objection because the defendant's statement is admissible as a party admission. A party admission has two elements: (1) sufficient evidence that the statement was made by the party, and (2) that the statement is being offered against that party by someone on the other side of the case. The plaintiff's witness can lay the foundation to show that there is sufficient evidence that the defendant made the statement. The statement is being offered by the plaintiff, against the defendant. Therefore, it satisfies both elements of the exception.

2. The mechanic's statement could be admissible for a non-truth purpose, to show that the defendant had notice of the dangerous condition of his brakes. If the plaintiff wanted to use the statement for its truth, to show that the brakes were indeed faulty, then she must find a hearsay exception. The two statements are admissible together as an adoptive admission. The mechanic's statement is not admissible as a party admission standing alone, because it is the mechanic's statement, not the party's statement. The defendant's statement about praying manifests a belief in the truth of the mechanic's statement that the brakes need to be fixed. Because the statements are being offered against the party, by the plaintiff on the other side of the case, and the adoption or belief has been established by a sufficiency standard, the statements will be admissible for the TOMA as adoptive admissions. The defendant's statement is admissible alone because it is an admission of the party, but it makes less sense without the mechanic's statement to provide context.

3. Statements a and b would be admissible against D1 and D2 as party admissions. If there was sufficient evidence of a conspiracy, then the statements would be admissible against all of the defendants in the conspiracy. The sentence in c is a question and thus not a statement. It does not make an assertion and therefore does not implicate the Hearsay Rule. If relevant, it would be admissible. The sentence in d is another question, but when said with a smile it contains an implicit message that the declarant does know what they are talking about, and therefore it might be admissible for the TOMA as an implicitly adoptive admission. It would not be admissible as a statement of a co-conspirator because questioning the plan is not likely to be considered "in furtherance of the conspiracy," and the statement itself cannot be used to establish the conspiracy under the sufficiency test. Under the FRE, the conspiracy would need to be proven by a preponderance of the evidence, but the statements themselves can be part of that proof. Also, the admissible statements would be admissible as exclusions from the Hearsay Rule, not exceptions.

4. Ibrahim's statement "you look familiar" is a party admission and is admissible against Ibrahim. Ibrahim's question is not a statement and therefore might not be hearsay. Still, an argument can be made that the implicit message of Ibrahim's question was that Ibrahim knew someone who looked like a younger version of Jacob. If the court is convinced by that argument, then that indirect assertion would be an admission, and the party admission exception would apply to admit the question as well.

5. Kaleb's statement can be offered for a non-truth purpose as circumstantial evidence of his emotional issues. If the prosecution wanted to offer

the evidence for the TOMA, to prove that Kaleb is depressed and therefore should not have weapons, then Kaleb's statement would be hearsay. Still, it would be admissible as a party admission if offered by the prosecution against Kaleb. (In addition, Kaleb's statement would be admissible to prove that he was depressed under the state of mind hearsay exception that is discussed in Chapter 7.)

6. Liam was present during Nuala's confession and heard what she said. He had the opportunity to contradict her if she misstated how the crime was committed. Most people would respond to such a confession if it were untrue. Therefore, Liam's silence can be construed to be an adoptive admission in this circumstance. If Liam had expressed his view that it could have happened that way but he did not remember, some would argue that he is not adopting Nuala's statement because he is admitting that he does not know for sure. On the other hand, others will argue that if it did not happen that way, it was in Liam's obvious interest to make that discrepancy clear; so his failure to do so constitutes an adoption. When the California Supreme Court addressed this issue, it determined that a statement like Liam's was adequate to constitute an adoptive admission, making the co-defendant's statement admissible against him.

7. Omar should respond that the report is an authorized admission, made by the county investigator, who was authorized to investigate the altercation. However, it will be difficult to establish that the investigator was authorized to speak on behalf of, or for, the police department in this situation. A one-time investigation usually does not give rise to such authorization under the substantive law of agency. However, if the county investigator has a history of working for the police and speaking on their behalf, then that might be enough to find implicit authorization. The court most likely will sustain the objection and prevent Omar from offering the report as an authorized admission. The report may be admissible under the public official records exception that is discussed in Chapter 7.

8. A statement can be authorized only when the individual making the statement has decision-making power or when the employee is a part of the decision-making process. The human resource representatives were advising Petra as to which positions she would be qualified to hold. They were not making the decision about whether to rehire her, which shows their lack of involvement in the decision-making process. Without their involvement, there is insufficient evidence that the human resources representatives are authorized to speak about rehiring Petra. An argument could be made that the human resources personnel are the ones logically assumed to have the authority to speak about personnel

matters. However, it is unlikely that an employer would authorize the human resources people to speak for that company by explaining that they are retaliating against a former employee who exercised her workplace right to file a grievance.

9. Ugo's statement to William is not admissible as a co-conspirator admission. First, it is not "in furtherance of the conspiracy." A statement cannot be in furtherance of the conspiracy if the objectives of the conspiracy have been completed or abandoned at the time the statement was made. Here, Ugo made the statement after the crime had been completed, and therefore this element is not met. Second, the only evidence of the conspiracy is the statement itself about the "plan" to rob. In California courts, the hearsay statement cannot be used to substantiate the existence of the conspiracy, and in the absence of sufficient evidence of a conspiracy, the statement cannot meet the co-conspirator admission exception.

   If this case were tried in federal court, then the statement itself can be used as evidence of the existence of the conspiracy, but the statement alone will not be enough to meet the preponderance test. The fact that Ugo and Shinto planned to rob someone, in addition to their conduct of hanging around waiting in the dark parking lot, might provide some additional evidence of conspiracy. The counterargument is that the homicide seems to be spontaneous because the gun was not brought out until after the victim attacked one of the robbers. If the preponderance test is met in federal court, the prosecution still has a problem because the statement was not made in furtherance of the conspiracy. Instead, it was made after the conspiracy to rob, if there was one, had already succeeded (if they got the man bag, cell phone, or laptop), or failed (if they ran away after the gunshot).

10. There was sufficient evidence of a conspiracy, without using the statements themselves, based on the fingerprints and the receipt, linking both Yolanda and Zuniga to the ranch. In addition, their statements were in furtherance of the conspiracy because the conspiracy was ongoing. Their answers were an attempt to protect the other members of the conspiracy as well as to minimize their own roles in anything going on at the suspected laboratory site by calling it a social visit. At the time that they made the contradictory statements, they were furthering the conspiracy by trying to avoid detection of the methamphetamine laboratory. The goal of the conspiracy had not yet been achieved because they had not completed their manufacture and distribution of the illegal drug. Thus the court should admit Yolanda's statement under the hearsay exception for co-conspirator declarations.

OTHER EXCEPTIONS TO THE HEARSAY RULE: PRIOR STATEMENTS OF WITNESSES

With prior statements of witnesses, the reference to the word *witnesses* is important because this group of exceptions applies *only* to hearsay statements made by *declarants who actually testify at the trial*. The witness's out-of-court statement is being offered in the trial, but the witness herself also will be there to testify, and thus there will be an opportunity for cross-examination, under oath, in front of the jury.

Prior Inconsistent Statements

When a witness testifies at trial in a way that is inconsistent with a statement that the same witness made at some time prior to trial, the out-of-court statement will be admissible as an exception to the Hearsay Rule. That prior *inconsistent* statement will be admissible for the TOMA as long as there remains an opportunity for the witness to explain or deny the inconsistency.

CEC §1235: Inconsistent statement

Evidence of a statement made by a witness is not made inadmissible by the hearsay rule if the statement is inconsistent with his testimony at the hearing and is offered in compliance with section 770.

How do you decide if the statement is inconsistent? An express contradiction is the easiest case. In court the witness testifies, "The light was red!" and at a prior time that witness told an investigator "The light was green!" Note that an express contradiction is not required, as long as there is *inconsistency in effect*. Evasive answers, silence, and changes in the level of detail or in the important details have been found by courts to be inconsistent in effect, adequate to implicate this hearsay exception. However, a witness's mere refusal to answer does not make the prior statements inconsistent.

Claims of forgetfulness can go either way. If there is reason to believe that the witness is lying about claiming to forget, then the court might find inconsistency in effect. However, if the witness says, "I don't remember" and there is no reason to disbelieve the witness's claim as to his loss of memory, then the prior statement is not inconsistent, and thus this hearsay exception will not apply. Nevertheless, the prior statement then becomes

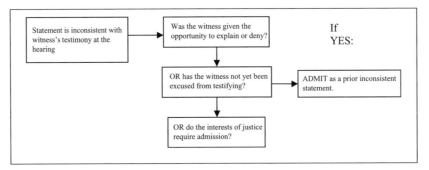

Figure 6.4. Admitting Prior Inconsistent Statements as Hearsay Exceptions

admissible for the non-truth purposes of impeachment (which are addressed in more detail in Chapters 4 and 8).

Figure 6.4 shows the process for determining whether a statement can be admitted under the prior inconsistent statement hearsay exception. The witness must testify at the hearing and must have made an earlier statement that is inconsistent with the testimony. Next, the witness must have had an opportunity to explain or deny the inconsistency, or the witness has not yet been excused from testifying in this case, or the interests of justice require admission. If any one of these three questions is answered in the affirmative, then the statement can be offered under the prior inconsistent statement exception.

Note that CEC 770 does not require that the witness be confronted with the statement before it is offered into evidence, as long as the witness has not been excused. However, as a practical matter, most lawyers do confront the witness while she is on the stand. Some are going for the Perry Mason type of recantation, "You're right, I am lying now. What I said before was the truth!" and others are just making the witness squirm to discredit that witness in front of the jury. If the witness refuses to concede to making the statement, the impeaching party is able to bring in hearsay testimony of the statement because the witness has just been granted the opportunity to explain or deny the statement, thus fulfilling the first condition of CEC 770.

Federal Rules of Evidence Compared: Notable Differences

There are three important differences in how the FRE deals with prior statements of witnesses. First, FRE 801(d)(1)(A) requires that the prior inconsistent statement was given under oath, subject to perjury, at a proceeding or deposition.

Second, the FRE requires that the witness be subject to cross-examination about the prior inconsistent statement. Being subject to "cross concerning the statement" is important. What is the scope of cross-examination? The scope of cross-examination (as is explained in Chapter 8), is testimony within the scope of the direct as well as questions about credibility issues. If this statement is not within the scope of the direct, then the witness still should be subject to cross on it to examine credibility. In the rare case in which the witness is not subject to cross-examination (for instance, when the witness dies after giving direct examination testimony but before being cross-examined), then it would not meet this requirement.

Under the FRE, if the statement satisfies all of these conditions, it can be offered for the TOMA. If it does not satisfy these conditions, then it may be offered for impeachment purposes only. *For impeachment purposes only* means it can be used show an inconsistency, but not to show that the prior inconsistent statement is the true one. The FRE also has a similar rule requiring an opportunity to explain or deny, FRE 613(b).

Third, as noted above, prior inconsistent statements are excluded from the definition of hearsay and are considered to be non-hearsay. In contrast, under the CEC, these statements are admissible hearsay under an exception.

Prior Consistent Statements

Prior consistent statements can be relevant to the issue of credibility, and credibility is a path that must be built in every case. When a witness keeps telling the same story, both inside and outside of court, the fact finder has heightened confidence that the witness is telling the truth. Consistency need not be absolute in terms of telling the story in exactly the same way, but it must be close enough to the current testimony to help rebut a charge of recent fabrication or improper influence.

These out-of-court statements constitute hearsay when they are being offered to show that the out-of-court statement is true. Using the statement to prove its truth is different from using the statement to show consistency or inconsistency. When using the statement to show consistency, the party is not relying on which of the statements is true, but is simply arguing that the witness is more credible because she has told the same story more than once. The consistent statement would therefore be circumstantial evidence of the truth of the testimony in court.

In contrast, when the party wants to use the consistent statement as evidence that the consistent statement is substantively true, then this hearsay exception is needed. Because the statement was made out of court, it is already less reliable than the in-court testimony. The risks of overwhelming the jury and clogging the courts with multiple repetitions of the same story are significant as well, so the CEC places some limitations on the use of a prior consistent statement as an exception to the Hearsay Rule.

CEC §1236: Prior consistent statement

Evidence of a statement previously made by a witness is not made inadmissible by the hearsay rule if the statement is consistent with his testimony at the hearing and is offered in compliance with Section 791.

The main use of a prior consistent statement is to rehabilitate a witness who was impeached, or undermined, on cross-examination. Often that impeachment occurs by the use of a prior inconsistent statement, as discussed above. CEC 1236 refers to compliance with CEC 791, which provides that the party can offer the witness's prior consistent statement after the witness has been *impeached*. This impeachment can happen either

1. by confronting the witness with a prior inconsistent statement, or
2. by expressly or
3. implicitly accusing the witness of bias, recent fabrication, or another improper motive.

Once impeachment has occurred, a party can offer a prior consistent statement into evidence. There is a time limitation on the prior consistent statement. It must have been made before the inconsistent one or before the motive to fabricate or other improper influence arose.

Determining Whether It Is a Prior Consistent Statement

These are the steps to analyze whether a statement fulfills the requirements:

1. The statement is consistent with the witness's testimony at the hearing and
2. Complies with CEC 791, which requires:
   a. It is offered after the witness was impeached with a prior inconsistent statement, and the prior consistent statement was made before the inconsistent one, or
   b. The witness has been accused of bias, or recent fabrication, or improper motive, and the prior consistent statement was made before that improper motive arose.

There are two instances when a prior consistent statement will be admissible. First, when a witness is confronted on cross-examination with a prior inconsistent statement, that cross-examination opens the door on the redirect examination for this prior consistent statement hearsay exception to help rehabilitate the witness and bolster her credibility. If the witness testifies on direct examination that "the traffic light was green," and then is confronted on cross-examination with her prior inconsistent statement from the day after the accident when she stated "the traffic light was red," then the stage has been set for using a prior consistent statement to rehabilitate the witness. The redirect examination of the witness can use the prior consistent statement as long as the prior consistent statement was made prior to the prior inconsistent statement.

If on the day of the accident the witness said, "the traffic light was green," then that statement will count as a prior consistent statement and will be admissible through this hearsay exception. On the other hand, if the "light was green" statement had not been made until three days *after* the accident, then it would not be admissible under this hearsay exception because the prior consistent statement was made after the prior inconsistent statement.

The second instance occurs when the witness has not been explicitly confronted with a prior inconsistent statement, but rather has been accused of either bias, recently fabricating the testimony, or being swayed by an improper motive. An explicit charge of bias would be the question "Isn't it true that you are changing your story now to protect your new boyfriend, the defendant?" If instead of confronting the witness on cross-examination with a prior inconsistent statement, the cross-examiner had asked, "Isn't it true that you began dating the defendant after his so-called accident?" this question amounts to an implicit charge of bias or improper motive, and will be adequate to trigger the prior consistent statement exception if the prior consistent statement was made prior to the time that the bias or motive arose.

The next question, then, to ask is whether the witness made the prior consistent statement *before* the potential bias began. In the example above, the implicit charge of bias relates to dating the defendant. If the witness made the consistent statement *before* she started dating the defendant, then there is an argument that dating the defendant did not have an impact on her testimony about the accident because she told the same story before she started dating the defendant. Thus, when the witness is confronted with either an implicit or an explicit charge, a prior consistent statement that was made *prior to* the time that the allegedly improper bias or motive arose will be admissible under this exception. In this case, as long as the witness said "the traffic light was green" before she started dating the defendant, the prior consistent statement will be admissible.

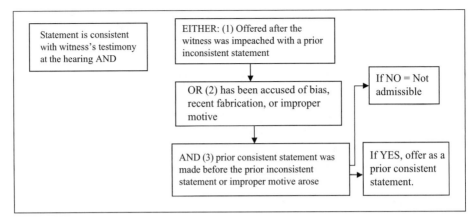

Figure 6.5. Admitting Prior Consistent Statements as Hearsay Exceptions

Figure 6.5 shows the process for admitting prior consistent statements. First, the witness must testify at the hearing and give a statement that is consistent with that testimony. Next, that statement can be offered only after the witness has been impeached in this case with a prior inconsistent statement or after the witness has been accused of bias or improper motive. Finally, the prior consistent statement must have been made earlier than the prior inconsistent statement was made or before the improper motive arose. Only then will the statement be allowed under the prior consistent statement hearsay exception.

Federal Rules of Evidence Compared: No Significant Differences

There are no significant differences in FRE 801(d)(1)(B) as to prior consistent statements, but the language "improper influence" is added to the FRE. Note that while the FRE does not explicitly require that the consistent statement have been made during any particular time period, such as before the motive arose, subsequent case law has determined that to be a requirement. In addition, under the FRE, this is defined as non-hearsay, rather than as an exception to the Hearsay Rule as it is under the CEC.

Refreshing Recollection

When a witness cannot remember something in answer to the attorney's question, the attorney is entitled to *refresh* the witness's recollection. When the attorney refreshes the witness's recollection, the witness can then respond to the unanswered question. Because the witness is now testifying from *present* (refreshed) recollection in court, there is no hearsay problem.

Sometimes the refreshing occurs by using a document. The procedure for refreshing recollection is as follows: ask the witness whether she remembers enough to respond accurately and, if not, ask whether a particular document would refresh her recollection. If she answers affirmatively, the common practice is to seek permission from the court to show the witness a document to refresh her recollection. If granted, then the attorney has the document marked for identification, hands it to the witness, and asks the witness to read the document to herself.

Why not let the witness read the document aloud? Because then the statement in the document would be hearsay (and might violate the secondary evidence rule, which is addressed in Chapter 11). After she reads the document, the attorney asks her if her memory is refreshed. If so, then the attorney takes the document away and asks the witness to now answer the question.

Past Recollection Recorded

When the missing information is more detailed or complex, the attorney may not be able to refresh the witness's recollection about the details. If the attorney is not successful in refreshing the recollection, or the details are something that the witness no longer remembers, then the *past recollection recorded hearsay exception* in CEC 1237 can be useful. This exception applies when the witness wrote a memo with the details or directed someone else to write such a memo. It is important that the memo was made at a time when the witness still remembered those details. That memo can be admissible for the TOMA if it meets the requirements of the past recollection recorded hearsay exception.

 CEC §1237: Past recollection recorded
(a) Evidence of a statement previously made by a witness is not made inadmissible by the hearsay rule if the statement would have been admissible if made by him while testifying, the statement concerns a matter as to which the witness has insufficient present recollection to enable him to testify fully and accurately, and the statement is contained in a writing which:

(1) Was made at a time when the fact recorded in the writing actually occurred or was fresh in the witness' memory;

(2) Was made (i) by the witness himself or under his direction or (ii) by some other person for the purpose of recording the witness' statement at the time it was made;

(3) Is offered after the witness testifies that the statement he made was a true statement of such fact; and

(4) Is offered after the writing is authenticated as an accurate record of the statement.

(b) The writing may be read into evidence, but the writing itself may not be received in evidence unless offered by an adverse party.

The proponent of the written statement must persuade the judge that the witness's statement would have been admissible, if she were able to give it (based on personal knowledge and relevance) and that the witness's perception was reduced to writing at a time when the information was fresh in the witness's memory.

The witness need not be the person who created the writing, as long as that witness provides some input into the making of the document at a time when the underlying facts were fresh in the witness's memory. If the document was made based on the witness's instructions or for the purpose of recording her statement, and the witness testifies that the statement was a correct reflection of what she perceived and that the written statement is an accurate record of that perception, then the foundation will be established.

These requirements seem a bit difficult to apply because the witness must testify and also must testify to a loss of memory. Some may ask how a witness who does not have a current recollection can be sure now that the statement accurately recorded the information. This concern is the reason why the witness must testify at trial as to the making of the document. The credibility concerns are mitigated by the fact that witnesses do not prepare these written statements to avoid cross-examination, and second, that in many instances, the recorders are police officers, traffic officers, or emergency personnel, and thus they have little or no motive to prepare a false report.

Is It Past Recollection Recorded?

There are six elements required for this exception:

1. The witness had personal knowledge
2. No longer has sufficient recollection to testify accurately or fully
3. Made or directed to be made
4. A statement in writing
5. While the matter was fresh in the witness's memory
6. Intending to be a true and accurate record.

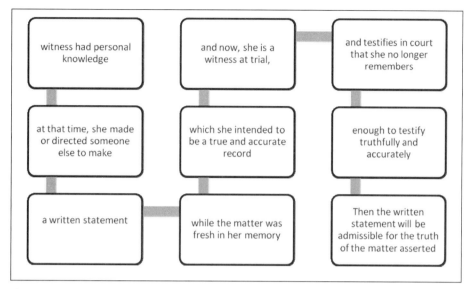

Figure 6.6. Meeting the Elements of the Past Recollection Recorded Exception

Figure 6.6 shows the steps in the process for determining whether the past recollection recorded hearsay exception is met. Follow the gray line from box to box to establish whether evidence falls within this exception.

Use these clauses as a checklist of the questions that you need to ask: The witness *must have had firsthand knowledge* of the information. Ask: Did you know this information at one time? The witness *must presently lack recollection*, and the judge has some leeway in evaluating whether the claimed memory loss is real or fake. Ask: Do you currently have sufficient recollection to testify as to this matter? The *witness made or adopted* the statement. Ask: Did you write this, or sign or initial someone else's writing? Was the *matter fresh in your memory* at that time? How do you know it was accurate? What did you do to make sure it was accurate at the time that you signed it? For instance, did you read the document? Did you understand it? If the judge is persuaded that there is sufficient evidence to support these foundational requirements, then the writing may be read into evidence. Only the other side can try to admit the writing into evidence as an exhibit.

Federal Rules of Evidence Compared: No Significant Differences

FRE 803(5) is less specific about the testimony required to substantiate the loss of memory and does not mention authentication. As a practical matter, the result is the same in federal court.

Statements of Identification

Another category of witness statements are statements of identification. What is a *statement of identification*? It can be pointing and saying "He's the man who did it"; picking out someone from a photo or police lineup; naming someone ("It was Fred"); or hearing a voice and saying "that's him." CEC 1238 creates an exception for witnesses identifying participants in a crime or other incident.

CEC §1238: Prior identification
Evidence of a statement previously made by a witness is not made inadmissible by the hearsay rule if the statement would have been admissible if made by him while testifying and: (a) the statement is an identification of a party or another as a person who participated in a crime or other occurrence; (b) the statement was made at a time when the crime or other occurrence was fresh in the witness' memory; and (c) the evidence of the statement is offered after the witness testifies that he made the identification and that it was a true reflection of his opinion at that time.

It does not matter whether the witness is currently able to testify as to the identity of the perpetrator. The out-of-court identification can be repeated in court, to bolster credibility, and thus is distinguishable from prior consistent statements. Recall that a prior consistent statement can be admitted for the truth only as far as it applies to rehabilitating the witness *after* her credibility has been attacked.

The following elements establish the statement of identification exception:

1. Statement would have been admissible if said while testifying
2. Statement is identification of a party or participant in crime or other occurrence
3. Made at a time when fresh in witness's memory
4. And the evidence of the statement is offered after the witness testifies
   a. That she made the identification, and
   b. That it was a true reflection of her opinion at that time.

What is the rationale for permitting statements of identification as an exception to the Hearsay Rule? Reliability of the out-of-court identification probably is higher than the reliability of an in-court identification would be, for several reasons. First, the in-court identification is *suggestive*. The attorney asks, "Do you see the person who committed the crime here in this courtroom?" and the witness answers, "Yes, I do." The attorney then asks, "Will you point to that person?" and the witness usually ends up pointing to the person sitting next to the defense lawyer. Maybe that is the person, but there is some cause for concern that the witness is pointing based on what is already known about that person. In many cases, what is known about that person is that he is now on trial for that crime.

Second, the prior statement has a *higher probative value* than the in-court statement because that prior statement was made closer in time to the actual event or crime. It is thus less likely to be affected by fading memory or some undue influence over the course of the intervening months until the trial. Third, the reliability of the out-of-court statement can be tested because the witness is on the stand and thus subject to cross-examination about perception, memory, narration, and sincerity. Still, where the witness has now forgotten, the effectiveness of cross-examination is not high. Where the witness has forgotten, the prior statement is much more necessary because it may be the only identification available to the prosecution.

Federal Rules of Evidence Compared: Minor Differences

For prior statements of identification, FRE 801 (d)(1)(C) does not require any particular conditions other than it "was made after perceiving that person," and so it is less specific than the CEC. The CEC has an increased focus on reliability because the witness must testify as to the accuracy of the statement in reflecting what she perceived at the time. In addition, statements of identification under the FRE are considered exclusions from the definition of hearsay, rather than as exceptions.

Examples

1. Vito asked his coworker, Xerxes, to kill Vito's boss so Vito could get the payout on the life insurance policy he had recently purchased without his boss's knowledge. Xerxes asked his neighbor Willemina to help him with the killings. After initially agreeing, Willemina backed out when she found out she would not be paid in advance. Xerxes then asked his neighbor on the other side of the house, Yohan, if he would help kill Vito's boss, and Yohan agreed. Xerxes and Yohan broke into the office where Vito worked while Vito was out of town. They killed Vito's boss. At trial, Willemina testified that she knew nothing about the murder-for-hire plot. Then, another witness testified that he overheard Willemina say that she had "backed out of something and so Yohan had to take care of

it." Yohan objected to the witness's statement as hearsay, and the prosecution responded that it was a prior inconsistent statement and should be admitted. How should the court rule, and why?

2. Jackie broke into Ilana's house late one night, intending to steal some antique jewelry that Ilana had been wearing at a recent charity event. When Ilana awoke and confronted Jackie, Jackie shot her and wrapped a red scarf around Ilana's neck. Ilana's body was found by her son Giraurd the next morning, and the red scarf was still around her neck. During the investigation, Giraurd told the police that he had never seen his mother wear a scarf of any color, and that he did not think that his mother owned any scarves. The police officer wrote down "victim's red scarf" in her police report. Jackie, who often wears a red scarf, was eventually caught and tried for felony murder. At Jackie's trial, Giraurd testified that he had seen his mother at dinner the night of her death, and she was not wearing a red scarf. He also testified that his mother did not own a red scarf. On cross-examination, Jackie's defense lawyer offered the police report as a prior inconsistent statement that Ilana did own a red scarf. On redirect, the prosecution offered Giraurd's statement to another police officer that his mother did not own a red scarf. Jackie's defense lawyer objected on the grounds of hearsay and improper rehabilitation. How should the court rule, and why?

3. Oliver robbed four stores in the span of three weeks. In each robbery, Oliver walked up to the cashier, claimed to have a gun inside his sweatshirt, and then demanded money from the cashier. While Oliver had pulled up the hood of his sweatshirt, he did not otherwise disguise his face. During the fourth robbery, Oliver was bold enough to commit the robbery while there were other customers in the store. Paolo, a customer who also happened to be a portrait artist, was watching Oliver in the overhead mirror, and dialed 911 from his cell phone as soon as Oliver left the store with the money. Paolo provided a detailed description of the robber to the 911 operator, and that call was audiotaped as is the usual practice for all 911 calls. Oliver was eventually caught and put on trial for the robberies. The prosecution called Paolo to the witness stand, and Paolo testified that he called 911, gave a detailed description of the robber, and later picked Oliver out of a photo lineup. When asked to repeat the exact description he had given the 911 operator, Paolo stated that he could no longer remember the exact description. Oliver's lawyer objected to Paolo's testimony about his description as inadmissible hearsay and a lack of foundation (personal knowledge). The prosecution responded that the description and subsequent identification by Paolo is admissible for the TOMA as a prior statement of identification. How should the court rule, and why? Would the ruling or analysis change in federal court?

4. Stanley robbed a gas station, and the gas station attendant Tino got a good look at Stanley's face. Tino met with a police sketch artist and gave a detailed description of the robber. Officers circulated the sketch, and one of Stanley's business rivals gave the police Stanley's full name and address, but Stanley was not at home when they went to make the arrest. Stanley had heard about the sketch, and he went back to the gas station and shot and killed Tino. The next day, Stanley told his friend Uli, "I robbed that gas station, and then I had to go back and kill the guy who identified me." Uli responded, "Don't worry, Stanley. I'd never rat you out." During the investigation, the police contacted Uli and tape-recorded a conversation in which Uli said, "Stanley told me, 'I was the guy who did the robbery and killing at the gas station.'" Stanley eventually was caught and is now on trial for robbery and murder. At trial, Uli is called to the witness stand, and he testifies that he cannot remember whether he ever talked to Stanley about robbery or murder. Uli also testified that Stanley never told Uli that he had killed someone. The prosecution offers Uli's recorded statement into evidence. Stanley's attorney objects on hearsay grounds. How should the court rule, and why? How would the analysis change in federal court?

5. Roberta was riding around with her friend Nancy when a car pulled up next to them and the driver said, "Yo-home girls, get back to your side of town or you won't make it back!" Roberta pulled out her gun and shot the driver of the other car, killing her and wounding two of the passengers. Nancy drove Roberta away from the scene, but both were later caught and put on trial separately. At the preliminary hearing in Roberta's case, Nancy testified that it was Roberta who had done the shooting. During Roberta's trial, Nancy claimed her Fifth Amendment right not to incriminate herself and refused to testify. The prosecution sought to admit Nancy's preliminary hearing testimony identifying Roberta under the prior inconsistent statement hearsay exception. Roberta's defense lawyer objected. How should the court rule, and why?

6. Kyle assaulted his girlfriend, Leslie, and her son, Morton. Leslie filed for a restraining order. A few weeks later, Kyle violated the restraining order and attacked Leslie and Morton, and the police arrested him later that same night. The police officers interviewed Leslie and Morton that evening and conducted a videotaped interview later that week. At trial, after Leslie testified about the assaults, Kyle's attorney asked her on cross-examination, "Isn't it true that you made up the assault story to get back at Kyle for refusing to repay the money he took from you before you got the restraining order?" Leslie answered, "No." On redirect examination, the prosecution asked Leslie whether she had told anyone else about Kyle's assaults before she got the restraining order, and Leslie answered, "Yes," and then began to describe earlier conversations with

her mother and sister. Kyle's counsel objected on the grounds of inadmissible hearsay. How should the prosecution respond, and how should the court rule?

7. Edwin was driving down Highway 5 from Sacramento to Los Angeles when he needed to use the restroom, so he stopped at a rest area off of the highway. While Edwin was in a bathroom stall, Franco burst through the stall door and shot Edwin in the chest. Edwin died instantly, and Franco removed Edwin's wallet and took his money and credit cards. Franco used Edwin's credit card to rent a limousine to drive him back to Sacramento to pick up his friend, Harry. As the limousine driver took them around the city, Franco told Harry all about the shooting at the rest stop. At the end of the limo ride, Franco passed Edwin's credit card to Harry. When Harry tried to use the credit card again the next day to rent his own limousine, Harry was arrested. While Harry was out on bail, he received a telephone call from Franco. When the police interviewed Harry, he said, "My friend Doug said he shot Edwin." After the prosecution offered Harry immunity, Harry said, "It was really Franco who said, 'I killed Edwin,' but Franco threatened me, and so I lied to the officers earlier." Harry testified at Franco's trial that "Franco said, 'I killed Edwin.'" Franco's lawyers offered Harry's first interview statement to the police into evidence as a prior inconsistent statement. The prosecution then sought to offer evidence of other statements Harry had made to the police, indicating that Franco, not Doug, was the shooter. Franco's defense lawyers objected as inadmissible hearsay. How should the court rule, and why?

8. Chandra was in an abusive relationship with her boyfriend Allen, who intimidated and threatened her until she agreed to help Allen kidnap, rob, and murder a young man whom they found passed out outside of a neighborhood pub. Chandra and Allen were eventually caught by the police. When interrogated, Chandra said that she helped Allen only because he threatened to beat her again and she was tired of the beatings. At the preliminary hearing, Allen's sister, Bernice, testified that Allen and Chandra had a loving relationship, and Allen was never abusive toward Chandra. She also testified about which shirt Allen was wearing on the day of the killing and the blood spots that she found on that shirt after the killing. At trial, Bernice testified that she did not remember testifying about the killing at the preliminary hearing. The prosecution tried to refresh Bernice's recollection with the transcript of the preliminary hearing, but after reading the transcript silently to herself, Bernice stated that her recollection was not refreshed. The prosecution then sought to offer the transcript of Bernice's preliminary hearing testimony, and the defense objects as inadmissible hearsay. How should the court rule, and why? Would the ruling change in federal court?

Explanations

1. The court should admit the prior inconsistent statement because it is inconsistent with Willemena's trial testimony that she knew nothing about the murder plot. While the statement does not indicate what was backed out of, there is a reasonable inference for the jury to make that Willemena's out-of-court statement referred to the murder plot.

2. The court should overrule the hearsay objection and admit the statement for the TOMA under the prior consistent statement exception. After a witness has been impeached with a prior inconsistent statement, as the police report appears to do here, then the witness may be rehabilitated on redirect examination with a prior consistent statement. Improper rehabilitation refers to efforts to bolster the credibility of a witness with a prior consistent statement before that credibility has actually been attacked. In this case, the confrontation with a prior inconsistent statement is an explicit attack, which then triggers the proper use of the prior consistent statement exception.

3. Paolo's description to the 911 operator and identification of Oliver from the photo lineup should be admissible under the prior identification exception to the Hearsay Rule. Paolo's description was made after perceiving the robber, while it was fresh in his memory, and Paolo has taken the witness stand to testify about his perception. Paolo is a portrait artist and perhaps would be more likely to remember faces and facial features. As long as Paolo testifies that the description was a true and accurate reflection of his opinion at the time, the statement should be admitted for the TOMA. The fact that Paolo cannot currently remember the exact description that he gave to the 911 operator does not make the statement inadmissible because it is his past personal knowledge rather than his current personal knowledge that is a prerequisite for using this hearsay exception. Nevertheless, his current lack of memory may impact the jury's evaluation of his credibility. There is no difference in the analysis in federal court except that the statement would be non-hearsay rather than an exception.

4. The prosecution should respond that the statement is a prior inconsistent statement and should be admissible for the TOMA. The defense will argue that the statement is not inconsistent with Uli's current testimony because Uli stated that he did not recall having a conversation with Stanley about murder and robbery. A mere lack of recall is not enough to constitute an inconsistency. However, the court will likely rule the statement admissible for two reasons. First, the evidence suggests that Uli is feigning a lack of recall, given that he made a tape-recorded statement and because of his friendship with Stanley and his hesitancy to "rat out"

his friend. Second, the second part of Uli's trial testimony, that Stanley never told Uli he killed or robbed someone, actually is expressly inconsistent with the prior statement that Stanley told Uli that he had robbed and killed the gas station attendant. The court should admit the prior statement under the prior inconsistent statement hearsay exception.

The statement also may be admitted as past recollection recorded if Uli testifies that it was made at or near the time when the memory was fresh in his mind, and that he tried to be truthful in that statement. In federal court, to be admissible as non-hearsay, the prior inconsistent statement must have been made under oath at a deposition or prior proceeding, and unless Uli's tape-recorded statement to the police was made under penalty of perjury, such as in a preliminary hearing, it will not meet the requirements to be admissible non-hearsay. Instead, the statement can be offered for impeachment purposes to show an inconsistency in the testimony, but will not be admissible for the TOMA.

5. The court should sustain the hearsay objection because it does not meet the requirements for a prior identification given that the declarant, Nancy, did not testify on the witness stand at the trial. Therefore, her statement is not admissible as a prior identification hearsay exception. Some lawyers may try to admit Nancy's identification as a prior inconsistent statement, but that argument will fail because the prior inconsistent statement must be inconsistent with current court testimony. Nancy did not testify at the current trial, so there is no current court testimony for the prior statement to be inconsistent with. Nancy's prior statement might meet the former testimony exception (which was discussed in Chapter 5). Recall that the elements of the former testimony exception are (1) unavailable declarant, (2) testified under oath in a former proceeding or hearing, (3) and the party in the current proceeding had an opportunity to cross-examine the declarant about the statements. Nancy satisfies the first and second elements because she is constructively unavailable based on her assertion of the privilege and the testimony was made in a prior proceeding. However, unless she and Roberta were codefendants at that preliminary hearing, Roberta likely did not have a prior opportunity to cross-examine Nancy, and therefore the third element is not met. The statement will not meet the elements of the former testimony exception and therefore will not be admissible for the TOMA. In addition, admitting the statement will violate Roberta's confrontation rights because the statement is testimonial.

6. The prosecution should respond that Leslie's statements about her prior conversations with her mother and sister are prior consistent statements, offered after she has been impeached on cross-examination with an implicit attack on her credibility. That attack was due to bias or improper

motive in seeking to retaliate against Kyle for taking her money and refusing to repay her after she got the restraining order against him. The prosecution would need to establish that the conversations with her mother and sister happened before any improper motive might have arisen, and thus before Kyle stated that he would not repay her money or before Leslie filed for the restraining order. As long as the prior statements were made before the time when Leslie had a motive to lie about the assault, then the statements can be admissible under the prior consistent statement exception for the TOMA.

7. Offering Harry's first statement does not violate the Hearsay Rule because it is being offered for the non-truth purpose of impeachment — to show that Harry has given conflicting accounts of the homicide. The prosecution then will try to offer Harry's other statements for the TOMA as prior consistent statements. Franco's attorney will object that the statements are inadmissible rehabilitation under CEC 791. The court should sustain the objection unless the prosecution can show that Harry's consistent statements were made prior to the grant of immunity, which is when the improper motive may have arisen, and prior to the inconsistent statement, in order to be relevant to the issue of rehabilitation and credibility. If, for instance, Harry were testifying that he told a friend that "I know Franco said he was the shooter, but Franco called and threatened me, and said that if I didn't name Doug as the shooter, I'd be dead meat," then Harry's prior consistent statement still would not be admissible because the consistent statement was made after the motive to lie first appeared (with the threat from Franco).

8. The court should overrule the objection and admit Bernice's preliminary hearing testimony as a prior inconsistent statement. Because Bernice is testifying in court now, her prior inconsistent statement will be admissible as long as she has the opportunity to explain or deny it. Being on the witness stand and not yet excused from testifying gives her that opportunity to explain or deny. Recall that an actual explanation is not required, and so the fact that Bernice claims a lack of memory and therefore would not be able to explain what she cannot remember does not prevent the use of this hearsay exception.

To establish the inconsistency, the court will evaluate whether Bernice seems to be deliberately evasive. If so, that evasiveness would be adequate evidence of implied inconsistency. Bernice's behavior suggests deliberate evasiveness given that she read her entire preliminary hearing transcript and still stated that her memory was not at all refreshed. If there were some medical reason for her lack of short-term memory such as a prescription medication, then the court might not find deliberate evasiveness and therefore would not find an inconsistency. However, on these facts, the court will most likely find that the preliminary hearing testimony is admissible to the extent that it contains prior inconsistent statements.

If this case were tried in federal court, the ruling on the prior inconsistent statement exclusion from the Hearsay Rule would not change. The preliminary hearing testimony was given under oath, Bernice is a witness subject to cross-examination, and thus the requirements of the FRE also are met. The former testimony exception in California (which was addressed in Chapter 5) would not apply unless Bernice was unavailable, and the lack of memory, if believed to be feigned, is not adequate to constitute unavailability. If the court believes her memory is truly faulty, however, then California cases provide precedent for the witness to be deemed unavailable. In contrast, in federal court, if a witness testifies to a lack of memory on the subject matter and the court finds by a preponderance of the evidence that she lacks such a memory, then she would be considered unavailable, and thus the former testimony exception would apply and her preliminary hearing testimony would be admissible.

Other Hearsay Exceptions

This chapter discusses hearsay exceptions that are based on the *content* of the statement. Recall that the exceptions in Chapter 5 apply only when the declarant is unavailable, and those in Chapter 6 apply only to parties or witnesses at trial. Unlike those exceptions, the exceptions in this chapter do not focus on the identity or availability of the declarant, but on the content of the statement. The exceptions described in this chapter apply regardless of whether the declarant is a party or witness and regardless of whether he is available or unavailable to testify. When using one of these exceptions in a criminal case, however, you must consider Confrontation Clause issues (as discussed in Chapter 5) if the declarant does not testify at trial.

This chapter is organized in two sections. The first section addresses statements that are usually spoken aloud rather than written down. These exceptions include spontaneous and contemporaneous statements, dying declarations, and statements expressing then-existing, direct states of mind. Statements made in these types of situations are admissible under a hearsay exception because they are deemed to be more reliable. Their reliability is heightened because the statements relate to a particular subject matter and occur under circumstances that make people less likely to lie.

The second half of this chapter discusses hearsay exceptions for statements found in written documents. These exceptions are for business records and public records. The rationale for these exceptions is that if the business or government relies on these written records, the records are also reliable enough to be admitted into a court of law.

In determining whether a statement meets the elements of these hearsay exceptions, the judge has to apply both the sufficiency and the preponderance standards. The sufficiency standard applies to the question of whether the statement was actually made by the declarant. (Recall from Chapter 6 that sufficiency is a low threshold.) Next, if there is sufficient evidence that the declarant made the out-of-court statement, then the judge applies the preponderance test to the other elements of the exception. (Recall from Chapter 6 that the preponderance test is a higher standard.) The rationale for this double standard is that the other elements determine how reliable the statement is, so the judge should determine whether these other elements are met before allowing the jury to hear the hearsay statement. The interaction of these two tests is addressed for each exception below.

Let us now turn to the oral statements.

SPONTANEOUS STATEMENTS

People often blurt things out when excited, scared, or surprised. When someone sneaks up behind another person and yells "Boo!" the other person may exclaim, "Ahh! You scared me!" Similarly, when riding in a car with a careless driver, the passenger might say in a shrill voice, "When that other car swerved into our lane just now, you didn't even notice! Good thing he swerved back into his own lane." These statements are made outside of a court hearing. The party seeking to offer any of these statements to prove their truth must consider the Hearsay Rule. However, CEC 1240 provides an exception for statements with this kind of content.

CEC §1240: Spontaneous statement
Evidence of a statement is not made inadmissible by the hearsay rule if the statement:
 (a) Purports to narrate, describe, or explain an act, condition or event perceived by the declarant; and
 (b) Was made spontaneously while the declarant was under the stress of excitement caused by such perception.

A spontaneous statement must have the following elements to be included under this exception:

1. the statement must purport to narrate, describe, or explain
2. an act, condition, or event

3. that was perceived by the declarant; and
4. the statement was made spontaneously
5. while the declarant was under the stress of excitement
6. caused by that perception.

Narrate, describe, or explain is the first element of the exception and requires that the statement must be an attempt to put into words what the declarant has observed. A description of a car accident or of a car that ran the red light would be the kind of statement that fits under this definition. However, statements that simply comment, such as "Uh-huh," would not meet the definition of spontaneous statements because they do not describe or explain anything.

The *act, condition or event* element refers to the situation that provoked the comment. Something must have happened, to prompt the declarant to speak. That something need not be an accident or injury, but applies to any sort of action. When a driver swiftly presses the accelerator on a car, the passenger might say "You're being a lead-footed driver!" Conditions are included to cover situations where someone observes a result, rather than an act. For instance, the statement "I didn't realize my car was that dented," would satisfy this element. Events can be positive (a wedding) or negative (a rear-end collision) and the definition broadly covers all of these situations.

The *perceived by the declarant* requirement reminds us that the declarant had to somehow observe the event with one or more of her five senses. Opinions and other statements lacking personal knowledge would not be admissible under this exception.

Made spontaneously means that the statement cannot be the product of thoughtful reflection. This is because time for reflection also provides an opportunity for fabrication. Generally, statements given in response to questions, such as in an interview, will not meet the spontaneous element. However, California courts have found that some statements that are a result of police or other questioning still can fit the exception if

1. the questions are not suggestive;
2. the victim or witness is still agitated and under the stress; and
3. other facts suggest reliability under the circumstances.

The *while under the stress* requirement helps to ensure that the statement was not fabricated or made after the opportunity for reflection about what would be best to say. While the declarant is still shaking, perspiring, woozy, or even in substantial pain from an accident, the declarant is deemed to still be "under the stress." Statements made during that time will meet this element. However, the longer the time lapse between the stressful event and the statement, the more opportunity for reflection and creative fabrication — thus the less reliable the statement may be. If the time lapse is because the declarant is unconscious or had not fully "returned to his senses," and was still under the stress, then deliberation and reflection are less likely, so the reliability remains at an acceptable level.

The statement must also be *caused by that perception*. The heightened reliability of spontaneous statements is predicated on the statement being somehow related to the stress. The causal link between the reason for the declarant's stress and the stressful act, event, or condition is important.

The Standards for Determining Whether the Elements Are Met

The judge will use the sufficiency standard to determine whether the declarant made the statement. Then, she will use the preponderance standard to determine whether each of the other elements is met. As discussed with other hearsay exceptions in Chapter 6, *only admissible evidence* can be used to lay the foundation for this hearsay exception. If the only evidence of the event in question is the statement itself, the California judge will not find an adequate foundation to support admitting the statement under this hearsay exception. If, on the other hand, there is testimony from a witness about the wreckage of the cars, that testimony is other evidence of the event (the crash). That testimony may provide sufficient support to allow the California judge to admit the spontaneous statement about the car crash accident under this hearsay exception.

The Rationale for this Exception

What is the rationale for this exception? When people observe things that startle them, they are often moved to describe what they see. People who see a car run a red light and almost hit another car may exclaim something like "Oh my gosh, that car just ran the red light and almost hit another car!" There is less opportunity to fabricate this spontaneous statement because the declarant is describing what she has just observed. Furthermore, the person she spoke to can tell right away whether the statement is true. For instance, if the declarant mentions to the passenger that a car just ran a red light when they have been driving on the freeway for the past ten miles, the passenger would say something like, "There are no street lights on the freeway. What are you talking about?" For that reason, the drafters of the CEC decided that the declarant is less likely to make an untrue statement describing what she has just observed, and therefore the CEC has an exception to the Hearsay Rule for these types of statements.

The obvious counterargument on the reliability issue is that even under the stress of excitement, people can still be concerned about promoting their self-interest and may think before they blurt something out. This exception thus provides an opportunity for quick thinkers to fabricate statements and use them later at trial. In addition, sometimes people are so freaked out due to their excitement or the stress of the event that they do not say what they mean, or they do not really know what they are saying. Either situation can lead to a credibility problem. For instance, while the car is skidding during an accident, the stressed-out driver may be yelling out a play-by-play ("Now we're spinning again and we're going to hit the tree!"), but the accuracy of the driver's perceptions may be impacted by the excessive stress of the impending collision.

Federal Rules of Evidence Compared: Notable Differences

There are two notable differences between FRE 803(2) and CEC 1240. Under the FRE, the content of the statement can be more broad. The statement must merely relate to the startling event. In contrast, under the CEC, the statement must purport to narrate, describe, or explain the event. In addition, to establish the foundation for the exception, the FRE permits the judge to consider inadmissible evidence when using the preponderance standard, whereas the CEC does not give the judge this option.

CONTEMPORANEOUS STATEMENTS

Some statements that describe or explain an event that is not necessarily exciting can be admitted under the contemporaneous statement exception. When the declarant is describing her own conduct *as it is occurring*, this hearsay exception can apply.

CEC §1241: Contemporaneous statement
Evidence of a statement is not made inadmissible by the hearsay rule if the statement: (a) Is offered to explain, qualify, or make understandable conduct of the declarant; and (b) Was made while the declarant was engaged in such conduct.

The timing of the statement is important because it must be made at the same time as the conduct or action that the statement is describing or explaining. For example, a passenger in a car asks the driver, "Why are you swerving so much?" and the driver responds "I'm swerving because there are deer crossing the road." The driver's response would satisfy the contemporaneous statement exception because the driver is explaining her own conduct of swerving while she is engaged in that conduct. Her conduct is contemporaneous with her statement about her conduct, and therefore it meets the requirements of this hearsay exception. However, the driver's response, although said during the event, would not be spontaneous since the event is not *stressful*. Thus that statement would not meet the spontaneous exception.

To meet the elements of the contemporaneous statements exception to the Hearsay Rule, the statement must

1. explain, qualify, or make understandable
2. conduct of the declarant, and
3. be made while the declarant was engaged in such conduct.

The Standards for Determining Whether the Elements Are Met

The judge will use the sufficiency standard to determine whether there is enough evidence to show that the declarant made the statement. In the swerving example above, the court likely will use the passenger's testimony that the driver made a statement while they were driving to meet the sufficiency test on the identity of the declarant. Then, the judge will apply the preponderance standard to evaluate the other elements. Here, the statement: (1) explains conduct (swerving so much), (2) of the declarant (the driver was the declarant and the one swerving the car), and it was (3) made while the declarant was engaged in that conduct (the driver was swerving as he was making the statement about swerving). If the judge finds it more than 50 percent likely that each element is met, then the preponderance test will be satisfied, and the statement will be admissible under the contemporaneous statement hearsay exception.

The Rationale for this Exception

The rationale for this exception is similar to that of spontaneous statements — there is less of an opportunity to fabricate when the declarant is describing what she is doing at the same time she is doing it. This reliability is assured by requiring that the statement be contemporaneous with the conduct and about that conduct. Thus, there is no problem with faulty memory or memory loss as time elapses. In the swerving car example above, if no deer were crossing the road, the passenger likely would say something like, "What are you talking about? Are you seeing things? There are no deer on this road." Because the declarant can be caught in a lie easily if the statement is inaccurate and someone else is present, the courts have enhanced confidence that the declarant is telling the truth.

However, this rationale does not hold true in all circumstances. For instance, imagine a situation where the declarant is speaking on the telephone. She may say, "I am walking out of my office door right now to meet you," when she is actually still sitting behind her desk checking her email. The listener on the other end of the phone conversation has no idea what the speaker is actually doing, so the speaker has less incentive to avoid lying. She cannot be caught as easily in a lie as she would if she described her actions to someone in person. Thus, the reliability of the statement can be lower in these circumstances.

As long as the preponderance standard is met for each of the elements, the statement will be admissible under this hearsay exception. The opposing party can then make an argument to the jury to discount the reliability of the hearsay statement, but this type of argument is about the weight of the evidence, not its admissibility.

Federal Rules of Evidence Compared: Substantive Differences

There are substantial differences between the CEC and FRE 803(1), which is entitled "present sense impression." FRE 803(1) focuses on the fact of description of an external matter, and includes statements about any event or other people's conduct as long as made while or shortly after personally perceiving that conduct. In contrast, under the CEC, the statement must be about the declarant's own conduct while she was engaged in that conduct.

STATE OF MIND DECLARATIONS

Indirect State of Mind Is Non-hearsay

Chapter 4 discussed some common non-truth (non-TOMA) purposes of hearsay and explained when a statement of one's state of mind can be offered for a non-truth purpose, which does not implicate the Hearsay Rule. When the statement refers to the declarant's "indirect state of mind," it is being offered as circumstantial evidence to prove the truth of something else, and the statement is non-hearsay.

For example, if offered to prove that the person was fearful, the statement "I thought he had a gun" would be indirect state of mind and therefore non-hearsay. Similarly, if offered to prove that someone was sad, the statement "I was crying at the time" would be indirect state of mind and non-hearsay. The statement "Smoke was practically coming out of my ears" can be admitted as non-hearsay to prove that a person was angry.

Direct State of Mind Requires a Hearsay Exception

However when the statement actually asserts the matter to be proven — such as "I am fearful," "I am sad", or "I am angry" — then technically these statements would be offered to prove the truth of the matters asserted in them. This is direct state of mind evidence, and these statements implicate the Hearsay Rule. For these types of statements, we can use the then existing state of mind exception to the Hearsay Rule. In summary, this hearsay exception applies to direct state of mind statements; indirect state of mind statements do not implicate the Hearsay Rule at all. Both types of statements are admissible in court.

CEC §1250: Statement of declarant's then existing mental or physical state

(a) Subject to 1252, evidence of a statement of the declarant's then existing state of mind, emotion, or physical sensation (including a statement of intent, plan, motive, design, mental feeling, pain, or bodily health) is not made inadmissible by the hearsay rule when:

(1) The evidence is offered to prove the declarant's state of mind, emotion or physical sensation at that time, or at any other time when it is itself an issue in the action; or

(2) The evidence is offered to prove or explain acts or conduct of the declarant.

(b) This section does not make admissible evidence of a statement of memory or belief to prove the fact remembered or believed.

For the then existing state of mind exception, there must be a statement of declarant's then existing state of mind, emotion, or physical sensation that is either

1. offered to prove declarant's state of mind at that time or at any other time at issue in the case, or
2. offered to prove or explain the declarant's own conduct or acts.

Note that a statement containing a *memory or belief is not admissible* to prove the fact remembered or believed under this exception. For instance, when a person says, "I have been in so much pain since the car accident," she is talking about several things. First, she is talking about her current pain in the phrase "so much pain." Second, she is talking about her past pain because of the phrase "have been in." Third, she is relying on her memory that the pain has been with her "since the car accident."

If the statement is offered to prove her *current* pain, those portions of it that refer to her current pain are admissible under CEC 1250. However, if she wants to prove her past pain, the statement would not be admissible under this hearsay exception because this exception does not cover previously existing pain. (Refer to Chapter 5 for a discussion of the hearsay exception for past state of mind.)

If she seeks to offer the statement to prove that the car accident was the cause of her pain, then that would involve her memory of the car accident, her memory of when her pain first began, and her belief that the car accident was the cause. Because this hearsay exception cannot be used to prove her memory or belief, those portions of the statement would not be admissible under this exception.

Determining Whether the Content of the Statement Involves Declarant's State of Mind

Of the declarant's means the statement must be about the person speaking (like the contemporaneous statements under CEC 1241 discussed above). Here, there is no need to prove firsthand knowledge because every person is presumed to know her own thoughts, fears, emotions and pain. The sufficiency test is used to determine whether the statement was made by the declarant herself.

State of mind is the shorthand reference used in the book and by many evidence professors for all types of feelings, emotions, pain, and sensations. "State of mind" also includes intent, motive, plan, and design. Was the conduct intentional or reckless? Did the declarant plan this out before doing it or act in the heat of passion? Sensation or physical condition includes pain as well as bodily health. Statements such as "My head hurts," and "I feel better now" fit within this definition. Emotion includes mental feeling like being happy, sad, or angry.

The Timing Element of the Statement: *Then Existing*

The phrase *then existing* refers to how the declarant feels at the time that she made the statement. Some students get confused because the phrase suggests a past time period, but the word *then* in this context means at the time that the declarant is saying the words that are sought to be offered in court. The fact that the statement was made out of court means that it was made prior to getting to trial, and thus in the past, but that is not the relevant inquiry. Instead, looking at the statement itself, the words must describe how the declarant felt at the time that she originally said the words in that statement.

For example, if the declarant says, "I am so happy right now!" she is describing how she is feeling while she is speaking the words. If the declarant says, "I was so upset yesterday," then she is not describing how she feels as she speaks, but rather how she felt at some time prior to the moment in which she uttered the words. Describing how one felt at a prior time requires reliance on memory, and memories can fade or falter, even from day to day. Because of this decreased reliability, statements based on memory are specifically excluded by CEC 1250. Some will be admissible under CEC 1251 (which is addressed in Chapter 5).

Using the Statement to Prove Subsequent Conduct

The alternative *or when offered to prove the declarant's conduct or acts* refers to using statements as circumstantial evidence to prove *subsequent* conduct by the declarant. How many times have you talked to a friend, explained your plans for the evening, and heard him say, "I'll meet you there," but then the friend never shows up? If you told another friend, "My best friend and I are going to meet you at the club," we can use your statement later in court to prove that you intended to meet at the club. We can also use your statement as circumstantial evidence that you probably went to the club. However, we cannot use your statement to prove that your best friend probably went to the club as well.

This specific limitation on the declarant's own conduct is important because courts presume people know their own plans, pains, feelings, thoughts, and desires, but not that they know someone else's. For example, when a declarant says, "I plan to travel to China with my friend Michelle, and we are leaving our cell phones behind," that statement can be circumstantial evidence that the declarant actually did go to China without a cell phone, and therefore is unreachable. But this statement cannot be used to prove that Michelle went to China with the declarant or that Michelle left her cell phone behind. At trial, the portion of the statement describing the declarant's plan will be admissible. However, the court will redact, or cut out, the portions of the statement relating to Michelle and her plans.

The Trustworthiness Element

The reference in CEC 1250 to CEC 1252 makes statements about then existing state of mind inadmissible if made under circumstances such as to indicate its lack of trustworthiness. The courts will consider factors such as coercion or undue influence, the passage of time, motivations to lie or misrepresent, self-serving expressions of remorse, as well as bias and grudges in deciding whether the circumstances indicate a lack of trustworthiness.

Federal Rules of Evidence Compared: Substantive Differences

There are two differences in FRE 803(3). The first minor distinction is that the FRE provides an exception to memories or beliefs about wills. While the CEC has a similar provision, it is contained separately in CEC 1260 and 1261 (both of which are discussed in Chapter 5).

The second difference is that the FRE does not contain the language about "conduct of the declarant," so litigants have tried to use this exception to help prove the intentions or conduct of people other than the declarant. These efforts resulted in what is known in federal courts as the *Hillmon* doctrine (which refers to using the declarant's state of mind to prove the declarant's own subsequent conduct) and the prohibition against second party *Hillmon* (which is when the declarant's state of mind is used to prove the someone else's subsequent conduct). Thus, the result is the same as under the CEC, excluding statements used to prove the conduct of someone other than the declarant.

FRE 803(4) contains a related exception for statements about medical conditions made for the purpose of diagnosis or treatment. There is no corresponding CEC section (except CEC 1253, which applies to medical information in the context of child abuse only).

Multiple Levels of Hearsay

Now that you have learned a number of hearsay exceptions, you are ready to consider the issue of multiple levels of hearsay. For instance, Larry is on trial for the murder of Sheri. At some point prior to the trial, Larry told his friend Maria, "I knew she was going to die because Sheri said, 'You're killing me Larry!' right before she passed out." At Larry's murder trial, the prosecution wants Maria to testify to exactly what Larry told her about Sheri's death. A portion of Larry's statement is quoting an out-of-court statement made by Sheri. As discussed in Chapter 6, Larry's own words ("I knew she was going to die because Sheri said") would constitute a party admission and thus would be admissible as an exception to the Hearsay Rule.

But the portion of the statement where Larry is quoting Sheri's out-of-court statement ("You're killing me Larry!") is not a party admission because Sheri is not a party to the litigation. The prosecution would need to find another hearsay exception to admit Sheri's statement. One possibility is to consider admitting Sheri's words under the spontaneous statement exception. Recall that this exception requires that the statement be made (1) describing an act perceived by the declarant, (2) while the declarant was under the stress of excitement, (3) caused by that perception. If Sheri felt Larry mortally wound her, was stressed about that situation, and made her statement as a result of that mortal wounding, then her words would be admissible as a spontaneous statement. Thus, the prosecution could use Maria's testimony to prove the truth asserted in both Sheri's words and Larry's words under the multiple hearsay doctrine.

Another possibility would be to admit Sheri's statement as a dying declaration. As noted in Chapter 5, a dying declaration requires that

1) a dying person
2) make a statement about the cause or circumstances of his death
3) while under the belief of impending death.

If Sheri was dying at the time she made the statement and believed that her own death was impending, then this statement that Larry is killing her can be admissible to prove the truth of the matter asserted (TOMA).

Keep in mind that if there are multiple layers of hearsay, you must analyze each layer of hearsay to look for an exception or a non-truth purpose. If each layer meets the requirements for a hearsay exception, then the Hearsay Rule will not bar admission of the entire statement, including the various levels of hearsay.

SOME LESS COMMON HEARSAY EXCEPTIONS

The CEC contains several additional hearsay exceptions, but these arise much less frequently. (The full text of the following CEC sections is included in the appendix.) CEC 1310 provides an exception for statements concerning the declarant's own family history, which includes birth, marriage, divorce, race, and ancestry. CEC 1311 similarly applies to the family history of a relative or intimate associate of the declarant, if the declarant is unavailable. Evidence of the reputation within the family or the community concerning family history is covered under the exceptions of CEC 1313 and 1314. Statements about property boundaries have an exception through CEC 1323.

The CEC provides a number of other exceptions for statements about reputation, including reputation concerning community history (CEC 1320), public interest in property (CEC 1321), boundary or custom affecting land (CEC 1322), and reputation concerning the character of a person in the community in which he habitually associates (CEC 1324). While CEC 1324 provides the hearsay exception, such evidence will still be susceptible to a character evidence objection (which is addressed in Chapter 2).

Examples

1. Zento worked as an attendant at a gas station, which was robbed one night while he was on duty. The police arrived about 15 minutes later and asked why Zento had called. Zento was visibly shaking and kept wiping sweat from his forehead while he described the robber's height, weight, eye, skin, and hair color. Zento also remembered the license plate number of the motorcycle on which the robber had sped away. Zento's description helped the police to focus their search on Yuri, who was subsequently arrested for the robbery. At Yuri's trial, the prosecution put the police officer on the stand to repeat Zento's statement describing the robber and the motorcycle. Yuri's counsel objected to the police officer's testimony as hearsay. How should the prosecution respond, how should the court rule, and why?

2. One night after drinking a 12-pack of beer and watching a disappointing Monday night football game, Ronald beat his wife Sally and then threatened to kill her if she went to the police. Ronald passed out a few minutes later from all of the beer, and Sally gathered up her son Quentin and went straight to the nearest police department. Before any-one could say anything to her, she burst into tears and started speaking very quickly and quietly. Sally told the police, "My husband Ronald beat me tonight, and he also choked me. Then he threatened to kill me if I came to the police. So I waited until he passed out to come here. Can you please help me? I am afraid that he will kill me." The police arrested Ronald, and he is now on trial for spousal abuse. Sally was too scared to show up in court, and therefore the prosecution seeks to offer the tes-timony of a police officer who heard Sally's statement when she showed up at the station on the night of the beating. Ronald's attorney objects to this evidence as inadmissible hearsay. How should the prosecution respond? How should the court rule, and why?

3. Portia poured gasoline over her sleeping husband Ollie and then lit a match, engulfing Ollie in flames. Their son Nathan wrapped Ollie in a blanket and called 911. The firefighters quickly doused the flames, and the emergency medical technicians came to tend to Ollie within ten minutes of the call. While the EMTs were dressing Ollie's wounds, Ollie said, "My wife, Portia, is the one who lit me on fire." When the police arrived, they questioned Ollie for about five minutes. Ollie could respond with only "yes" or "no" answers because he was in too much pain to speak. Ollie asked the officers if he was going to die, and the rookie officer responded, "Anything can happen, sir. But we'll catch the person who did this to you, with you or without you." Ollie then murmured the name, "Nathan," and then he passed out from the pain medication. Ollie died on the way to this hospital. The police arrested Nathan and Portia and charged both with murder. At trial, the prosecution seeks to put the EMT on the witness stand to testify to Ollie's statement that Portia is the culprit. Portia's defense counsel objects. How should the prosecution respond, and how should the court rule?

4. Assuming the same facts as in Example 3, how would your answer change in federal court? Assume too that Portia's defense counsel also seeks to offer the rookie police officer's statement that he heard Ollie murmur "Nathan" before he passed out. Nathan's defense counsel objects. How should the court rule, and why?

5. While updating her Internet dating profile, Irena told her friend Gena, "I only go out with men who are at least 6 feet 4 inches tall, with blue or green eyes, and they need to be muscular, too." Irena saw the Internet profile of a man whose physical description seemed to match her preferences, started emailing him through the Internet dating service, and decided to go out with him on Friday night a few weeks later. Irena told Gena, "I found a guy whose profile is exactly what I'm looking for. We are meeting at the bar at TGI Saturdays this weekend. If when he shows up I can tell he lied on his profile, I'll just stay for one drink and then leave." Irena never returned from that first date. The Internet service provided information about the men who had been chatting with Irena in the last few weeks before her disappearance, and Hammond's name was on the list. Hammond is 5 feet 8 inches tall, very thin, and has brown eyes, but his Internet profile describes him as 6 feet 4 inches tall, with green eyes. A few days later, Irena was found tied up in an extra bedroom at Hammond's home. Hammond is now on trial for the kidnapping of Irena, and his defense is that she consented to being tied up and held hostage because that is a "turn on" for her. The prosecution calls Gena to the witness stand, so she can testify to Irena's statement about who she would be willing to date and from whom she would walk away.

Hammond's defense counsel objects to the evidence as irrelevant and inadmissible hearsay. How should the court rule, and why?

6. Ursula was shopping in her favorite department store, admiring a leather coat in the dressing room mirror, when she heard the sales clerk standing outside the dressing room door yell, "What are you doing with that gun? Please don't hurt us!" Ursula then heard a man's voice say, "Just give me the cash and some gift cards, and I'll leave you all alone." Ursula ducked down in the dressing room stall, called 911 on her cell phone, and exclaimed, "The department store is being robbed!" Victoria was in the stall next to Ursula, and when she heard Ursula speaking on the phone about the robbery, Victoria whispered, "The robber is the same guy who was buying six bottles of aftershave at the cosmetics counter about five minutes ago. Have them check with the cosmetics sales clerk." Ursula repeated Victoria's statement to the 911 operator. The robber was gone by the time the police arrived, but when the police checked with the cosmetics clerk, only one person had purchased six bottles of aftershave that afternoon, and he had paid with a credit card. The police were able to track down the address of the credit card holder, and went to the home of Tommy, where they found stacks of gift cards and cash. Tommy was arrested and put on trial for robbery, and the prosecution sought to admit Ursula's statements to the 911 operator. Tommy's counsel objected on the grounds of inadmissible hearsay. How should the prosecution respond, and how should the court rule?

7. Cherie, Dani, Edna, and Fran are in the same study group. Given the commitment of time and energy for their joint outlines, the members decided to get life insurance policies on one another so that if one member died, the others would have enough money to get by without staying in law school to get their degrees. After their first midterm examination, Dani asked Edna, "Will you meet me at Chowdy's restaurant for dinner tonight? We can celebrate acing our first law school exam!" Edna responded, "That sounds great. I'll definitely meet you there." Dani then told Fran, "Edna and I are going to meet at Chowdy's tonight for dinner to celebrate. Do you want to join us?" Fran said, "Sure, I'll meet you there at 8 p.m." While walking from the parking lot to the restaurant, Dani called Cherie, and said, "Hey, I'm here at Chowdy's. Edna and Fran are planning to meet me there. I hope they get here soon." About 30 minutes later, at 8:15 p.m., a bomb exploded in Chowdy's restaurant, killing everyone inside. The bodies were too obliterated to be positively identified. Cherie filed a claim to collect on the three life insurance policies of her fellow study group members, but the insurance company paid only on Dani's policy. Cherie used what she learned in the first year of law school to sue the insurance company to get payments on the other policies also. She sought to admit her own testimony about the phone

call she received from Dani shortly before the explosion. The insurance company objected to Cherie's testimony as inadmissible hearsay. How should the court rule, and why? Is there any difference in the analysis or outcome if the case were tried in federal court?

8. Alicia told her husband Brad, "I wish we were no longer married." Brad, shocked and surprised, collapsed into a chair and moaned, "I'll change. I'll do whatever you want. Just don't leave me." Alicia had had enough of Brad's "drama" and promises to change and replied, "I cannot forgive you for the past. I want to end this marriage." Three days later, Alicia disappeared, leaving her clothes, purse, and car behind. The police questioned Brad, and he explained that Alicia had planned to leave him, and so she probably just decided to walk away, instead of trying to deal with the breakup in person. Despite never finding a body, the district attorney charged Brad with the murder of Alicia. In his defense, Brad seeks to offer his own testimony that Alicia said, "I cannot forgive you for the past. I want to end this marriage," to help prove that Alicia voluntarily moved away and therefore did not meet with foul play. The prosecution objected based on hearsay. How should the defendant respond, and how should the court rule?

9. A patient tells her doctor, "My head is killing me. It has been hurting badly, and I have been having severe neck and back pain since the speeding blue Mercedes SLK-500 rear-ended me on the freeway. If this turns out to be no big deal, I plan to work for another decade to support my family." Moments later, the patient suffered a seizure and went into a coma. She died several days later from a brain hemorrhage. The patient's husband, a stay-at-home father, sued the owner and driver of the blue Mercedes for wrongful death and sought damages for lost future earnings. The plaintiff husband called the doctor to the witness stand, to testify about the cause of the patient's death and her statement just before her coma. The defendant Mercedes driver objects as inadmissible hearsay. The plaintiff responded that the state of mind exception permits the evidence. How should the court rule? Would the ruling be different in federal court?

Explanations

1. The prosecution should argue that Zento's statement is admissible under the spontaneous statement exception. The statement meets the first requirement of spontaneous statements because it describes an event (the robbery) perceived by the declarant (Zento) and explains who conducted the robbery (in the description of Yuri). Because Zento was visibly shaking at the time that he gave his statement, it is likely that he was still under the stress of excitement of having been robbed at the time that he spoke, even though 15 minutes had passed. The other element is whether the statement was "made spontaneously." If the police officer

asked Zento any leading questions, this element may not be met. However, some California courts have found that a 15-minute interval between the stressful event and the statement is sufficiently close to meet the spontaneous requirement as long as the police officer's questions to the victim were not suggestive. Here, the police officer asked an open question, "Why did you call us?" which is not suggestive. As long as there is other evidence of the robbery in addition to Zento's description of "the robber," the foundation will be established and the spontaneous statement exception will apply.

2. The prosecution should respond that Sally's statement meets the requirement for the hearsay exception for a spontaneous statement. The statement is spontaneous because it purports to describe the stressful event (the beating), which was perceived by the declarant (Sally experienced the pain and fear of the beating). The only question is whether Sally was still under the stress of excitement caused by such perception. The fact that she was crying and speaking quietly and very quickly all support the prosecution's argument that she was still under the stress of the beating when she spoke to the police. Still, some time had passed between the beating and her statement.

   The defense will likely argue that too much time passed, and that the passage of time would make the statement less reliable. While she waited for Ronald to pass out, she could have had time to fabricate a story. If a substantial amount of time has passed, then the statement will not meet the spontaneous element. If less than 30 minutes have elapsed (as in the real court case), then spontaneity still can be established. Sally made her statement without any prompting or suggestive questions from the police, and because of her physical symptoms it is likely that the court will find that she still was under the stress of excitement and will admit the statement about the beating. Sally's statement regarding her fear that Ronald will kill her is a statement of her then existing state of mind and would be admissible under that exception.

3. The prosecution should respond that Ollie's statement about Portia meets two hearsay exceptions. First, it meets the spontaneous statement exception because it is explaining an event (his being lit on fire), and it was made while he was still suffering from the pain and stress of that event. Not more than about 15 minutes have passed since he was lit on fire, and Ollie still was experiencing the pain of his burns when he made this statement. Therefore, the statement will be admissible under the spontaneous statement exception. The "yes" or "no" answers to questions may not meet the requirement of spontaneity because questions that can be answered "yes" or "no" are likely to be suggestive or leading. If the specific questions actually asked were not suggestive, then the spontaneity element could be met. The contemporaneous statement exception

will not work because the statement is not explaining conduct of the declarant, but rather explains the conduct of his wife. If any of the "yes" or "no" questions were directed at Ollie's own conduct, then they still will not be admissible because they were not made contemporaneously while he was engaged in that conduct. Second, the dying declaration exception (discussed in Chapter 5) could also apply as long as Ollie subjectively believed that he was dying based on his personal knowledge regarding the extent of his injuries and pain. Being in severe pain with burns over a significant portion of one's body can lead a person to believe that death is imminent, and the rookie police officer's comment, "with you or without you," could contribute to the belief of impending death. The judge will have to determine whether she finds that Ollie had this belief, and if so, the statement will be admitted for the jury's consideration.

4. If the case in Example 3 were tried in federal court, the statements and responses to questions could be admitted as present sense impressions (immediately thereafter) or as excited utterances made while Ollie still was under the stress of excitement caused by the event. The statement under belief of impending death exception would apply in this murder prosecution because in criminal court it applies only in homicide cases. The question about Nathan's name brings up reliability issues. When the statements are prodded or the questions are suggestive or closed, there is a greater chance that the questioner manipulated the statement. The mere fact that the victim uttered his son's name should not be enough to link his son to the murder committed by the victim's wife.

5. The court should overrule both objections and admit the statement. The statement is relevant to show that Irena was less likely to go through with a date with Hammond once she saw his lack of height and undesirable eye color. Thus, it is less likely that she would have accompanied him willingly to his home or let him tie her up in the spare bedroom. It would be relevant also to show the identity of the kidnapper. Under the state of mind hearsay exception, the statement could be offered to show the declarant Irena's plan (to date men with a certain height and eye color), and to help prove the declarant's own conduct — that she did not want or plan to accompany a man who looked like Hammond to his home.

6. The prosecution should explain that Ursula's statement to the 911 operator that the store was being robbed is a spontaneous statement narrating or describing a stressful event. While Ursula did not actually see the robbery occurring, the fact that she heard the voices during the robbery is enough to meet the "perceived by the declarant" element. The robbery was ongoing when Ursula made the telephone call to 911, and thus she

was still under the stress of excitement caused by finding out the store was being robbed. Tommy's lawyers may argue that Ursula had no personal knowledge of whether the store actually was being robbed, but as long as there is evidence other than her statement that there was a robbery, her lack of personal knowledge about the fact of a robbery will not be fatal to the use of this hearsay exception.

In addition, the defense counsel may argue that the second statement describing the man who had purchased the aftershave was not based on Ursula's perception, but rather was Victoria's perception and thus the statement would not be admissible through Ursula. This gets into the issue of multiple levels of hearsay. You must examine each level of hearsay to see whether there are exceptions that apply to each level. Here, Victoria's statement to Ursula would also meet the requirements of the spontaneous statement exception because it describes an act (the robbery) that she perceived, while she (Victoria) was under the stress of excitement caused by that robbery. Ursula's statement to the 911 operator also meets this exception. Therefore, both levels of hearsay have applicable exceptions, and the court should admit the statements.

7. The court should overrule the hearsay objection to Dani's phone call if it is used to prove Dani's contemporaneous conduct — that she was actually in the restaurant shortly before the time of the explosion. However, the court should sustain the objection to the extent that it is used to prove the truth of matter asserted — that Edna and Fran also were at the restaurant. If Cherie or someone else had overhead Fran's statement to Dani, or Edna's statement to Dani, then those statements could be admitted to show Edna and Fran's plan to join Dani, which would be circumstantial evidence that they actually did follow through on their plan to join Dani at Chowdy's restaurant at about 8 p.m. In federal court, the result would be the same because the present sense impression hearsay exception would allow the statement that Dani is there at Chowdy's. The *Hillmon* doctrine (specifically the second party *Hillmon* rule) prevents the use of the state of mind statement by Dani to prove that Edna and Fran acted in conformity with the plan (to meet at 8 p.m.) that Dani articulated.

8. The defendant should respond that he is not offering his testimony about Alicia's statement for the TOMA, but rather as circumstantial evidence of Alicia's state of mind in terms of her plan to leave him. As indirect state of mind evidence, it will be admissible without the need for a hearsay exception. Strategically, however, Brad may prefer to offer Alicia's statement for the TOMA — that she was leaving him. In that case, the statement would be direct state of mind evidence, which requires a hearsay exception. The direct state of mind exception would permit Brad to offer the evidence of her then existing state of mind, which is that she planned

to leave him. That exception would not permit Brad to offer a statement of memory or belief to prove the fact remembered or believed.

Thus a question arises about the portion of her statement about not forgiving him for the past. Because her statement is in the present tense — that she cannot, at the time that she is speaking, forgive Brad for past events, it will be admissible under this state of mind exception. If Alicia had commented on those past events, however, then the substance of her comment would include her statement of memory or belief as to the existence of those past unforgivable events and would not meet the requirements for the state of mind exception. Brad could turn to the exception for past state of mind (as addressed in Chapter 5). That exception requires unavailability and that Alicia's state of mind is an issue in the litigation, which is not certain based on the facts provided.

9. The state of mind exception can be used to prove the direct state of mind, which includes the patient's feelings of pain and other bodily sensations about which she spoke. In addition, her statement of her plan to work for decades would be admissible to show her own future plans and would be relevant to the lost future earnings claim in the lawsuit. However, the patient's statement of past facts (the car hit me, from behind) would not be admissible under this hearsay exception because they are statements of memory or belief, to prove the fact remembered or believed.

    In *federal court*, the plaintiff could use the medical diagnosis hearsay exception to admit the portion of the statement about the cause of the injury as long as it was pertinent to the diagnosis or treatment. Knowing someone was hit by a car from behind is pertinent to a diagnosis of head, neck, and back pain. Knowing that the car was speeding on the freeway might be pertinent given that the speed at impact influences medical diagnosis and treatment. It is unlikely that the make, model, or color of the car (blue Mercedes SLK-500) would have any relevance to the diagnosis or treatment, and therefore that part of the statement would not be admissible under this hearsay exception and would have to be redacted.

HEARSAY EXCEPTIONS FOR DOCUMENTS

The CEC contains additional hearsay exceptions that generally apply to documents that were created outside of court. When a party seeks to admit the statements in the documents for the truth of a matter asserted in the documents, then a hearsay issue arises. The CEC has several exceptions to permit a party to admit these documents under certain circumstances.

Recall that Chapter 6 explains how to use the past recollection recorded hearsay exception. That exception applies when a person writes down information while it is fresh in his memory or directs someone else to record the information while it is fresh. If that writing was created by or on behalf of a person who is a witness at trial, and that witness cannot remember enough to testify fully and accurately at trial, then the writing can be read into evidence for the TOMA. Recall that this exception applies only when the person who made the writing or directed that the writing be made is present to testify at trial.

The exceptions in the remainder of this chapter need not have been created by a person who is a witness at trial. Because there is not necessarily an opportunity to cross-examine the person who created the documents, the courts require other indicia of reliability. With these exceptions, the indications of reliability stem from the fact that the records were made, and how they are used, kept, and stored for business or public purposes.

BUSINESS RECORDS

Business records are out-of-court written statements. When they are offered into evidence to help prove the TOMA in the business record, admitting the document implicates the Hearsay Rule. The necessity of using evidence in the form of business records is high because it would be impossible in many circumstances to find an employee of the business who remembers a particular transaction such that she is able to testify competently about it.

To the extent the matters really are routine — such as an insurance company sending out a renewal notice to a customer whose policy will expire soon — it is not likely that any witness can testify accurately from memory and personal knowledge as to whether and when she mailed out an individual renewal notice. Moreover, because many businesses have a division of labor, it would be unduly burdensome to require each individual who played some role in a particular business transaction to come to court to testify about the role that she played. Therefore, an exception was created to help satisfy the need for such documents in trials.

For instance, if a homeowner in a foreclosure action needs to prove that he made a payment on his mortgage each month during the calendar year, there are several ways that he can do so. Bringing a copy of his check register with the dates, check numbers, and amounts of payments would be one way. The check register will show that the homeowner made a notation about writing a check, but does not prove whether the checks actually were written, or if written, whether they were actually sent to the financial institution that holds the mortgage.

The homeowner's bank statement would be a better form of proof because a bank statement shows the date and amount for all checks cashed, thus proving that certain checks were written for the amount of the mortgage and cashed by someone. The bank statement might not include the payee information, so it would at most prove that the homeowner did write checks to someone for that amount. Still, an unscrupulous homeowner could be writing the checks to cash, and pocketing the money.

Even more reliable proof would be the end-of-year mortgage statement from the financial institution, showing the date each payment was received and the amount. That mortgage statement is an out-of-court statement, and if offered to prove that certain payments were made on certain dates, it constitutes hearsay. If a party tried to use witnesses in court to prove up each payment, she would need numerous witnesses. The first might be the mail clerk who opened the letter containing the check. Second, she would call the delivery clerk who sent the check to the accounting office. Third, she would bring in the accounting personnel who input the date and amount of the check. Fourth would be the person who delivers the actual check to the bank for payment. The fifth witness would likely be the person who is informed when the check clears. The final witness would be the person who credits the amount to the homeowner's account.

If the business is a large financial institution or has a significant amount of business each day, it is unlikely that each of these people will have a specific memory of this particular homeowner's check to be able to testify based on personal knowledge. Hence, there is a need for a hearsay exception to permit the use of the mortgage statement instead of requiring the testimony of numerous witnesses.

The reliability of business records is high because the courts assume that if businesses depend on their own internal record-keeping to make the business work, then the courts should be able to rely on that record-keeping in the search for truth. Still, trustworthiness is the important consideration. The record must have been prepared by individuals whose job is to accurately prepare those records in the regular course of business. These records often include multiple layers of hearsay (addressed in the section above), and thus you should analyze them in a step-by-step manner.

The Elements of the Hearsay Exception for Business Records

First, there must be a business. *Business* is defined rather broadly to include commercial enterprises as well as churches and synagogues, governmental activities, and even non-profit organizations.

CEC §1271: Business record

Evidence of a writing made as a record of an act, condition, or event is not made inadmissible by the hearsay rule when offered to prove the act, condition, or event if:

(a) The writing was made in the regular course of a business;

(b) The writing was made at or near the time of the act, condition or event;

(c) The custodian or other qualified witness testifies to its identity and the mode of its preparation; and

(d) The sources of information and method and time of preparation were such as to indicate its trustworthiness.

The requirement that the writing be *made in the regular course of business* is important because the reliability stems from the fact that the record is regularly made or kept, systematically checked, and relied on by the business enterprise. Records made in response to a special event or divergence from normal practice would not fit within this element of this exception. Such special records are not systematically made, checked, and relied on and therefore are not created in the regular course of the business's operation.

Next there is a temporal requirement that the writing was made *at or near the time of the act, condition, or event recorded.* Because the record is only as reliable as the person who makes it and because memories deteriorate over time, this element is important to support reliability. There is no set time limit to define *near* because businesses have such different practices as to when and how often various records are generated. The judge has discretion to decide if the record was made near enough in time to satisfy the reliability concern.

A custodian or other qualified witness must either *testify as to identity and mode of preparation* of the record or use the subpoena-affidavit exception described below. The proponent of the business record must produce sufficient admissible evidence to support a finding that the business record is authentic, which means that the record is what it purports to be. (The specifics of the authentication requirement and its elements are discussed in Chapter 11.) The custodian is the person in charge of ensuring that the records are maintained and could include an administrative assistant, a supervisor, or even the owner of the company. The custodian or other qualified witness does not have to have personal knowledge about the making of the record because that would defeat much of the usefulness of the rule. The witness must have enough specific knowledge to sufficiently describe how such records are made and kept, and to identify the particular document as that type of business record.

The subpoena-affidavit exception of CEC 1562 permits offering business records without first calling a knowledgeable witness or custodian when a subpoena duces tecum is issued and the records are accompanied by an affidavit from the custodian or other qualified witness, setting out the information required under CEC 1271.

Finally, the *sources of information* and *method and time of preparation* must indicate *trustworthiness*. The judge has substantial discretion here. The judge can exclude information that is provided by those with no business duty to report it, as well as information prepared in contemplation of litigation.

Computer data is considered to be within the definition of *writing*, and thus is also subject to the best and secondary evidence rules that are discussed in Chapter 11. CEC 1552 creates a presumption that a computer program or printout is an accurate representation of what it purports to represent. People input much of the data. People can make mistakes or misinterpret the data, and they can intentionally misrepresent data that the reliable computer program then uses to come up with an unreliable result. If the opponent presents contrary evidence, then the proponent must convince the judge by a preponderance of the evidence that the record is what it purports to be.

Federal Rules of Evidence Compared: Notable Differences

One difference between the CEC and FRE 803(6) on business records is that the FRE is more specific and explicit about the personal knowledge requirement for the person transmitting the information and also requires that the record be not only made, *but also kept in the ordinary course of the business*. In addition, the CEC and FRE have different default assumptions about trustworthiness for both business records and the absence of an entry in a business record. Under the CEC, the proponent first must convince the judge that the record is sufficiently trustworthy, whereas under the FRE, if the record is made in the course of regularly conducted business activity, it will be admissible *unless* the opponent provides enough information to convince the judge of a lack of trustworthiness.

THE ABSENCE OF AN ENTRY

Is the *absence* of an entry an assertion? When the person who inputs payments received by a business fails to make a notation that a payment was received, that lack of a notation may be tantamount to the assertion that "no payment was received." For that reason, the absence of an entry in a business record can constitute hearsay. Because so many larger businesses consider the absence of such an entry to be a substitution for the assertion that no payment was received and because preexisting case law supports this argument, the CEC contains a hearsay exception that applies to permit evidence of the absence of a record to be used to prove that the act or event, such as a payment, was never made.

CEC §1272: Absence of an entry

Evidence of the absence from the records of a business of a record of an asserted act, condition, or event is not made inadmissible by the hearsay rule when offered to prove the nonoccurrence of the act or event, or the nonexistence of the condition, if:

(a) It was the regular course of that business to make records of all such acts, conditions, or events at or near the time of the act, condition, or event and to preserve them; and

(b) The sources of information and method and time of preparation of the records of that business were such that the absence of a record of an act, condition, or event is a trustworthy indication that the act or event did not occur or the condition did not exist.

If a business *regularly* makes a particular type of entry into its records under CEC 1271, then the absence of that type of entry for a particular client or transaction will be the equivalent of the assertion that the act or event did not occur and therefore will be admissible under the absence of an entry exception. Use CEC 1271 to identify when a particular absence might constitute hearsay, and if it does, then use the checklist below to determine whether the requirements for the hearsay exception are met.

To meet the absence of an entry exception, there must be

1. an entry absent from the business record
2. where, under CEC 1271, such an entry would have been recorded
3. that is offered to prove either the nonoccurrence of the act or event or the nonexistence of the condition.

RECORDS BY A PUBLIC EMPLOYEE

Many public records also would meet the business records exception, as many business records of governmental agencies can satisfy the public records exception. When public employees record information as part of their public duties, however, then there is no need to rely on the business records exception because there is a specific exception for public employee records.

 CEC §1280: Record by public employee
Evidence of a writing made as a record of an act, condition or event is not made inadmissible by the hearsay rule when offered in any civil or criminal proceeding to prove the act, condition, or event if all of the following applies:

(a) The writing was made by and within the scope of duty of a public employee.

(b) The writing was made at or near the time of the act, condition, or event.

(c) The sources of information and method and time of preparation were such as to indicate its trustworthiness.

The rationale for this exception is that reliability is increased based on the fact that the public employee has a duty to make or provide certain records of public activities, knowing that those records can be relied on in governmental activities. In order for it to be a record by a public employee, it must be

1. made by and within the scope of duty
2. of a public employee
3. at or near the time of the act, condition, or event, and
4. the sources must indicate trustworthiness.

The public employee record exception requires that the report be *made by and within the scope of duty of a public employee*, and thus is not as broad as the language of the business record exception of *in the regular course of business*. The public records exemption does not require the testimony of a witness as to the identity and mode of preparation for the record as long as the trustworthiness element is satisfied in some other way.

The *scope of duty* refers to the job description or general duties assigned to the employee on a regular or even irregular basis. As long as the employee was performing her job by creating the record, it will satisfy this element. For instance, coroners have a duty to accurately record death information while court clerks have a duty to accurately record court decisions, rulings, and case dispositions.

The timing and trustworthiness factors are the same as those discussed above for the business records exception.

PUBLIC EMPLOYEE RECORDS IN CRIMINAL CASES

Remember from Chapter 5 that the Confrontation Clause provides a federal constitutional right that protects criminal defendants when the prosecution seeks to use testimonial hearsay statements against them. Business records and public records generally are not considered to be testimonial and therefore do not implicate the Confrontation Clause analysis when used against criminal defendants. However, when the record is from a law enforcement agency, the surrounding circumstances and substance of the record must be analyzed to determine whether the Confrontation Clause is implicated. When the public record is prepared by crime scene laboratory technicians, it likely will be testimonial.

For instance, a blood analyst collects samples from a crime scene and performs tests to determine whether the blood type matches that of the defendant. When the analyst performs the tests and reaches a conclusion about a blood match, that analyst will prepare a report that describes the collection of the evidence, the testing methodology, and the results.

At trial, the prosecution may wish to offer the report into evidence to prove the truth of that conclusion and will attempt to use this hearsay exception for public records. The report is a hearsay statement that is being offered against a criminal defendant. It is also testimonial because it was prepared not in the throes of an ongoing emergency, but rather to help investigate the crime, apprehend the right suspect, and convict that suspect at trial. A reasonable person would expect that this report would be used at trial.

The U.S. Supreme Court agrees that these types of reports are testimonial. Recall from Chapter 5 that a testimonial statement can be admitted for the TOMA against a criminal defendant only if the declarant is a witness at trial or if the declarant is unavailable *and* the defendant had a prior opportunity to cross-examine the declarant about that report. The common practice prior to this Supreme Court decision was to admit the report as a public record or business record and obviate the need to bring each technician to testify at trial. Now the prosecutor must call the technician to the witness stand, unless she is unavailable. Even where the technician is unavailable, if the defendant did not have a prior opportunity to cross-examine that technician about that report, the report will not be admissible for the TOMA.

Absence of an Entry in Public Employee Records

CEC 1284 also provides a hearsay exception for the absence of an entry in a public record. The exception permits the admission of a written statement, from the custodian of the public record, attesting to a "diligent search and failure to find a record" to prove the absence of a record in that office. The rationale for this exception is that such a statement from the custodian of the public records is likely to be accurate, and omitting the requirement of witness testimony helps conserve public resources.

Federal Rules of Evidence Compared: Notable Differences

The CEC and FRE 803(8) have notably different requirements for official records. The FRE provides a greater limit on the use of such records against criminal defendants and a greater scope of admissibility for opinions when offered in civil cases or in criminal cases when offered against the government.

In addressing the absence of an entry, FRE 803(10) provides a hearsay exception for either a certification or testimony about the absence of the entry in a record regularly made and preserved by a public office or agency. The Confrontation Clause issues are the same in federal court.

Examples

1. Peter sued the LAPD for employment discrimination. In preparing for their exit interviews, other police officers corroborated Peter's complaints and had their own complaints of discriminatory treatment, which they wrote down on exit questionnaires. Peter sought to admit the written exit interview questionnaires. The LAPD objected that the questionnaires constituted hearsay. Peter responded that they met the business records exception. How should the court rule, and why?

2. Ophelia sued Mutual Insurance Company for failure to pay the full benefits on the life insurance policy she held on her now deceased husband Nestor. The policy provided for an additional payment of $10,000 in the case of a death resulting from an "accidental bodily injury." Ophelia sought to admit a copy of the coroner's death certificate as a public employee record. The death certificate listed the cause of death as "accidental drug overdose." Mutual Insurance Company argued that the term *accidental* was subject to different interpretations and that an accidental drug overdose when the drug was both illegal and self-administered, as was the heroin in this case, does not constitute an accidental death.

Mutual objected to the death certificate as inadmissible hearsay. How should the court rule, and why?

3. Roscoe is on trial for the murders of two teenage girls. Their bodies were found about a month apart, in the early morning hours, off of two different local highways. Roscoe is a truck driver, and he usually shows up for work between 4:00 and 4:30 a.m. The gate guard at the facility where Roscoe works is responsible for logging in the arrival and departure times of all truck drivers. The prosecution sought to admit in evidence the logs for each of the two days that a teenage girl's body was found. The first day's log shows Roscoe logged in at 6:30 a.m., and the second day has no listing for Roscoe being logged in at all that day. Roscoe objects on the grounds of hearsay and argues that the trustworthiness of the record has not been established for purposes of meeting the business records exception because some trucks were not logged in at all on those days, and the usual gate guard was absent on each of those days. How should the prosecution respond, and how should the court rule?

4. Officer Jackson observed the car in front of him swerving and making illegal U-turns on the highway. Jackson flashed his lights and instructed the driver to pull to the side of the road. When the driver, Barry, lowered his window, Jackson smelled alcohol and called Officer Killian for backup. When Killian arrived, Jackson explained to Killian what he had observed, and Killian then arrested Barry. Killian wrote up a police report, including his own and Officer Jackson's observations. The Department of Motor Vehicles held an administrative hearing and determined that Barry's driver's license will be suspended based on the DUI. Barry appeals to Superior Court. The City Attorney seeks to admit Killian's police report, with Jackson's observations, as well as a report prepared several weeks after the arrest by a forensic technician, listing Barry's blood alcohol level as three times the legal limit for driving. Barry objects to both items of evidence as inadmissible hearsay. How should the City Attorney respond, how should the court rule, and why?

Explanations

1. The court should sustain the LAPD's objection because the questionnaires do not meet the elements of a business or an official record. The exit questionnaire is not made in the normal course of business because it is prepared only when an employee is leaving a job. Furthermore, the exit questionnaire is not an official record because it is not made within the scope of duty of the public employee. Exit questionnaires do not impact the current duties, although they might affect future employment policies and procedures. The reliability element is difficult to satisfy without knowing the circumstances of the employees' reasons for

exiting. If they had been fired, their exit questionnaires might be less candid or more negative. If they had left voluntarily to go work for another police department, their exit questionnaires might be less candid in a more positive way to avoid "making waves." Because the questionnaires fail to satisfy the reliability element, the court should exclude them.

2. The court should overrule the hearsay objection because the death certificate meets the hearsay requirement for a public employee record (as well as the "vital statistics" exception in CEC 1283). It was made by a public employee (the coroner), in the course and scope of his duties (to identify and record causes of death), and was made at or near the time that he discovered that cause of death through the autopsy. The trustworthiness can be established by the practices of the office and the way the document was filed and kept. Mutual's argument about the various interpretations of the term *accidental* does not impact the admissibility of the document pursuant to a hearsay exception. However, Mutual may wish to seek a limiting instruction to the jury, to note that the term *accidental* has different meanings such that the coroner's definition is not coextensive with the insurance company's definition.

3. The prosecution should establish the basis for the business records exception by showing that the logs constitute a "record of an act, condition, or event" (namely the arrival and departure of truck drivers), that the log was made in the regular course of business (as a daily requirement for all truck drivers to be logged in and out), and that the writing was made at or near the time of the act (which would make sense if the log is time stamped or has the time noted for each arrival and departure). In addition, the exception requires that the custodian or *other* qualified witness testifies to its identity and the mode of its preparation, and so the substitute gate guard might need to testify to satisfy this element.

The final element is that "the sources of information and method and time of preparation were such as to indicate its trustworthiness," and Roscoe takes issue with this element due to the omission of some records. However, if the log is accurate as to the trucks noted, then without further evidence that it was inaccurate as to trucks noted or not noted, the court is likely to admit the first log document under the business records exception. The reliability is higher in this case if the log is used to record employees' hours for purposes of paychecks. If a log incorrectly noted the employee as arriving later than he really arrived, it is likely that he would have corrected that log or brought the error to someone's attention when his paycheck arrived. The failure to complain about the log being wrong where it would be in one's interest to do so is further evidence that the log is correct and reliable.

The second log document shows an absence of an entry for Roscoe and can be offered as long as the reliability prong is met. To the extent that other truck drivers were not logged in who were actually there that day, the reliability of the absence of an entry is undermined. It may be enough for the court to sustain the hearsay objection because the reliability for the business records exception has not been satisfactorily established on the issue of an absence of an entry. More likely, the court will find that these omissions affect the weight of the evidence, not its admissibility. If so, the court will admit the evidence and then the jury can decide how reliable it finds the log evidence.

4. The City Attorney should respond that the police report is admissible because Killian had firsthand knowledge and a duty to report what he observed about Barry and because Jackson also had firsthand knowledge as well as a duty to report what Jackson had observed about Barry. Thus, the chain of reliability was intact when Killian recorded Jackson's statements into the police report. The court should overrule the hearsay objection to the police report. As for the technician report, both the business records exception and the records by a public employee exception require that the record was made at or near the time of the event, and the City will be unable to establish the proper timing if the report was signed and dated several weeks after Barry's arrest. If the blood was not tested until several weeks later, at or near the time the report was signed, then there would be room for error and unreliability, given that the level of alcohol in blood dissipates with time. Based on the inability to meet the requirements for the hearsay exception and the potential lack of reliability, the court should sustain the objection to the report about Larry's blood.

CHAPTER 8

Witness Testimony Foundations

This chapter explains the mechanics of the most common form of evidence — witness testimony. The first part of the chapter covers who may testify in court and the methods for disqualifying witnesses. Only witnesses who understand the duty to tell the truth, have personal knowledge of what they testify about, and are capable of expressing themselves in an understandable manner will be qualified to testify. Interpreters and translators will help others in the court proceeding to understand the testimony, if needed. In addition, this chapter discusses the limits on jurors and judges testifying at trial.

The second part of the chapter addresses witness questioning techniques and methods for attacking and supporting the credibility of witnesses. For a witness to give evidence in court, a foundation must be laid to establish whether and how the witness is qualified to testify, as well as a foundation for the witness's credibility. On cross-examination, the attorneys will try to undermine the credibility of the witness using conflicting statements such as prior inconsistent statements, or contradictory testimony. Because the credibility of the witness is always at issue in the litigation, this chapter explores some additional rules on using character evidence to support or attack the witness's credibility. These witness character rules provide exceptions in addition to those that Chapter 2 addresses.

WITNESS COMPETENCY

The general rule stated in CEC 700 is that all people are qualified to be witnesses, unless there is a reason for them to be disqualified. The primary reasons for disqualification are when the witness cannot fulfill one of the factors from the credibility checklist discussed in Chapter 4:

1. perception
2. memory
3. narration, and
4. sincerity.

A witness who did not perceive the crucial events or who is forgetful may not be qualified to testify if she lacks personal knowledge as required by CEC 702. A witness who does not understand the idea of "truth" or who cannot communicate in a way that the jury understands can also be disqualified from testifying under CEC 701.

CEC §701: Disqualification of witness
(a) A person is disqualified to be a witness if he or she is:
    (1) Incapable of expressing himself or herself concerning the matter so as to be understood, either directly or through interpretation, by one who can understand him; or
    (2) Incapable of understanding the duty of a witness to tell the truth.
(b) In any proceeding held outside of the presence of a jury, the court may reserve challenges to the competency of a witness until the conclusion of the direct examination of that witness.

The language of CEC 701(a)(1) is a bit circuitous ("understood . . . by one who can understand him"), but the point is simple. As long as the expressions of the witness *can be understood*, the witness will not be disqualified on this ground. For example, a witness with a hearing loss who communicates in sign language can be understood by those who can read sign language — therefore the witness is not disqualified from testifying. The phrase *through interpretation* means that other people could understand the witness through an interpreter or translator. An interpreter explains what the witness is trying to communicate. Translators help others to understand witnesses who testify in a language different from that of the court proceeding.

Whether the witness can communicate in an understandable way is up to the judge to decide. If the objecting party wishes to challenge the witness's competency, that party will have to persuade the judge, by a preponderance of the evidence (i.e., it is more than 50 percent likely), that the witness is not qualified. The challenges must be resolved before the jury is allowed to hear the witness's testimony. If there is no jury present, the challenge can be reserved until the conclusion of the witness's testimony, after which the judge will decide whether the testimony is admissible. There is no minimum IQ nor is there a minimum or maximum age for qualification. Witnesses with mental impairments may be permitted to testify, and the jury can evaluate the strength of the witness's testimony taking into consideration the impairment. Similarly, witnesses who are temporarily impaired — such as those under the influence of drugs or alcohol — could testify as long as they are not so impaired that the jury cannot understand what they are saying.

Some additional considerations arise when hearsay testimony is admitted. If a witness gives testimony in one proceeding and a party offers that testimony in a later proceeding under one of the hearsay exceptions for former testimony (discussed in Chapter 5), then the opposing party can challenge the witness's competency at the time of the first proceeding in an attempt to render the hearsay testimony inadmissible in the later proceeding. For instance, an elderly victim of abuse testifies against his assailant at a preliminary hearing. By the time of trial, if the elderly victim has severe dementia, he may be deemed not competent to testify and thus is unavailable as a witness. The prosecutor then would seek to admit the preliminary hearing hearsay testimony under the former testimony exception, and the defendant may challenge the victim's competency at the time he made that statement on the grounds that he may have been suffering from a less severe form of dementia when he gave the original testimony.

Truth-Telling

In evaluating the *truth-telling* abilities or *sincerity* or *veracity* of witnesses, the CEC asks whether a person understands the duty to tell the truth. To testify, each witness must take an oath or affirmation to tell the truth. This requirement is important because it impresses on the witnesses the importance of being truthful in their testimony. The oath also lays a foundation for a potential perjury prosecution if the witness lies under oath. Children under the age of ten and certain people with cognitive impairments are allowed to "promise to tell the truth" under CEC 710, instead of taking the oath. A witness with a mental or physical infirmity may be able to take and understand the oath, and if so, would be permitted to testify. Children below a certain age and people with diminished mental faculties may not understand what it means to tell the truth. If this lack of comprehension is established by a preponderance of the evidence, then that witness will be disqualified from testifying. The determination is made by the court on a case-by-case basis.

Personal Knowledge

The personal knowledge requirement in CEC 702 ensures that witnesses testify about what they have observed with their own five senses rather than repeat what they heard from someone else. Personal knowledge is governed by a sufficiency standard. This means that viewing the evidence in the light most favorable to the proponent, the judge will consider whether there is enough evidence that a reasonable jury *could* find that the witness has personal knowledge of the matters she is testifying about. Note that the judge does not have to think that a reasonable jury *would* find the witness has personal knowledge — that would be a higher standard. The witness's own testimony may be used to prove whether the personal knowledge requirement is met.

CEC §702: Personal knowledge of witness
(a) Subject to Section 801, the testimony of a witness concerning a particular matter is inadmissible unless he has personal knowledge of the matter. Against the objection of a party, such personal knowledge must be shown before the witness may testify concerning the matter.
(b) A witness' personal knowledge may be shown by any otherwise admissible evidence, including his own testimony.

To determine whether a witness has personal knowledge, consider the scope of the testimony and the scope of the witness's perception. Ask whether the witness saw, heard, touched, tasted, or felt the event or condition about which the witness seeks to testify. A witness who saw two cars crash into each other has personal knowledge about the car crash but may not have personal knowledge about the parties' injuries (for instance, if the witness drove away before anyone emerged from the crashed cars). Examining the scope of a witness's knowledge may require some preliminary questions to lay the foundation for the witness's testimony. Those questions can be asked of the witness herself. For instance, with the car crash, the questioning may go something like this:

Lawyer: What, if anything, happened on your drive home?

Witness: I saw two cars get in an accident.

Lawyer: Did you see the cars in the moments leading up to the accident?

Witness: Yes.

Now the lawyer has laid a foundation for the witness's personal knowledge of the car crash, and the lawyer can now proceed to ask the witness to describe the car crash. If the lawyer wants the witness to describe more, then she must lay more foundation. The lawyer can ask, "Did you see the accident victims after the crash?" and "Where did you see them?," and then "How did they behave?"

In limited circumstances, a witness is allowed to give her opinion instead of her personal knowledge. This exception to the personal knowledge requirement is in CEC 801 (which is discussed in Chapter 9).

Translators

Translators, under CEC 750, are subject to the same rules as witnesses because the translator is testifying on behalf of the witness. It is important for the translator to have personal knowledge of what the witness said, which means that the translator heard and understood the witness's testimony. It is also important that the translator understands the duty to tell the truth by relating the witness's words and meaning accurately and precisely to the court. These specific rules are necessary to have confidence that the translator is making an accurate rendition of the witness's actual testimony in another language.

Most courts have special procedures to certify translators as qualified to translate in court. Because many translators work in a particular courtroom for hours handling whatever cases come to that courtroom, once a certified translator has been sworn in for one case in that courtroom the court generally recognizes a continuing duty to abide by the oath, even in a subsequent case later that day.

The CEC contains several specific sections addressing translators, including requirements for the translator's oath (CEC 751), the circumstances under which translators must be provided for witnesses (CEC 752), and requirements for documents offered into evidence (CEC 753). In addition, the CEC provides a detailed procedure for interpreters for the deaf in criminal and civil commitment hearings (CEC 754 and 754.5), in domestic violence and family law proceedings (CEC 755), and for medical examinations requested in civil cases (CEC 755.5). (The CEC sections about translators are contained in the appendix.)

Federal Rules of Evidence Compared: Minor Differences

FRE 601 provides a similar general rule of competence for all cases, but notes that in civil cases where state law governs, federal courts apply the state law for determining competence. FRE 602 contains a similar personal knowledge requirement also using a sufficiency standard.

FRE 603 requires a similar oath or affirmation, but omits any special language for children.

FRE 604 subjects an interpreter to the same oath or affirmation requirement, but also requires that the translator or interpreter be qualified as an expert.

Under FRE 605, the witness's personal knowledge may be established after the witness finishes testifying. The FRE does not contain any corresponding additional sections on written translations, interpretations for the deaf, or domestic violence and medical examinations.

JUDGES AS WITNESSES

In the current proceeding: CEC 703. When a judge has personal knowledge of the disputed facts in a case over which she is presiding, she should disqualify herself. If there is any inference of impropriety, such as the judge having a relationship with one of the parties or a financial interest in a corporate defendant, for instance, a judge should disqualify herself. These situations would be reasons for the judge to excuse herself under the ethical rules (which you study in a separate law school course). If the judge does not recuse herself, parties have the opportunity under the civil procedure rules to make a motion to disqualify the judge. Under the laws of evidence, however, there is no requirement that a judge recuse herself. If neither party objects, the CEC allows the judge to testify as a witness in the case over which she presides.

However, if the non-calling party objects to the judge being a witness, the result will be a mistrial, and the case will be reassigned to begin the trial again under the direction of another judge.

In a subsequent proceeding: CEC 703.5. When a judge has presided over a hearing, trial, or other court proceeding, she is disqualified from testifying about that proceeding in a subsequent proceeding unless an exception applies. The exceptions include when the testimony involves statements or conduct that could lead to contempt filings, constitute a crime, or give reasons for a judicial investigation or disqualification proceedings. Arbitrators and mediators must also abide by CEC 703.5, with a limited exception for certain family law mediators. (The CEC sections about judges as witnesses are contained in the appendix).

JURORS AS WITNESSES

In the current trial: CEC 704. Jurors are not automatically disqualified from testifying in the trial in which they serve. However, if a juror has personal knowledge about the case, then she must disclose that information to the parties. Typically, the jurors reveal this information in voir dire, the jury selection process. If the juror already has been selected and is hearing evidence in the case, this disclosure must be done outside of the presence of the rest of the jury. If neither party objects, the juror may be compelled to testify — however, in most cases, it would be tantamount to malpractice to permit a juror to testify for the other side of a case and then continue on to deliberate about the evidence in the same trial. If either party objects, the judge must declare a mistrial, and the case will be reassigned to another jury. (The CEC section about jurors as witnesses is contained in the appendix).

In post-trial proceedings: CEC 1150. After the trial has ended, jurors may be called to testify about the trial. If there is a dispute about the validity of the verdict, jurors will sometimes testify in a post-trial hearing or other proceeding. For example, if the jury foreperson announces the unanimous verdict of guilt and one of the jurors bursts into tears, the defense attorney will likely want to talk to that juror after the trial. If that juror then states that the foreperson brought a knife into the jury room and threatened to stab anyone who did not vote "guilty" within the hour, the defense lawyer would wish to challenge the jury verdict. To do so, he would need to have the jurors testify under CEC 1150 about the foreperson's conduct as an improper influence on the verdict.

CEC §1150: Evidence to test a verdict
(a) Upon an inquiry as to the validity of a verdict, any otherwise admissible evidence may be received as to statements made, or conduct, conditions, or events occurring, either within or without the jury room, of such a character as is likely to have influenced the verdict improperly. No evidence is admissible to show the effect of such statement, conduct or condition, or event upon a juror either in influencing him to assent to or dissent from the verdict or concerning the mental processes by which it was determined.

(b) Nothing in this code affects the law relating to the competence of a juror to give evidence to impeach or support a verdict.

The CEC permits jurors to testify about matters that are likely to have improperly influenced the prior jury verdict, but it prevents the jurors from testifying about the *effect* of such misconduct or improper influence on the vote or deliberations. This means that a juror can testify about the substantive problem but cannot testify about the ways in which that problem affected or influenced *how* the jurors reached the eventual decision. In the example above, the juror can testify that the foreperson had a knife and threatened to stab them. The juror cannot testify about how the threats made her feel or how the violence affected her deliberation.

Federal Rules of Evidence Compared: Substantive Differences

FRE 605 disqualifies the judge from testifying in the trial over which she presides and, unlike the CEC, does not require a party to object. FRE 606(a) disqualifies jurors from testifying in the trials in which they serve. FRE 606(b) provides a procedure similar to CEC 1150 for permitting jurors to testify when the validity of a verdict is challenged. The FRE is more restrictive because it prohibits testimony about "any matter or statement occurring during the course of the jury's deliberations," in addition to testimony about the effect of those matters. The FRE permits jurors to testify about extraneous prejudicial information and improper outside influences, such as newspaper articles about the case, but not about things like alcohol or drug use occurring in the jury deliberation room. The FRE recently was amended to allow testimony on whether the jurors made a mistake when they entered their verdict on the verdict form.

Examples

1. Mora was a court-certified interpreter, and he was sworn in to translate for a hearing in Nelson's case. Oliver's case was the next on the docket, and the clerk forgot to re-swear Mora. Mora translated for Oliver's trial. Oliver was convicted and appealed on the grounds that the translator was not properly sworn under CEC 710 and 750. How should the court rule, and why?

2. Denny was the general manager of a car dealership. He was fired after working there for 20 years, and he sued for breach of his employment

contract. During the discovery phase of the litigation, Denny sought to take the deposition of Edsel, the owner of the car dealership. The defense counsel objected on the basis of CEC 701, providing an affidavit from a doctor stating that Edsel suffered from dementia, which hampers his short-term memory and causes him to make up stories to explain things he cannot remember. Denny responds that because Edsel attends shareholder meetings and occasionally still works at the car dealership, he is competent to testify under oath. How should the court rule, and why?

3. Paul was on trial for possession with intent to distribute illegal drugs. The jury deliberated for two days before convicting him. Paul filed a motion to set aside the verdict on the grounds that some of the jurors smoked marijuana, sniffed powder cocaine, and drank alcohol in the restroom during the two days of deliberations. Paul argued that under CEC 1150, he could introduce affidavits from two jurors who saw the others use drugs and alcohol. How should a California court rule? How would the ruling differ in federal court?

4. Frankie is a minor child living with his aunt Hilda and uncle Greg. The court appointed Greg and Hilda to be Frankie's guardians while his parents were battling health and addiction problems. Two years later, Frankie's parents sought to terminate the guardianship so that they could regain custody of Frankie. At the hearing on the guardianship termination, Hilda and Greg called several of Frankie's relatives, including his mother's sister, Juno, and brother, Ivan, who had lived with Frankie and his parents for several years. Frankie's parents objected that Juno and Ivan had no personal knowledge about who should have custody of Frankie and thus CEC 702 barred them from testifying. How should the court rule, and why?

5. Kerry is a juror in the murder trial of a famous television actor, Robert, who is accused of killing Laney, the actress who played his wife on the television series. Robert claims that he was showing Laney his gun, and that it accidentally went off when she held it close to her face. When the jury was selected, the judge instructed the jury to avoid any television, news, or Internet access during the time that they served as jurors in the case. During the course of the jury deliberations, one of the other jurors started playing a U-Tube video on her I-Phone and some other jurors starting watching it. The video was a reenactment of the murder, created by some fans of the television show that Robert and Laney had starred in. Kerry refused to look at the video and threatened to tell the judge if they did not turn off the video immediately. The other juror turned off her I-Phone right away, and assured Kerry that she knew the video was fake and that it would not impact her deliberations. When the jurors resumed their discussion of the case, two of the jurors said that that U-Tube video

helped to convince them that the defendant killed the victim intentionally. The jury convicted Robert of murder, and his lawyer spoke to several of the jurors afterward. The lawyer filed a post-trial motion to challenge the verdict and sought to have Kerry testify about the U-Tube video and the comments that the jurors made about the video. The prosecution objects that this testimony would violate CEC 1150. How should the court rule, and why?

6. Adelaide says that she was with her husband Barry and her son Collin when Barry kidnapped a gas station attendant. Barry kicked Adelaide and the attendant out of the car, and then shot the attendant, killing him. At Barry's murder trial, Adelaide testifies as a prosecution witness and provides numerous details about the circumstances of the kidnapping and murder. She took the police to the scene of the murder, where they found shell casings matching Barry's gun. She also took police to the gas station and pointed to the exact spot where the initial kidnapping had occurred. On cross-examination, Barry's attorney asks Adelaide about Collin, and she reiterates that Collin was present during the kidnapping, and also testifies that a few weeks after the murder, she gave birth to triplets. Barry's attorney then provides evidence that Adelaide is delusional and that there are no birth records for any child named Collin or for any triplets. He moves to disqualify Adelaide as incompetent under CEC 701 and as lacking personal knowledge under CEC 702. How should the court rule, and why?

Explanations

1. The court should overrule the objection on the grounds that Mora was court-certified and was properly sworn in just a short time before Oliver's trial unless there is some evidence to suggest that Mora took his duties less seriously in the second trial because he was not re-sworn at that time. Oliver should have objected to this during the trial instead of waiting until the end of the case.

2. The court should sustain the objection and rule that Edsel is not competent under CEC 701 because he cannot understand the duty to tell the truth. His dementia causes him to make up untruthful stories whenever his memory fails him.

3. A court applying CEC 1150 should admit the evidence that the jurors were ingesting alcohol and drugs during their deliberations if that conduct was likely to have improperly influenced the verdict. The CEC does not permit the jurors to testify about the effects of the alcohol and drugs on them or their mental processes, but would let them testify to the fact that such substances were ingested. A federal court applying the FRE

would decline to admit the evidence about drug and alcohol use because it occurred during the deliberations and because it is not considered to be an improper "outside influence." One example of an "outside influence" would be finding a newspaper with articles about the case in the jury deliberation room with markings indicating that someone had read it.

4. The court should overrule the objection and permit Ivan and Juno to testify about any matters for which they have firsthand knowledge. Living with Frankie and his parents means they both observed firsthand how Frankie was treated, whether he was well fed and clothed, and whether his academic and other needs were being addressed properly. These issues would be relevant in a custody case.

5. The court should overrule the objection as to the existence of the U-Tube reenactment but sustain the objection as to the comments the jurors made. In a post-trial proceeding that challenges the verdict, a juror can testify about matters that may have improperly influenced the verdict. The U-Tube reenactment is an improper influence because the judge instructed the jurors to stay away from Internet information about the case. Moreover, as the video was created by fans and not crime scene investigators, it may be completely inaccurate about the details of the crime. Thus, the video would be both irrelevant and unduly prejudicial, and any influence it had on the jurors would be an improper one. However, the jurors are not allowed to testify about the effect of the improper influence on their verdict. The juror's statement that the video would not influence her is a statement about the effect of that improper influence. Similarly, the jurors' statements that the video convinced them that the killing was intentional are also statements about the effect of that improper influence. Because these two statements involve the effect of that improper influence, they would be inadmissible under CEC 1150.

6. The court should overrule the defense objection and rule that Adelaide is competent to testify about the circumstances of the murder. The permissible grounds for disqualification are not established on these facts because Adelaide is capable of expressing herself in an understandable way, and she is capable of understanding the duty to tell the truth under CEC 701. Her delusions about the existence of children do not make her incapable of understanding the duty to tell the truth. Rather, she has a different perception of the truth about the presence of her imaginary children. The specific details that Adelaide provided support a ruling that she meets the personal knowledge requirement of CEC 702 because she knew important details about the crime, which help confirm her testimony that she was present at the crime. Still, her delusions can be used as impeachment material to undermine her credibility.

QUESTIONING WITNESSES: DIRECT, CROSS-, AND REDIRECT EXAMINATIONS

The Types of Witness Examinations

It is important to know when an attorney is conducting a direct, redirect, or cross-examination. *Direct examination* refers to the first examination of a witness on a particular matter by the party that called that witness. In most cases, each witness is subject to only one direct examination, but under CEC 760, the court can, in the interests of justice, let a different party recall that witness to conduct a second direct examination as long as it is on a different matter than the first. In a criminal case, the defendant may not be placed on direct examination by the prosecution or a codefendant without consenting first (CEC 772).

After each direct examination, the opposing party has the opportunity to conduct a *cross-examination* of the witness. On cross-examination, the scope of the questioning is limited to matters that were already covered in the direct examination and to credibility issues, under CEC 761 and 773. *Redirect examination* (CEC 762) follows cross-examination, and the scope of the redirect is limited to the scope of the cross-examination and to rehabilitating the witness on credibility issues. The CEC permits *re-cross-examination* after the redirect (CEC 763), and the courts have discretion to allow re-re-direct, and re-re-cross, ad nauseum (CEC 774). (The CEC sections about examinations are contained in the appendix).

The Order of Witness Examinations

The order of examinations is governed by CEC 765 and 772. Generally, the prosecution (or plaintiff in a civil case) will call the first witness for direct examination. Then the defense will cross-examine that first witness. Then the prosecution (or plaintiff) will conduct the redirect examination of that witness. When the first witness is excused, the prosecution (or plaintiff) will call the second witness, and repeat the process with each of the witnesses. That process is known as the prosecution or plaintiff's *case in chief*. Afterward, the defense presents its case in chief by calling its first witness for direct examination, and then the other side will conduct a cross-examination of that first defense witness. The defense will then conduct the redirect of that first witness and then move on to the next witness as the defense progresses through its case in chief.

CEC 765 requires the court to exercise reasonable control over the questioning of witnesses to serve the interests of judicial economy, as well as to protect witnesses from undue harassment or embarrassment. Judicial economy refers to the need to conserve court time and resources with efficient use, as described in the Chapter 1 discussion of conditional relevance. For instance, a special provision restricts the unnecessary repetition of questions posed to witnesses younger than age 14 when a person of their age might not understand them. CEC 772 permits deviations or interruptions in examinations in the discretion of the court or for good cause — which includes judicial economy.

When a witness discloses new information during an examination, the court has discretion to permit a party to reexamine that witness about the new information, even if that party has already conducted and completed its examination of the witness (CEC 774). Courts also have discretion under CEC 775 to call and examine witnesses on their own — but courts rarely exercise this discretion fully. Sometimes courts will use this discretion to ask additional questions of a witness already called by one of the parties. If the court does examine a witness, the parties have the same right to object as if the opposing party had called the witness, and then each party has the right to cross-examine the witness about any matters inquired into by the court.

The court may prevent people who will be witnesses from hearing the testimony of other witnesses in that case. Courts do this by excluding them from the courtroom under CEC 777. However, this exclusion does not apply to parties who may be witnesses or to the officer or designated employee if the party is not a natural person. When a witness completes her direct, cross-, and any redirect or re-cross-examinations, the party calling that witness will ask the court to excuse the witness. Once a witness has been excused from testifying, a party may not call that witness again without leave of court under CEC 778.

Using Leading Questions in Witness Examinations

A *leading* question is one that suggests the desired answer (CEC 764). Leading questions are permitted (and in fact encouraged) on cross-examination, but they are prohibited on direct and redirect examinations except in very limited circumstances. Leading questions during direct examination are acceptable only for *preliminary matters*, for children less than ten years old, or for dependent people with cognitive impairments in certain actions, and as the interest of justice otherwise requires (CEC 767). *Preliminary matters* include introducing the witness or asking about the reason for being in court today (e.g., "You have been a physician for ten years, right?" or "You are testifying today because you were in a car accident on July 3, is that correct?").

Witnesses are required to give an answer that responds to the question asked, and if they fail to do so, the counsel asking the question can object and move to strike the non-responsive portion of the answer from the record (CEC 766).

Federal Rules of Evidence Compared: Minor Differences

FRE 611 explains the mode and order of interrogation and corresponds to CEC 760-765, 767, and 773. The FRE does not contain specific provisions on responsive answers, the order of examination, reexamination, examinations by an adverse party, or the recall of witnesses, but the practice is the same. FRE 614 permits the court to call and question witnesses, similar to CEC 775.

IMPEACHING AND SUPPORTING CREDIBILITY

Witness credibility is an important issue in every case. Much as the hearsay exceptions were designed to ensure that more reliable evidence is presented to the jurors, the credibility statutes are designed to give each party a fair opportunity to explore a witness's credibility — and therefore reliability. CEC 785 allows any party to support or attack the credibility of a witness. However, unrestrained inquiries into credibility issues would detract from the primary issues in the litigation. Therefore, there are two important sets of limitations: one on the kinds of evidence that can be used to support or attack credibility of witnesses, and the other on the circumstances under which a party can use this evidence. CEC 780 provides a list of the types of information that the fact finder can use to evaluate the credibility of witnesses in California courts.

CEC §780: General rule as to credibility
Except as otherwise provided by statute, the court or jury may consider in determining the credibility of a witness any matter that has any tendency in reason to prove or disprove the truthfulness of his testimony at the hearing, including but not limited to any of the following:

   a. His demeanor while testifying, and the manner in which he testifies.
   b. The character of his testimony.
   c. The extent of his capacity to perceive, to recollect or to communicate any matter about which he testifies.
   d. The extent of his opportunity to perceive any matter about which he testifies.

e. His character for honesty or veracity or their opposites.

f. The existence or not, of a bias, interest, or other motive.

g. A statement previously made by him that is consistent with his testimony at the hearing.

h. A statement made by him that is inconsistent with any part of his testimony at the hearing.

i. The existence or nonexistence of any fact testified to by him.

j. His attitude toward the action in which he testifies or toward giving testimony.

k. His admission of untruthfulness.

a. Demeanor

How the witness behaves while testifying can be an important clue to whether the witness is being truthful or untruthful. For instance, a witness who appears nervous when asked certain questions, takes a long time to answer, or provides vague answers may appear to be hiding something. Conversely, a witness who looks counsel in the eye and answers promptly and clearly with detailed responses will appear to be more credible.

b. Character of Testimony

This broad category evaluates the purpose or goal of the witness testimony as well as its general tenor. For instance, in determining whether testimony is reliable, courts may consider whether the witness describes a situation that is plausible or one that is very far-fetched. Similarly, the character of the testimony helps provide clues as to potential bias, which is discussed below.

c. Capacity to Perceive, Recollect, or Communicate

Chapter 4 discusses the credibility interests in hearsay evidence (capacities for perception, memory, narration, and sincerity), and similar concerns that apply to the credibility of all witness testimony. Ways to impeach the witness's *capacity* include impairments such as poor eyesight or hearing, unreliable short-term memory, and inarticulate communication skills. Evidence of mental disorders can also be used to impeach a witness. Drugs and alcohol distort perception and memory, and they can impact the ability to communicate effectively. Experts can provide testimony on the capacity of another witness in any of these areas to help the jurors evaluate the witness's credibility.

Be sure to limit any inquiry about impairments to the relevant time period, which may be while testifying (to impeach capacity to recollect and communicate) or the time when the events or conditions that the witness is testifying about actually occurred (to impeach capacity for perception and memory). Drug use at the time of perception or shortly before the perception can affect perception or memory of the events and therefore is relevant and useful in evaluating the witness's testimony. Being under the influence of drugs or alcohol while testifying may also affect memory and the ability to communicate.

Be aware that inquiring about the witness's drug or alcohol use may prompt a character evidence objection from opposing counsel. As discussed in Chapter 2, the response to this objection is that evidence about drug or alcohol use on a particular occasion is not character evidence as long as it is not being offered for a propensity purpose. The propensity purpose of evidence of drug and alcohol use would be to prove that because the witness drank or did drugs on one occasion, she must have been drinking or doing drugs at the relevant time. When using the evidence to impeach a witness's capacity to perceive or recollect, however, it is being used for a non-propensity purpose. Rather, the party seeks to use this impairment evidence to show the specific defect in perception or memory while the relevant events were occurring. Thus, opposing counsel can ask, "Isn't it true that you could hardly see because you had five Cosmopolitan cocktails before you were robbed at the ATM machine?" but not "Isn't it true that you drank five cocktails like you do every day?"

However, if the cross-examining counsel wishes to inquire about *repeated* drug or alcohol use, then the character evidence rules and exceptions from Chapter 2 regarding opinion, reputation, and habit character evidence may be implicated. The California Supreme Court has not decided whether prior drug use specifically should be admissible under the Right to Truth in Evidence provision because the relevance is not always clear and the prejudicial effect is high.

d. Opportunity to Perceive

The opportunity to perceive can be affected by circumstances like poor lighting or an obstruction to the eyewitness's view. If the witness was looking in a different direction at the time the events occurred, or standing or driving in some other place at that time, she would not have the opportunity to perceive the event. Sometimes witnesses will say that they saw an accident when they saw only the aftermath, and questions seeking to establish that the witnesses arrived at the accident scene minutes after the accident rather than before it will be useful impeachment material.

e. Character for Honesty or Veracity or Their Opposites

Recall the general rule that character evidence is not admissible to prove conduct in conformity with that character, unless an exception applies.

Chapter 2 discusses exceptions for criminal defendants, victims, and when character was at issue. There are additional exceptions for witnesses at trial. These exceptions allow a very limited use of character evidence when offered on the issue of witness credibility. In civil cases, the permissible use of reputation and opinion character evidence is very narrow, and only evidence probative of honesty or veracity or their opposites is permitted. However, the use of character evidence about honesty or veracity of witnesses in California criminal cases is less restricted because of the Right to Truth in Evidence state constitutional provision, also known as Proposition 8. (These differences are explained in greater detail below.)

f. Existence of Bias or Other Motive

Impeaching based on bias involves establishing that the witness has some motive or interest to testify in a particular way. Anything that makes the witness testify inaccurately will be sufficient. Bias does not address the ability or capacity to perceive or to remember accurately but rather the witness's willingness to testify truthfully and accurately as to what really happened.

The bias can be in favor of one side or against the other side and is sometimes called *partiality* or *partisanship*. An improper motive for testifying inaccurately can include giving testimony for money or revenge. Other examples of bias and improper motives are being related to or employed by a party, having a financial stake in the litigation, and testifying to get special favors or recommendations for a lesser sentence in your criminal case. Being in the same gang is questionable under some California cases because of the potential prejudice of exposing the jury to gang evidence, but living in the same neighborhood and having the same friends can be brought out.

A threat is another improper interest or motive. Evidence that the witness was intimidated or threatened can come in to impeach the witness because it is relevant to credibility. Evidence of a threat against the witness cannot be offered against the accused as consciousness of guilt, however, unless there is sufficient evidence to connect the accused to the threat. In the case of plea bargains and immunity offers granted by the prosecution to a witness in exchange for his testimony against the accused, counsel can inquire as to whether the agreement with the prosecution requires truthful testimony, or something more specific such as testifying "consistently with the grand jury testimony."

Extrinsic proof of these biases or interests is allowed only if the witness denies being biased. If the witness admits to having a bias, no extrinsic evidence of that bias is allowed. However, if the witness denies bias and extrinsic evidence is admitted, that evidence is still subject to exclusion at the judge's discretion under CEC 352 (see Chapter 1). The rationale for admitting such proof is that the bias directly affects the truth of the testimony in court, and so some inquiry into the basis for that bias is appropriate. If the witness is important and this bias is the only way to discredit him, the judge is more likely to allow a greater inquiry into the basis for the bias.

g. Prior Consistent Statements

Recall from Chapter 6 that CEC 791 provides that when a witness has been impeached, either with a prior inconsistent statement or by an express or implicit charge of bias, recent fabrication or improper motive, a party may rehabilitate the witness's credibility by offering a prior statement that is consistent with the current in-court testimony. The timing of the prior consistent statement is very important — it is admissible only if it occurred before the inconsistent statement or before the reason for the bias, recent fabrication, or other improper motive arose. (CEC 791 is discussed in Chapter 6 along with the hearsay exceptions for prior consistent statements.)

When the prior consistent statement is in writing, CEC 768 permits counsel to inquire about consistent statements without mentioning that written statement. For instance, if counsel has a written statement that the witness gave to the police that states "the light was red," counsel can ask the witness whether the witness told the police that the traffic light was red. Counsel does not need to show the written statement to the witness, read it to him, or even disclose the existence of that written statement. However, if counsel does show the writing to the witness, then all parties must have a chance to review that writing before counsel can question the witness about that written statement.

h. Prior Inconsistent Statements

Another impeachment mechanism is to use an inconsistent statement that the witness made prior to her testimony. CEC 770 permits a party to offer a prior inconsistent statement for impeachment purposes as long as the witness was given the opportunity to explain or deny the statement, or has not yet been excused from testifying or unless the interests of justice require otherwise. In addition, a prior inconsistent statement can be admitted for the truth of the matter asserted when it meets the requirements for the hearsay exception. (The hearsay exception for prior inconsistent statements is addressed in Chapter 6.)

CEC 768 also applies to prior inconsistent written statements. Counsel may ask a witness about inconsistencies and need not show, read, or even mention the written statement to the witness. In the traffic light example above, if opposing counsel has a written statement that the witness gave to the insurance company that states "the light was green," counsel may ask the witness about what he told the insurance company. Counsel need not disclose that she has the written statement. However, if counsel does show the written statement to the witness, the parties must have a chance to review it before counsel asks the witness any questions about that writing.

A similar provision about inconsistent oral statements or conduct is in CEC 769. Counsel does not need to disclose any information about the inconsistent oral statement or conduct before asking the witness about the inconsistency.

i. Non-existence of Facts

When the witness testifies to facts that do not exist, pointing out their non-existence is another way to impeach that witness's credibility. For instance, imagine that a person who saw a car crash testifies that one car swerved around a giant statue of a horse before the accident. Imagine also that the intersection where the accident occurred does not have any statues. Opposing counsel can use the evidence of the non-existence of the horse statue to impeach the witness's credibility. This technique is often referred to as *impeachment by contradiction*.

j. Attitude

A witness with a surly, pompous, or similarly negative attitude may be less credible, and counsel can point that out to the jury to impeach the witness.

k. Admission of Untruthfulness

Sometimes counsel will confront a witness with a prior inconsistent statement, and the witness will admit that he lied. That admission can be evidence to impeach the witness.

Civil Cases: CEC 786, 787, and 790

In civil cases, character evidence about witnesses is admissible for the very narrow purpose of attacking or supporting credibility. Because of that limitation, only evidence involving the witness's character for honesty and veracity (or the opposite) is allowed under CEC 786. The evidence of a witness's bad character for dishonesty or lack of veracity is admissible during or after the witness's testimony. Under CEC 790, good character evidence of a witness's honesty or veracity is not admissible until after evidence of bad character for honesty or veracity has been admitted to attack that witness's credibility. In other words, the good character evidence for truth-telling is admitted only as rebuttal after a credibility attack using evidence of bad character for dishonesty.

CEC §786 Character evidence generally

Evidence of traits of his character other than honesty or veracity, or their opposites, is inadmissible to attack or support the credibility of a witness.

CEC §790 Good character of witness

Evidence of the good character of a witness is inadmissible to support his credibility unless evidence of his bad character has been admitted for the purpose of attacking his credibility.

Thus, proving a witness's character for honesty or veracity generally will begin on cross-examination because the good character evidence will not be admissible until the witness has been impeached with bad character evidence. The types of character evidence (as you will recall from Chapter 2) are opinion, reputation, and specific instances of conduct.

Establishing a Witness's Bad Character for Dishonesty

Opinion and reputation evidence of a witness's character usually will be offered through the testimony of another witness. For instance, imagine a civil case in which Tad is a witness. The opposing side wants to attack Tad's credibility by having its own witness, Kelly, testify that in her opinion, Tad is a liar. To introduce this opinion evidence, counsel will need to establish during direct examination that Kelly is sufficiently acquainted with Tad that she is qualified to form an opinion on Tad's character for being dishonest. Counsel will ask questions of Kelly such as, "How long have you known Tad?" and "In what context?" to help to lay this foundation. Similarly, if counsel wishes to offer reputation character evidence about Tad's character for dishonesty, she will need to establish that Kelly is qualified to testify about Tad's reputation by asking questions such as "Are you familiar with Tad's reputation in the area of honesty?" "How are you familiar with his reputation?" to show that Kelly has heard others talking about Tad and his dishonesty and has some knowledge about Tad's reputation for a lack of veracity. Once this foundation is established, then counsel can ask "What is Tad's reputation on the issue of honesty?"

Cross-Examining the Character Witness

After Kelly testifies about Tad's reputation for dishonesty or her opinion that he is a dishonest person, Tad's counsel will cross-examine Kelly to try to undermine the basis for her opinion or her knowledge about Tad's reputation. Some of those cross-examination questions would likely focus on revealing that Kelly actually knows very little about Tad and his reputation. For example, maybe Kelly heard about only two people who think Tad is dishonest, and she never had any negative interaction with him herself.

Responding with Evidence of the Witness's Good Character for Honesty

Once Kelly has completed her testimony about Tad's character for dishonesty, Tad's counsel may decide that he needs to counter that evidence by calling witnesses to testify about Tad's good character for honesty. When it is time for Tad's case in chief, Tad's counsel may wish to call the defense witness, Judy, to the stand to give opinion or reputation evidence of Tad's honest character. The same process described above applies for opinion and reputation evidence of a good character trait. Judy's testimony on Tad's good traits is allowed now, after Kelly's negative testimony, to rebut the bad character evidence that paints Tad as a liar.

Limitations on Using Specific Instances of Character for Honesty

The same technique is used to qualify Judy to talk about the good character of Tad once his character for honesty has been impeached by Kelly's testimony. The opposing counsel may cross-examine Judy in an attempt to discredit her opinion or her knowledge of Tad's reputation for honesty. For example, opposing counsel might ask Judy if she knew that Tad lied to an insurance company to get money and time off work. Counsel is stuck with Judy's answer and cannot offer extrinsic evidence about those acts. Just as with the criminal defendant "mercy rule" character exception discussed in Chapter 2, the inquiry into the specific instance is permissible, but proving the specific instance through questions or extrinsic evidence is not permissible.

The attorney may inquire about these past misdeeds to test the qualifications of the character witness, but not to prove the underlying misdeed. The question seeks relevant information because it impacts Judy's credibility as a witness and impacts the persuasiveness of her testimony. If Judy has not heard about this specific misdeed, then how well does she know Tad's reputation? If Judy has heard about this misdeed and still gives an opinion that Tad is honest, then less weight should be placed on Judy's good character evidence because the basis is not as strong.

While the reputation or opinion witness can be asked about these types of specific instances of another witness's conduct, specific instance evidence of that same witness's past misdeeds is not admissible to prove a character trait to support or attack that witness's credibility. The only exception is if that prior misdeed is a conviction of a crime that meets the requirements of CEC 788, discussed below.

CEC §787 Specific instances of conduct

Subject to Section 788 [for criminal convictions], evidence of specific instances of his conduct relevant only as tending to prove a trait of his character is inadmissible to attack or support the credibility of a witness.

This limitation means that counsel cannot ask Judy whether she ever lied to an insurance company to attack her credibility. Counsel can ask Judy only whether she heard about Tad lying to the insurance company and took that into account in forming her opinion about his honesty. Asking the question about a specific instance to test the basis for the reputation or opinion testimony is permissible; however, asking the specific instance question to prove the underlying fact (that Tad lied to the insurance company) or to prove dishonesty itself is not permissible in civil cases under the CEC. Remember that these rules above apply only to civil cases in California. The next section discusses the rules for criminal cases.

Prior Felony Convictions as Permissible Specific Instances

When a witness in a civil case has a prior criminal conviction, that evidence may be admissible to impeach the witness. Under CEC 788, to use a prior conviction as specific instance evidence relating to honesty or veracity, the conviction must be for a felony. The conviction is not admissible if it was pardoned, was a perjury conviction that was later dismissed, or if the felon earned a certificate of rehabilitation. Furthermore, the felony must involve "moral turpitude," or a readiness to do evil. For example, the courts classify these crimes as having moral turpitude: perjury, child molestation, and torture. Crimes that do not involve moral turpitude include statutory rape, involuntary manslaughter, assault, and battery. Importantly, these specific instances of felony convictions are still subject to the CEC 352 balancing test (discussed in Chapter 1). The convictions may be proved through the witness's own testimony or copies of the record of conviction admitted under CEC 452.5 and the hearsay business records exception (discussed in Chapter 7). It is important to recognize that the attorney cannot make up alleged past misdeeds or felonies to ask questions about. The attorney must have at least a good faith belief that the misdeed occurred before asking the character witness about it. (The CEC section about prior convictions is contained in the appendix).

Criminal Cases: Proposition 8/The Truth in Evidence Provision

The Right to Truth in Evidence provision of the California Constitution was enacted by the voters as Proposition 8 in 1982. The Truth in Evidence provision overturns the limitations in CEC 786, 787, and 790 in criminal cases. In other words, when impeaching witnesses in criminal cases, both sides can offer opinion or reputation character evidence of traits, even if it is unrelated to character for honesty or veracity (as long as the evidence is somehow related to credibility), can offer good character evidence without waiting for bad character evidence first, and can use character evidence of specific instances to prove honesty or veracity.

Notwithstanding the Truth in Evidence provision, the character evidence used for impeaching witnesses in criminal cases must relate to the witness's credibility to avoid the general character evidence ban of CEC 1101. Recall from Chapter 2 that the general ban on using character evidence to prove conduct in conformity does not apply to the character of witnesses for credibility purposes. All character evidence that does not involve witness credibility is governed by the rules and exceptions addressed in Chapter 2, which were not overturned by the Truth in Evidence provision and remain in effect.

Furthermore, any evidence that Proposition 8 permits still may be excluded based on relevance and the CEC 352 balancing test for undue prejudice, wasting the court's time, or confusing issues for the jury (as discussed in Chapter 1). For instance, a witness in a criminal case has a reputation for having numerous girlfriends at the same time, and he testifies that he was with "my one and only girlfriend" all night. Having multiple girlfriends does not involve character for honesty or veracity, but his reputation for having multiple girlfriends contradicts the implication that he has only one girlfriend. Thus, the evidence that he has a reputation for having multiple girlfriends impacts the witness's credibility. However, the probative value of this evidence on his credibility is not very high (just because he has a reputation for having multiple girlfriends does not mean he had multiple girlfriends at the time he testified), and the undue prejudice may be substantial (particularly if the jury has a number of members who believe in monogamous relationships). When the character evidence is on a trait unrelated to honesty but related to credibility, the court can still exclude the evidence as unduly prejudicial under CEC 352, even though it is technically permissible under the Truth in Evidence provision of Proposition 8.

Proving Specific Instances of Honesty and Dishonesty in Criminal Cases

Specific instance inquiries relating to the witness's character for truth-telling are permitted in criminal cases. Unlike the rule in civil cases, in criminal court, the specific instance evidence is not limited to prior felony convictions, as long as the evidence is still relevant to truth-telling. What kinds of specific instances are probative of credibility? Counsel can ask about anything that the witness has done that might tend to show that she is a dishonest person — like previous lies, cheating, and tax fraud — as long as there is a good faith basis for the inquiry. The court has discretion about which questions to permit and which to exclude. Courts have found that drug use, violence, committing sex crimes, and being a sex worker are specific acts that do not bear on truthfulness.

Asking about an *arrest* is not permitted because that is not a specific act that the witness *committed*, but rather an act that was committed on the witness. Counsel can easily resolve this problem by asking about the substantive act that led to the arrest rather than the arrest itself. For example, instead of asking "You were arrested for stealing money from a cash register, weren't you?" counsel should ask "You stole money from the cash register, didn't you?"

The Truth in Evidence provision did not overturn CEC 788 as it applied in criminal cases, so the same requirements in civil cases for using specific instances of prior convictions to prove character for truthfulness apply. Thus, convictions offered under CEC 788 in criminal cases must be felonies that involve moral turpitude, and the evidence is still subject to the CEC 352 balancing test (discussed in Chapter 1). However, while misdemeanor convictions are not allowed in civil cases, they are allowed in criminal cases through the Truth in Evidence provision, as long as the conviction is relevant to the witness's character for truthfulness and the admission does not violate other constitutional rights.

Federal Rules of Evidence Compared: Substantive Differences

FRE 607 on who may impeach corresponds to CEC 785. On the issue of using reputation or opinion character evidence, FRE 608(a) permits good character evidence on truthfulness after any attack on "character by reputation, opinion or otherwise." Thus, the FRE allows a more broad attack, with non-character evidence as well, to trigger the good character response. In contrast, under the CEC in civil cases, the witness must be attacked with character evidence before the good character response will be permitted.

Specific Instances Under the FRE   When considering specific instances of character evidence, FRE 608(b) provides that specific instances on the character for truthfulness may be asked about, but may not be proven by extrinsic evidence, which the Ninth Circuit defines as "[e]vidence not presented at trial, acquired through out-of-court experiments or otherwise."[1] These specific instances can be inquired into on cross-examination to test the character for truthfulness of the witness herself or of some other witness in the case.

For example, in federal court on cross-examination, Ed could not be asked, "Isn't it true that you got into a fight with the defendant last week?" because the fight has nothing to do with his Ed's character for truthfulness. Ed could be asked, "Isn't it true that you lied in court once before?" If Ed denied the lie, the attorney could not provide testimony from the court clerk in the prior court hearing to prove that Ed lied under oath before because having another witness testify about the lie would constitute extrinsic evidence. Counsel is stuck with the witness's answer about these specific instances on credibility issues in federal court.

Contrasting with California   In a criminal case in a California court, counsel could ask Ed whether he lied in court before and also whether he got in a fight with the defendant (as long as counsel can establish some link to credibility), and the court has discretion to permit the court clerk or someone else to testify about either matter if Ed denies the allegation. The in-court lie is a specific instance of character for dishonesty and thus is admissible under Proposition 8. The fight is a specific instance of character for violence, and it could be admissible under Proposition 8 only if it relates to credibility. Otherwise, it is governed by the general character prohibition of CEC 1101. An argument could be made that the fight shows a bias against the defendant because a person is more likely to fight someone whom he does not like, and thus the fight relates to credibility. The court likely would find that the probative value of evidence of the fight is low on the issue of witness credibility and the prejudicial effect is high, and therefore will exclude the evidence under CEC 352.

Convictions Admissible Under the FRE   FRE 609 also permits impeaching a witness with prior convictions and provides a different standard

---

1. United States v. Navarro-Garcia, 926 F.2d 818, 821 (9th Cir.1991).

depending on whether the witness to be impeached is the criminal defendant in the current case and whether the conviction involved dishonesty. If the witness is the accused in a criminal case, then he may be impeached with evidence of a conviction for a crime if it can be readily determined that the elements of the crime required an act of dishonesty or false statement by the witness. This provision applies when the prior conviction was either a misdemeanor or a felony.

On the other hand, if it cannot be readily determined that the elements of the crimes as proved or admitted required an act of dishonesty or false statement by the witness, then the FRE permits evidence of a felony only and requires that the government show that the probative value of the felony conviction as impeachment evidence outweighs the prejudicial effect to the accused. The evidence will be admitted only if the probative value weighs more than the prejudicial effect to the criminal defendant in the case.

If the witness is not the accused in a criminal case, then you perform a similar two-step analysis. First, if it can be readily determined that the crime required dishonesty or false statement, then the conviction is admissible regardless of whether it is a felony or a misdemeanor. Second, if the conviction did not require dishonesty or a false statement, then only a felony may be used for impeachment — if it passes the balancing test of FRE 403. This balance will be based on how relevant the felony is to veracity and the weight of the prejudicial effect of admitting the conviction evidence. The federal court will exclude the conviction under FRE 403 only if the probative value is substantially outweighed by the prejudicial effect. It does not matter whether the current case is civil or criminal.

Other Limitations on Convictions Under the FRE   The FRE contains some other limitations on the admission of convictions. If more than ten years have passed since the date of conviction or release from confinement, the conviction will not be admissible unless the court determines that in the interests of justice, the probative value of the conviction substantially outweighs its prejudicial effect, and the proponent has given adequate advance written notice of intent to use that conviction. Like the CEC, convictions may not be used if there was a pardon, an annulment, a certificate of rehabilitation, or another equivalent procedure, and the person has not been convicted of a subsequent felony grade offense. As for juvenile convictions, under the FRE they usually are not admissible to impeach the witness, but in a criminal case where the witness is not the accused, the judge has discretion to allow the evidence in if such evidence would be admissible against an adult witness and the court finds it necessary to a fair outcome. The fact that an appeal is pending is admissible, but it does not render the underlying conviction inadmissible.

FRE 613(a) is analogous to CEC 768(a) and FRE 613(b) to CEC 770, but does not apply to party admissions. There is no FRE corresponding to CEC 791.

LIMITATIONS ON CREDIBILITY ATTACKS: RELIGIOUS BELIEFS, SEXUAL HISTORY, AND HYPNOSIS

Religious Beliefs Evidence of a witness's religious beliefs or non-beliefs cannot be offered to prove that the witness is more or less likely to tell the truth because of those convictions or lack thereof. Some may argue that this evidence is relevant to truth-telling because a religion may prohibit lying, and therefore a person of that religion is more likely to tell the truth. However, the CEC does not allow these uses of evidence of a witness's religious background.

The CEC does permit the use of religious affiliation to impeach the witness when offered to prove something other than character for truth-telling, such as bias or interest in the litigation. For instance, in a case involving attacks on animal research facilities in the name of a certain religion, opposing counsel may ask a witness testifying on behalf of the attackers if she subscribes to the same religion. This question may reveal that the witness is biased in favor of the attackers and their actions because she shares the same religious beliefs against animal experimentation.

Victim's Sexual History In a case in which the defendant is blamed for a sexual offense and seeks to attack the credibility of a witness who is also the alleged victim, the defendant may want to use evidence of the witness's past sexual conduct. There must be a separate hearing under CEC 782 to determine whether that evidence will be admitted. In most cases, the evidence of the victim's past sexual conduct is limited — the defendant can bring up evidence only of their past sexual conduct together. CEC 1103(c) does not allow using evidence of the witness's past sexual conduct with other people to prove that what happened between the alleged victim and defendant was consensual (see Chapter 2).

The CEC 782 hearing is governed by a sufficiency standard, which means that the proponent of the sexual conduct evidence must persuade the judge that the evidence is sufficiently probative of the alleged victim's lack of credibility. CEC 782 is specifically exempted from the Truth in Evidence provision and thus still applies in criminal cases in California. CEC 783 provides a similar procedure in civil cases involving sexual torts such as sexual harassment. The sexual history evidence is also subject to the exclusion under CEC 352. The judge examines the evidence and then rules on whether the probative value of the evidence of her sexual history is not substantially outweighed by the prejudicial effect based on the balancing test of CEC 352. (The full text of this hearing statute is contained in the appendix.)

Witnesses Who Were Hypnotized   In criminal trials, CEC 795 permits the use of a previously hypnotized witness's testimony if certain requirements are met. These requirements help ensure that the hypnotized testimony is credible and reliable. Those requirements include that

1. the matters were related and recalled by the witness prior to hypnosis;
2. the pre-hypnotic memory was recorded or transcribed;
3. the hypnosis session was videotaped;
4. the hypnosis session was conducted with notice and according to established protocols by a licensed professional; and
5. the court holds a hearing to determine the reliability of the witness's testimony before admitting the testimony.

When the hypnotized witness is the criminal defendant, the courts allow a broader use of the testimony to avoid unduly hampering the defendant's right to testify on his own behalf. (The full text of this hyponosis statute is contained in the appendix.)

In civil cases, the use of post-hypnosis testimony is governed by case law. Based on the *Shirley-Hayes* line of cases[2], a trial court must conduct a hearing to determine (1) whether the witness underwent hypnosis (2) for the purpose of restoring memory about the subject of the hypnotic session, and (3) whether any proposed testimony is about events recalled and related to other pre-hypnosis events. Then, the court will use its discretion to determine whether to admit the evidence.

Federal Rules of Evidence Compared: Substantive Differences

There is no substantial difference in FRE 610 preventing the use of religious affiliation. On the issue of sexual offenses, FRE 412 is narrower than CEC 782, permitting the accused to offer evidence of specific instances of his own conduct with the alleged victim if the judge determines in a separate hearing that the probative value outweighs the prejudice to the victim. The FRE also permits evidence of the sexual conduct of the victim with

---

2. People v. Shirley, 31 Cal. 3d 18, 723 P. 2d 1354 (1982); People v. Hayes, 49 Cal. 3d 1260, 783 P. 2d 719 (1989).

others to prove someone else is responsible for the charged offense. FRE 412 does not permit the use of the sexual history information merely for impeachment of her character for truthfulness. The FRE has no provision for hypnotized witnesses.

Examples

1. Ben and his extended family got into a heated argument on Easter Sunday. One of their neighbors overheard the family yelling, using racial slurs, and threatening to "go postal" on an African American neighbor later that night. The neighbor called the police, and Ben was arrested for disturbing the peace. At his criminal trial, Ben offered the testimony of each of his family members, who all testified under oath that they were not planning to hurt anyone and that they had been drinking and were simply "doing some family bonding and having a good time together." On cross-examination of each family member, the prosecution asked about previous arrests. Each family member who testified had been arrested once before on misdemeanor charges including disturbing the peace, assault and battery, domestic violence, and forgery. Ben objected that these questions were improper impeachment of his family members. How should the court rule on the disturbing the peace charge? On assault and battery? On domestic violence? On forgery?

2. Mrs. Tista was sexually molested by her pastor Reverend Bauto when she met with him privately to obtain marriage counseling. Reverend Bauto told Mrs. Tista that if she told on him she would destroy their church because he would kill himself. Mrs. Tista eventually told the police about the sexual abuse, and the pastor was put on trial for molestation. At trial, Reverend Bauto sought to discredit Mrs. Tista's testimony by asking about her past sexual history of having sexual encounters with many men that led to her need for marriage counseling. The prosecution objected that this is not proper impeachment. How should the court rule?

3. Using the same facts as Example 2, consider the following: At trial, Mrs. Tista testified about the molestation. When asked why she waited so long to report the crime to the authorities, Mrs. Tista explained that Reverend Bauto had told her that she would be destroying the church. The defense then objected to any inquiry about the defendant's or Mrs. Tista's religious beliefs as impermissible under CEC 789. How should the court rule?

4. Sue was on trial for armed robbery. Sue drove to the local Chase bank branch and rammed her car into the glass partition in the front of the building. Then she leaned out of the car window and yelled to the tellers to put all the money in the trunk. After they had done so, Sue backed out

of the bank and started to drive away, but a Highway Patrol Officer flashed his lights and pulled her over. At trial, the prosecution seeks to offer evidence of Sue's two prior felony bank robbery convictions. Sue's defense counsel objects. How should the court rule?

5. Foster was a single father with a teenage daughter named Cindy. He started dating Becky, who had been physically and mentally abused by her parents and had a strong aversion to yelling, screaming, and physical violence of any kind. When Cindy misbehaved, Foster would yell and rant while he lashed Cindy with a belt. When Becky observed this behavior, she would have to leave the room and play loud music to block out the noise. Eventually, a case worker came and removed Cindy from the home. At Foster's trial for child abuse, the prosecution called Becky as a witness, and she testified about Foster yelling, screaming, and hitting Cindy. On cross-examination, Foster asked Becky whether it was true that she was beaten up by her parents and whether she had a morbid fear of yelling, screaming, and hitting. The prosecution objected that these questions were outside the scope of the direct examination and thus improper on cross-examination. How should Foster respond, how should the court rule, and why?

6. Several priests were accused of sexual abuse, and the plaintiffs sued the Archdiocese for negligent supervision of the accused priests. In the defense case in chief, Father Pisci testified about his role in supervising these priests. On cross-examination, the plaintiffs' attorneys sought to impeach Father Pisci by admitting his misdemeanor conviction for committing a lewd act. The defense attorneys objected that in a civil case, only felony convictions are admissible. The plaintiffs responded that they were using the conviction to show bias. How should the court rule, and why?

7. Oscar is on trial for arson and attempted murder. He allegedly had broken into the home of elderly Rose, hit her on the head, and then set the building on fire. Rose was able to get out of the building, and when the paramedics arrived, she told them, "I was hit on the head by a white man who set the building on fire." Later, when Rose gave a statement to the police, she said, "I was hit on the head by a tan man." Oscar, who has tan skin color, was bragging about setting a building on fire, and his bragging came to the attention of the police. After an investigation, the police arrested Oscar for the arson and attempted murder of Rose. Rose testified at trial that her attacker was tan. At trial, Oscar wanted to offer Rose's first statement that the man was white. The prosecution objected. How should the defendant respond, and how should the court rule?

Explanations

1. The court should sustain all of Ben's objections. The question of whether a witness has been arrested is not proper impeachment material. Being arrested is not a prior bad act, but rather is something that was done to the witness. If the questions instead had asked whether the witness committed an assault, domestic violence, or battery, then those questions would be about the witness's own past acts. These questions still would be improper as irrelevant, however, because these prior bad acts show violence and disruption, not the family members' character for truth-telling. While the Truth in Evidence provision permits inquiry into character other than honesty or veracity in a criminal case, only prior bad acts demonstrating credibility or its lack thereof will pass the CEC 352 balancing test and be admissible. The prior forgery crime does involve credibility. Therefore, a question asking whether the witness had engaged in forgery (but not whether she was arrested for it) would be proper on cross-examination for the purpose of impeaching that witness's credibility in this criminal case.

2. The court should grant a CEC 782 hearing to evaluate the evidence that Reverend Bauto seeks to admit about Mrs. Tista's sexual history. When the defendant in a sexual offense case seeks to attack the credibility of a witness who is the alleged victim with evidence of her past sexual conduct, a separate hearing must first be held according to the requirements of CEC 782 (or CEC 783 for civil cases). Here the court will likely decide during the CEC 782 hearing that the evidence is not admissible to impeach the witness. Not only does the evidence involve her past sexual conduct with people other than the defendant (which may violate CEC 1103(c) if the defendant uses that evidence to prove the victim consented), but the evidence also fails the CEC 352 balancing test. Based on the facts given, the prejudicial effect of evidence that the witness is promiscuous would outweigh the probative value of those affairs on the witness's credibility, and the judge will exclude the evidence under CEC 352.

3. The court should sustain the objection to prevent any criticism or denigration of their religious beliefs for the purposes of impeaching or supporting credibility. However, to the extent the religious beliefs help to explain Mrs. Tista's delay in reporting the crimes, some inquiry about religion can be appropriate and would be permitted by the court to prove matters other than the impact of Mrs. Tista's religion on her credibility.

4. The court should overrule the objections only if Sue testifies at trial. In a criminal case, specific evidence of convictions is admissible to

impeach a witness at trial. While Sue is the defendant in the criminal case, she is not required to testify. If she does not testify, then she is not a witness, and the specific instance evidence of her past conviction cannot be admitted to impeach her. The general character evidence ban would apply to prevent the use of specific instances of her character to prove conduct in conformity. The prosecution may try to offer the prior armed robberies for a non-conduct in conformity purpose, such as evidence of a common plan or scheme under CEC 1101(b) (which is discussed in Chapter 2), but the prejudicial effect of such a use may substantially outweigh its probative value.

5. There are several responses that Foster can make. On the first objection, the prosecution is right that the questions exceed the scope of the direct examination. Becky's direct testimony did not include evidence of her childhood or her fears. Foster may argue that it is permissible to exceed the scope of the direct to inquire into credibility issues, and that these questions go to show bias or motive. The prosecution can respond that her past experience does not make her a less credible witness to someone else's potential child abuse, but the court likely will allow the questions on this basis.

Second, Foster could argue that Becky has an unrealistic perception of what constitutes abuse based on her oversensitivity. These questions suggest that Becky might be biased in her interpretation of what constitutes child abuse, given her oversensitivity. This argument would form an appropriate basis for overruling the objection. However, the evidence seems more relevant to attack Becky's character for being fearful or overly sensitive to yelling, rather than her character for truthfulness. While other character traits can be addressed in a criminal case under Proposition 8, if the trait does not relate to credibility, then it will be excluded under CEC 1101(a). An objection on that basis likely would be sustained. Instead, Foster can inquire about whether Becky had an impaired opportunity to perceive the alleged abuse because she left the room when it started. This question inquires about what actually happened in the home, not about Becky's character.

6. The court should sustain the defense's objection. In civil cases, only felony convictions are admissible to impeach credibility, and the felony must involve moral turpitude. Misdemeanor convictions are not admissible in civil cases. It does not matter whether the conviction is being offered to show a bias because all convictions in civil cases are governed by CEC 787. Misdemeanors implicating credibility are admissible in criminal cases due to the Truth in Evidence provision. However, the conviction for a lewd act is a misdemeanor that does not directly relate to credibility. Thus, even if this was a criminal case, the misdemeanor conviction would be inadmissible.

7. The defendant should respond that he is offering Rose's first statement under CEC 770 as a prior inconsistent statement and that the jury is allowed to consider a prior inconsistent statement when evaluating a witness's credibility (CEC 780). The court should then overrule the prosecution's objection as long as Rose has not yet been excused as a witness or already had a chance to explain or deny the prior inconsistent statement.

9 CHAPTER

Opinion Testimony: Lay and Expert

People often express themselves in the form of an opinion, drawing inferences and even conclusions from facts they observe. However, when the facts are sparse, opinion evidence may be necessary to help the jurors make sense of the limited factual evidence. In such cases, it would be counterproductive in the search for justice to forbid witnesses from giving opinions when they testify at trial. Thus the CEC permits both lay witness and expert witness opinion testimony under certain conditions.

Whenever confronted with testimony in the form of an opinion, first consider whether the person is giving a lay opinion or an expert opinion. Opinions based on common experience are referred to as *lay opinions*, and opinions based on technical, scientific, or other specialized knowledge are called *expert opinions*. Figure 9.1 shows these two categories of opinion testimony.

CEC 800 permits witness testimony containing lay opinions on relevant matters only when the opinion is

1. "rationally based on the perception" of the witness, *and*
2. is "helpful to a clear understanding" of the testimony.

For expert opinions, where the information is based on technical, scientific, or other specialized knowledge, CEC 801 requires that the opinion be about subject matter "sufficiently beyond common experience" and be based on material that is reasonably relied on by other experts in that field. For instance, a medical history is information that doctors use to help diagnose an illness. A reasonable doctor relies on medical histories, and thus a medical history is material that is reasonably relied on by medical experts.

When the expert testimony involves techniques and procedures that are relatively new to science, and new to the law, then reasonable reliance is not sufficient. The courts apply the *Kelly* test in these circumstances, which evaluates whether the technique or procedure is generally accepted in the relevant expert field. This chapter discusses the differences between the reasonable reliance and generally accepted standards, and explains how to determine which standard applies to your expert testimony.

Building on the questioning techniques described in Chapter 8, this chapter also shows you how to establish the expertise of your expert witness and how to cross-examine an opposing expert. The chapter concludes with a brief section on experts on specific issues.

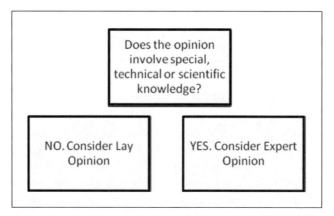

Figure 9.1. Categorizing Opinion Testimony

LAY OPINIONS

Lay opinions are governed by CEC 800. The statute's first requirement is that the lay opinion must be "rationally based on the perception" of the witness. In evaluating this first criterion, determine whether the witness used one of her five senses to perceive an act or event. For instance, imagine a case in which the defendant allegedly smashed a person's head with a bat during a drunken bar brawl. One witness might have seen the defendant's face turn crimson and inferred that the defendant suddenly got very angry. As a result, she might testify, "In my opinion, the defendant was very angry when he smashed the victim in the head." Another witness may have heard the defendant slur his words and smelled the defendant's breath as the defendant stumbled into him and inferred that the defendant was intoxicated. A third witness may have felt the bat used to smash the victim in the head and give an opinion that the bat was made of foam rubber. A fourth witness may have tasted the defendant's margarita and give an opinion that the drinks were very watered down. In each case, the witness perceived something about the defendant, whether it be seen, heard, smelled, felt, or tasted.

CEC §800: Opinion testimony by lay witness
If a witness is not testifying as an expert, his testimony in the form of an opinion is limited to such an opinion as is permitted by law, including but not limited to an opinion that is:
(a) Rationally based on the perception of the witness, and
(b) Helpful to a clear understanding of his testimony.

Opinion Rationally Based on the Witness's Perception

After establishing the witness's perception, ask whether the opinion that the witness seeks to give is *rationally based* on that perception. As long as the opinion is logically connected to that which the witness perceived, this first criterion will be met. For example, inferring sudden anger from an emerging crimson complexion is rational just as inferring intoxication from the sound of slurred words and the smell of alcohol is rational. Tasting is a rational way to determine whether a drink is watered down, and touching an item is a good way to feel whether the item is hard or soft.

On the other hand, if the witness saw the defendant pick up some coins that had fallen on the floor and, from that observation, inferred that the defendant was fearful, there is no rational connection. Similarly, if a witness watched a man stumble three times while trying to cross the room and inferred that he was very sure-footed and stone-cold sober, an opinion of sure-footedness could not be rationally based on watching someone stumble multiple times.

Witnesses can use lay opinions to estimate the value of their own property or their own services, but when that value is speculative or intangible, expert testimony may be necessary. For instance, a woman without any special training can potentially estimate the value of a diamond ring she inherited from a family member. The jury can evaluate how much weight to give her lay opinion, based on the support for her value estimate. If the witness instead were asked to provide the projected value of her stock portfolio in the year 2020, she would need to have some experience in that area before her lay opinion about that value would be useful to the trier of fact.

Lay opinions can be admitted about another person's weight, age, or approximate height; to estimate time and distance; and to describe basic emotions like fear and anger. Depending on the mode of perception, a witness can also give an opinion on whether a substance was an illegal drug (by tasting or otherwise ingesting it) and can describe apparent intoxication, drowsiness, or hyperactivity as long as the witness has personal knowledge about how an intoxicated, drowsy, or hyperactive person behaves (meaning she has seen one before).

Opinion Helpful to the Trier of Fact

The second criterion further limits opinion testimony to that which is helpful. If the opinion is not helpful to a clear understanding of the witness's testimony, then the opinion should not be admitted into evidence because it is of no use to the fact finder. For instance, when the opinion testimony merely supports information that can be proven with established facts, the opinion itself may not be helpful under CEC 800.

Often a witness will try to testify to the opinion, without providing the underlying information needed to assess whether the witness perceived something and rationally based her opinion on that perception. For instance, if the witness merely says, "In my opinion, he suddenly got angry," opposing counsel may wish to object on the basis of a lack of foundation for the opinion testimony because the witness did not explain what made her think the defendant was angry. The court likely will sustain the objection, but give the examining counsel the opportunity to lay the foundation for the opinion testimony.

EXPERT OPINIONS

When the subject matter of testimony is beyond common experience, expert opinion testimony can be offered to assist the trier of fact in understanding the evidence. Expert testimony that adds nothing to the jurors' common knowledge and experience will not be admissible. For instance, expert testimony about driving a car in "stop and go" traffic will not be outside the common experience, unless the car is a race car or the jury is made up of people who have never had drivers' licenses. Expert testimony about riding a bicycle or walking up a hill is unlikely to be outside the common experience of the jurors. Testimony about landing a malfunctioning airplane or parachuting from a perfectly good airplane is outside of common experience, and relevant expert testimony in these areas will be allowed.

CEC §801: Opinion testimony by expert witness

If a witness is testifying as an expert, his testimony in the form of an opinion is limited to such an opinion as is:

(a) Related to a subject that is sufficiently beyond the common experience that the opinion of an expert would assist the trier of fact; and

(b) Based on such matter (including the specialized knowledge, skill, experience, training, and education) perceived by or personally known to the witness or made known to him at or before the hearing, whether or not admissible, that is of a type that reasonably may be relied upon by an expert in forming an opinion upon the subject to which his testimony relates, unless precluded by law from using such matter as a basis for his opinion.

Expert opinion testimony about uncommon experiences or knowledge must be based on matters of a type reasonably relied on by experts in the field generally. The underlying information that forms the basis for the expert opinion can be obtained in a variety of ways, including by the expert's own perception or personal knowledge or by being told about it before or during the hearing in the case.

This is a crucial difference from lay opinion testimony, which can be based only on the witness's own perception. The expert must have perceived the information or otherwise had the information revealed to her before or during the hearing. Thus there are multiple ways for an expert witness to learn the information that forms the basis of her opinion. The expert can observe the plaintiff in court and listen to the plaintiff's testimony about symptoms and pain and then render her expert opinion. Or an expert can read a report written by some other doctor who had examined the victim and testify about her expert opinion without ever having seen or examined the victim herself.

Figure 9.2 summarizes how to evaluate opinion testimony.

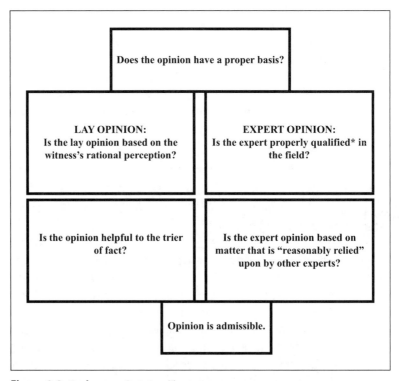

Figure 9.2. Evaluating Opinion Testimony

*Reasonable reliance and expert qualifications are discussed in the sections below.

THE BASIS FOR THE EXPERT OPINION AND THE REASONABLE RELIANCE TEST

For a witness to provide an expert opinion, the proponent must show a proper basis for the expert testimony. This showing involves an examination of the underlying information that helped the expert to form her opinion. If that information is the type of information *reasonably relied on* by other experts in that field, then that will be a proper basis for the expert opinion. Courts are comfortable with expert opinions relying on the same matters that the experts use in their fields of expertise to make diagnoses and other decisions and are less comfortable with innovative or unusual approaches. The information that the experts rely on can be admissible or inadmissible and can be based on personal knowledge, secondhand knowledge, and even hypothetical questions, as long as the information is the type of information that other experts reasonably rely on in making their opinions, such as an actuarial chart or a medical treatise detailing a list of symptoms for various diseases.

This proper basis or foundation is similar to that discussed for the hearsay exceptions in Chapters 5 through 7 and permits the court to evaluate whether the requirements of the opinion statute are met. For this reason, CEC 802 allows the court to require opinion witnesses to disclose the matter on which the opinion is based, such as the perception of "seeing the defendant's crimson face" or "smelling alcohol." In addition, CEC 803 permits the court to exclude the opinion or any portions of it that are based on improper material, such as the opinion that "picking up change" means that one is "fearful." These sections apply to all opinion testimony, regardless of whether the testimony is given by a layperson or an expert witness.

CEC §802: Statement of basis of opinion

A witness testifying in the form of an opinion may state on direct examination the reasons for his opinion and the matter (including, in the case of an expert, his special knowledge, skill, experience, training, and education) upon which it is based, unless he is precluded by law from using such reasons or matter as a basis for his opinion. The court in its discretion may require that a witness before testifying in the form of an opinion be first examined concerning the matter upon which his opinion is based.

CEC §803: Opinion based on improper matter

The court may, and upon objection shall, exclude testimony in the form of an opinion that is based in whole or in significant part on matter that is not a proper basis for such an opinion. In such a case, the witness may, if there remains a proper basis for his opinion, then state his opinion, after excluding from consideration the matter determined to be improper.

If the expert relies on information that is unusual or different from that of other experts, then the reasonable reliance element is not met. For instance, if most experts rely on actuarial charts to estimate the future earnings of a 40-year-old engineer, then an expert who gives an opinion about future earnings and relies on actuarial charts in forming that opinion will have a proper basis for his opinion. By contrast, if an expert seeks to offer an opinion about future earnings based on the length of the engineer's palm, that information would not be a proper basis for the expert opinion. Where the basis is not proper, then the foundation for the expert opinion is not adequate. In such cases, the court will sustain an objection to the expert's opinion testimony. If the opinion is not based on matters reasonably relied on by experts in that field, then the judge should exclude the opinion.

Experts must also avoid omitting factors that would be reasonably relied on by other experts. For example, if it is reasonable for an expert forensic scientist to rely on his sense of smell in identifying a particular chemical, the expert's testimony about smelling a particular substance can provide an appropriate basis for his expert opinion about the identity of the substance. However, when most experts rely on their sense of smell in this situation and the testifying expert does not, then that expert's opinion testimony may be excluded because it fails to consider methods that are reasonably relied on in the field.

Using Hypothetical Questions with Experts

Hypothetical questions are another way to make facts known to an expert at the hearing. For instance, the plaintiff's attorney calls the expert and asks what her prognosis would be if a person testified to a set of hypothetical symptoms, and then the plaintiff's attorney repeats the plaintiff's list of symptoms. The expert opinion testimony about those same symptoms is helpful to ensure a clear understanding of the plaintiff's testimony. However, if the hypothetical excludes several symptoms that the plaintiff testified about or otherwise inadequately represents the evidence presented in the case, then the opinion should not be allowed because it may be irrelevant and also may exclude matter (symptoms) reasonably relied on by other experts in the field. Thus, the hypothetical question must not be pulled from thin air, but must be related to the facts presented at trial.

Using Inadmissible Information with Experts

It does not matter whether the information that forms the basis for the expert opinion is admissible, as long as it is the type of information reasonably relied on by experts in that field (and is not based on impermissible matter that violates statutory, constitutional, or case law). Thus, inadmissible information still can be a proper basis for an expert opinion.

For instance, records that constitute hearsay can be a proper basis for the expert opinion if the records are the type of information reasonably relied on by others in the medical field. If the expert testifies that in her opinion the defendant did not commit malpractice, the expert may disclose the underlying basis for that opinion using statements contained in the medical reports under CEC 803. If a hearsay objection is made and sustained, the medical report statements would not be admissible for the truth of the matter asserted, but they would be admissible to show the basis for the expert opinion. The opposing counsel should make this request in the form of a limiting instruction to the jury (limiting instructions are explained in Chapter 1).

The court retains discretion to exclude any mention of the hearsay statement, even for a non-truth purpose, where the matter is irrelevant, incompetent, or unreliable.

If the expert testifies that her opinion is based on the opinion or statement of another person, such as the written statement of another doctor who is not a party, is not identified with a party, and has not been a witness in the case, then that other person may be called as a witness to testify about that statement or opinion under CEC 804.

Experts also may rely on unduly prejudicial information to form the basis for their opinions, as long as that basis passes the reasonable reliance test. In such situations, opposing counsel should object to prevent the expert from disclosing to the jury the prejudicial material that forms the basis for that expert opinion. Where the information is irrelevant, unreliable, or poses an undue risk of prejudice, the court should exclude the information under CEC 352 (see Chapter 1). When the underlying evidence is a hearsay statement and that statement is also unduly prejudicial, the court has the discretion to exclude the hearsay statement and need not admit it with a limiting instruction. Profile evidence is generally precluded as unduly prejudicial along with irrelevant or speculative matters and polygraph evidence.

For instance, if a homicide defendant exercises her constitutional right not to testify in her own trial, but seeks to admit her own statements about the killing through the testimony of her expert psychiatrist, the court may find that a limiting instruction would not be adequate. If the jury considers those statements for the truth of the matter asserted, then the risk of potential prejudice might substantially outweigh the probative value of the defendant's hearsay evidence. Unsubstantiated hearsay has a lower probative value, and exculpatory statements that are not subject to cross-examination (because the hearsay declarant declined to testify) might lead the jury to decide based on passions and prejudices, rather than the law.

Federal Rules of Evidence Compared: Minor Differences

FRE 701 adds that the testimony also can be helpful to the determination of a fact in issue, and that the testimony must not be based on technical, scientific, or other specialized knowledge, to ensure that expert opinions are admitted only under the expert witness rules discussed below. This first addition merely reiterates a version of the relevance rule. The second difference in the FRE has no practical impact because in California, if the matter involves technical or specialized knowledge, it too is governed by the expert witness CEC sections.

FRE 703 provides some additional detail on the proper bases for opinion testimony, but is limited to expert opinion testimony and therefore is included in the Federal Rules of Evidence Compared section within the "Kelly Test" section below.

FRE 705 takes a different approach to the disclosure of the basis for the opinion and also is limited to expert opinion testimony.

QUALIFYING THE EXPERT

To testify as an expert, a witness must possess *special knowledge, skill, experience, training, or education* on the subject matter of his testimony. When there is an objection by the opposing party, CEC 720 requires that the expert witness's background be proven before the opinion testimony is offered. Most attorneys prefer to establish the expert witness's background and credentials before the other side objects. They do this by asking a series of questions to trace through the witness's resume, describing his education, experience, additional training, publications, and other information to support that the expert is knowledgeable in the particular area of inquiry. The judge uses the preponderance of the evidence standard to determine whether the expert is more likely than not qualified to give an opinion on the subject matter.

CEC §720: Qualification as an expert witness
(a) A person is qualified to testify as an expert if he has special knowledge, skill, experience, training, or education sufficient to qualify him as an expert on the subject to which his testimony relates. Against the objection of a party, such special knowledge, skill, experience, training, or education must be shown before the witness may testify as an expert.
(b) A witness' special knowledge, skill, experience, training, or education may be shown by any otherwise admissible evidence, including his own testimony.

Recall from Chapter 5 that the preponderance standard is satisfied if something is more likely than not — meaning 50.1 percent likely is enough, and 49.9 percent likely is not enough. An expert is qualified to give expert opinion testimony under CEC 720 if it is more likely than not that she has the knowledge or skill necessary to form her expert opinion. How to meet the preponderance test will vary with the type of expert. For instance, in medical malpractice cases, deciding whether an expert is qualified to speak about the "standard of care" requires an inquiry into the expert's training and experience in similar cases under similar circumstances. The expert need not have experience with cases at the particular hospital or medical center where the alleged malpractice occurred. However, location can be important in situations where there are large geographic differences in accepted medical practices.

In a case involving lost future earnings, an economics expert would have to have experience evaluating the salaries and trends in a particular labor market, but other labor markets may have similar trends. On the other hand, expert testimony in a products liability case about a defective automobile part would not require the expert to have experience with that particular broken part in the past because a broken part is a broken part, regardless of where or when it occurred.

CROSS-EXAMINING THE EXPERT

Once the expert is deemed to meet the preponderance standard for qualifications, she can give her opinion on the matter at issue. Then, the opposing side can cross-examine the expert. The cross-examination provisions of the CEC discussed in Chapter 8 also apply to expert witnesses. However, an additional CEC provision permits cross-examining experts about their qualifications, the subject of their testimony, and the matters on which their testimony is based. Recall from Chapter 8 that the scope of cross-examination generally is limited to what was asked on direct examination and credibility. Under that rule, if an expert's qualifications are not discussed on direct examination, then the cross-examination could not address the expert's qualifications. Because the expert's qualifications must be established for the expert to give her opinion, CEC 721 permits "fully cross-examining" the expert in this area. This full cross-examination may exceed the scope of direct and credibility.

CEC §721: Cross-examination of expert witness
(a) Subject to subdivision (b), a witness testifying as an expert may be cross-examined to the same extent as any other witness and, in addition, may be fully cross-examined as to (1) his or her qualifications, (2) the subject to which his or her expert testimony relates, and (3) the matter upon which his or her opinion is based and the reasons for his or her opinion.

(b) If a witness testifying as an expert testifies in the form of an opinion, he or she may not be cross-examined in regard to the content or tenor of any scientific, technical, or professional text, treatise, journal, or similar publication unless any of the following occurs: (1) The witness referred to, considered or relied upon such publication in arriving at or forming his or her opinion. (2) The publication has been admitted in evidence. (3) The publication has been established as a reliable authority by the testimony or admission of the witness or by other expert testimony or by judicial notice. If admitted, relevant portions of the publication may be read into evidence but may not be received as exhibits.

This full cross-examination allows not only delving into the expert's qualifications to testify on the particular subject matter, but also inquiring into whether the expert sufficiently considered matters that are inconsistent with her opinion. For instance, a medical doctor may give an opinion about her diagnosis of a particular illness and testify that her diagnosis was based on five symptoms that the patient had experienced. Under CEC 721, the opposing party may cross-examine the expert about additional symptoms the patient experienced, to see if those symptoms are consistent with a different diagnosis or are inconsistent with the doctor's current diagnosis. If so, opposing counsel can ask the doctor to explain why she made the diagnosis given the inconsistencies. The answers affect the weight of the expert testimony. The jury can decide how much credibility to place on the expert's opinion in light of other symptoms either not considered or dismissed by the expert.

Examining the Basis for the Expert Opinion

The basis for an expert opinion often includes treatises and other established reliable sources routinely consulted by experts, such as the *Diagnostic and Statistical Manual of Mental Disorders* (DSM-IV)[1] for psychiatrists and psychologists, and perhaps *Gray's Anatomy* for surgeons and other medical doctors. The CEC permits cross-examination about treatises and other similar sources when they were

1. consulted by the expert,
2. admitted into evidence,
3. established by testimony to be reliable, or
4. considered to be reliable by judicial notice (which is addressed in Chapter 10).

Special care must be taken to avoid unlimited questioning on any treatises because that would put evidence before the fact finder without any opportunity for cross-examination of the proponents of that content.

---

1. The DSM-IV is published by the American Psychiatric Association and is commonly used as a resource by mental health professionals. The DSM-IV lists recognized mental disorders and the criteria required to diagnose the disorders.

A party may bring material to the jury's attention that is relevant to the expert's opinion and that the expert was either unaware of or did not consider. The jurors can be instructed that they must not consider the treatise for the truth, unless it has been admitted under some hearsay exception. The jury should consider how the questions based on those treatises affect their weighing of the expert's testimony and the basis for his opinion.

Offering statements from treatises can implicate the Hearsay Rule. CEC 1341, which provides a hearsay exception for publications concerning facts of general notoriety and interest, covers some expert materials. CEC 1341 states: "Historical works, books of science or art, and published maps or charts, made by persons indifferent between the parties, are not made inadmissible by the hearsay rule when offered to prove facts of general notoriety and interest." Medical journals generally will not fit under this definition because the science of medicine is constantly evolving and changing.

Examining Bias and Other Interests

Another aspect of expert witness cross-examination involves potential bias or interest in the outcome of the litigation. This line of questioning affects the credibility of the expert witness, which is always relevant. For this reason, under CEC 722 the opposing party may ask questions about whether the expert is court-appointed or hired by a party, as well as questions about the compensation the expert receives for her testimony. CEC 723 permits the court to limit the number of expert witnesses called by any party.

Federal Rules of Evidence Compared: Some Substantive Differences

For qualifying an expert, FRE 702 applies the same standard as CEC 720, requiring a preponderance of evidence to show that the proffered expert has the "knowledge, skill, experience, training, or education" to qualify her as an expert in a particular field.

In the area of cross-examination, FRE 705 permits the expert to testify about his opinion without first testifying as to the underlying facts or data, but recognizes that the expert may be required to disclose that information on cross-examination. The FRE does not contain any counterpart to the portions of CEC 721(a) about "full" cross-examination, but in practice most judges permit the same inquiry under FRE 402 as long as it is relevant to issues in the litigation, including the credibility of witnesses.

Typically in federal court, the proponent of the expert witness establishes the witness's qualifications, and the adverse parties have a chance to immediately voir dire the expert about her qualifications, just as they do in California court. Generally the federal courts give counsel some "elbow room" in cross-examining an expert as to the basis for his inferences.

As for cross-examination about publications, the FRE permits broader inquiry into other sources when cross-examining an expert witness with authoritative books in the field under FRE 803(18) than is available under CEC 1341. The FRE permits cross-examination of experts about statements in these treatises regardless of whether the expert relied on that treatise in forming her opinion. In addition, the statements from these treatises may be admitted for the truth of the matter asserted if

1. the statements are established as reliable authority by expert testimony or by judicial notice (which is addressed in Chapter 10), and
2. the expert witness either testified during direct examination that she relied on that treatise or had that treatise called to her attention on cross, as long as an expert is available on the witness stand to assist the jury in applying the treatise.

FRE 706(c) provides for the disclosure of court-appointed experts, and federal case law permits an inquiry into fees paid to experts, thus covering both aspects of CEC 722. The FRE has no specific rule corresponding to CEC 723.

Examples

1. Officer Ron arrested Brandy, a minor, for possession of a concealable firearm and live ammunition. At trial, the prosecutor sought to qualify Ron as an expert in identifying live ammunition, based on his police academy training and five years' experience as an officer handling live ammunition. Brandy's counsel objected that Ron was not properly qualified under CEC 720. How should the court rule?

2. Rachel sued the hospital where her recent surgery was performed, alleging fraudulent billing practices that charged uninsured patients higher rates than insured patients. In the civil trial, Rachel offered into evidence a document stating that in the opinion of the reviewer, Rachel's medical bill for $20,000 would have been only $6,000 if she had had health insurance. That document was created by Regin Medical Review Company, and no one from Regin appeared in court to testify about the review. The hospital objected that there was no properly qualified expert under CEC 720 because there was no witness from Regin at trial. What other objections might the hospital make, and how should the court rule? (Hint: Review Chapter 7, "Other Hearsay Exceptions," before answering this question.)

3. Tova fell down the stairs while on a visit to California and consulted an American doctor, Chris, who prescribed pain medication and put a splint

on her arm. A few weeks later, Tova returned to her home in Israel, and her regular doctor Elijah examined her arm. Elijah determined that the splint did not properly set the fractures in her arm and would result in some permanent injury. Tova sued Chris for medical malpractice in California court and sought to offer expert testimony from Elijah. Elijah attended medical school in Israel and has been practicing there for more than 20 years. He has treated numerous fractures successfully. Chris objected that Elijah was not qualified to speak about the standard of care in California because all of his experience was in Israel. How should the court rule?

Explanations

1. The court should overrule the objection. Five years of experience in addition to the training at the police academy meets the preponderance test for qualifying Ron as an expert in identifying live ammunition. Once the court determines that Ron's expert opinion is admissible, the jury still has to consider how much weight to give the expert opinion testimony. With only five years of experience, the jury may find that Ron's opinion does not carry much weight in their deliberations.

2. The court should sustain the objection and decline to admit the document as an expert opinion. The document itself does not provide the necessary information to qualify an expert because it does not explain the education, experience, or training of the person who performed the analysis. The document also would constitute hearsay unless a foundation is established for an exception. See Chapter 7 for a review of the business records hearsay exception.

3. The court should overrule the objection and permit Elijah to be qualified as an expert witness as long as he has experience dealing with similar injuries. The difference in geographic locations of his experience does not render his opinion less valid as long as the standards of medical care are similar in Israel and California. If Tova had fallen in a third world country, for instance, and been treated by Chris there, the standards may be different due to a lack of resources and supplies. In that case, Elijah's experience might not be similar enough for his testimony based on his past experience to be helpful in the current case.

THE *KELLY* TEST FOR NEW SCIENTIFIC TECHNIQUES AND PROCEDURES: GENERAL ACCEPTANCE

California courts require more than the reasonable reliance test when *new* (sometimes referred to as *novel*) scientific techniques, procedures, or methods form the basis for the expert opinion. In such cases, you must analyze the evidence using the *Kelly*[2] test. The *Kelly* test applies only to "that limited class of expert testimony which is based, in whole or in part, on a technique, process, or theory which is *new* to science and, even more so, the law."[3] The term *science* also includes social science techniques and psychological theories.

The *Kelly* test applies to all expert evidence that carries a "misleading aura of scientific infallibility"[4] because the court is concerned with unproven, new techniques or procedures that appear to have some definitive answer for the jurors. The question for the court is not which techniques are best, but which techniques are accepted as reliable by a significant number of experts in the field and which are subject to substantial criticism for unreliability by experts in the field. Expert testimony must establish that the correct scientific procedures were used and that the expert is properly qualified to testify about the reliability of the technique or procedure. There is no set time period on how new the process must be to require an analysis under the *Kelly* test.

Commonsense observations that jurors can make along with the expert witness do not implicate the *Kelly* test because they are less likely to be misleading and are not new to science or the law. For instance, when a procedure isolates physical evidence such as a shoe print and simply involves putting a clear overlay copy of one shoe print tread pattern on top of a copy of another, the comparison is very straightforward. The jurors do not need an expert opinion to assist them in visually comparing the collected shoe print with another shoe print. The jurors can look and see the relative size for themselves, and thus there is no "misleading aura of infallibility." This type of procedure would not be subject to the *Kelly* test. (Note: Expert opinion testimony would still be necessary to help the jurors understand the methods of collecting, preparing, and processing the shoe print evidence.)

Examples of the Misleading Aura of Infallability

The court analyzes the misleading aura of infallibility to address procedures and techniques that would be beyond the understanding of a juror, even with explanations by experts on each side of the case. For instance, some statistical analysis contains a misleading aura of infallibility and may thus be subjected to the *Kelly* test before expert opinions in that field will be admissible.

Consider expert testimony that renders an opinion that the chances of a particular DNA match are 100 billion to 1. The inference is that because

---

2. People v. Kelly, 17 Cal. 3d 24, 549 P.2d 1240 (1976).
3. People v. Stoll, 49 Cal. 3d 1136, 1156, 783 P. 2d 698 (1989).
4. Id. at 1157.

there are not 100 billion people on the planet, this blood must belong to the defendant. However, probability is not the same as causation. Even where there is an extremely high probability that the DNA in the blood from the crime scene matches the DNA in the defendant's blood, that probability does not mean that the defendant is the culprit. That probability simply means that the defendant's blood sample is very similar to the culprit's blood. The blood sample might have degraded or been tampered with, and human intervention could result in a false positive match. Thus the technique is fallible and just appears to be infallible. Certain DNA matching evidence still is novel and is subject to the more rigorous *Kelly* test to determine its admissibility.

The *Kelly* test also helps to curb the introduction of so-called junk science into the courtroom by subjecting new techniques to this more rigorous test. For instance, an expert purports to have a new technique for determining whether a person suffers from a mental incapacity — measuring the size of his waist. In a breach of contract trial in which Fred raises the affirmative defense of incapacity to contract, Fred's counsel may seek to offer the expert opinion that Fred suffers from a mental disability based on the evidence of Fred's waist size. If the court permits this expert opinion and the decision is upheld on appeal, then there would be precedent for using waist size to determine mental competence. The *Kelly* test requirement of general acceptance in the relevant professional community prevents one or two court decisions from changing the course of acceptable scientific analysis.

How to Satisfy *Kelly*

When the *Kelly* test applies, how does one analyze the *Kelly* test? The *Kelly* test adopted the federal standard from the *Frye*[5] case. It requires the proponent of the expert opinion testimony to persuade the judge that the novel scientific principle or technique "has been sufficiently established to have gained *general acceptance* in the particular field in which it belongs." General acceptance in the particular field is a much higher standard than the reasonable reliance test that is applied to expert testimony based on non-novel techniques and procedures. The reason the courts have a higher standard for new techniques and procedures is to help ensure reliability of the new tests, techniques, and procedures when they have not been subjected to years of peer review or extensive litigation in the courts.

A technique or process that is very new to science would implicate the *Kelly* test because of its novelty, but that same process would likely fail the *Kelly* test because it has not had enough time to become generally accepted.

---

5. Frye v. United States, 293 F. 1013, 1014 (1923).

It is very difficult to establish the reliability of such a novel process when the person who invented it is the only person who knows enough to testify about it. Additionally, when the inventor of a process has a financial or professional interest in having her test become generally accepted, any testimony by that expert may be biased in favor of promoting acceptance of the technique. Thus, in cases in which the sole or the crucial witness on a scientific process or technique has a substantial financial or professional interest in promoting that new technique, her testimony alone may not be adequate to establish the general acceptance necessary to meet the *Kelly* standard. In such a case, the court will decline to admit expert opinion testimony based on that novel technique.

Choosing the Right Test: *Kelly* or Reasonable Reliance?

Some criticisms of the *Kelly* test are based on the difficulty of determining which techniques are novel yet also generally accepted and which are established techniques that are reasonably relied on by experts in the field. How does one decide whether to apply the reasonable reliance test or the *Kelly* test of general acceptance?

Mere criticism of how a technique or process was used by a testifying expert is not the same as a misleading aura of infallibility, and thus will not implicate the *Kelly* test. For instance, a competing expert may criticize the way the other side's expert conducted a study or interpreted data. This type of criticism affects how much the fact finder should rely on that expert opinion or what weight the expert opinion carries. It does not implicate *Kelly* because criticism of how a technique was applied in one case does not imply that the technique itself is novel or has a misleading aura of infallibility. The court will leave to the jury the task of resolving competing expert approaches as long as the approaches meet the reasonable reliance threshold.

Examples of scientific techniques and processes that do trigger the *Kelly* test and are considered generally accepted are footprint and teeth or bite analysis, tests of bodily fluids, blood splatter analysis, and intimate partner battering evidence.

The following techniques and methods also triggered the *Kelly* test but failed to satisfy the general acceptance requirement:

1. Expert opinions on the cause of a minor's injury based on observations of a stuffed mannequin thrown down stairs

2. Methods of determining mold levels when only one lab used that particular method

However, the following types of expert opinions are not subject to the *Kelly* test and must meet only the reasonable reliance test:

1. Why witnesses making identifications may be mistaken
2. Why the personality of a defendant is inconsistent with the charged offense
3. Why rape victims do or say things that are inconsistent with their claims at trial
4. Shoe print analysis
5. The "cold hit" method of matching DNA from a crime scene to an existing DNA database

The bottom line is that if the technique is not novel or does not carry a misleading aura of infallibility, then the *Kelly* test does not apply. If the technique is new or has that misleading aura, then *Kelly* does apply, and the court must determine whether the technique is generally accepted in the relevant scientific community before admitting the expert opinion into evidence. Figure 9.3 summarizes these distinctions.

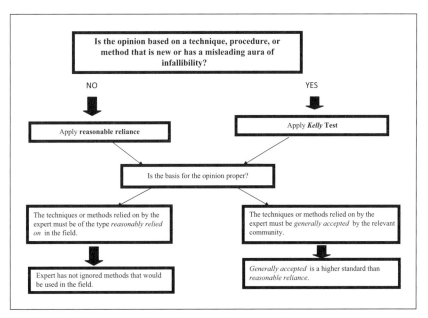

Figure 9.3. *Kelly* or Reasonable Reliance? Making Sure the Expert Opinion Has a Proper Basis

Federal Rules of Evidence Compared: Substantive Differences

FRE 702 combines the expert qualifications of CEC 720 with the testimony limitations of CEC 801 and has a modified standard for determining what expert opinion testimony is admissible: (1) the testimony must be based on sufficient facts or data, (2) the testimony must be the product of reliable principles and methods, and (3) the witness has applied the principles and methods reliably to the facts of the case.

FRE 703 applies a similar test to that of CEC 801. FRE 705 permits the expert to testify about his opinion without first testifying as to the underlying facts or data unless the court orders otherwise. In contrast, CEC 802 permits an expert witness to testify about the basis for his opinion unless he is precluded by law from doing so.

In areas new to science, federal courts used to apply the *Frye*[6] test to evaluate the admissibility of expert evidence. The *Frye* test used the same generally accepted standard that the *Kelly* test used in California. However, that changed in *Daubert v. Dow Chemicals*,[7] where the U.S. Supreme Court determined that *Frye* should no longer be applied in federal trials because it conflicts with the liberal admissibility approach of the FRE. FRE 702 was amended to reflect this new standard, which in contrast to the CEC applies broadly to all expert opinions, regardless of whether they are based on new or established scientific techniques.

EXPERT OPINIONS ALLOWED ON ULTIMATE FACTUAL ISSUES BUT NOT LEGAL ISSUES

Experts can give opinions on ultimate factual issues if the opinion will help the jurors to decide an issue that is beyond their scope of common knowledge. Experts cannot give opinions on ultimate legal issues, such as whether the defendant had a legal duty to the plaintiff or whether the plaintiff herself was negligent. However, experts can give opinions about ultimate issues of fact. Thus, an expert may testify that in her opinion the defendant was depressed, but she cannot testify that in her opinion the defendant had intent to commit murder.

---

6. Frye v. United States, 293 F. 1013 (1923).
7. 509 U.S. 579, 113 S.Ct. 2786 (1993).

CEC §805: Opinion on ultimate issue
Testimony in the form of an opinion that is otherwise admissible is not objectionable because it embraces the ultimate issue to be decided by the trier of fact.

Some issues seem to fall in the middle of these two, and in those cases the court will examine whether the expert opinion "invades the province of the jury to decide a case."[8] When the expert opinion is "amounts to nothing more than an expression of his or her belief on how a case should be decided,"[9] the opinion is not helpful to the trier of fact because it impinges on the jury's job of making that decision during deliberations. In that situation, the expert testimony would not be allowed.

On the other hand, when the issue is important but not the ultimate decision in the case, expert testimony can be admissible. For instance, an expert can offer opinion testimony on the issue of whether a crime was committed "to benefit or promote a gang" or whether a crime was "in furtherance of a conspiracy." However, that expert opinion must be based on sufficient facts to satisfy the reasonable reliance test. An expert cannot testify that a crime was committed to benefit a gang based on the single fact that the defendant was a gang member. More evidence is required for this opinion to meet the reasonable reliance test. Thus, if the defendant admitted gang membership and has gang tattoos, engaged in the crime with the help of several other known gang members, and committed the crime in gang territory, this additional information would be an adequate basis to support an expert opinion that the crime was for the benefit of the gang.

Expert profilers can testify, but the profile evidence may amount to inadmissible character evidence or unduly prejudicial evidence. For instance, an expert may describe a typical profile of a drug courier. If this expert opinion testimony is used to show that the defendant acted in a manner that corresponds to the profile and therefore he is the kind of person who is a drug dealer, it involves an impermissible propensity purpose, and the expert testimony will not be admitted to prove that proposition unless it meets one of the character exceptions discussed in Chapter 2. The underlying evidence could be admitted for a non-character purpose — such as possessing relevant knowledge under CEC 1101(b) (see Chapter 2) — but still will be subject to an objection as unduly prejudicial in violation of CEC 352 (the probative value/prejudice balancing test discussed in Chapter 1).

---

8. Summers v. A. L. Gilbert Co., 69 Cal. App. 4th 1155, 1182, 82 Cal. Rptr. 2d 162, 178 (1999).
9. Id. at 1183.

CEC 870 has carved out some exceptions to the ultimate issue rule. One exception involves opinion testimony about the sanity of another person. A witness who is intimately familiar with the person whose sanity is at issue is permitted to offer opinion testimony. This intimacy includes not only spouses but also close friends. When the validity of a document is disputed and the person whose sanity is at issue signed that document, a witness who also signed the document can give an opinion on whether the other person was sane at the time of signing.

In addition, when a witness can base an opinion on the sanity of another person on her own perception and that opinion is helpful to the trier of fact, the lay opinion on sanity is admissible under CEC 800. Also, an expert who is properly qualified and bases her opinion on matters that satisfy the reasonable reliance test can give an opinion on the sanity of another. However, a Penal Code provision prevents any witness from giving an opinion on the mental state of a criminal defendant.

Federal Rules of Evidence Compared: Minor Differences

FRE 704 adds a specific provision to the general rule about ultimate issues to prohibit an expert witness from testifying about whether the defendant did or did not have the mental state or condition constituting an element of the crime charged or of a defense in a criminal case. A similar provision prohibits such testimony by experts in California courts, but it is in the Penal Code, not the CEC.

COURT-APPOINTED EXPERTS: CEC 730–733

CEC 730 permits judges to appoint experts as needed to testify as well as to investigate and prepare reports. Court-appointed experts may be appropriate when experts in a controversial field have vastly different opinions from one another or when the parties' experts are biased in some way that suggests they are not able to provide a neutral assessment of the technical or specialized information. For instance, when a social worker has been involved with a family for years and is called as an expert witness to testify about the best placement for the children, the non-custodial parent may object that the ongoing relationship might interfere with the social worker's ability to provide a credible expert opinion. In such cases, the court has the discretion to grant a party's motion to appoint an expert or make the appointment on the court's own motion. The reports submitted by court-appointed experts are not confidential and therefore can be provided to the court as well as to the parties on both sides.

CEC 731 provides for the payment of court-appointed experts. In criminal and juvenile cases, the county pays the fees for the court-appointed expert, while in civil cases the court determines the proper apportionment between the parties. Under CEC 732, the court or either party can call a court-appointed expert to the stand to testify, and the non-calling party can cross-examine a court-appointed expert and object as he would with any other expert witness. The court-appointed expert process does not prevent the parties from hiring their own experts to evaluate the opinion of the court-appointed expert. Those experts are called *rebuttal experts* under CEC 733. However, the parties must pay the fees for these additional experts. A party who hires a rebuttal expert is not necessarily entitled to redo any physical and other examinations on which the court-appointed expert based her opinion. The court has the discretion to grant a reexamination or limit the rebuttal expert to reviewing the court-appointed expert's notes, tests, and reports. (The code sections on court-appinted experts are contained in the appendix.)

Federal Rules of Evidence Compared: Minor Differences

FRE 706 provides for court-appointed experts and payment for those experts and also states that the rule does not prevent the parties from calling their own expert witnesses. There are no substantive differences between the FRE and CEC 730 through 733. The FRE also authorizes the court to disclose to the jury which experts are court-appointed, but does not specifically address the fees paid to the expert, though that inquiry is permitted in most courts.

EXPERT OPINIONS ON SPECIFIC ISSUES: CEC 810–824

The CEC contains numerous specific provisions that apply to any legal action in which the value of property is to be determined. These property provisions apply to real property, interests in real property, and tangible personal property valued together with real property. The CEC permits expert opinion testimony on market value, comparable sales and leases, capitalization, and non-profit valuations. These code sections also specify the proper and improper bases for such opinions. The FRE does not contain any corresponding rules. (These code sections on specific expert opinions are contained in the appendix.)

THE INTIMATE PARTNER BATTERING EXCEPTION: CEC 1107

CEC 1107 permits the use of expert testimony regarding battery by an intimate partner and its effects in criminal cases. The effects of such battering include physical, emotional, and mental abuse and how that abuse impacts the victim's beliefs, perceptions, and behavior. This type of evidence once was commonly referred to as *battered woman* or *battered spouse syndrome evidence* and is now called *intimate partner battering evidence*.

CEC 1107(a): Intimate partner battering and its effects; expert testimony in criminal actions

In a criminal action, expert testimony is admissible by either the prosecution or the defense regarding intimate partner battering and its effects, including the nature and effect of physical, emotional, or mental abuse on the beliefs, perceptions, or behavior of victims of domestic violence, except when offered against a criminal defendant to prove the occurrence of the act or acts of abuse which form the basis of the criminal charge.

The prosecution may use this evidence to show the victim's fear of the defendant accused of domestic violence. However, such evidence is not admissible when offered against that defendant to prove the acts of abuse that form the basis for the underlying criminal charge.

When the battered spouse has been charged with harming or killing her batterer, the defense may wish to offer this evidence to show the defendant's fear of the victim or to show the reasonableness of her fear of death or great bodily injury to justify killing in self-defense.

CEC 1107(b) also explicitly lists a simple foundational requirement for admitting such evidence — the proponent must establish the relevancy of the evidence and the qualification of the expert witness. The section also specifically prevents the court from treating expert opinion testimony on intimate partner battering and its effects as a "new scientific technique" with unproven reliability. The code section also defines which "abuse" fits into this category, and notes that what was formerly referred to as battered women's syndrome would be covered by this intimate partner battering statute. The FRE has no corresponding provision for CEC 1107.

Examples

1. Fodam Investment Securities Fund sued QualWorld investment bank for fraud, misrepresentation, and securities violations resulting in a financial loss of more than $50 million. At the civil trial, the Chief Financial Officer of Fodam testified that the value of the securities was listed as over $55 million when Fodam and QualWorld entered into the transaction, but that when Fodam learned of the fraud and misrepresentation, the securities were worth only a little over $5 million. QualWorld's attorneys objected to the CFO's testimony as an improper lay opinion and moved to strike the opinion testimony. How should Fodam respond, and how should the court rule?

2. Maggie was on trial for attempted burglary. Her intended victim awakened to the sound of glass breaking and saw a woman's legs and black high heels with a red sole kicking through her bedroom window. The victim screamed, and the perpetrator ran away. When police responded to the homeowner's 911 call, they examined the shoe prints at the scene and noted that the shoe prints had spike heels and a faint imprint of "Christian Louboutin" on the sole. Maggie was arrested running down the street in high-heeled shoes. The police officer sought to testify about his opinion that the shoes Maggie was wearing at the time of her arrest matched the size and heel depth of the prints at the scene of the crime, and that the shoes had a slightly raised signature of Christian Louboutin on the bottom of the sole. Maggie's lawyer objected on the grounds that the lay opinion by a police officer was improper. How should the prosecution respond, and how should the court rule?

3. Larisa called the police one day when her husband, Milton, failed to come home from work. After several days, police investigator Ivan came to talk to Larisa about her husband's possible whereabouts. After a few more days, the police discovered Milton's body, and a credit card trace led them to Harry, who was arrested while driving Milton's van. Harry was charged with capital murder for killing Milton. Ivan met with Larisa frequently in the weeks leading up to the trial and called her almost every day during the trial. Larisa died of a heart attack during the penalty phase of Harry's death penalty trial. The prosecution sought to put Ivan on the stand to testify that Milton's murder left Larisa "heartbroken and overwhelmed," that she was "totally devastated" by the brutal killing of her husband. Harry's lawyer objects that Ivan's testimony is an impermissible lay opinion. How should the prosecution respond, and how should the court rule?

4. During the penalty phase of Harry's trial in Example 3, Harry seeks to offer mitigation evidence from his pediatrician, who will testify that in

his expert opinion, Harry's academic development was set back because of his unstable family life, which began when he was forced to take an extended family trip to Canada in the middle of his fifth grade school year. The prosecution objects that this is not the proper subject of expert testimony because it is not outside the common experience of the jury. How should the defense respond, and how should the court rule?

5. Opal called 911 one evening and told the operator that she had an argument with her husband, Sandy. After the argument, Sandy had beaten Opal when she declined to have intercourse with him, and then he forced himself on her. Sandy was charged with intimate partner battering and spousal rape. When the prosecution called Opal to testify at his trial, she simply said that Sandy had been "rough" with her, but that he did not "rape" her. Sandy's defense attorney sought to put on expert testimony from a psychology professor specializing in marriage counseling. The professor would give her opinion that the "rough" sex was actually consensual "make-up sex," which had been part of the couple's pattern of interaction over the years. The prosecution objected to the expert's opinion testimony on the grounds that it was not sufficiently beyond the common experience of the jurors to help them decide the issue of consent. How should the court rule?

6. Lexi is being prosecuted in criminal court for insurance fraud. Numerous documents were seized from his law office, and the court appointed a special master (magistrate judge) to review the boxes of documents to take out any privileged material before turning the evidence over to the prosecution. The special master spent weeks reviewing the documents and submitted a bill for over $25,000. The court apportioned the bill at 50/50 between Lexi and the district attorney's office. Should either party object to this apportionment, and if so, on what grounds?

7. Lindy wrote a letter to his cousin, Bert, trying to convince Bert to join him in his white supremacist club. Lindy's letter also bragged about killing a Chinese man by beating him to death. Bert turned the letter over to the police, who obtained a search warrant and searched Lindy's home. The police found articles, flyers, and books about white supremacy as well as a social networking website with "friends" pages linking Lindy to other known white supremacists in the area. Lindy was eventually charged with capital homicide. Lindy, along with three of his online "friends," also was charged with multiple counts of conspiracy to commit hate crimes. At trial, the prosecution seeks to offer the expert opinion testimony of a police sergeant who works with the Department of Homeland Security and specializes in monitoring white supremacist organizations. The sergeant would testify about the organizational structure of the groups and provide some insight

about the symbols and statements that were found among Lindy's possessions to explain the link between Lindy and his "friends" — the alleged co-conspirators. The expert also seeks to deliver his opinion that Lindy is a white supremacist. Lindy's counsel objects to the expert testimony on the grounds that it is not helpful to the trier of fact and embraces the ultimate legal issue to be decided by the jury in violation of CEC 801 and 805. How should the court rule?

8. Rick was on trial for criminal fraud based on operating an illegal pyramid scheme. The prosecution alleges that Rick defrauded people into buying products and contributing money with the promise of future profits as long as they maintained secrecy about the business plan and helped recruit new members into the club. The members received more than 75 percent of the funds in the form of investment returns. Rick offered the testimony of an expert witness who was properly qualified as an expert in pyramid schemes. In response to a hypothetical question by defense counsel, the expert gave his opinion that pyramid schemes are not secret organizations, do not sell products, and do not provide a return of 60 percent or more of the funds. The prosecution objected and moved to strike that answer. Before the court could rule on the objection, Rick's counsel then asked the expert, "In your opinion, is Rick's organization a 'pyramid scheme?'" The prosecuting attorney leapt from his seat and shouted, "Objection! Invades the province of the jury, Your Honor." How should the court rule?

9. Atuk sued Manny for legal malpractice alleging that Manny's incompetence caused Atuk to lose his patents on several new inventions for the automobile industry. During the civil trial, Atuk called Lisa as an expert witness to testify on damages. Lisa's expertise was as a CPA and business appraiser specializing in patent evaluations. She testified about the number of units that could have been manufactured per year and the approximate royalty rate per unit. The product had not yet been manufactured, so when she testified about the expected market penetration level for the product, an area in which she admitted she had no expertise, Manny's counsel objected that this was impermissible opinion testimony under CEC 801 and 803. Atuk's counsel responds that Lisa's opinion is based on market share projections that Atuk supplied to her. How should the court rule?

10. Gary underwent vasectomy surgery under the care of Dr. Tammy so that he and his wife would no longer be able to conceive children. After the surgery, Dr. Tammy assured Gary that the procedure had gone as planned. Six months later, Gary's faithful wife discovered that she was pregnant. When the baby was born, DNA testing revealed that the baby was Gary's son. Gary sued Dr. Tammy for malpractice,

emotional distress, and economic damages. Dr. Tammy filed a summary judgment motion, asserting that there was no triable issue of material fact, using the declaration of Dr. Bay. That declaration included a summary of Dr. Bay's resume and stated the following: "After reviewing Gary's medical records, in my expert opinion, Dr. Tammy complied with the standard of care and did nothing improper. The surgery just did not work." Gary's counsel objects to the declaration as an impermissible opinion based on improper matter under CEC 801 and 803. How should Dr. Tammy respond, and how should the court rule?

11. Cookie was arrested for the suspected homicide of his former teacher, and the police officers found a woman's purple shoe in his closet. The purple shoe had minute blood spatters on it. John, the criminologist, tested the blood stains on the purple shoe. Because the blood stains were very small, John combined several blood stains from that shoe into one sample, and then tested that sample to find out whether it matched the blood of the victim. At trial, John was qualified as an expert witness and sought to give his opinion that the blood on the purple shoe matched that of the victim. Cookie objected on the following grounds: the blood testing is a novel technique subject to the *Kelly* test, combination of blood splatters is not a generally accepted method, and John is not qualified to testify as an expert in blood splatter. What additional information would the judge need to have to decide whether to sustain or overrule Cookie's objection? How would the analysis differ if this case were tried in federal court?

12. Deon is the defendant in a civil lawsuit for personal injury damages from an automobile collision in which several people were injured and the driver at fault fled the scene. Deon claims that he was not the driver of the car involved in the hit and run, explaining that he has a very popular car (a black 2009 Mini Cooper convertible) and his car was at the car wash at the time of the accident. Presley is a crime scene analyst who specializes in tire tread analysis. Presley's technique is to make a plaster cast of the tire tread, pour a liquid rubber substance into the plaster cast to make a rubber mold, and then use that to make a tire print in the dirt at the crime scene. After checking to make sure that the original print and the rubber-made print match up, Presley scans the rubber tread pattern into a computer and uses a computer search engine to compare that print to tire prints from various automakers until he finds a match. At trial, the prosecution calls Presley as an expert on tire tread analysis. Presley testifies to his qualifications, and the court is satisfied that Presley is an expert in that field. Presley then seeks to offer his opinion that the tire print from the crime scene matches that of a 2009 Mini Cooper. Deon's lawyer objects on the grounds that Presley's technique is new to science and the plaintiff has not met

the burden of the *Kelly* test. How should the plaintiff's counsel respond, and how should the court rule?

13. Donnie is accused of shooting several sex-workers and is on trial for multiple murders and the attempted murder of another victim who survived. Donnie's expert, Dr. Terrie, was properly qualified as an expert in serial killer profiles and offered evidence that Donnie did not match any established serial killer profiles. On cross-examination, the prosecution sought to ask Dr. Terrie the following questions: (a) "Weren't you aware that Donnie carried a duffel bag filled with numerous guns on many occasions?" (b) "Were you not aware that Donnie showed others photos of women he claimed to have killed?" and (c) "Didn't you know that Donnie called sex-workers his 'girlfriends' and got upset when they worked for other men?" The defense objected to each of these questions as impermissible character evidence. The prosecution responded that these questions were permissible inquiries to test the credibility of the expert witness and the basis for her opinion. How should the court rule, and why? (Hint: Review Chapter 2, "The Character Evidence Exclusion Rules," before answering this question.)

Explanations

1. Fodam should respond that the lay opinion is admissible because non-expert witnesses are permitted to testify about the value of their own property or services under CEC 800. QualWorld may argue that the value of securities requires specialized knowledge and thus is a proper subject of expert opinion. However, the notes and cases interpreting CEC 800 provide that as long as the witness is testifying about his own property, his lay opinion as to the value is admissible if it is based on his own perception and helpful to the trier of fact. Here, the opinion was based on his studying of his own securities prior to and subsequent to the transaction, and his value assessment was rationally based on that perception, along with his financial training. Law Revision comments to CEC 800 make clear that a lay witness may give his opinion as to the value of his property or the value of his own services as long as it rationally based on perception and helpful to the trier of fact. The court should overrule QualWorld's objection and allow the CFO's testimony about value.

2. The prosecution should respond that the police officer's opinion is rationally based on his perception of the shoe prints and his observation of the shoes Maggie was wearing. The opinion will help the trier of fact so that they do not need to examine the shoe print photo and the shoes themselves to determine whether they match. Maggie may further

argue that the shoe print identification is the subject of specialized knowledge, experience, and training, and therefore the officer should not be able to testify as to his opinion unless he is qualified as a shoe print analysis expert. However, the court likely will find that the lay testimony as to the size and general description of the shoes and how they match the prints is not so far beyond the common experience of the jurors to require expert testimony.

3. The prosecution should argue that Ivan's testimony is a permissible lay opinion because it is rationally based on his perception of Larisa from interviewing her numerous times and his almost daily telephone calls with her. From that contact, Ivan would be able to form an opinion of how Larisa was feeling, including her mental and emotional state. That opinion is helpful to the trier of fact because Larisa is not able to testify to her own feelings due to her recent death. The defense may counter that the testimony about mental health should be the subject of an expert opinion because it requires some technical or scientific knowledge. The prosecution will respond that the concept of being heartbroken, overwhelmed, and devastated are not so far out of the common experience that expert testimony should be required. The court should overrule the objection and permit Ivan's lay opinion testimony.

4. The defense should respond that the opinion is the proper subject for expert testimony because it requires specialized knowledge to diagnose the origin of a child's subsequent antisocial behavior. The prosecution will respond that the testimony does not constitute a diagnosis, but rather consists of observations that are well within the common experience of most jurors. Leaving school for an extended period of time can rationally be linked to stunted academic development. Therefore there is no need for expert testimony on that point. The prosecution will argue further that the opinion is not helpful to the trier of fact because the jurors can deduce for themselves whether the family trip had a notable impact on Harry's academic development as they determine whether that should mitigate against imposing the death penalty for his crime. The court should sustain the objection and decline to admit the pediatrician's opinion.

5. The court should sustain the objection because the concept of whether a married couple engaged in "make-up sex" is not so far beyond the common knowledge of the jurors, and expert testimony would not be helpful to them in determining whether there was consent. Most jurors are aware of the phrase "make-up sex" and its characteristics — that it occurs after an argument in a sort of consensual, conciliatory gesture. The expert's testimony was not needed to explain to the jurors that the sexual act could have been consensual "make-up sex."

The evidence would be relevant only to the witness's credibility, and because her credibility was the primary issue for the jury to decide, it was not the proper subject of expert testimony. If the evidence had been offered to rebut a charge of fabrication (as discussed in Chapter 8), then it may have been relevant in much the same way that battered women and rape trauma syndrome evidence is admitted in those types of cases to address issues of delays in reporting the alleged crime.

6. Both parties should object to the apportionment. Lexi should object to this apportionment because this is a criminal case. Under CEC 731, in criminal cases, court-appointed experts are to be paid by the government. The prosecution should object to the apportionment because the statute mandates that the payment be made from the county treasury, not the district attorney office's budget.

7. The prosecution should respond that while the concept of white supremacy may be generally known to jurors, the specific details and beliefs may be outside of their common knowledge. The expert opinion would be helpful to the trier of fact in interpreting the white supremacist symbols and in understanding the way the organization operates. Provided that the police sergeant is properly qualified in this area, the court should overrule the objection and admit the police sergeant's expert opinion testimony about the white supremacist beliefs, symbols, and organizational structure. The court should overrule the objection on CEC 805 grounds as well because the ultimate legal issue is not whether Lindy is a white supremacist, but whether he committed a brutal murder with a hate crime special circumstance that justifies imposing the death penalty. This opinion testimony about an ultimate factual issue of his white supremacist classification is not prohibited by CEC 805.

8. The court should overrule the first objection and deny the motion to strike. The expert can testify about which factors, in his opinion, are not indicative of a pyramid scheme. However, the court should sustain the second objection and prevent the expert from giving his opinion that the scheme was a pyramid scheme. That was the ultimate issue for the jury to decide, and an expert opinion on that question would invade the jury's province.

9. The court should sustain the objection under CEC 800, 801, and 803. Lisa's admission that she has no experience in market penetration evaluation means that she is not qualified to render an expert opinion on that topic. If she sought to deliver a lay opinion about market penetration, it would have to be rationally based on her perception and helpful to the trier of fact. Since the product has not yet been manufactured, she has no perception of what market share the product

might eventually obtain, and her lay opinion would be inadmissible as well. Lisa's reliance on Atuk's own estimation of market share is not reasonable reliance because Atuk has no experience with the actual product or with market share calculations. Even if Atuk testified, it is unlikely that his lay opinion about the market share impact on the value of his proposed product would be admissible because he too has no perception on which to rationally base his opinion.

10. Dr. Tammy should respond that the medical records are the type of information reasonably relied on by experts in the field, and therefore those records are a permissible basis for the opinion. Gary should counter that the records were not admitted into evidence, constitute hearsay, and therefore cannot be admitted for the truth of the matters asserted therein. Because Dr. Bay is relying on the statements in those records about what sort of procedure was performed and what steps were taken, and because no witness has testified to those underlying facts, there is no admissible evidence on which Dr. Bay has based his opinion. The reliability of the medical records has not been established, and therefore they should be excluded under CEC 803 unless or until a proper foundation is laid. If the medical records had been admitted under the business records hearsay exception (see Chapter 7), their reliability could have been established and the records could form a proper basis for the expert opinion. If Dr. Bay had examined Gary to determine whether the procedure was properly performed, that would be a proper basis for his opinion. In this case, Dr. Bay simply relied on the statements contained in the hearsay document as independent proof of the facts, and that is not an adequate evidentiary basis for the opinion. The court should strike the expert testimony of Dr. Bay and deny Dr. Tammy's summary judgment motion.

11. The judge would need to know three categories of information. First, as to John's qualifications, the court must know how long he has worked in the crime lab and his education, training, and experience with blood type analysis. Second, the judge would need to know whether blood matching is a technique that is novel or carries a misleading aura of scientific infallibility. If so, then the judge would need to hear witness testimony to determine whether the technique is generally accepted by experts in the relevant community. If the technique was not novel, then the judge would need to get expert testimony about whether the technique of combining the blood splatter samples is reasonably relied on by experts in the field. If so, then the expert testimony should be admissible.

   If the case were tried in federal court, the court would apply the same basic analysis to John's qualifications as an expert witness, but would analyze the blood matching technique under FRE 702. Recall that

FRE 702 no longer distinguishes between novel techniques and established techniques, and has the same requirements for all expert evidence: (1) the testimony must be based on sufficient facts or data, (2) the testimony must be the product of reliable principles and methods, and (3) the witness has applied the principles and methods reliably to the facts of the case. Here, testimony would need to be offered to show that the blood matching method is reliable and that John has applied the method reliably to the blood in this case. If the judge finds by a preponderance of the evidence that this expert testimony complies with FRE 702, then John's opinion will be admissible.

12. The plaintiff's counsel should respond that tire tread analysis itself is not new to science and does not carry a misleading aura of infallibility; therefore it would be improper to subject Presley's testimony to the *Kelly* test. The procedure that Presley used is similar to a visual comparison of shoe prints, which the jurors can easily do themselves, making it possible for the fact finder to check the reliability of the expert's comparison. Like the shoe print case discussed in Example 2, the process is an obvious one and need not be subjected to the *Kelly* standard. The court should overrule the objection on *Kelly* grounds and admit the expert opinion as long as the court is satisfied that Presley's technique constitutes, or is a variation of, one that is reasonably relied on by experts in that field.

13. The court should overrule the objection and permit the prosecution to ask the questions. Recall from Chapter 2 that the prosecution can rebut the character evidence offered by the defendant under the "mercy rule." By putting on a defense expert to testify to the defendant's own character (that he does not act in conformity with a serial killer profile) the defendant opened the door to the use of character evidence on this relevant character trait. In addition, the expert may be "fully cross-examined" about the basis for her opinion and that includes whether she considered matters that were inconsistent with her opinion. The answers to those questions can help the jury to evaluate the strength of Dr. Terrie's testimony. However, Donnie is entitled to seek a limiting instruction to ensure that the jury does not consider the questions for the truth — as evidence that Donnie actually did carry guns, show pictures of the alleged victims, and call sex-workers his girlfriends.

The Burden of Proof, Presumptions, and Judicial Notice

This chapter analyzes three basic concepts of evidence law:

1. The burden of proof
2. Presumptions
3. Judicial notice

First, the *burden of proof* is the standard for convincing the judge or jury which party should prevail in the litigation. There are different burdens for civil and criminal cases. A plaintiff or prosecution prevails by producing evidence to persuade the fact finder that the elements of the cause of action or crime have been met. A defendant prevails either when the plaintiff or prosecution fails to meet its burden or when the defendant produces evidence that convinces the fact finder to decide in his favor.

Second, *presumptions* are assumptions that the law requires to be made when certain basic facts are shown to exist. Presumptions provide a shortcut to proving facts in litigation because once a party establishes the basic facts, certain other facts are presumed to exist as well. Some presumptions are *rebuttable* and others are *conclusive*.

Third, *judicial notice* is another shortcut to proving a certain fact. It is a procedure in which the court can recognize both facts and laws to be true, without requiring the parties to provide evidence in court to establish that truth. Judicial notice applies to state laws and court cases, as well as to commonly known facts and other facts that are readily verifiable.

The sections below discuss each of these concepts in more detail.

THE BURDEN OF PROOF

The *burden of proof*, or the burden of persuasion, is allocated to the party who needs to convince the fact finder in order to win on a particular claim or defense. In civil cases, the plaintiff has the burden of proof as to each element of a cause of action, and the defendant has the burden of proof as to each element of an affirmative defense (e.g., contributory negligence, excuse for non-performance, or expiration of the statute of limitations). In a criminal case, the prosecution has the burden of proof as to each element of the crime charged, and the criminal defendant has the burden of proof on any affirmative defenses (e.g., insanity, necessity, or self-defense).

CEC §500: Party who has the burden of proof

Except as otherwise provided by law, a party has the burden of proof as to each fact the existence or nonexistence of which is essential to the claim for relief or defense that he is asserting.

The CEC also provides four specific statutes, applying in both civil and criminal cases, that place the burden of proof on the party who claims that

1. another is guilty (CEC 520);
2. a person did not exercise due care (CEC 521);
3. any person, including the party herself, was insane (CEC 522); and
4. the dispute concerns the boundaries of real property or the validity of land grants, in certain circumstances (CEC 523).

The Level of Proof The standard for meeting the burden of proof varies with the type of case. There are three different baseline thresholds for the burden of proof: beyond a reasonable doubt, clear and convincing, and preponderance. The court is required to instruct the jury as to which is the appropriate standard in each case.

CEC §502: Instructions on burden of proof

The court on all proper occasions shall instruct the jury as to which party bears the burden of proof on each issue and as to whether that burden requires that a party raise a reasonable doubt concerning the existence or nonexistence of a fact or that he establish the existence or nonexistence of a fact by a preponderance of the evidence, by clear and convincing proof, or by proof beyond a reasonable doubt.

Beyond a reasonable doubt does not mean that there is no doubt, but rather means that the jurors feel "an abiding conviction of the truth of the charge."[1] Beyond a reasonable doubt is the standard that applies to the prosecution in criminal cases. Criminal defendants are required to prove their affirmative defenses, like insanity, necessity, and self-defense, by a preponderance of the evidence. It is not enough for a criminal defendant to merely raise a reasonable doubt about his own sanity or whether he was in reasonable fear for his life.

Clear and convincing is defined as a "high probability of the truth of the facts,"[2] and thus is a lower standard than beyond a reasonable doubt. The clear and convincing standard applies in certain California civil cases that involve the impairment of some liberty right, such as proceedings for civil commitments to mental institutions and for removing children from the home. California also applies the clear and convincing standard to cases involving punitive damages, requiring clear and convincing proof of oppression, fraud, or malice before a jury may award punitive damages.

The *preponderance baseline* is defined as "evidence that has more convincing force than that opposed to it"[3] and thus it is lower than both the beyond a reasonable doubt and clear and convincing standards. The preponderance test, also referred to as the *more probable than not* standard, is the burden of proof in the majority of civil cases and is also the standard for some judicial rulings on evidentiary issues (as discussed in Chapters 5 through 7 for hearsay exceptions and in Chapter 9 for expert opinions). *More probable than not* means that there is greater than a 50 percent likelihood that the fact is established. When the evidence appears to weigh equally on both sides, the preponderance standard is not met, and the party with the burden of proof loses.

Sufficiency   The *sufficiency* standard means that a reasonable juror *could* find the existence of the fact to be true. Note that the language is *could* rather than *would*, and thus is a low threshold. Sufficiency is never the appropriate threshold for the burden of persuasion to resolve the litigation, but it is used to determine the outcome of many evidentiary issues within the course of the litigation. Recall that Chapter 1 introduced the concept of the sufficiency test when explaining the doctrine of conditional relevance.

---

1. CALJIC 2.90.
2. BAJI 2.62.
3. BAJI 2.60.

This doctrine applies when the relevancy of some evidence is conditioned on proving some other preliminary fact or when evidence is admissible to prove one proposition but not to prove some other proposition.

Satisfying the Burden of Proof In a criminal case, the prosecution satisfies the burden of proof when it has convinced the fact finder of the elements of the crime beyond a reasonable doubt. Satisfying the burden of proof on an affirmative defense in a criminal or civil case means that the defendant has convinced the fact finder by a preponderance of the evidence that the defense is more likely true than not true.

If the evidence adds up to less than the baseline, the party with the burden of proof loses. If all of the evidence adds up to meet but not exceed the baseline threshold, the party with the burden of proof also loses the case. Only if the evidence exceeds the baseline threshold will the party with the burden of proof win. The jury (or judge if there is no jury) decides whether the burden of proof has been met when reaching a verdict or decision in the case.

THE BURDEN OF PRODUCING EVIDENCE

The *burden of production*, or *burden of producing evidence*, determines which party must provide the evidence on a particular issue. Whichever party has the burden of proof on a particular issue also starts off with the burden of production on that issue. Then, the burden of producing evidence can later shift as evidence is presented at trial. In a civil case, the plaintiff has the burden of proof and thus also begins with the burden of production as to each element of her causes of action and must prove any essential facts. The substantive law in the relevant area, not the evidence rules, determines which facts are essential.

CEC §550: Party who has the burden of producing evidence
(a) The burden of producing evidence as to a particular fact is on the party against whom a finding on that fact would be required in the absence of further evidence.
(b) The burden of producing evidence as to a particular fact is initially on the party with the burden of proof as to that fact.

When a party makes an objection to evidence offered by another party, the party offering the evidence has the burden to produce evidence to overcome the objection. For instance, when a hearsay objection is made, the party who is offering the hearsay statement has the burden to produce evidence to meet the requirements of a hearsay exception (or to show that the statement is not hearsay).

There are two standards for meeting the burden of producing evidence: sufficiency and preponderance. The sufficiency standard applies in a limited number of areas, and the preponderance standard applies more broadly.

Sufficiency The following areas of producing evidence are governed by the sufficiency standard: relevancy (CEC 350), all categories of party admissions (CEC 1221-1227), prior statements of witnesses (CEC 1235-1236), the identity of a hearsay declarant, personal knowledge (CEC 702), and convictions to attack witness credibility (CEC 788), as well as authentication (which is addressed in Chapter 11).

CEC §403(a): Determination of foundational and other preliminary facts where relevancy, personal knowledge, or authenticity is disputed

The proponent of the proffered evidence has the burden of producing evidence as to the existence of the preliminary fact, and the proffered evidence is inadmissible unless the court finds that there is evidence sufficient to sustain a finding of the existence of the preliminary fact, when:

(1) the relevance of the proffered evidence depends on the existence of the preliminary fact;

(2) the preliminary fact is the personal knowledge of a witness concerning the subject matter of his testimony;

(3) the preliminary fact is the authenticity of a writing; or

(4) the proffered evidence is of a statement or other conduct of a particular person and the preliminary fact is whether that person made the statement or so conducted himself.

Chapters 5 through 7 on hearsay exceptions further explain when the sufficiency standard applies for determining whether a hearsay exception is appropriate in a particular situation. Some hearsay exceptions require that the foundation be established with sufficient evidence under CEC 403. In other areas, a preponderance of evidence establishes the foundation under CEC 405. The judge determines whether the preponderance test is met before the jury is permitted to hear the evidence.

Preponderance The preponderance standard applies more broadly and covers all evidence that is not included under the sufficiency standard.

Recall that Chapter 6 explains the preponderance test in the context of hearsay exceptions whose foundations required more than the sufficiency test.

CEC §405(a): Determination of foundational and other preliminary facts in other cases

When the existence of a preliminary fact is disputed, the court shall indicate which party has the burden of producing evidence and the burden of proof on the issue as implied by the rule of law under which the question arises. The court shall determine the existence or nonexistence of the preliminary fact and shall admit or exclude the proffered evidence as required by the rule of law under which the question arises.

The kinds of issues that are decided by the judge under the preponderance standard of CEC 405 include admissions during compromise negotiations; elements of hearsay exceptions, such as dying declarations and spontaneous statements (other than the identity of the declarant); the disqualification of witnesses for mental incapacity (CEC 701); whether a pardon or rehabilitation has been granted for a conviction (CEC 788); qualifications of expert witnesses (CEC 720); opinion evidence on sanity (CEC 870) and handwriting matches (CEC 1416-1419); whether secondary evidence of documents can be admitted (discussed in Chapter 11); as well as the existence of privileges and exceptions (discussed in Chapters 12 and 13).

Meeting the Burden of Production   The judge decides whether the standard for the burden of production has been met. Courts have some discretion to alter the burden of production when the interests of justice require, such as when one party has much greater access to the necessary information than the party who has the burden to prove those facts.

The burden of production varies with the evidence provided. For instance, if the defendant objects to the plaintiff's testimony on the grounds of hearsay, and the plaintiff responds that the statement is a party admission, the plaintiff has to provide sufficient evidence to show that the statement was made by a party. If the plaintiff does not provide sufficient evidence from which a reasonable juror could find that the statement was made by a party to the case, then the judge will rule against the plaintiff and sustain the hearsay objection. The plaintiff will have failed to meet her burden of production on the hearsay statement.

On the other hand, if the plaintiff's response to the hearsay objection is "spontaneous statement," then the judge must apply both tests (as discussed

Sufficiency	Preponderance
Relevancy (CEC 350)	Admissions during compromise negotiations
Party admission (CEC 1221-1227)	Dying declarations, spontaneous statements
Witness's prior statements (CEC 1235-1236)	Elements of hearsay exceptions other than identity of hearsay declarant
Identity of hearsay declarant	Witness's mental capacity (CEC 701)
Personal knowledge (CEC 702)	Pardon or rehabilitation granted for conviction
Conviction to attack credibility (CEC 788)	Qualifications of experts (CEC 720)
Authentication of evidence	Opinion as to sanity (CEC 780)
	Handwriting matching (CEC 1416-1419)
	Whether secondary evidence admissible
	Existence of privileges and exceptions

Figure 10.1. Burdens of Producing Evidence on Particular Issues

in Chapter 7). The sufficiency test applies to the identity of the hearsay declarant, and the preponderance test applies to the other elements of the exception, such as whether there was a startling event and whether the statement was made while the declarant was under the stress of that startling event. Figure 10.1 lists the categories of evidentiary rules that fall under each test.

Examples

1. Mo suffers from migraines and debilitating arthritis. When the medical marijuana law was enacted, Mo obtained a license to grow medical marijuana and planted three marijuana bushes in his backyard. Mo added more each month until he had over 30 plants. The law limited medical use to 3 plants per person for personal use, and Mo was prosecuted for violating the law. Mo claimed that he was providing the marijuana to several other extremely ill people with marijuana prescriptions. He argued that even though the extra plants were not for his personal use, they were for the personal use of other people who also had licenses to grow marijuana, and he was just saving energy by growing them all in one place. In closing argument, the prosecutor stated that Mo should be found guilty unless Mo proves by a preponderance of the

evidence that he was growing for other ill people as well. Mo's counsel objects that this is an improper instruction on the burden of proof. How should the court rule, and why?

2. Poppy is on trial for the murder of his ex-wife. At trial, Poppy claimed that he was insane at the time of the killing, which is an affirmative defense to the murder charge. The prosecution said that Poppy needed to prove his insanity by a preponderance of the evidence. Poppy argued that he needed to raise only a reasonable doubt about his sanity to avoid conviction. Which side is correct?

Explanations

1. The court should sustain the objection and strike that portion of the prosecution's argument. While Mo should not be convicted of the marijuana charge if he is providing it to other extremely ill patients under a proper license, Mo simply has the burden to produce evidence that he was providing for other ill patients. If he raises reasonable doubt as to whether he was using it all for himself, he should not be convicted. A criminal defendant never has the burden to prove his innocence by a preponderance of the evidence.

2. The prosecution is correct. Insanity is an affirmative defense to a homicide charge, and the defendant has the burden of proving his affirmative defenses by a preponderance of the evidence. This example is different from Example 1 because Example 1 involves *negating an element of the crime* (for personal use). Proving an affirmative defense is different from negating an element of the charged crime. Defendants must simply provide reasonable doubt to negate an element of the charged crime, but must provide greater proof to establish an affirmative defense-like insanity.

PRESUMPTIONS AND INFERENCES

One shortcut that parties can use to help meet the burden of proof is called a *presumption*. A presumption is defined in CEC 600(a) as "an assumption of fact that the law requires to be made from another fact or group of facts found or otherwise established in the action." A presumption involves two parts: (1) the basic facts that are established in the case, and (2) the presumed facts that the law requires to be found. Some presumptions affect the burden of proof, while others impact the burden of production. Some presumptions are rebuttable and others are conclusive.

A second shortcut is called an *inference*. The main difference between inferences and presumptions is that inferences are permissive. The jurors may make the inference if they wish, but they are not required to. We make common everyday inferences all the time. For instance, when class time has arrived and there is only one person in the room, that person may infer that class must be somewhere else. She may decide to pick up her books and wander the halls looking for someone from the class to tell her where to go. That lone student is not required to infer that class is in another room. She could infer that class was cancelled and go home for the day. Like the student, jurors are permitted to make inferences in their deliberations and can exercise their own judgment in doing so. Presumptions, however, require the jurors to make certain inferences when the basic facts are established.

Conclusive Presumptions

A *conclusive* presumption is a rule of substantive law that states that if the basic facts are found, then the presumed facts must be found. Any evidence to the contrary does not matter, even if it is very strong. Most conclusive presumptions are governed by substantive law and not the CEC, but several are contained in the CEC. These include the presumptions that

1. a party cannot later contradict his own statement if he has induced another to believe the statement is true and that other has relied on it to his detriment (CEC 623);
2. a tenant cannot deny the title of the landlord at the time of entering into the landlord-tenant relationship (CEC 624); and
3. facts recited in a written instrument like a settlement agreement are determined to be conclusively true as between the parties to the document (CEC 622).

When the social policy basis for the presumption would not be served by applying it in a particular case, the courts can decline to apply a conclusive presumption. In some such cases, courts may treat conclusive presumptions as rebuttable. Consider, for example, a tenant who entered into a lease with a person he believed was the landlord and to whom he paid the rent for several months. Then, the tenant was evicted by another person who turned out to be the true owner of the property. The tenant may file a lawsuit alleging fraud and seeking to recover the rental payments made to the non-owner. The alleged landlord will assert that the conclusive presumption of CEC 624 prevents that tenant from denying the landlord's title to the property.

Applying the presumption in this situation would not serve the social policy behind the statute, which is to ensure that tenants do not dispute ownership to remain living in a unit once they have stopped paying rent. Here, the tenant did not stop paying rent, but rather was paying rent to the wrong person based on a fraudulent misrepresentation. Thus, the court might choose not to apply the presumption at all or might treat the conclusive presumption as a rebuttable presumption, thereby permitting the jury to consider the contrary evidence about ownership.

Rebuttable Presumptions

Unlike a conclusive presumption, a rebuttable presumption does not foreclose the presentation of contrary evidence. *Rebuttable* means that the other side is permitted to introduce evidence to disprove the presumed facts, even if the basic facts are established. The opponent can also attempt to disprove the basic facts, and then the jury will have to weigh the evidence to determine whether the basic facts exist and thus whether the presumption should apply.

There are two types of rebuttable presumptions: *Thayer* and *Morgan* (named after famous evidence scholars). The Thayer presumptions affect the burden of producing evidence, while Morgan presumptions affect the burden of proof and are less common.

CEC §601: Classification of presumptions
A presumption is either conclusive or rebuttable. Every rebuttable presumption is either (a) a presumption affecting the burden of producing evidence or (b) a presumption affecting the burden of proof.

Thayer Presumptions

Thayer presumptions are those that shift the burden of producing evidence to the opposing party. CEC 603 makes clear that these presumptions are designed to avoid requiring proof of facts that are likely to be true. This means that when one side has produced enough evidence of the basic facts to trigger the presumption, the likelihood is that the presumed fact is true.

Examples of Thayer rebuttable presumptions include the following:

1. A letter properly addressed and mailed was received (CEC 641); a date on a writing is accurate (CEC 640).
2. Money delivered by one to another was due (CEC 631).
3. A thing delivered belongs to the person to whom it was delivered (CEC 632).
4. An obligation to repay given to the debtor has been repaid (CEC 633).

5. An obligation still in the possession of the creditor is unpaid (CEC 635).
6. The earlier rent was paid when there has been receipt for later rent (CEC 636).
7. Possessions of a person are owned by her (CEC 637).
8. A writing creating an interest in real property is authentic if at least 30 years old (CEC 643).
9. Books purporting to be published by a public authority were published by that authority (CEC 644).
10. Newspaper articles purporting to be from a particular newspaper company are published by that newspaper company (CEC 645.1).
11. A civil defendant is negligent if the plaintiff establishes facts for res ipsa loquitur (CEC 646).
12. The return of process served by a registered process server is valid service (CEC 647).

For example, in a negligence case, the res ipsa loquitur presumption applies when three criteria are met:

1. the accident is the kind that does not occur unless someone is negligent
2. the accident was caused by some agent or instrumentality that was under the control of the defendant, and
3. the plaintiff or injured party committed no negligent or contributory negligent act.

Imagine, for instance, a construction company that is repaving a two-lane road. After closing one lane, construction workers direct cars to take turns driving in opposite directions in the remaining lane. At each end of the lane closure is a construction worker with a fluorescent vest and a sign that reads "Stop" on one side and "Slow" on the other. Two workers take turns directing one lane of traffic to stop so that cars coming from the other direction can use the lane. Two cars enter the lane from opposite directions and have a head-on collision. The res ipsa loquitur presumption may apply here against the defendant construction company because this is the kind of accident that would not occur unless someone was negligent; the construction company workers had the signs to direct drivers, and the lanes of traffic were under their control. As long as neither driver was negligent in following the instructions of the construction workers, the rebuttable Thayer presumption should apply.

Another example is a breach of contract case in which the plaintiff proves that she mailed the acceptance of an offer. Once this fact is proved, the plaintiff does not have to introduce additional evidence that the defendant received the acceptance to meet her burden of production.

311

Using the presumption that mail properly addressed and sent is received (CEC 641) permits the judge to instruct the jurors that if they find the existence of the basic facts to be true (that the letter was properly addressed and mailed), then they must find the presumed facts to also be true.

Remember there are numerous presumptions contained in other California statutes. While some presumptions are listed in the CEC, other California Codes contain numerous additional presumptions.

Rebutting a Thayer Presumption

If the opposing party fails to introduce evidence sufficient to sustain a finding that the basic or presumed facts do not exist, then the judge instructs the jurors about the presumption, stating that if the jurors find the existence of the basic facts to be established they must also find the presumed fact to be established. Where the presumed fact is an essential element of the cause of action, the jury has to find that the basic facts exist by the governing standard for the case. In most civil cases, the governing standard is a preponderance of the evidence.

CEC §604: Effect of presumption affecting burden of producing evidence

The effect of a presumption affecting the burden of producing evidence is to require the trier of fact to assume the existence of the presumed fact unless and until evidence is introduced which would support a finding of its nonexistence, in which case the trier of fact shall determine the existence or nonexistence of the presumed fact from the evidence and without regard to the presumption. Nothing in this section shall be construed to prevent the drawing of any inference that may be appropriate.

The phrase *and without regard to the presumption* in CEC 604 means that if the opposing side produces enough evidence to override the presumed facts, the presumption "bursts" (disappears), and the jury does not receive any instruction about the presumption. The jurors then simply weigh the competing evidence on both sides to decide whether the fact is true, just as they would in the absence of any presumption.

In the contract example above, the presumption about the contract acceptance did not affect the burden of persuasion because the plaintiff still has to persuade the jury by a preponderance of the evidence that the defendant did receive the acceptance. Unless the defendant presents evidence that he did not receive the acceptance, there will be enough evidence for the jury to decide this issue in favor of the plaintiff.

Morgan Presumptions

Morgan presumptions are those that also shift the burden of proof or persuasion to the other side to prove the nonexistence of the presumed fact. When a Morgan presumption applies, the court instructs the jury to find the presumed fact unless the other side produces enough evidence to meet the appropriate standard for the burden of proof. In most civil cases, the appropriate standard of proof will be the preponderance of the evidence standard. Morgan presumptions recognize the social policy goals of presumptions and do not focus so much on the probability of the presumed fact being true given the existence of the basic facts. The policy considerations underlying Morgan presumptions include favoring parent-child relationships, the validity of marriages, and the stability of titles to real property (CEC 605). Another Morgan presumption promotes a policy against abuse of elders and the infirm by creating a presumption that caregivers are disqualified from inheriting from the decedent unless the caregivers provide clear and convincing evidence that the inheritance was not the result of fraud, duress, or undue influence during the time they were giving care.

Rebuttable Morgan presumptions that impact the burden of proof include the following:

1. The owner of legal title to property is the owner of the full beneficial title unless clear and convincing evidence indicates otherwise (CEC 662).
2. A ceremonial marriage is valid (CEC 663).
3. A person intends the consequences of her own voluntary act (CEC 665).
4. An official duty has been performed properly (CEC 664).
5. A person not heard from in five years is dead (CEC 667).
6. A person failed to exercise due care if that person violated a statute and proximately caused injury to person or property of the type that the statute sought to protect (CEC 669).
7. Payment by check was made if a copy of both the check and bank statement showing payment are provided (CEC 670).

Presumptions in Criminal Cases

Morgan presumptions (those that shift the burden of proof or persuasion) and conclusive presumptions are unconstitutional in criminal cases. Conclusive presumptions would relieve the prosecution of part of its burden to prove the presumed facts beyond a reasonable doubt, thus violating the constitutional rights of the accused. If the prosecution proves the basic facts and then the jury gets to presume certain other facts, the prosecution is not proving those presumed facts beyond a reasonable doubt.

CEC §607: Effect of presumption that establish an element
When a presumption affecting the burden of proof operates in a criminal action to establish presumptively any fact that is essential to the defendant's guilt, the presumption operates only if the facts that give rise to the presumption have been found or otherwise established beyond a reasonable doubt and, in such case, the defendant need only raise a reasonable doubt as to the existence of the presumed fact.

Because Morgan presumptions shift the burden of persuasion, in a criminal case they would put the burden on the defendant to disprove some element of the crime. Disproving an element is a higher burden than the defendant's normal burden of simply undermining the prosecution's case by identifying reasonable doubt. For this reason, CEC 607 was enacted to prevent the prosecution from using this shortcut to proof in criminal cases. Morgan presumptions that affect the burden of persuasion now can be used only where the basic facts are proven beyond a reasonable doubt, and the jury is instructed that they *may* find the presumed facts, but only if the defendant did not raise a reasonable doubt as to the existence of the presumed fact.

Federal Rules of Evidence Compared: Substantive Differences

There are no corresponding FRE sections on the burden of proof that are analogous to CEC 500, 502, or 550. FRE 301 explains that presumptions in federal court shift only the burden of production and do not shift the burden of proof. Therefore, the FRE does not recognize Morgan presumptions. In addition, FRE 302 notes that in federal civil actions, presumptions affecting the elements of a claim for relief or defense shall be governed by the applicable state law.

Examples

1. Bernie and Fergie were longtime friends. When Fergie became ill and could no longer take care of herself, Bernie moved into Fergie's mansion and began helping with personal care, cooking, feeding, and running errands. Fergie did not pay Bernie for these services, but she allowed Bernie to live in her condo without paying any rent or utilities expenses. A year after Bernie moved in, Fergie amended her trust to include as beneficiaries "any friend who is living in my home and providing care for me." When Fergie died, her grandchildren challenged Bernie's

entitlement to be a beneficiary of Fergie's trust, relying on the presumption that "a person who takes care of a decedent is disqualified from inheriting from that decedent unless she provides clear and convincing evidence that her inheritance was not the result of fraud, duress, or undue influence." Who has the burden of production?

2. The California Business Code contains the following conclusive presumption: "A physician having more than two misdemeanor convictions involving alcohol consumption constitutes unprofessional conduct." Dr. Griffy had three misdemeanor convictions for driving while intoxicated, and the medical board rescinded his medical license. At his medical malpractice trial, the plaintiff offered evidence of Dr. Griffy's three convictions. Dr. Griffy argued that he should be permitted to offer contrary evidence to show that he is a careful doctor and does not drink alcohol when he is seeing patients. The plaintiff's attorney objected, stating that no further evidence should be allowed on this issue. How should the court rule, and why? Would the ruling be different if this were a manslaughter case involving criminally negligent medical treatment?

3. Ramon sued Maritime Co. for conversion and trespass when Ramon's boat was engulfed in flames while at Maritime Co.'s repair yard. Ramon offered evidence that Maritime had taken the boat from its slip and moved it into its own repair yard. Maritime offered evidence that it was properly in possession of the boat because it held a lien on the boat, and that it properly collected the boat when Ramon was three months behind on his repair loan payments. Maritime offered the original note for the loan and the presumption that an obligation held by the creditor is presumed to be unpaid. Because Maritime still held the original note and Ramon did not have it, Maritime argued that the presumption should apply. Ramon stated that he had repaid the loan, so the boat was rightfully his. Who has the burden of production?

4. Alex and Andy are graduate students at a local university, and they were married the day before the California voters passed a ban on same-gender marriage. The university seeks to expel Alex and Andy from married student housing on the ground that their marriage is no longer valid. Alex and Andy seek to apply the presumption that "a marriage performed under the laws of the state is presumed to be valid." How should the university respond?

5. Defendant Cally was charged with possession of materials with intent to manufacture methamphetamine. Hydriotic acid is a necessary ingredient for manufacturing methamphetamine. The California Health & Safety Code contains a statute that states "possession of immediate precursors sufficient for the manufacture of . . . hydriotic acid . . . shall be deemed

to be possession of the derivative substance." The prosecution presented evidence that Cally was found with the ingredients to make hydriotic acid. In closing argument, the prosecution told the jury about the presumption. The defendant objected that the presumption impermissibly lessened the prosecution's burden of proof and was improper in a criminal case. How should the court rule, and why?

6. Thad was driving a red Mercedes CLK and ran a red light. Officer Morris saw the traffic violation and put on his lights and siren, but Thad continued to drive, turned the corner, and pulled into a parking lot. Officer Morris cautiously approached the car and asked Thad for identification. Thad said he was on his way to the liquor store and had forgotten his wallet. Thad also said that he did not see any flashing red light on the police car, so he did not think that the officer was trying to pull him over. As Thad was speaking, Officer Morris noticed a red purse partially hidden under the back seat of the car. Recalling that a red purse and a red Mercedes had been reported stolen earlier in the day, Officer Morris decided to search Thad and found a crow bar and several new car keys with the Mercedes logo. Thad was arrested and subsequently put on trial for grand theft auto and evading the police. When Thad tried to offer evidence that the police officer did not follow his duty to have a red flashing light to alert Thad that he was trying to pull him over, the prosecution objected, stating that the presumption "an official duty is presumed to have been properly performed" prevented Thad from introducing that evidence. Thad argued that the prosecution did not meet its burden of proof to show that the presumption should apply. How should the court rule, and why?

7. Bauman filed a malpractice lawsuit against Dr. Yusef, alleging that the surgeon had left a sponge in Bauman's leg after a surgical procedure. Nurse Eva testified that she helped the doctor to count the sponges once at the beginning of the surgery, but that he did not ask her to help count the used sponges before he stitched up the wound. Bauman argues that the res ipsa loquitur presumption should apply to shift the burden of production to the defendant. Dr. Yusef objects. How should the court rule, and why?

8. Kenny's family filed a petition to have him declared dead so that they could collect on his life insurance policy. The family relied on the presumption that "a person who has not been heard from in five years is presumed dead." Kenny had been missing for more than ten years after a suicide note was found in his car, which was parked at a local airport. The car contained a suitcase, medication, clothing, books, his passport, and wallet. The insurance company countered that the presumption that a person not heard from in five years is dead should not apply because Kenny disappeared just before he was set to be indicted on 100 counts of securities fraud and likely just assumed a new identity and fled the jurisdiction. Who has the burden of production?

Explanations

1. The plaintiffs are relying on the presumption previously noted in this chapter that people who take care of a decedent are disqualified from inheriting from that decedent unless they provide clear and convincing evidence that their inheritance was not the result of fraud, duress, or undue influence. Once the plaintiffs establish that Bernie was taking care of Fergie before she died and that Bernie is now a beneficiary of the trust, the basic facts are proven and the presumption will take effect. The presumption then shifts the burden of production to Bernie to show that he did not use fraud, duress, or undue influence to convince Fergie to include him as a beneficiary. The presumption also contains a higher standard of proof — clear and convincing evidence — which means that Bernie has to disprove duress or undue influence on Fergie with a "high probability of the truth of the facts." This higher standard will be difficult to meet, especially if Bernie was the only other person living with Fergie during her illness. There would be no one to comment on how Bernie treated and interacted with Fergie during the time leading up to the change in her trust documents. Thus, Bernie is not likely to prevail.

2. The court should preclude evidence on the issue of Dr. Griffy's unprofessional conduct because of the conclusive presumption. The basic facts — more than two misdemeanor convictions involving alcohol — have been established by the testimony. Thus the presumed fact — that Griffy engaged in unprofessional conduct — should be presumed. Because this is a conclusive presumption and not rebuttable, that fact is established for purposes of this civil litigation. However, if this was a criminal case, then conclusive presumptions would not be allowed, and they would turn into permissive inferences. The jury would be instructed that they may, but are not required to, find that Dr. Griffy engaged in unprofessional conduct. (Recall from Chapter 8 that the prior misdemeanor convictions would be admissible because the Truth in Evidence provision permits such evidence in criminal cases.)

3. Ramon had the initial burden to prove that his boat was taken improperly. When he presented that evidence, the burden of production shifted to Maritime to put forward evidence to show that Maritime was entitled to take the boat. The note that Maritime offered triggers the presumption that a note possessed by a payee, without any endorsement of payment, is presumed to be unpaid. Once the note is paid, the original document is usually returned to the borrower instead of being held with the lender. Here, because the lender still had the original document and it was not marked "paid in full," the presumption applies to shift the burden of production back to the plaintiff Ramon. Ramon now has the burden to prove that he actually had paid off the note before he can recover for damages to the boat.

4. The presumption applies to shift the burden of production to the university to prove that the marriage was not valid. The university would have to show that there was some irregularity in the wedding ceremony to invalidate the marriage and properly expel Alex and Andy from married student housing.

5. The court should overrule the objection and permit the use of the presumption. The presumption is a legislative enactment, and thus it creates a rule of substantive law — that possession of ingredients is the same as possession of the final product. In stating that the possession of the precursor ingredients "shall be deemed," the legislature did not create a presumption of possession, but instead created a substantive rule of law that possession of the ingredients to make hydriotic acid was the legal equivalent of possessing hydriotic acid itself. The presumption does not also give the prosecution a shortcut to prove that Cally had the intent to manufacture methamphetamines. Therefore this is not an impermissible conclusive presumption in a criminal case.

6. The court should rule that the presumption cannot apply this shortcut to proof in a criminal case. The prosecution must prove that Thad knowingly evaded the police, meaning Thad knew that Officer Morris wanted him to stop but still continued to drive. The principal way motorists know that an officer wants them to pull over is the signal of flashing lights or a siren. Unless the prosecution provides evidence of a flashing light or siren, the charge of evading arrest cannot be proven. Thus, the prosecution must present evidence to show beyond a reasonable doubt that Thad knew that Officer Morris was trying to pull him over. The mere statement of the presumption that official duties are properly performed is not enough, standing alone, to meet this standard.

7. The court should overrule Dr. Yusef's objection. The three elements of the res ipsa loquitur presumption are met because (1) a sponge would not be left in a patient's leg without someone being negligent, (2) the doctor who conducted the surgery and closed up the wound had control over the nurses as well as his own behavior in checking for lost sponges, and (3) the plaintiff was under anesthesia and therefore unable to commit any negligent act during the surgery. Therefore, the presumption applies to shift the burden of production to the defendant Dr. Yusef to prove that he was not negligent.

8. The burden of production shifted from the family to the insurance company once the family established that Kenny had been missing and not heard from for ten years. The presumption applied to shift the burden of production to the insurance company to provide evidence that counters that presumption of death. The risk of substantial jail time is enough to provide a reasonable explanation for Kenny's absence, and

thus the burden of production shifts back to the plaintiffs to produce evidence that it is more likely than not that Kenny is deceased.

JUDICIAL NOTICE: CEC 450–460

Judicial notice is another shortcut to proof. It is a process that allows the court to recognize certain facts and other information as true without either party having to present evidence at trial to establish that information. When a judge *takes judicial notice of* or *notices* a fact, the party who had the burden to prove that fact no longer has to introduce evidence to establish that fact.

There are two types of facts that a California court can judicially notice: legislative facts and adjudicative facts. *Legislative facts* include

1. the law;
2. data and information used to interpret the law, like legislative histories;
3. facts that relate to the meaning of the law; and
4. evidence of historical, societal, or social policies and practices.

Adjudicative facts are those that are significant to the present case. These are the facts to which the law will be applied in determining the outcome.

Mandatory Judicial Notice

There are certain matters that are *mandatory* for judicial notice, while others are *permissive*. According to CEC 451, the court *shall* take judicial notice of the following, whether or not a party requests such notice:

1. Decisional, constitutional, and public statutory law of California and the United States
2. Regulations of state and federal agencies
3. Rules of court, the state bar, and professional conduct
4. The true meaning of English words, phrases, and legal expressions
5. Universally known facts that cannot reasonably be disputed.

Universally known facts do not need to be known by everyone, but rather are facts known by "persons of reasonable and average intelligence and knowledge." Many geographic, historical, and political facts as well as current events will fit within this category.

Permissive Judicial Notice

For *permissive* judicial notice, the court has discretion to notice certain other matters. According to CEC 452, permissive matters include

1. laws, regulations, and court decisions of other states;
2. official acts of the United States or departments of other states;
3. court records of California and other courts;
4. laws of other nations and international covenants; and
5. locally known and easily verifiable facts (CEC 452).

Locally known facts are those that are "of such common knowledge within the territorial jurisdiction of the court that they cannot reasonably be the subject of dispute." *Easily verifiable* facts may be not widely known, but can be verified easily using sources of "reasonably indisputable accuracy."

Under CEC 453, permissive matters may be treated as mandatory if two criteria are met:

1. Proper notice is given to the other side.
2. Sufficient information is provided to the court to show that taking judicial notice of that matter is appropriate.

The types of information that can be used by the court to determine whether judicial notice is proper include calendars, commercial telephone directories, almanacs, treatises, encyclopedias, expert witnesses, court decisions, court records, and the laws of another state or nation. The information must note the propriety of taking judicial notice and the tenor of the matter to be noticed (CEC 454).

Determining Whether Judicial Notice Is Appropriate

Each party to the case has an opportunity to present information to the judge before she makes a decision on a request for judicial notice. If the judge relies on material that was not presented by the parties, then the judge must permit the parties to review that material to make their arguments and must also make that material part of the record in open court. Under CEC 460, the court may appoint an expert for the purpose of giving information and advice as to the taking of judicial notice.

The limitations on the matters the judge may consider are the rules of privilege (which are discussed in Chapters 12 and 13) and the probative value/prejudicial effect balancing test of CEC 352 (which is discussed in Chapter 1). When a party requests judicial notice of privileged information or information whose probative value is substantially outweighed by the prejudicial effect, the court can decline to judicially notice the matter even in cases of mandatory judicial notice. The privilege and prejudice evaluations should be part of the court's consideration of whether it is proper to take judicial notice of the matter.

The source used to verify the information does not become evidence itself but rather is used by the judge only as an aid in deciding whether judicial notice is appropriate. When documents like court records are judicially noticed, the judge recognizes the existence of the court record but does not make a determination that assertions made in those records are true because that could violate the Hearsay Rule (discussed in Chapter 4). A separate hearsay exception would have to be satisfied for the document to be admitted for the truth of the matter asserted. There is a special exception for certified computer-generated criminal conviction records, which are admissible to prove the truth of the matter asserted under CEC 452.5 (discussed in Chapter 8). If the records are offered for a non-hearsay purpose, such as notice of a similar lawsuit, then the judge can take notice of the content for that non-hearsay purpose. Similarly, with agency records, the judge can notice the existence of the record but not the truth of the assertions therein.

If the court grants the request for judicial notice, then it should instruct the jury about the matter that has been noticed. CEC 457 provides that judicially noticed matters are binding on the jury in California civil and criminal cases if the trial court so instructs, which it may do on its own or must do if requested by a party. In criminal cases, case law prohibits judges from taking judicial notice of facts that the prosecution must prove beyond a reasonable doubt.

Denying Judicial Notice

When the court denies judicial notice, it must advise the parties of its denial "at the earliest practicable time" so that the parties have time to acquire the necessary evidence to prove the matter at trial (CEC 456). A denial of a request for judicial notice does not preclude the trial court from taking judicial notice in a subsequent proceeding in that action (CEC 458). A reviewing court must notice items that were or should have been noticed by the trial court and thus must take notice of mandatory matters. The reviewing court also has the discretion to notice the permissive matters specified in CEC 452. Where the trial court was not provided the appropriate information to substantiate a request for permissive judicial notice, the appellate court retains discretion as to whether to notice the matter if presented with the necessary information on appeal (CEC 459).

Federal Rules of Evidence Compared: Substantive Differences

The FRE applies like the CEC to adjudicative facts, but does not address the issue of legislative facts. FRE 201 has slightly different definitions for mandatory and discretionary notice. *Discretionary* means that a court may take judicial notice whether requested or not. *Mandatory* means that a court shall take judicial notice if requested by a party and supplied with the necessary information. The FRE also converts judicial notice in criminal cases into permissive inferences with an instruction that the jury may, but is not required to, find the judicially noticed fact. In contrast, CEC 457 prevents the judge from taking judicial notice of any fact that the prosecution is required to prove beyond a reasonable doubt.

Examples

1. Fred's former employer, Indemnity Insurance Co., sued him for misappropriation of company funds. At trial, Fred produced a letter agreement in which Indemnity gave him permission to draw money from the insurance company bank accounts for certain outside expenses. Fred argued that the letter agreement was proof that he had permission to the use the company's money for these purposes. Fred asked the court to take judicial notice of the letter agreement to support his argument. Indemnity objects that the letter agreement is not a proper subject of judicial notice. How should the court rule, and why?

2. Len is a jailhouse informant who spies on fellow inmates and reports incriminating comments to the prison guards, who then put Len in contact with the district attorney's office. Samir is on trial for robbery and attempted murder at a Taco Bell. Len testified that he overheard Samir say that he "really enjoyed hearing the Taco Bell employees beg for their lives" after he "shot their supervisor in the leg." Samir's counsel argued that Len got the information from a newspaper article, not from Samir, and asked the court to take judicial notice of the two newspaper articles that were published the day before Len allegedly overheard Samir's statement. Both articles say that the Taco Bell employees begged for their lives while the robber laughed and shot their boss. The prosecution objects. How should the court rule?

3. Bowen is on trial for assault with a deadly weapon in a school zone, and the prosecution has requested a street gang enhancement to the charge. His four codefendants all pleaded guilty to the charges. The prosecution asked the court to take judicial notice of the four guilty pleas. The jury was told to treat the judicially noticed evidence as facts proven

conclusively. Bowen objected that the jury instruction regarding judicial notice was erroneous. How should the court rule, and why?

4. Hass was offered a job as a police officer. The employment contract with the City contained a clause that said Hass would have to repay the City for the cost of his training if he did not remain in the job for at least one year. Hass was aware of the clause when he signed the employment contract. Eight months later, Hass resigned from the police force. Hass ignored repeated requests and bills from the City to repay the training costs. The City sued Hass and won a judgment against him. Hass appealed and asked the appellate court to take judicial notice of two items: (1) a California case overturning a state non-competition statute, and (2) excerpts from the City's law enforcement employment manual. How should the court rule on Hass's two requests, and why?

5. Mannie was convicted on several sexual assault charges. After a psychiatrist testified that Mannie had a mental disorder that could be treated, Mannie was found to be a sexually violent predator and sentenced to a state mental hospital where he was subjected to involuntary treatment. Mannie hired another psychiatrist, Dr. Ozz, to testify in a hearing to determine whether Mannie could discontinue the involuntary treatment. At the hearing, Ozz testified that labeling Mannie a sexually violent predator was incorrect. The state asked the court to take judicial notice of the prior court finding that Mannie was a sexually violent predator to prove that Mannie should remain subject to involuntary treatment. Mannie objects that this is an improper use of judicial notice. How should the court rule, and why?

Explanations

1. The court should sustain the objection. The letter agreement is not in the mandatory or permissive categories for judicial notice. It is not a law or rule, not a fact of common knowledge or one that is universally known, and it is not something that is not reasonably subject to dispute. The interpretation of the meaning of the letter agreement is a crucial issue in the case, and therefore is subject to dispute. Judicial notice is improper in this case.

2. The court should sustain the objection. The substance of a newspaper article is not a proper subject for judicial notice because newspaper articles are not matters generally known and the facts are not capable of ready and easy verification by reliable sources. There is a presumption that a news article purporting to be from a particular newspaper is from that newspaper, but that presumption addresses only the source of the article, not the reliability of the article's substance.

3. The court should overrule the objection and take judicial notice of the guilty pleas so that the prosecution does not need to waste court time to prove the other convictions.

4. The court should grant the request to notice the California case law and most likely will deny the request to notice the employment manual. The California case law is a matter of mandatory judicial notice. Under CEC 459, the reviewing court must notice matters that the trial court was required to notice. Because the trial court would have been required to take judicial notice of this statute, the reviewing court must do so even though the request was not mentioned at trial. The employment manual is not a proper subject of mandatory or permissive judicial notice, and it was not presented to the trial court. Hass may argue that the manual is not reasonably subject to dispute because it is an accurate and reliable source. If the court accepts this argument, then the court may take judicial notice of the manual, but it is not required to do so.

5. The court should deny the request for judicial notice because the state is seeking to prove the truth of the finding rather than merely taking notice that a previous finding was made. While a court can take judicial notice of prior decisions and findings, it is merely the *existence* of those findings and decisions that are the proper subject of judicial notice. The shortcut of judicial notice is not available to prove the truth of the underlying facts leading to the court finding. Here the state seeks to use the fact that Mannie was determined to be a sexually violent predator in the past to prove that he is actually is a sexually violent predator. That amounts to an impermissible lessening of the prosecution's beyond a reasonable doubt burden in a criminal commitment case.

Authentication and the Secondary Evidence Rule

This chapter discusses two other evidentiary rules that were designed in part to address the common law fear of forgeries: the authentication requirement and the Secondary Evidence Rule. Authentication, like the concept of relevance discussed in Chapter 1, is a preliminary issue that needs to be resolved before other evidentiary issues can be addressed. Preliminary issues like authentication are sometimes referred to as *foundation* issues. When a party offers some tangible evidence, that party must provide information for the judge to decide whether the evidence is authentic because evidence that is not authentic should not be admitted at trial. For instance, if the plaintiff offers a contract into evidence, the plaintiff would need to provide evidence to show that the contract is the actual contract signed by the parties and not a forgery or an altered version of the contract.

The authentication requirement is governed by the sufficiency test, which means that as long as a reasonable juror could find the evidence to be authentic, the requirement will be met. Then the evidence will be admissible, subject to other evidentiary objections. There are numerous ways to authenticate evidence, and the most popular method is witness testimony. All of the methods are discussed in the first half of this chapter.

The Secondary Evidence Rule is implicated whenever a party seeks to prove the *contents* of a document. It evolved from the Best Evidence Rule, which provided that a party should offer into evidence the original document instead of a copy, a duplicate, or oral testimony about the content of that document. California replaced the Best Evidence Rule with the Secondary Evidence Rule after recognizing that original documents are not always available and that duplicates can be as reliable as originals, particularly when the documents are on a computer file. The rule provides limitations on when copies, duplicates, and oral testimony can be used as proof instead of the original document. This rule and its exceptions are discussed in the second half of this chapter.

AUTHENTICATION

When a party offers a writing or other tangible evidence at trial, courts require some assurance that the evidence is authentic before letting the jury consider it. The authentication requirement states that the party offering the evidence must provide sufficient information for a reasonable juror to find that the evidence is what that party claims it is. The authentication requirement involves questions of relevance and undue prejudice. For instance, if the prosecution in a homicide trial wishes to admit a threatening letter from the defendant to the victim, the prosecution will need to authenticate the letter. If the prosecution does not provide sufficient evidence from which a reasonable juror could find that this letter was the letter written by the defendant to the victim, then the letter should not be presented to the jury. A forged document may not be relevant to the case, or it may have a lower probative value and a higher prejudicial effect. If the letter was not written by the defendant, then it may be irrelevant. If the letter was actually written to someone other than the victim, it would be less probative in the current homicide trial.

CEC §1400: Authentication defined
Authentication of a writing means (a) the introduction of evidence sufficient to sustain a finding that it is the writing that the proponent of the evidence claims it is or (b) the establishment of such facts by any other means provided by law.

CEC §1401: Authentication required
(a) Authentication of a writing is required before it may be received in evidence.
(b) Authentication of a writing is required before secondary evidence of its content may be received in evidence.

The judge fulfills a gate-keeper role in the authentication process by determining which evidence is reliable enough to be presented to the jurors. If there is not sufficient evidence from which a reasonable juror could find that the letter was written by the defendant or written to the victim, then the jurors should not hear about the letter. A letter written by someone else would not help the jurors decide this case and may confuse the issues. On the other hand, when the judge finds that there is sufficient evidence from which a reasonable juror could find that the letter is what it purports to be — a letter written by the defendant to the victim — then the judge can "open the gate" to admit the letter into evidence.

Once the authentication threshold has been met, the letter could still be subject to other objections, such as hearsay (discussed in Chapter 4). The court will address any objections made by the parties before determining whether to admit the evidence, even *after* it has passed the sufficiency test for authentication. If the evidence overcomes all objections, then the jurors can consider the letter and are free to decide whether they believe that the letter was written by the defendant to the victim.

What Is a *Writing*?

While the language of the statute says "writing," letters and other written documents are not the only subjects of authentication procedures. The California Evidence Code (CEC) broadly defines a *writing* to include not only typewriting and handwriting, but also photostating, photographing, electronic mail and facsimiles, including "[e]very other means of recording upon any tangible thing and any form of communication or representation," regardless of the manner in which the record was created (CEC 250). Graffiti also constitutes a writing if there are "words, insignia, symbols or any other markings that convey a particular meaning" (CEC 1410.8). Though the CEC specifically refers to writings, as a matter of practice and case law, all tangible real evidence is subject to an objection for lack of authentication prior to being admitted into evidence. Relevancy is at issue whether the item is a document or writing or some other form of tangible evidence.

Methods of Authentication

There are various ways to authenticate documents and other writings. The CEC provides a non-exhaustive list of these methods (CEC 1410–1421).

A Witness with Knowledge

The most common way to authenticate a document is by a *witness with knowledge*. The attorney can ask the witness several standard questions to lay the foundation:

1. Does the witness recognize the document?
2. If so, how does the witness recognize the document?
3. Have there been any changes or alterations to the document?

327

These three questions usually are enough to lay a foundation that meets the sufficiency standard for authenticating the document. If the answer to the third question reveals that there have been changes, then additional questions will be asked of the witness to explain what alterations were made and whether they impact the accuracy or meaning of the document. CEC 1402 specifically addresses writings that have been altered by requiring the party seeking to admit the writing to explain the circumstances under which the alterations were made and the effect of the alterations on the meaning or language of the document in order to authenticate the altered document.

Signature Recognition

Another common way to authenticate a document with a signature is to have one of the people who were present when the document was signed testify that the document is genuine. This process is known as *authentication by a witness to the execution of a writing* or *authentication by a subscribing witness* (CEC 1413). The courts no longer require this method of authentication for all documents with signatures, but some special statutes require the signatories to testify about authenticity in certain circumstances (CEC 1411). However, if the person who signed the document denies or does not recollect executing the document, the CEC allows the use of other means to authenticate the document (CEC 1412).

Handwriting Comparison

Handwriting recognition or comparison is another authentication method, but it is becoming less common because so many documents are printer-generated. In a will contestation, for instance, if sufficient evidence is presented from which a reasonable jury could conclude that the will was hand-written by the decedent, Marguerite, it will meet the authentication requirement.

Some methods of proving that the will is in Marguerite's handwriting include

1. hearing testimony from Marguerite's daughter, who is familiar with her mother's handwriting;
2. permitting the jury to compare a letter known to be written by Marguerite to the will sought to be admitted; and
3. qualifying an expert witness to provide an expert opinion that the will is genuine based on a handwriting analysis performed either while on the witness stand or outside of court (CEC 1415–1418).

When a will at issue is more than 30 years old, CEC 1419 allows comparison with other documents that have been considered and acted on as though they were genuine when deciding the will's validity.

Party Admission

Authentication by party admission is another way to meet the sufficiency test. Recall from Chapter 6 that a party admission is used to admit a statement made or adopted by a party on the other side of the case. If the party against whom a writing is being offered has admitted its authenticity or acted as though it were authentic at any time, then that admission or conduct will be sufficient to satisfy the authentication requirement (CEC 1414).

Context, which includes *timing* and *location* in addition to other circumstances, is another method of authenticating writings. Authentication of a letter can be accomplished when the writing appears to be a reply to another letter (CEC 1420) and when the content of the writing suggests its authenticity because it includes information that would be known only to the writer (CEC 1421). In addition, a sales receipt found in a woman's purse may provide sufficient evidence to admit that receipt as evidence that the woman made a purchase. The fact that police found lock-picking tools next to a burglarized home may be sufficient evidence to admit the tools as those possibly used in the burglary.

Presumptions for Authentication

Several presumptions (of the Thayer type, which affect the burden of producing evidence, as discussed in Chapter 10) are available as shortcuts to authentication. The writings subject to presumptions of authenticity include

1. those with a certification of acknowledgment (CEC 1451);
2. those with official seals of the United States, federal agencies, public agencies, admiralty courts, or notary publics (CEC 1452);
3. domestic official signatures of public employees of the United States or any of its public entities or by a notary public (CEC 1453); and
4. foreign official signatures if accompanied by additional certifications from the consulate or embassy (CEC 1454).

For the presumption to attach when a document bears an official seal, a signature is required in addition to a stamp or other identifying mark. These rebuttable presumptions burst if there is sufficient evidence to demonstrate the lack of authenticity of the writing at issue.

Chain of Custody

One component of authentication that is especially important with non-documentary tangible evidence is the *chain of custody*, which helps to ensure the tangible evidence was not substituted, replaced, or otherwise tampered with. For instance, when a blood drop is collected from a crime scene and later analyzed to show how closely it matches the blood of the defendant, it is important to know that the blood drop taken from the crime scene is the same blood drop that was analyzed and compared to the defendant's blood sample. This knowledge can be established by presenting evidence of the chain of custody. The chain of custody would include where, when, and to whom the blood drop was transferred—from the time it was gathered at the crime scene until it was analyzed and found to match the defendant. Each transfer from a person or a place is a link in the chain of custody.

Gaps in the chain of custody are not necessarily fatal to admissibility because of the low sufficiency standard for authentication. However, those gaps will affect how reliable the jurors determine the blood match evidence to be. If the gap is large, the judge may determine that there is insufficient evidence to establish the authenticity of the blood match and exclude that evidence. If the blood drop that was compared to the defendant's blood was not the same drop that was taken from the crime scene, then the evidence of a match is not necessarily relevant to the present homicide case. If it is not relevant, then it is not admissible.

Authenticating Photographs, Maps, and Moving Pictures

The process of authenticating a photo or map is similar to that of documents. The attorney will get a witness to testify that the photo correctly represents what it purports to depict. To do this, the proponent must call a witness familiar with what is being represented (such as the intersection where a traffic collision occurred) who can testify that the photo accurately depicts the intersection. Maps and other diagrams also require authentication by a knowledgeable witness to show that the map or diagram provides a correct representation of locations. Similarly, computer reconstructions must be explained so that the court can determine whether they accurately depict the computer data or programs that they purport to depict.

Videotapes and DVDs capture more information than photographs and should be treated as a series of photographs. Frame-by-frame authentication is not required, but a witness must testify that the tape or DVD accurately depicts what was actually occurring. Any changes or edits to the tape or DVD would need to be explained in the same way as alterations to documents. Distortions based on camera height, lenses, and other equipment may also need to be explained to provide sufficient evidence for authentication, and expert testimony may be necessary in some cases.

330

Federal Rules of Evidence Compared: Minor Differences

FRE 901 is very similar to the CEC. It provides a similar non-exhaustive list of ways to authenticate items, adding voice identification, telephone conversations, distinctive characteristics, and public records and processes. Instead of the presumptions of authenticity that are used in the CEC, however, FRE 902 has a list of items that are "self-authenticating" and therefore need no additional foundation to satisfy the authentication requirement. In addition to the documents presumed authentic under the CEC, the following items are self-authenticating under the FRE: trade inscriptions, commercial paper, and presumptions under Acts of Congress.

Examples

1. Gaby was arrested in a hotel room for facilitating prostitution by her classmates at the law school Barrister's Ball. A search of her hotel room revealed a document that had three columns. The first listed names, the second listed attributes, and the third listed "limitations." There were prices and times noted in pencil next to each name. The document did not have Gaby's name on it. The prosecution called a police officer to the witness stand, and he testified about where he had found the document and why he had been searching the hotel room. He also explained that the document contained the names of female classmates, their measurements, and their sexual likes and dislikes. The prosecution then sought to admit the document at trial as evidence that Gaby was operating as a madam pimping out her law school classmates. Gaby's lawyer objected on the grounds of a lack of authentication. How should the court rule, and why?

2. Connie sued Ving for quiet title. Connie claimed a prescriptive easement over Ving's land, and Ving claimed that the easement was permissive. Ving sought to admit a quitclaim deed, allegedly signed by the previous owner, which states that the ownership of the easement belongs to Ving. The previous owner testified that he does not remember signing that quitclaim deed and that he had never seen it. The notary whose seal is on the deed also does not have a record of that deed in her notary book. Connie objects to admission of the quitclaim deed on the grounds of a lack of authentication. Ving responds that there is a presumption of authentication for documents recorded in a public office and therefore the deed should be admitted. How should the court rule?

3. Rod was charged with insurance fraud after allegedly signing some forms in an attempt to collect life insurance on an uncle he knew was living

abroad. At trial, the prosecution sought to admit the fraudulent form so that the jury could compare the signature on Rod's driver's license with the signature on the forms. Rod objected that the forms were not properly authenticated and that the jury needed expert testimony to reach a conclusion about the handwriting comparison. How should the court rule, and why?

4. Jazz Chicken Company supplies live chickens by the pound to the Yeri Canning facility. Yeri cooks, cleans, debones, and packages the chickens into lunch-sized cans sold at grocery stores around the nation. The contract between Jazz and Yeri specifically states that some chickens will die in transit and that the total weight of deceased chickens will be deducted from the invoice Yeri must pay for each shipment. Food safety regulations require a Poultry Condemnation Certificate (PCC) be filled out and submitted to the Food and Drug Administration (FDA) whenever a shipment arrives with some dead chickens. Yeri filled out the PCC, noting 40 pounds of dead chickens, and filed the PCC with the FDA. Then, a Yeri employee altered the PCC to note 400 pounds of dead chickens and sent a copy of that altered PCC with the invoice payment. Jazz was surprised to learn that 400 pounds had been deducted from the last shipment and sued to recover the additional money. Jazz sought to produce the original PCC that was on file with the FDA. Yeri objected on the grounds that since the weight listed on the FDA original was different from the weight listed on the copy, the original could not be authenticated. How should the court rule, and why?

5. Hartoon and his buddy shot two people one night and were promptly arrested. While in jail awaiting trial, the buddy wrote a letter to Hartoon, asking him what story they should go with when they talk to their lawyers. Hartoon wrote back to his buddy with detailed instructions on what to say to the lawyers and the district attorney. At trial, the prosecution sought to admit Hartoon's letter as a party admission. Hartoon objected that the letter had not been authenticated. How should the court rule, and why?

6. Jacob was arrested for DUI and submitted to a blood test. The test results showed that he was over the legal limit, and he was prosecuted for that DUI charge. At trial, the prosecution sought to admit a document that contained Jacob's name, the names of three other drivers, and the results of their blood tests. The document contained a signature line at the bottom, but instead of a signature there was a rubber stamp with the sheriff's name and the department address and telephone number. The sheriff was not present at trial. Jacob objected that the document had not been properly authenticated. The prosecution responded that there was a presumption of authenticity because the document had an official seal. How should the court rule, and why?

Explanations

1. The court should overrule the objection and find that the authentication standard has been met. The location of the document and the content of the columns provide sufficient evidence that it is what it purports to be: an aid for a madam pimping out her classmates. The facts that it was found in Gaby's hotel room in the hotel where some of the prostitution activities were occurring and listed several of her classmates are adequate to meet the sufficiency standard.

2. The court should sustain the objection. The presumption is a rebuttable presumption, and adequate evidence has been provided to rebut that presumption. When the notary does not have a record of the document and the person who allegedly signed the document does not remember signing or even seeing the document, that contrary evidence is enough for the court to rule that there has not been sufficient evidence that the deed is what it purports to be — an authentic deed detailing the rights to the easement. Thus, the court should decline to admit the deed.

3. The court should overrule Rod's objection. Lay witnesses and even jurors can look at two signatures and make a determination as to whether the signatures are similar enough to meet the low sufficiency test threshold for authentication.

4. The court should overrule the objection and admit the original PCC from the FDA files. Authentication requires sufficient evidence that a document is what it purports to be. Obtaining the document from the files of a governmental agency will be adequate to meet the sufficiency test. The fact that there are conflicting interpretations about the accuracy of the evidence — whether 40 pounds or 400 pounds of dead chickens arrived in the shipment — does not make the document inadmissible. The conflict suggests that the evidence may not be as reliable, and therefore may not be as probative, but does not render the evidence inadmissible for lack of authentication.

5. The court should overrule the objection. Authentication by evidence of a reply is an appropriate method of authentication. Hartoon's letter is in reply to his buddy's letter, and therefore the sufficiency threshold has been met.

6. The court should sustain the objection. The presumption for documents under official seal requires a signature along with the stamp to constitute an official seal. Because there was no signature, the basic facts for the presumption have not been established, and the presumption does not apply. The document itself is not enough without the presumption to meet the sufficiency threshold. Thus, unless there is additional evidence,

the document should be excluded as lacking authentication. The defendant also should object that admitting the document would violate the Confrontation Clause (see Chapter 5 to review the Confrontation Clause requirements). The blood test report is hearsay because it is an out-of-court statement offered for the truth of the matter asserted — that Jacob's blood alcohol content was over the legal limit. The report is testimonial because it was created with government involvement for the purpose of use at trial. Admitting a hearsay testimonial statement against a criminal defendant violates the Confrontation Clause unless the declarant appears as a witness at trial, or the declarant is unavailable and the defendant had a prior opportunity to cross-examine the declarant about the statement. Thus, unless the blood analyst is unavailable and Jacob had a prior opportunity to cross-examine him about the report, the Confrontation Clause is not satisfied, and the report will be excluded on that ground as well.

THE SECONDARY EVIDENCE RULE

The Secondary Evidence Rule applies when the parties seek to prove the *content* of a writing. The types of writings to which the Secondary Evidence Rule applies include documents, photos, and recordings.

One way to prove that a document states what one party asserts that it states is to offer the original document into evidence. CEC 1520 states that "the content of a writing may be proved by an otherwise admissible original." The rule derives from the federal Best Evidence Rule, which was based on the notion that the best evidence about the content of a writing was the original writing itself. Thus, the federal courts prefer to have the original contract to prove the content of that contract.

 CEC §1521: Secondary evidence rule
(a) The content of a writing may be proved by otherwise admissible secondary evidence. The court shall exclude secondary evidence of the content of writing if the court determines either of the following:
    (1) A genuine dispute exists concerning material terms of the writing and justice requires the exclusion.
    (2) Admission of the secondary evidence would be unfair.
[Subsection (b) provides that oral testimony is not made admissible unless it complies with Section 1523. Subsection (c) notes that this section does not excuse the authentication requirement, and (d) provides the title.]

For instance, if a plaintiff in a breach of contract case wants to prove that the contract specifically states a price of $10 per unit, she can do so by admitting the original signed contract into evidence. To admit the contract, the plaintiff would first have to authenticate it under the procedures described in the first section of this chapter. Then, the jurors can read the contract and decide for themselves whether it says "$10 per unit" or some other price.

When the original contract document has been lost, however, the plaintiff will not be able to use the original contract itself to prove the price under CEC 1520. In such a case, the plaintiff will need to use other evidence to prove that contract term. This other evidence is called *secondary evidence*. Because of the frequent need for secondary evidence, the California legislature revised the Best Evidence Rule and replaced it with the Secondary Evidence Rule in California courts.

Types of Secondary Evidence

Secondary evidence can include a copy or duplicate of the contract, a computer printout of the contract file, and even a photo or recording of the contract terms. In an effort to accommodate the digital age, a CEC provision was added to permit admission of other types of copies. If a writing meets the requirements of a business record (see Chapter 7, CEC 1270), then a non-erasable optical image reproduction, a photostatic copy, a microfilm or miniature, or any other photographic copy will be as admissible as the original writing itself (CEC 1550). Reproductions of files, records, photos, fingerprints, and other matters maintained in the criminal justice system will be as admissible as the original (CEC 1550.1). When an original photo print of an original writing or video has been lost or destroyed, a copy will be admissible if properly attested or certified (CEC 1551). In addition, properly authenticated copies or translations of original Spanish title documents about land claims will be as admissible as the originals would be (CEC 1605).

CEC §260: Duplicate

A "duplicate" is a counterpart produced by the same impression as the original, or from the same matrix, or by means of photography, including enlargements and miniatures, or by mechanical or electronic rerecording, or by chemical reproduction, or by other equivalent technique which accurately reproduces the original.

The Secondary Evidence Rule permits the use of such other evidence, unless the court determines that

1. a genuine dispute exists over material terms, or
2. admitting secondary evidence could be unfair.

Where the "other evidence" is oral testimony, its admissibility is governed by CEC 1523, described below.

To determine whether material terms are in dispute, examine the substantive issues and claims in the case. In the contract example above, if the lawsuit involves a dispute over the correct price, then the price is a material term of the contract in dispute, and secondary evidence would not be admissible if justice requires exclusion.

Evaluating Unfairness

In determining whether unfairness or injustice would result, the California courts look at several factors, including whether

1. the writing is being used in an unanticipated manner;
2. one party suppressed the original in discovery;
3. the original was not produced in reasonably diligent discovery;
4. the original and the secondary evidence are dramatically different (such as where a copy of a photo has fading colors or is in black and white when the original was in color);
5. the original is unavailable and, if so, why; and
6. the writing is central to the case.

When one party is accused of purposefully destroying the original writing, courts will find it to be unfair to permit that party to offer secondary evidence on the content of that writing.

Additional Limitation in Criminal Cases Criminal cases place another limitation on the use of secondary evidence. When the judge determines that the proponent has the original in his possession, custody, or control and did not produce it to the other side or make it *reasonably available* before trial, the proponent will not be allowed to offer the secondary evidence. The phrase *possession, custody, or control* is a common phrase used in discovery requests to ensure that all available responsive documents are produced. Whether a party has satisfied the reasonably available standard depends on the time, place, and manner of allowing the inspection of the original. More time should be provided for the case in chief, but a shorter time frame, even moments before using the secondary evidence, has been found to be sufficient when a criminal defendant is surprised by a rebuttal witness.

CEC §1522: Additional grounds for exclusion of secondary evidence
(a) In addition to the grounds for exclusion authorized by Section 1521, in a criminal action the court shall exclude secondary evidence of the content of a writing if the court determines that the original is in the proponent's possession, custody, or control, and the proponent has not made the original reasonably available for inspection at or before trial. This section does not apply to any of the following:
 (1) A duplicate as defined in Section 260.
 (2) A writing that is not closely related to the controlling issues in the action.
 (3) A copy of a writing in the custody of a public entity.
 (4) A copy of a writing that is recorded in the public records, if the record or a certified copy of it is made evidence of the writing by statute.
(b) In a criminal action, a request to exclude secondary evidence of the content of a writing, under this section or any other law, shall not be made in the presence of the jury.

This criminal limitation applies to the prosecution as well as to the defense lawyers. It does not apply if a duplicate of the writing is offered, the writing is not closely related to important issues, or a copy is in the custody of a public entity or in a public record. Any request to exclude secondary evidence must be made outside the presence of the jury. This requirement helps to avoid any potential prejudice that might result if the jury feels that one party was hiding evidence from the other side.

Figure 11.1 explains what types of writings are subject to the Secondary Evidence Rule, when the rule is triggered by an attempt to prove the contents, and when unfairness may nonetheless prevent the use of secondary evidence.

Oral Testimony as a Form of Secondary Evidence

CEC 1523 applies specifically when the type of secondary evidence a party seeks to offer is in the form of oral testimony. The general rule is that oral testimony is not admissible to prove the content of a writing, but there are several exceptions. The first three exceptions are triggered when the party who seeks to offer secondary evidence about the writing does not have the original or a copy of that writing. Oral testimony can be admissible if

1. the original was either lost or destroyed without any fraudulent intent, or

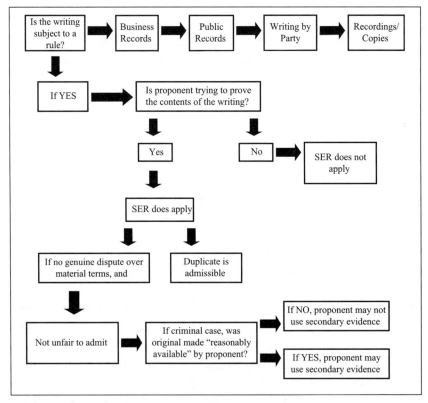

Figure 11.1. Applying the Secondary Evidence Rule

2. the proponent does not have the original or a copy *and* was not able to reasonably procure the original or a copy using the court process or other means, or
3. the proponent does not have the original or a copy *and* the writing is not closely related to controlling issues in the litigation.

CEC §1523: Oral testimony of the content of a writing; admissibility
(a) Except as otherwise provided by statute, oral testimony is not admissible to prove the content of a writing.
(b) Oral testimony of the content of a writing is not made inadmissible by subdivision (a) if the proponent does not have possession or control of a copy of the writing and the original is lost or has been destroyed without fraudulent intent on the part of the proponent of the evidence.
(c) Oral testimony of the content of a writing is not made inadmissible by subdivision (a) if the proponent does not have possession or control of the

original or a copy of the writing and either of the following conditions is satisfied:

(1) Neither the writing nor a copy of the writing was reasonably procurable by the proponent by use of the court's process or by other available means.

(2) The writing is not closely related to the controlling issues and it would be inexpedient to require its production.

(d) Oral testimony of the content of a writing is not made inadmissible by subdivision (a) if the writing consists of numerous accounts or other writings that cannot be examined in court without great loss of time, and the evidence sought from them is only the general result of the whole.

The fourth exception does not require that the originals be unavailable, but applies when the writings are so voluminous that it would waste the court's time to examine the entire batch. When the only evidence sought is the "general result of the whole," then courts find a thorough examination to be a waste of judicial resources. This fourth exception can apply when boxes of documents have been reviewed to determine whether some sort of pattern emerges. The general result might be that the documents indicate a pattern of fraud or of embezzlement. Some reference to the content of the documents is necessary to support the fraud or embezzlement accusation. Requiring a copy of every document to be admitted into evidence before allowing oral testimony about it would be unduly cumbersome. Thus, this exception permits oral testimony to summarize the general result of reviewing the entire batch of documents.

Figure 11.2 explains the different situations in which secondary evidence in the form of oral testimony will be admissible.

Remember that the Secondary Evidence Rule applies only when trying to prove the *content* of a writing. If an employer wants to show that the employee logged into work 15 minutes late each day during a particular

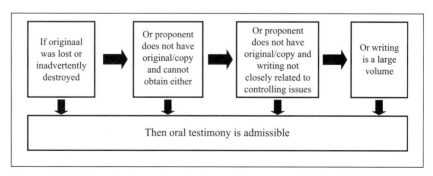

Figure 11.2. When the Secondary Evidence Rule Permits Oral Testimony

week, then the Secondary Evidence Rule would apply because the employer is trying to prove the content — that the writing shows the employee's signature with a particular time noted for each day that week. If a witness is going to testify that the landlord gave her a receipt that stated "payment in full," then the Secondary Evidence Rule is implicated by the attempt to prove the content of the receipt. Because the term *writing* applies more broadly to transcripts and recordings, if the prosecution wants to prove the actual substance of exactly what was said in a recorded conversation, then the Secondary Evidence Rule requires the prosecution to produce the original recording or a duplicate of the recording.

When the Secondary Evidence Rule Does Not Apply

In the contract example above, if the plaintiff merely wants to prove that she had entered into a contract with the defendant, rather than to prove the terms of that contract, then the Secondary Evidence Rule does not apply.

Proving the absence of content does not implicate the Secondary Evidence Rule. Thus, if an employer wants to show that an employee never logged into work one day, the Secondary Evidence Rule does not apply. The work log can be admitted to show the absence of the employee's sign-in.

The Secondary Evidence Rule is not necessarily implicated whenever oral testimony mentions a document. Parties can use witness testimony to state that a payment was made and will not run afoul of the Secondary Evidence Rule. In the landlord payment example above, if the original receipt was lost or destroyed without fraudulent intent, then the oral testimony can be admissible about whether the receipt indicated that the rent was paid in full. Similarly, a prosecutor may provide testimony about a conversation that was recorded as long as she is not trying to prove the substance of the recording. If the prosecution wants to establish that a conversation occurred on a particular topic, then oral testimony can be admitted, and the Secondary Evidence Rule is not implicated.

Presumptions for Proving Content

The CEC contains several rebuttable presumptions (Thayer-type, as you recall from Chapter 10) that are shortcuts to proving the contents of certain writings. For instance, if one party alleges that she has a copy of a writing (or a log entry) that is kept in the custody of a public entity, that will be sufficient evidence of the content of the writing if the copy is (or purports to be) published by a public entity or is a certified or attested copy kept in a public office (CEC 1530).

If that writing affects an interest in real property, the presumption applies to establish the existence and content of the original, its execution, and its delivery to all interested persons (CEC 1600).

The official record of a writing is sufficient evidence of the content of the writing as long the record is of a public entity and a statute authorizes the recording of that type of document in that public office (CEC 1532).

Printed information from a computer program is presumed to be an accurate representation, but if contrary evidence is presented, the proponent must establish the accuracy by a preponderance of the evidence (CEC 1552).

A similar code section applies to printed representations of images stored on a digital or video record (CEC 1553). Deeds of real property conveyance purporting to have been executed properly will be presumed to have conveyed the interest as described (CEC 1603), as will a certificate of purchase for land (CEC 1604).

The requirements for a subpoena duces tecum (with documents) are detailed in CEC 1560 through 1567. This subject is covered in your civil procedure and pretrial discovery courses, and is not discussed in this book.

PUTTING IT ALL TOGETHER: MEETING THE AUTHENTICATION AND SECONDARY EVIDENCE REQUIREMENTS

Whenever a party seeks to admit a document into evidence, the party first should satisfy the authentication requirement. If that party also seeks to prove the contents of the document, then an original or duplicate, computer file, or photograph can be used to prove those contents. Oral testimony about the contents will be permitted only if one of the four exceptions exists. Once the document has been admitted into evidence, oral testimony to explain the documents and the parties' interpretations of the document will be admissible.

The authentication requirement forces the proponent to identify the document and provide sufficient evidence for the fact finder to determine that the document is what the proponent claims it is. Remember that a sufficiency standard means that the judge views the evidence in the light most favorable to the proponent.

To address the Secondary Evidence Rule objection, the proponent must persuade the judge that no genuine dispute exists concerning the material terms of the original and that admission of the secondary evidence would not be unfair. In making this determination, the California judge can weigh and consider the evidence on both sides of the issue and may take into account the credibility of the witnesses.

If these objections are overruled, the opponent may also wish to make a hearsay objection if the document is being offered to prove the truth of the matter asserted. The proponent will need to establish that a hearsay exception applies (see Chapters 5 through 7). If the hearsay objection is overruled, then the party may disclose the contents of the document to the jury by publishing it to the jury or having a witness read the document or relevant portions to the jury.

Federal Rules of Evidence Compared: Minor Differences

FRE 1002 once favored proof of the contents by using the original writing; it is called the Best Evidence Rule because the original writing itself was the best evidence of its content. Duplicates are now as admissible as the original in most circumstances (FRE 1003). Because of its many exceptions, the FRE is not substantially more strict about using originals and duplicates. However, it maintains a preference for the original document.

FRE 1004 provides exceptions that parallel the CEC. In addition, FRE 1005, like CEC 1530, provides an exception for the contents of an official record or a document that is recorded or filed in a public office. If the copy cannot be obtained by reasonable diligence, then other evidence will be admissible.

FRE 1006, like CEC 1523, provides that summaries are also permissible when the volume is large, but in contrast to the CEC, the FRE requires the originals or copies to be made available for examination or copying.

FRE 1007 provides that testimony or deposition of the party against whom the evidence is offered or by that party's written admission will be admissible proof, without requiring him to account for not producing the original.

THE COMPLETENESS DOCTRINE

When only portions of a document are read to the jury by one proponent, there is a chance that the jury will be misled. The CEC contains another provision referred to as the *completeness doctrine* that protects against some of the misleading impressions that can be created by lawyers taking words out of context. When one party admits a portion of a transcript, for instance, this provision allows the opposing party to admit another portion of that same transcript immediately afterward. The only limitation is that the additional information must be necessary to make the evidence understood. The opposing party does not need to wait until its next turn, which would be the cross-examination of the witness on the stand. Instead, the opposing party can object and immediately inquire about the omitted information or offer the omitted information into evidence.

This doctrine becomes important in considering statements that are admitted as exceptions to the Hearsay Rule where part of the statement can be admitted pursuant to an exception but another part of the statement is not admissible under the exception. If the admissible part would be misleading to the jury without the rest of the statement, then the completeness doctrine is a way to provide more context. This doctrine allows the opposing party to admit surrounding statements as long as they are necessary for a more complete understanding of the subject matter.

CEC §356: Entire act, declaration, conversation, or writing may be brought out to elucidate part offered

Where part of an act, declaration, conversation, or writing is given in evidence by one party, the whole on the same subject may be inquired into by an adverse party; when a letter is read, the answer may be given; and when a detached act, declaration, conversation, or writing is given in evidence, any other act, declaration, conversation, or writing which is necessary to make it understood may also be given in evidence.

Federal Rules of Evidence Compared: Substantive Differences

FRE 106 is significantly less broad than the CEC and applies only to writings or recorded statements, but not to acts, declarations, or conversations.

Examples

1. In a drug prosecution, the Government's informants testify as to the substance of conversations that they had with the defendants, but the Government does not produce the recordings of those conversations. The defendant objects, claiming a violation of the Secondary Evidence Rule. How should the court rule?

2. Arthur was a truck driver who was required to sign a log each day when he showed up at work. The log sheets are kept on file for one year and then routinely destroyed. Arthur was arrested on suspicion of kidnapping and murder. Arthur could not afford bail and was in jail awaiting trial.

While in jail, Arthur allegedly confessed to his cellmate that he did not log into work on the day of the kidnapping and stated that he was lucky that no one would know because the log sheets had been destroyed. At trial, the prosecution sought to admit a copy of the log sheet from the day of the kidnapping. Arthur objected that it violated the Secondary Evidence Rule because it would be unfair to admit the copy in his trial. How should the court rule?

3. Brad interviewed for a litigation position and was told that he had an offer, subject to getting satisfactory grades during his last semester of law school. Brad studied for weeks to prepare for his Evidence examination. After the test, he felt really good about his performance, and he told his roommates that he "aced" the test. A month later, when grades were posted, he saw that he had received a D+ in the Evidence course. The firm rescinded his offer because of Brad's grade in Evidence. Two months after that, when the exams were released, Brad picked up his exam and saw the grade written on the front cover was an A+. Brad showed the examination to his roommates, who confirmed that that grade was an A+. Brad then sued his professor and his law school for interference with prospective economic advantage and negligent infliction of emotional distress. At trial, Brad called one of his roommates to the witness stand and asked him what grade was written on Brad's evidence examination. The defense counsel objected that the testimony would violate the Secondary Evidence Rule. How should the court rule?

4. Dart was exposed to a dangerous chemical in his workplace, and his employer-provided insurance company denied coverage. Dart sued. Dart said that he did not have a copy of the insurance policy or the original, so he sought to offer the oral testimony of the insurance agent who had answered his questions when he was signing up for the policy. The insurance agent was about to testify about the terms of coverage when the defendant objected that the testimony violates the Secondary Evidence Rule. Dart responded that because the original policy was unavailable, the rule permitted oral testimony. The defendant responded that Dart had asked to see a copy of his policy before he filed the lawsuit, and after he was left alone with the file, the original and all copies were never seen again. How should the court rule?

5. Sam's girlfriend, Ula, asked him to kill her stepfather. Ever loyal, Sam did as he was asked and then dumped the body in the ocean. Ula was very grateful and offered to split her inheritance with Sam. When the body was found six months after the murder, the police came to talk to Ula and Sam. The next day, Sam called Ula on her cell phone and told her he was afraid the police were closing in and that he was feeling extremely remorseful. Sam also said that he was thinking of either leaving town

or confessing to the police. Neither Sam nor Ula were aware that the police had obtained a tap on Ula's cell phone and that Detective Peeps overheard and recorded their conversation. Sam and Ula were prosecuted for murder for hire. At trial, the prosecution called Detective Peeps to the witness stand and asked him to testify about the conversation between Sam and Ula. The defense objected that this oral testimony would violate the Secondary Evidence Rule. How should the court rule, and why?

6. Mr. and Mrs. Hepa set up a revocable trust that would become irrevocable on the death of either of them. Their house was listed as an asset of the trust. Mrs. Hepa died a few years later. Then, Mr. Hepa married the second Mrs. Hepa and moved her into the same house. When Mr. Hepa died, his son from the first marriage sued the second Mrs. Hepa, claiming that the house now belonged to him as the sole remaining beneficiary of his parents' irrevocable trust. At trial, the son testified that based on his examination of the ten boxes of trust documents, the house remained in the irrevocable trust and therefore belonged to him. He began to provide a detailed oral summary of the trust history when the second Mrs. Hepa objected on the grounds that the oral testimony violated the Secondary Evidence Rule. How should the court rule, and why?

Explanations

1. The court should overrule the secondary evidence objection because the rule does not apply here. What is at issue is the substance of the conversations, not the substance of the recording.

2. The court should overrule the objection. If the copy of the log sheet is sought to be admitted to show that Arthur did not log in that day, then the Secondary Evidence Rule is not implicated. The rule does not apply to show the absence of content in a document. If the log sheet is admitted to show a later arrival or for some other content purpose, then a copy or duplicate is admissible as long as admitting the copy or duplicate would not result in unfairness. Here, Arthur has not established any unfairness that might result. The simple fact that he thought the log sheets had been destroyed is not enough to constitute unfairness, and the log sheets should be admitted.

3. The court should sustain the objection. The Secondary Evidence Rule is implicated because Brad is trying to prove that his examination had a grade of A+ written on it. Brad would need to provide an original or a duplicate to satisfy the Secondary Evidence Rule. There is no evidence that Brad has lost or inadvertently destroyed the original, nor is unable to obtain the original examination answer or a copy, and so these avenues

for using oral testimony will not be open to him. The writing is closely related to the controlling issues in the case since the writing involves the grade he earned, and the error in properly reporting the A+ caused Brad's claimed damages. The grade is not voluminous, and therefore Brad cannot use this avenue for admitting oral testimony. Brad must produce the original or a copy of the examination answer to prove the grade that he earned.

4. The court should sustain the objection. The Secondary Evidence Rule permits oral testimony to prove the contents of the policy when the original is lost or inadvertently destroyed without fraudulent intent as long as it would not be unfair to admit such testimony. Here, there is an argument that Dart destroyed the original policy when he reviewed the file. Thus, it would be unfair to permit Dart to benefit from destroying the original policy. The Secondary Evidence Rule will not permit Dart to offer oral testimony in this situation.

5. The court should overrule the objection because the Secondary Evidence Rule does not apply. The prosecution is not using the detective's testimony to prove the contents of a transcript or recording of the phone conversation (the content of a writing). The detective is testifying about what the parties actually said, not what the transcript says they said. Thus, his oral testimony is not made inadmissible by the Secondary Evidence Rule. A hearsay objection would also be overruled because the statements of Sam and Ula are party admissions (discussed in Chapter 6).

6. The court should overrule the objection. Oral testimony about the content of documents is permissible when the documents are so voluminous that they could not be examined individually in court without great loss of time. Here, the son can testify about the general result of his analysis of the ten boxes of trust documents without requiring the court to go through all ten boxes of documentation.

Introduction to Privileges; Professional Relationship Privileges

The law of privileges recognizes that the need for justice must sometimes yield to professional, personal, and institutional interests. Privacy and confidentiality are hallmarks of many personal and professional relationships, and the law of privileges limits court intrusions into these private matters. For example, the attorney-client and physician-patient relationships depend on honest and frank discussions between the parties to get the best representation or treatment. Privileges described in the CEC aim to encourage those relationships and the open communication that is vital to their operation. Thus, the law of privileges precludes admitting these confidential communications at trial.

Privileges in California are purely statutory. California state courts recognize only those privileges enumerated in the CEC or other statutes (CEC 911). The courts do not recognize common law privileges that have not been codified by the legislature. Furthermore, judges cannot create new privileges or expand the scope of existing privileges.

The CEC allows 18 privileges, which apply in all proceedings in which testimony can be compelled, including civil and criminal litigation, coroners' inquests, legislative hearings, certain administrative hearings, grand jury proceedings, and even arbitration proceedings. The privileges apply not only in hearings and trials, but also in the course of discovery and depositions. California cases also hold that privileges apply when search warrants are issued requesting potentially privileged information. If the search warrant is directed at an attorney who is suspected of a crime but seeks disclosure of client files, the attorney is obliged to seek a court order to prevent disclosure of any protected documents.

The CEC privileges break down into three types:

1. Those that protect confidential communications made in the course of a relationship (*confidential communications privileges*)
2. Those that exempt certain people from giving evidence (*testimonial privileges*)
3. Those that exempt a witness from providing certain information (*content privileges*)

This chapter addresses confidential communications privileges and focuses specifically on those involving professional relationships. After a general overview of privilege law, this chapter explains the attorney-client, physician-patient, and psychotherapist-patient privileges. Other confidential communications privileges, as well as testimonial and content privileges, are discussed in Chapter 13.

THE GENERAL APPROACH TO ANALYZING PRIVILEGES

When facing a privilege issue, always ask the following four questions. These questions apply to every privilege in the next two chapters, with small but important variations:

1. First, ask whether the parties to the communication or from whom testimony is sought are *covered* by a privilege listed in the CEC.
2. If so, next ask whether the communication or evidence is *within the scope* of the privilege as defined in the CEC.
3. Third, ask whether the privilege has been *waived*, perhaps by disclosure.
4. Fourth, consider whether an *exception* to the privilege applies.

Are the Parties Covered? For a communication to be privileged, the parties to the communication must fit a definition in the CEC. Only certain people are exempt from testifying under the *testimonial* privilege. The CEC provides specific definitions for the purpose of a privilege. This chapter addresses the professional relationship privileges and the definitions for lawyers, clients, physicians, psychotherapists, and patients.

Is the Communication or Evidence Covered by the Privilege? The only protected communications are *confidential communications*. The content privileges protect only certain types of information from disclosure. Each privilege has a CEC section that describes the confidential communications or evidence that is protected under the privilege. For the privilege to apply, the communication must satisfy the requirements of that CEC section.

For professional relationships, communications made in the course of the relationship are presumed to be confidential under CEC 917(a). This is a rebuttable Thayer presumption, meaning the burden of proof shifts to the party objecting to the privilege. The mere delivery of the communication using electronic means that others may have access to does not defeat the presumption. (See Chapter 10 for more explanation of burdens of proof and presumptions.)

It is important to understand that *the communication between the parties to the privilege is what is protected*, not the subject matter of the communication. For example, just because a lawyer and client discuss a subject does not mean that all information on that subject is protected from disclosure. If a client tells his lawyer that he was not looking at the road when he hit the car in front of him, opposing counsel can ask, "Were you looking at the road?" or "What were you doing when you hit the car in front of you?" because both questions go to the subject matter underlying the communication, not the communication itself. Opposing counsel could not ask, however, "What did you tell your lawyer about the accident?"

Has the Privilege Been Waived?   If the first two questions are satisfied, then the communication is privileged and cannot be disclosed at trial. However, the privilege ceases to exist if it has been waived. Waivers are addressed in CEC 912. A waiver occurs when the holder of the privilege, without being coerced, either discloses or consents to someone else's disclosure of a significant part of the privileged communication. The holder of a certain privilege will be specified in the CEC sections about that privilege. In some cases, there may be more than one holder.

There are many different ways to waive a privilege. Voluntary disclosure can occur when the privilege holder either intentionally discloses the information to a third party or chooses to testify in court. Conduct can also indicate consent to disclosure, including the failure to claim the privilege when the holder has the opportunity to do so. A waiver can also occur by a negligent and inadvertent disclosure of privileged information because of a lack of due care. However, not all disclosures constitute a waiver. Most privileges allow for disclosure to third parties when it is "reasonably necessary." If there is more than one holder of the privilege — joint holders — then a waiver by one does not constitute a waiver by the other, and the non-waiving holder still can claim the privilege.

Is There an Exception that Destroys the Privilege?   There are two basic types of exceptions to privileges. The first type makes the privilege invalid in certain proceedings. For instance, if a client sues her lawyer for malpractice, there is an exception to the attorney-client privilege in that proceeding to

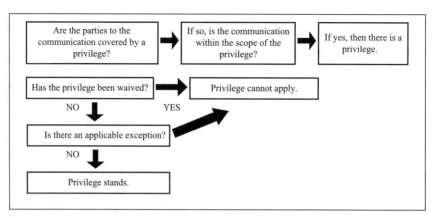

Figure 12.1. To Determine Whether a Communication Is Privileged in California

permit the attorney to disclose the communications to defend himself. Confidential communications made in the course of that attorney-client relationship will be allowed into evidence. The second type of exception is a blanket exception that applies no matter what type of proceeding. The best example is the crime or fraud exception to the attorney-client privilege. Under that exception, there is no privilege, no matter the proceeding, if the client sought the lawyer's services to aid in the commission of a future crime or fraud. Each privilege comes with its own specific exceptions, which are discussed below.

In evaluating privileges, consider the following questions illustrated in Figure 12.1: (1) Are the parties to the communication covered by a privilege? (2) If so, is the evidence or communication within the scope of the privilege? (3) Has the privilege been waived? (4) Is there an applicable exception to this privilege (considering both specific-litigation exceptions and blanket exceptions)?

RULING ON CLAIMS OF PRIVILEGE

If one party objects on the grounds of privilege, the judge decides whether a privilege applies. The person claiming the protection of a privilege has the burden to show that the elements of the privilege are all met. The burden of proof for establishing the existence of a privilege is by a preponderance of the evidence (see CEC 405 in Chapter 10). The party opposing the privilege is entitled to present evidence to negate the existence of the privilege. The opposing party may also argue that the privilege was waived or that an exception applies. The opposing party must prove the waiver or exception by a preponderance of the evidence. Then the judge determines whether the privilege applies.

To determine whether the privilege was waived, the judge will consider evidence offered by the opposing party on the issue of whether the "privileged" information was disclosed. However, not all disclosures amount to a waiver. A disclosure of the confidential information is generally not a waiver when disclosure to a third party is *reasonably necessary* for transmission of the information or to accomplish the goal of the professional relationship (CEC 912(d)). An inadvertent disclosure to an eavesdropper will not waive the privilege as long as the holder believed that the communication was confidential.

The judge or presiding officer does not usually require disclosure of the confidential information to rule on whether the privilege applies. The court has discretion to order review in chambers to determine whether the privilege exists and what it protects. When there is voluminous material, the courts often appoint a special master or discovery magistrate judge to perform the review.

To avoid punishing those who raise privilege claims, the presiding judge and lawyers cannot comment at trial about the use of a privilege (CEC 913(a)). If a party requests, the court must instruct the jurors not to draw any inferences from the use of the privilege and instruct that no presumption arises from its use (CEC 913(b)).

The judge should not compel disclosure of privileged information and should prevent disclosure of privileged information when possible. When no authorized holder of a privilege is in court and a witness seeks to disclose privileged information, the judge or presiding officer must exclude the information if there is no party there who is authorized to claim the privilege (CEC 916(a)). The only exceptions are when no privilege holder exists or when a holder authorizes the disclosure or waives the privilege (CEC 916(b)).

In non-judicial proceedings such as certain administrative hearings, CEC 914 authorizes the presiding officer at the hearing to fill the role of a judge to determine whether a privilege applies. If a person declines to disclose information despite the presiding officer's determination that the privilege does not apply, that person will not be held in contempt unless the presiding officer is from a public office with contempt power or a judge orders disclosure.

If a judge or other presiding officer makes an improper ruling on a privilege claim and compels disclosure, that disclosure will *not* operate as a further waiver of the privilege. The privilege is intact, and the holder can assert the privilege again in later proceedings (CEC 919).

Federal Rules of Evidence Compared: No Corresponding FRE

Unlike in California, where the only privileges are those specifically granted by statute, the FRE does not codify any privileges. FRE 501 states that federal law as to privileges is governed by the common law. FRE 501 also states that in civil cases with state law claims, federal courts will apply the privilege laws of the forum state. The proposed but unadopted FRE on privileges are included in many texts because they are illustrative of the majority common law position.

THE ATTORNEY-CLIENT PRIVILEGE: CEC 950–962

The attorney-client privilege allows the client the right to refuse to disclose confidential information between the client and the attorney. The lawyer has a separate ethical obligation, aside from this privilege, to avoid disclosing client confidences in any setting. The purpose of this privilege is to ensure that the attorney has the trust of the client and gets all the information needed to provide the most effective legal representation. The attorney-client privilege gives the client two privileges: (1) to refuse to disclose and (2) to prevent others from disclosing confidential communications, as long as the client, the lawyer, or other authorized person claims the privilege in that proceeding.

As outlined in the section above, there are four steps that must be taken as a general approach to California privileges. In accordance with those four steps, the attorney-client privilege will be explained by examining

1. the parties to the communication;
2. the requirements for that communication to be confidential;
3. waivers; and
4. exceptions.

The Lawyer

For purposes of the attorney-client privilege, the lawyer must be someone authorized to practice law in any state or nation. The term *lawyer* includes not only the actual attorneys but also their representatives, such as assistants, legal secretaries, clerks, and paralegals. *Note:* In criminal cases the prosecutor (a district attorney) is a public official who represents the state and has no "client" for purposes of the attorney-client privilege.

Reasonable Belief Under CEC 950, a lawyer may also be someone whom the client reasonably believed was authorized to practice law. This allowance is to protect confidences when a person misrepresents herself as an attorney or when the client has no reason to know that the person is not licensed to practice law. The party claiming the privilege will have the burden to prove that the belief was a reasonable one. In circumstances when a statute allows a person to have a lay legal representative, the client may reasonably believe the layperson to be a lawyer. The client's belief may be reasonable even if the client failed to ask whether the person was licensed to practice, as long as there were other indications that the person was a lawyer (such as that she gives legal advice, displays diplomas on her office walls, or has legal treatises on her bookshelves). However, a client's belief is not reasonable if the purported lawyer expressly stated that she is not a licensed lawyer.

"In Any State or Nation" This language protects a client who consults someone she reasonably believes to be an attorney in any legal system. The CEC will protect any confidential communication to a lawyer, regardless of where the purported lawyer is from and regardless of whether that jurisdiction recognizes such a privilege.

The Client

A *client* is a person, a corporation, or other business entity that consults a lawyer to get legal services or advice. The consultation can occur directly by the client or indirectly through an authorized representative. When there are *joint clients* who consult the attorney for the same purpose, all of the clients retain the privilege against third parties and other outsiders. However, shareholders and trust beneficiaries do not become clients of the corporate or trust attorney without a separate agreement.

The Corporate Context While a corporation can be a client and is a "person" in many legal contexts, a corporation itself cannot communicate with its attorney. It must communicate with its attorney through *natural persons*, like directors, officers, and other employees. However, only certain persons can be treated as the client for purposes of the attorney-client privilege. In a landmark case, the California Supreme Court laid out examples of persons who would be considered clients for the purpose of the corporate attorney-client privilege, such as employees who are also defendants, those who are acting solely as witnesses, those who are required to report, and those who would ordinarily speak on a certain matter. (This topic is explained in greater detail in the section below titled "Communications in the Corporate Context.")

Confidential Communications

A *confidential communication* is a communication made in confidence between a client and an attorney and made in the course of the attorney-client relationship. The communication must not, as far as the client is aware, be disclosed to anyone to whom disclosure is not reasonably necessary to transmit the information or accomplish the goal of representation. The communication must actually be transmitted — mere intent to transmit will not suffice.

Actual employment of the attorney is not required, and statements made by a prospective client to a lawyer she might hire are still confidential, even if she does not ultimately hire the attorney. However, when an attorney tells the potential client that he will not represent her, anything the potential client says after that point will not be privileged. If she does hire the attorney, all legal advice will be privileged, whether or not related to the original reason for retaining the lawyer. Non-legal advice, such as business or personal advice, is not privileged. If the advice is sought for more than one reason, the dominant purpose controls. If the dominant purpose is legal in nature, the attorney-client privilege will apply.

Communications made in the course of the attorney-client relationship are *presumed to be confidential*, and the opponent to the privilege has the burden of proving that the communication was not confidential.

Disclosure to Third Persons   Disclosure to third persons does not destroy confidentiality if the third parties are present to further the consultation or goals of the representation. Common third persons that fit within the protection are spouses, parents, business associates, interpreters, and experts used to help the attorneys prepare for trial. The general rule for disclosure to experts is if the facts and circumstances suggest that the expert was hired to evaluate and pass on to the attorney matters that were given to the expert by the client in confidence, both the expert's opinions and reports will be privileged. But if the expert is evaluating and examining matters that are not confidential communications from a client to attorney, then the expert report will not be protected by the privilege simply because a copy was sent to the attorney. Expert reports that are not protected by the attorney-client privilege still may be protected by the attorney work-product doctrine, which is governed by the California Code of Civil Procedure.

When the client is aware of disclosure to other third persons who are not necessary for transmission or accomplishing the goals of legal representation, then the communication is not confidential or privileged. Likewise, the mere presence of the attorney along with other persons in a meeting does not render the information disclosed in that meeting privileged. But, when the client is unaware and there is a third party eavesdropping, disclosure to the eavesdropper will not destroy the privilege.

What Counts as a Communication? The communication may be written or oral. It may even be a non-verbal act if the act was intended as a message. However, tangible items are not communications and therefore are not privileged (e.g., a bloody knife given to the defense attorney). Similarly, the attorney's impressions about the client are not confidential communications (e.g., the attorney's impression that the client was jumpy and anxious). Additionally, information that is not communicated by the client but is merely perceived by the attorney's senses is not privileged (e.g., seeing a cut on the client's hand or smelling gasoline on the client's clothes).

Generally the identity of a client is not protected by the privilege because it is not a confidential communication containing legal advice or strategy. However, there are two exceptions:

1. When disclosure of the client's name might implicate the client in unlawful activity or expose the client to civil or criminal liability
2. When enough is known about the reason for the representation that revealing the identity of the client also reveals something that normally would be confidential

Disclosure of identity might expose the client to liability if, for example, an attorney tries to negotiate a lesser charge for a client who wants to release a kidnapped victim. In that case, revealing the client's name would expose that client to criminal penalties. Disclosure of identity might reveal something confidential about the client if, for instance, an attorney who represents people seeking to adopt children is asked to disclose their identities. That disclosure would reveal the confidential information that the clients are seeking to adopt a child.

Communications in the Corporate Context

Whenever an officer, a director, a employee, or another person involved in the corporation has a communication with an attorney, the following two-step inquiry must be performed to determine if it is a confidential communication:

1. Is the communication for the purposes of giving or receiving legal advice or service?
2. If so, is the communication reasonably necessary for transmission or to accomplish the purpose of the legal consultation, or disclosed to persons who are present to further the interest of the corporate client?

The first question ensures that only legal communications are protected by the privilege. The second question ensures that the legal communications are also *confidential* ones, shared only with corporate officers or employees who are reasonably necessary to further the corporation's legal interests.

If a communication is made to, or even in the presence of, a person involved in the corporation who is not reasonably necessary, then that communication was not made to the client, and the privilege will not apply. In deciding whether a person at a corporation is reasonably necessary, California courts apply 11 principles set forth in the California Supreme Court's *Chadbourne* case.[1] Under *Chadbourne*, communications made by an employee who is a *codefendant* in a case against the corporation to the corporation's attorney are privileged. Even if an employee is not a codefendant, a communication he makes to the corporate attorney may still be privileged if the employee is the *natural person to speak* on the matter. For example, if a lawsuit alleging employment discrimination in hiring has been filed against the corporation and Frank is the human resources director, then he would be the natural person to speak about hiring discrimination. His statements to the corporate attorney, then, are protected under the privilege.

Also, corporate employees who are acting *solely as witnesses* in the legal matter can make privileged communications to the corporate attorney. Furthermore, the attorney-client privilege applies to *required reports or statements* that corporate employees must make confidentially in the ordinary course of business, as long as those reports and statements are actually transmitted to the corporate attorney. If the reports are made for more than one purpose, the dominant purpose controls.

Communications made to agents of the corporation with the knowledge and consent of the corporation may still be privileged despite being communicated to the agent rather than the corporate attorney. The inquiry is whether disclosure to that agent — a third party — was reasonably necessary to transmit the communication or accomplish the goals of the legal representation.

Communications made to the corporation's indemnity *insurance agents* can be considered privileged, depending on the reason for the communications and the particular facts of the case. The court will need to determine on a case-by-case basis whether the particular communications made to the particular agent are privileged under the unique circumstances of that case.

A final principle from *Chadbourne* is that the *intent of the person making the communication governs*. This means that if the person making the communication intends that it be kept confidential, that intent weighs in favor of the communication being confidential and privileged. If the employer instructs an employee to make a confidential communication to the corporate attorney, the employer's intent controls.

---

1. D.I. Chadbourne, Inc. v. Superior Court, 60 Cal. 2d 723, 388 P.2d 700 (1964).

Claiming the Privilege

The holder of a privilege can claim the privilege. With the attorney-client privilege, the client is the holder of the privilege, except when the client has a guardian, a conservator, or an executor, who then becomes the holder of the privilege. The holder is also the person who can waive the privilege. The attorney-client privilege is dual, allowing the holder both to refuse to disclose confidential information and to prevent others from disclosing the information.

The only other people who may claim the privilege are persons authorized by the holder or the professional who either made or received confidential communications. In addition, lawyers, doctors, and therapists have an affirmative obligation to claim the privilege — if the holder still exists, if the holder so authorizes, and if the professional is present when disclosure of the confidential communications is sought. If the holder of the privilege no longer exists, the privilege is terminated.

Note: An attorney might violate her statutory obligation to claim the privilege as described above. However, beyond a failure to claim the privilege, an attorney might affirmatively violate the privilege by choosing to disclose information. For instance, an attorney might disclose confidential information to the police that forms the basis of an arrest warrant for the attorney's client. The client may raise a federal due process violation claim arising out of the issuance of a warrant based on information gained by the government through the violation of the attorney-client privilege. In evaluating the due process claim, California courts apply the following analysis:

1. Did the government authority know about the attorney-client relationship between the attorney informant and the client/defendant?
2. Did the government deliberately intrude on that relationship?
3. Was the defendant prejudiced as a result of the government intrusion?

Waiver and Disclosures

The privilege can be waived when information is disclosed to people who are not reasonably necessary to transmit the communication or further the goals of the legal representation. A voluntary disclosure of privileged information to non-necessary third parties will waive the privilege, and the court can compel disclosure. People who are reasonably necessary may include expert witnesses, advisers, doctors, and family members.

Some disclosures to expert witnesses will still amount to a waiver, however. For instance, in a civil case, a party waives the privilege when he calls an expert witness to testify about matters the expert learned in the course of the attorney-client relationship. By calling the witness to the stand himself, the party forfeits the ability to object that the testimony reveals privileged information. In criminal cases, the defense must identify the expert witnesses that it plans to call to testify and produce expert reports. However, disclosure of reports is limited to information that is not protected by the attorney-client or attorney work product privileges. Other communications are protected by the privilege.

If disclosure of privileged information is coerced, perhaps by subpoena or a government agency request, there is no waiver, even if the information is actually disclosed, as long as the holder took reasonable steps under the circumstances to prevent disclosure. Those reasonable steps may include seeking a court order to prevent disclosure. What is reasonable will vary from case to case, depending on the specific facts and circumstances. However, the holder of the privilege does not have to go so far as refusing to comply with a court order to avoid a waiver of the privilege. Also, inadvertent production of privileged documents in response to a discovery request is not a waiver as long as the attorney identifies the error promptly, informs opposing counsel of the inadvertent disclosure, and requests that the documents be returned or destroyed.

Exceptions to the Attorney-Client Privilege: CEC 956–962

The CEC provides eight exceptions to the attorney-client privilege. The party asserting that an exception applies has the burden to produce enough evidence to prove by a preponderance of the evidence that the circumstances for the exception are met.

Future Crime or Fraud (CEC 956) If the client sought or obtained the attorney's services for help in committing what the client knew or reasonably should have known to be a future crime or fraud, then the privilege does not apply. The same is true if the attorney suggests a future crime or fraud to the client. However, the exception does not apply when a client consults an attorney about past crimes or frauds. Neither does the exception apply when the course of action is a tort, not a crime.

To establish that the future crime or fraud exception applies and that privileged communications should be disclosed, the party opposing the privilege must show (1) a prima facie case of the crime and/or fraud that the attorney's services were to assist with, and (2) a reasonable relationship between the crime or fraud and the attorney-client communication.

Reasonable Belief to Prevent Bodily Injury (CEC 956.6)   This exception applies when the lawyer reasonably believes that disclosure is necessary to prevent the client from committing a criminal act that the lawyer believes is likely to result in death or substantial bodily harm.

Same Deceased Client (CEC 957)   When two or more people are claiming money or property through the same deceased client and the issue involves a communication with that client who is now deceased, the privilege does not apply. The rationale for this exception is that the client would want to authorize the lawyer to disclose the information so the estate can be distributed properly. The court needs the client's thoughts as expressed to the lawyer to make an informed decision.

Attorney-Client Breach (CEC 958)   When the communication relates to breach of a duty of lawyer to client or client to lawyer and is relevant to the claims and defenses in that litigation, then the privilege will not apply. The kinds of duties that are usually implicated are the duty of the attorney to exercise reasonable diligence, the duty of the lawyer to faithfully account for the client's fees and property, and the client's duty to pay legal fees and costs. This exception applies in malpractice actions and claims of ineffective assistance of counsel.

Attorney as Attesting Witness (CEC 959)   An *attesting witness* is someone who watches another person sign a document. With many important documents, such as wills and powers of attorney, there is a place for the witness to sign the document also. When the attorney is also the attesting witness, this exception destroys the privilege as to certain information that the attorney may have learned when acting as the attesting witness for the execution of a document such as a will. There will be no privilege covering the intention or competence of a client who executed the document for which the attorney acted as an attesting witness. There is also no attorney-client privilege for communications about the execution or attestation of that document.

For instance, while signing his revised will in the presence of an attorney, a person says "I know you don't have a medical degree, but I want you to sign right here so you can say that I was of sound mind when I decided to I leave everything to the dog rescue organizations. After all, I am the Pope." The client is communicating with his attorney, but the communication is about the witnessing of the will and the competence of the client who executed the will. His statement that he is the Pope suggests that he may not be competent, and that information can be disclosed under this exception.

Similarly, there is no exception for communications relevant to issues involving the intention of a deceased client regarding a writing affecting an interest in property (CEC 960) or the validity of a deed, will, or other writing affecting an interest in property (CEC 961). These exceptions apply even if the attorney was not an attesting witness to the writings in question. However, the exception does not extend to other documents that are financial in nature, like tax returns, even if they are connected to interests in property or trusts.

Joint Clients (CEC 962)   When two or more clients have consulted the lawyer on a matter of common interest, there is no privilege in any civil litigation between or among those clients or their successors in interest.

Figure 12.2 summarizes the elements of the attorney-client privilege.

12.2   Attorney-Client Privilege

	Attorney-Client Privilege
Nature of Privilege	Dual. The holder can • refuse to disclose, and • prevent others from disclosing.
Parties to the Privilege	Lawyer: • Person authorized to practice law in any state or nation • Or someone whom the client reasonably believes is so authorized Client: • Person who consults lawyer to retain or to get legal service or advice • Can consult indirectly through a representative • Can include incompetents
Protected Communication	• Information transmitted in confidence between lawyer and client in course of that relationship, • Including the legal opinion formed and advice given, • As long as not disclosed (as far as client knows) to others to whom disclosure is not reasonably necessary for transmission or accomplishment of the purpose of consultation.
Who Can Claim?	• The holder, or • Person authorized by the holder, or • The lawyer, if authorized and the holder still exists • Whether or not the client is a party to the proceeding seeking disclosure.
The Holder	• The client, or • The client's guardian or conservator if he has one, or • For dead clients, the personal representative, or • Successor, assign, or similar representative of corporations and other entities that no longer exist.

	Attorney-Client Privilege
Exceptions	• Future crime or fraud • Prevent criminal act likely to result in death or substantial bodily harm • Parties claiming through deceased client • Breach of duty arising out of the relationship • Intention of deceased client concerning or the validity of a writing affecting property interest • Lawyer as attesting witness • Joint clients
CEC sections	950-962

Federal Rules of Evidence Compared: Notable Differences

As explained earlier, the FRE does not codify federal rules on privileges. FRE 501 instructs the federal courts to apply state privilege law for any state law claims in federal civil cases and the federal common law for federal claims and in criminal cases. FRE 502, enacted in 2008, limits actions that constitute waivers of attorney-client privilege in federal and state cases and proceedings (discussed in more detail below). However, there are proposed federal rules on privileges that, despite not being enacted law, are useful as a guide for the majority federal common law position in the various privileges.

Proposed FRE 503 describes the attorney-client privilege and provides the same basic protections to confidential communications between an attorney and a client. The U.S. Supreme Court has determined that under federal law the privilege does not die with the client as long as it is claimed by an executor or a representative. The proposed FRE 503(d) lists five of the same exceptions granted in the CEC:

1. Furtherance of a crime or fraud
2. Claimants through the same deceased client
3. Breach of duty by lawyer or client
4. Document attested by lawyer
5. Joint clients

The FRE section on lawyers as attesting witnesses exempts any communication about a document attested to by an attorney, whereas the CEC section limits this exception to communications relevant to the intention or competence of the client or the execution or attestation of the document itself.

In the Corporate Context

As for the attorney-client privilege in the corporate context, the majority of the federal courts apply the approach of the U.S. Supreme Court decision in Upjohn.[2] In Upjohn, the Court examined four factors to determine which communications among people in the corporation and the attorneys are privileged. Those four factors are whether the communication was

1. made for the purpose of obtaining legal advice;
2. made at the request of superiors;
3. related to a matter within the scope of the employee's duties; and
4. treated as confidential.

The FRE on Waiving the Attorney-Client Privilege

The newly enacted (not merely proposed) FRE 502 *applies to waivers in state and federal proceedings*, even when state law provides the rule of decision. If the disclosure is made in a federal proceeding or to a federal office or agency, FRE 502(a) limits the waiver to the communication or information actually disclosed. The waiver does not extend to any undisclosed information unless the waiver was intentional and the undisclosed information is on the same subject matter, such that the information, in fairness, should be considered together.

FRE 502(b) provides that an *inadvertent disclosure* does not operate as a waiver in a federal or state proceeding, if the holder took *reasonable steps to prevent disclosure* and *promptly took reasonable steps to rectify the error*. If the disclosure is made in a state proceeding, it is not a waiver in a federal proceeding as long as the disclosure either would not be considered a waiver in federal court or was not a waiver under the state law (FRE 502(c)).

When a court order requires disclosure that is not a waiver, it will not be a waiver in another state or federal proceeding under FRE 502(d). Agreements between the parties about disclosure are binding only on the parties to that agreement, unless incorporated into a court order under FRE 502(e).

Examples

1. Bert sued Al for breach of contract. Mumford was Al's attorney in that lawsuit. Al lost the lawsuit and appealed. Al lost the appeal and sued Mumford for malpractice. At the malpractice trial, Mumford sought to testify that Al had a losing case because Al had admitted to Mumford that he had planned all along to breach the contract with Bert. Al objected that the attorney-client privilege prevented Mumford from testifying

---

2. Upjohn Co. v. United States, 449 U.S. 383 (1981).

about Al's admission in that confidential communication. How should the court rule?

2. Employees of Tent Healthcare Corporation filed a class action lawsuit alleging violations of employee benefit laws. A questionnaire was sent out to all members of the class, and many of them contacted the class action lawyer to discuss how to respond to the questionnaire. During discovery, Tent's counsel requested the names, addresses, and phone numbers of the class members who had contacted the lawyer in response to the questionnaire. The attorney representing the class objected, stating that many of the class members had requested anonymity because they still worked for the corporation. Revealing their names would violate a client confidence that is protected by the attorney-client privilege. How should the court rule, and why?

3. Vela was convicted of murder and sentenced to life imprisonment. While in prison, Vela spoke with fellow inmate Squeeze, who called himself a "jailhouse attorney" and gave legal advice to numerous inmates. Squeeze advised Vela to fire his public defender and promised to help Vela prepare a petition for a retrial. While they were working on the petition, Vela told Squeeze that he had lied to the police when he told them that he was on heroin and did not remember killing the 80-year-old victim. When Squeeze heard the age of the victim, he told the guards that he would testify at Vela's retrial. Vela objected, claiming that the attorney-client privilege protected any disclosures Vela had made to Squeeze. How should the court rule, and why?

4. Guiermo was arrested for fraud when the "hedge fund" he was selling to clients turned out to be a Ponzi scheme. While out on bail awaiting trial, Guiermo drove while drunk to meet his attorney. A police officer pulled him over and asked him to step out of his car. Guiermo grabbed some papers off of the passenger seat and shoved them into his mouth. The officer, thinking Guiermo was trying to cheat a breathalyzer test, pulled the papers from Guiermo's mouth. Because drinking was a violation of Guiermo's bail, the officer gave the papers to the district attorney prosecuting Guiermo's fraud case. The papers had a list of names, addresses, and schedules of witnesses who were going to testify against Guiermo, along with a note reading "these are the ones to take care of before trial." At trial, the district attorney sought to admit the papers into evidence. Guiermo objected that they were protected by the attorney-client privilege because he prepared them for his attorney and was on his way to deliver them. How should the court rule, and why?

5. During Pierre's trial for robbery, his wife got into a fight with another witness in the courtroom. The court ordered Pierre's wife to leave, and Pierre's attorney said, "If you exclude his wife, he will be

unmanageable and will hurt someone in this courtroom." Pierre was convicted and argued on appeal that his attorney's statement was an improper disclosure of confidential attorney-client privileged information. How should the court rule on the privilege claim, and why? Would the ruling be different if the lawyer had prefaced his statement by saying, "Pierre told me that . . ."?

6. Chin was arrested on a date rape charge but claimed the intercourse had been consensual. Chin's attorney asked him to prepare a list of the dates and times that he had interacted with the alleged victim, and names of witnesses who had seen them together before the alleged rape. Chin prepared these documents on his computer at work and attached the files to an email he sent to his attorney. Chin's employer routinely reads employee emails to see whether they are work-related. On reading Chin's email and the attachment, the employer fired Chin and turned over the list to the district attorney's office. Chin objected that the list was protected by the attorney-client privilege. The prosecution responded that Chin waived the privilege by knowingly transmitting the files from work in a way that third parties could access. Furthermore, he knew his employer had a practice of reading some employee emails. How should the court rule, and why?

7. When Bing died, his executor formed a company to hold ownership of Bing's real property assets while they were being distributed to his heirs. Once the distribution of the estate was complete, the executor was discharged. A few years later, a recording company claimed that Bing had been overpaid and sued Bing's heirs to recover the alleged overpayments. In that lawsuit, the recording company sought to obtain copies of documents written by Bing's attorneys to Bing. Bing's heirs objected that the documents were protected by the attorney-client privilege. How should the court rule, and why? Would the outcome be different in federal court?

8. Rasha filed a discrimination claim against her employer Seag Corporation, alleging that she was demoted because her supervisor found out that she had married a woman. Rasha hired Kilroy, a lawyer who was already representing Techie, another Seag employee who claimed that Seag had discriminated against him when he married a man. Rasha, Kilroy, and Techie met for lunch one day and discussed both of their cases against Seag. Techie decided to settle his case, and as part of the settlement agreement, Techie told the Seag lawyer everything he had heard about Rasha's case during that lunch meeting. When Rasha's case went to trial, Seag tried to admit the evidence Techie had shared about Rasha's case. Rasha objected that the information was protected by the attorney-client privilege because she and Techie were joint clients of

Kilroy discussing matters of mutual interest with the lawyer. Seag claims that Rasha waived the privilege. How should the court rule?

9. Shareholders of Kess Company sued the company after it publicly disclosed that its auditors found improperly recorded revenues at one of its subsidiaries. Kess hired a law firm to investigate and represent the company in the shareholder lawsuit. Meanwhile, the Securities and Exchange Commission (SEC) began a formal investigation of the subsidiary for possible securities fraud. The law firm volunteered to share its final report and interview transcripts with the SEC subject to a confidentiality agreement. The shareholders moved to compel production of the report and interviews. Kess argued that the documents were protected by the attorney-client privilege. The plaintiff shareholders responded that Kess waived the privilege by sharing the documents with the SEC. How should the court rule?

10. Chandra sued the Bourne Corporation for the injuries she suffered when she fell on a sidewalk, alleging corporate negligence. Bourne called its attorneys and its insurer when Chandra fell. At the request of the corporate attorneys and the insurance company, an insurance agent interviewed company employees who were responsible for maintaining the sidewalk and surrounding grounds and made a report about his findings. As she prepared for trial, Chandra sought disclosure of that report. Bourne declined to disclose the report, claiming that it was protected by the attorney-client privilege. How should the court rule?

Explanations

1. The court should overrule the objection because there is an exception to the attorney-client privilege when the client and the attorney are in litigation against one another over matters that arose during the attorney-client relationship. Al has sued Mumford for malpractice, which triggers the exception; the privilege does not apply.

2. The court should overrule the objection and allow disclosure of the names because the identities of the clients generally are not confidential communications and thus are not subject to the privilege. The two exceptions to the general rule about disclosing clients' identities — when revealing the names subjects the clients to civil or criminal liability or reveals private information — do not apply here. The clients are not subject to any liability for this revelation unless there is a countersuit involved. In addition, revealing the clients' names would not reveal anything more than the clients' names and addresses. Because all of the clients are Tent employees, the company already has that information, and disclosure would not reveal private information. The privilege

will protect the substance of what they discussed in that conversation as long as it was for the purpose of seeking legal advice or representation.

3. The court should overrule the attorney-client privilege objection because Vela has not met his burden to establish a reasonable belief that Squeeze was licensed to practice law. A "jailhouse lawyer" does not meet the statutory definition of *lawyer*. The fact that Squeeze was in prison suggests that even if he once had a law license, that license likely would be suspended or revoked while he was in jail.

4. The court should overrule the objection for two reasons. First, the papers are not confidential communications between an attorney and a client because the attorney never received the notes. Second, even if the papers were confidential communications to the attorney, the list could be a communication seeking the lawyer's help to perpetrate a crime. The papers seem to be a hit list or a list for bribes or threats, and the statement about "witnesses to take care of" likely will be adequate to meet the preponderance test for the future crime or fraud exception to destroy the privilege.

5. The court should overrule the privilege objection because the attorney's statement that Pierre would be unmanageable is based on his impressions about his client's mental state. An attorney's impression is not a confidential communication and therefore is not protected by the attorney-client privilege. If the attorney had instead stated what Pierre had said ("Pierre told me that . . ."), then he would be repeating a confidential communication and might meet the necessary elements of the privilege. However, the exception allowing disclosure to prevent bodily injury could apply if the lawyer reasonably believed that Pierre would inflict a severe injury or even death. If that exception applies, then the disclosure would not violate the privilege.

6. The court should sustain the objection. An electronic transmission where others might have access is not enough to destroy the privilege. This is in contrast to a situation where the employee communicated on a crowded company elevator, for instance. In the case of an intercepted email, the employer is more like an eavesdropper, and an eavesdropper will not destroy the privilege. The employer knew that the materials were being transmitted to an attorney and should have declined to intrude on the employee's privacy by reading the privileged material.

7. The court should overrule the objection because the attorney-client privilege ends when the client has died, the final distribution of the estate has taken place, and the personal representative or executor has been discharged. At this point, there is no client in existence, and

therefore there is no attorney-client privilege. The documents should be disclosed to the recording company. In contrast, in federal court, the privilege can continue to exist after the death of the client, and thus the objection would be sustained.

8. The court should overrule the privilege objection because there is no evidence that the two were actually joint clients. If they were joint clients, then the matters they discussed with the attorney would be privileged against third parties. However, simply having the same lawyer and suing the same defendant over similar claims does not make them joint clients. The lawyer was representing them in separate lawsuits, and Rasha and Techie had different interests. Rasha waived the privilege by discussing her case in front of Techie.

9. The court should grant the motion to compel production of the documents and reports because Kess waived the privilege by voluntarily disclosing the documents to the SEC. The SEC was not a reasonably necessary third party to further the goals of the legal representation in the shareholder lawsuit. Although the SEC and Kess superficially appear to share somewhat overlapping interests in ferreting out potential securities fraud by the subsidiary, their interests are not really aligned. They would not be on the same side of any securities fraud litigation arising out of the investigation. If Kess were allowed to share information with the SEC, it would be like a defendant sharing information with one plaintiff but trying to maintain the privilege against other plaintiffs, which is not allowed. If the SEC had issued a subpoena and compelled disclosure, then Kess could argue that the disclosure was under coercion and would not operate as a waiver in a separate proceeding. However, Kess was not coerced into providing the reports to the SEC; Kess did so voluntarily, and therefore the waiver doctrine applies and the documents are no longer protected by the attorney-client privilege.

10. The court should overrule the privilege claim and compel disclosure of the report. Applying the *Chadbourne* principles, the material did not constitute a confidential communication between an attorney and a corporate client. The maintenance employees were not codefendants, and there was no evidence that they were the natural persons to speak for the corporation on this point. The head of the maintenance department, on the other hand, would be the natural person to speak for the corporation on this issue. In addition, there was no evidence that the insurance agent intended that his report be transmitted in confidence to the corporation's lawyers. The fact that the insurance agent may have prepared the report with the expectation that it would be given to the attorneys is not enough to establish the privilege.

THE PHYSICIAN-PATIENT PRIVILEGE: CEC 990–1007

The *physician-patient privilege* provides protection for communications between a doctor and a patient when those communications are made confidentially and for the purposes of medical diagnosis or treatment. Like the attorney-client privilege, there is a rebuttable presumption that a communication between a doctor and a patient is confidential. Also like the attorney-client privilege, the patient has a dual privilege — the right to refuse to disclose and to prevent others from disclosing the confidential communication.

The term *physician* means a person licensed to practice medicine in any state or nation. Even a person who is not a licensed doctor can still be a physician for purposes of the privilege if the patient reasonably believed the person was a licensed doctor (CEC 990). The patient does not have a duty to inquire about whether a physician is licensed in a particular jurisdiction.

A *patient* is defined as a person who consults a physician or submits to an examination for the purpose of medical diagnosis or treatment (CEC 991). The treatment involved may be of the type to prevent, cure, or treat the symptoms of an illness. However, a person merely participating in a research study is not a *patient* unless the primary purpose of the study is to diagnose or treat the participants. Likewise, persons who donate organs are not patients for purposes of this privilege because they consult doctors out of altruistic motives, not to seek diagnosis or treatment. Similarly, people who donate their genetic material in exchange for money are not patients. The privilege does not depend on whether there is a contract with the doctor or whether the patient is paying for the treatment.

The types of communications protected by this privilege include statements made between the physician and patient as well as information obtained by physical or mental examinations. Any diagnosis made or advice given by the physician is also protected. As with the other professional privileges, a rebuttable presumption of confidentiality applies as long as the statement, as far as the patient knows, was made without disclosure to anyone other than people reasonably necessary to accomplish the goals of the consultation.

The privilege, as stated above, is dual. The patient is entitled to refuse to disclose and to prevent another person from disclosing privileged information. The patient, or holder, can claim the privilege whether or not the patient is a party to the proceeding in which disclosure is sought. The holder is entitled to claim the privilege and can authorize others to claim the privilege on his behalf (CEC 994). The physician also may claim the privilege on behalf of the holder, as long as the holder still is in existence. In fact, the physician is required to claim the privilege whenever she is present when someone seeks disclosure of a privileged communication.

The patient is the holder of the privilege (CEC 993). If the patient has a guardian or conservator, that person becomes the holder of the privilege. If a patient dies, the patient's personal representative, such as an executor, becomes the holder. Once the estate is fully distributed and the personal representative is discharged, the holder ceases to exist, as does the privilege.

The physician-patient privilege can be waived in the same ways as privileges generally, usually by disclosing the confidential information to someone other than a person reasonably necessary to further the goals of that professional relationship.

Exceptions to the Physician-Patient Privilege

The CEC provides for 12 exceptions to the physician-patient privilege, including several that are analogous to those of the attorney-client privilege discussed above.

The first is the patient-litigant exception, which destroys the privilege when the patient tenders an issue related to his medical condition. For example, patients bring up such issues when they claim a mental defense. The exception also applies when any party claiming through or as a beneficiary of the patient brings up the medical condition, as often happens in a lawsuit for wrongful death.

The crime or tort exception applies when the physician's services were sought or used to help anyone plan, commit, or escape detection after already committing a crime or tort (CEC 997).

Importantly, the physician-patient privilege does not apply in criminal proceedings (CEC 998). Nor does it apply when damages are sought on account of the patient's conduct and good cause is shown for disclosure of communications about the condition of the patient (CEC 999). For instance, imagine the patient is an employee who drove a truck without his prescription glasses and injured a patron. In a negligence lawsuit in which the patron seeks damages for her injuries, only a showing of good cause will permit disclosure of the patient-employee's medical records about his eyesight.

The privilege does not apply when the issue involves a breach of duty in the physician-patient relationship (CEC 1001). A breach by the patient generally means non-payment for services rendered. Breach of duty by the doctor often involves allegations of malpractice.

The privilege does not apply in commitment or similar confinement proceedings (CEC 1004), for example when an elderly person is being involuntarily committed to a hospital because she can no longer take care of herself. The privilege does not apply in proceedings brought by or on behalf of the patient to establish the patient's competence (CEC 1005), such as when a person is deemed mentally unfit to control her own money. Similarly, where a public entity brings a proceeding to suspend, revoke, limit, condition, or terminate a patient's right, authority, license, or privilege, the privilege does not apply (CEC 1007). When the confidential information is part of a required report to a public employee or is recorded in the public record, then the privilege does not apply (CEC 1006).

When the patient is deceased, there are several additional exceptions to consider. When parties are all claiming through the same deceased patient, such as siblings whose parent has just died, there is no privilege (CEC 1000). Similarly, when the issue is over the intentions of a deceased patient in a deed, will, or other writing that affects a property interest or the validity of any such writing, the privilege does not apply (CEC 1002-1003).

Federal Rules of Evidence Compared: No Corresponding FRE

There is no corresponding FRE and no proposed FRE on this privilege.

Examples

1. John is an Ivy League alumnus who saw an advertisement noting that CryCorp would pay twice the going rate for sperm and egg donations from Ivy League graduates. John filled out a medical questionnaire, submitted to a medical evaluation, and discussed his health history with a CryCorp fertility doctor, who was licensed to practice medicine in the Bahamas. John donated sperm each month for several years under the pseudonym "Donor 76." Cindy selected Donor 76's sperm for her child, and the child was born with a rare and very serious kidney disease. Cindy sued CryCorp for negligence and sought discovery of the medical records of Donor 76. CryCorp objected, arguing that the medical records were protected by the physician-patient privilege. How should the court rule, and why?

2. Cali suffered from a terminal illness and had a lot of trouble with her medical insurance company delaying payment for medical expenses and denying her reimbursement requests for certain prescription drugs. When Cali died, her daughter Nia tried to follow up on her mother's grievances with the insurance company, but was told that only Cali's personal representative could obtain the information because it was protected by the physician-patient privilege. Nia was not the executrix or personal representative, but she claimed that as the next of kin, she was entitled to the information. How should the court rule, and why?

3. Elliot contracted AIDS, and his wife Shelly sued him for intentional and negligent infliction of emotional distress, seeking $2 million in damages when she found out that she was also infected with HIV. Shelly alleged

that Elliot had had unprotected intercourse with multiple men, contracted HIV during their two-year marriage, and then infected her through unprotected intercourse. Shelly sought discovery of all of Elliot's medical records for the previous ten years. Elliot objected that the information was protected by the physician-patient privilege. How should Shelly respond, and how should the court rule on the privilege claim?

4. Helmut Inc. is a medical corporation. Every time a patient threatens to file or actually files a medical malpractice action against a Helmut doctor or the hospital, Helmut sends the patient's entire medical file to its attorneys. Healthwatch, a non-profit consumer health organization, sued Helmut for breaching the physician-patient privilege when it used a blanket policy to disclose all medical information to the attorneys whenever a patient threatened to sue or actually sued. Helmut argued that the disclosures were protected because the breach of duty exception destroys the privilege whenever a patient files a malpractice lawsuit and the threat of such a lawsuit is close enough to fit within that exception. Healthwatch argues that the exception is not that broad and should not apply. How should the court rule, and why?

Explanations

1. The court should overrule the privilege objection and compel production of the medical records. The elements of the privilege have not been established because John was not a patient under CEC 991. He did not consult the CryCorp fertility doctor for the purpose of diagnosis or treatment but rather to determine whether he was fit to donate viable sperm in exchange for money. The fact that the fertility doctor is licensed only in the Bahamas is of no consequence even if John had been a patient because CEC 990 defines physicians as people authorized to practice medicine in "any state or nation."

2. The court should uphold the privilege claim because Nia is not the holder of the privilege or authorized by the holder to claim it. The privilege does not automatically revert to the next of kin when the patient dies. Rather, the personal representative of the patient's estate becomes the holder. Nia was not her deceased mother's personal representative, so she cannot claim the privilege.

3. Shelly should respond that an exception exists when there is good cause for disclosing information relating to the condition of the patient in a proceeding to recover damages for the patient's conduct under CEC 999. Here, Elliot is the patient and Shelly is suing him for damages based on his conduct (exposing her to HIV). Therefore, as long as Shelly can show good cause for the disclosure, the exception applies and the information

will not be protected by the privilege. Good cause would likely be shown by the short duration of the marriage, the fact that they both now have HIV, that his has progressed to AIDS, and that they had unprotected intercourse during their marriage. The court should overrule the privilege objection and order disclosure of the medical information relevant to Shelly's claim.

4. The court should permit disclosure of the files when the patient has filed a malpractice lawsuit or otherwise put the patient's medical condition at issue through the breach of duty and patient-litigant exceptions. However, when a patient merely threatens to sue but has not yet done so, the exception does not apply, and the information should remain privileged.

THE PSYCHOTHERAPIST-PATIENT PRIVILEGE: CEC 1010–1027

The psychotherapist-patient privilege is analogous to the other privileges discussed thus far. The patient has a dual privilege to refuse to disclose and to prevent another from disclosing a confidential communication between herself and her psychotherapist. The privilege contains a broad definition of the term *psychotherapist*.

Parties to the Communication The definition of *psychotherapist* is much more expansive than the definition of *physician*. It describes 13 types of psychotherapists for the purposes of the privilege (CEC 1010). For example, a psychotherapist could be a person who is authorized to practice medicine in any state or nation and devotes, or is reasonably believed to devote, a substantial portion of her time to the practice of psychiatry. The definition also includes licensed psychologists, clinical social workers, marriage and family therapists, associate clinical social workers, school psychologists with the requisite credentials; persons working under the supervision of a licensed psychologist or board certified psychiatrist; certain trainees and interns in the field; a registered nurse with a master's degree in psychiatric mental health nursing; and an advance practice registered nurse in the psychiatric field.

The *patient* for purposes of the psychotherapist-patient privilege is very similar to the patient for the physician-patient privilege. As with the patient in the previous privilege, here the patient must consult or be examined by the psychotherapist for the purpose of diagnosis or treatment. Again, the treatment may be of the type that prevents, cures, or alleviates the symptoms of an illness—but here the condition must be mental or emotional.

Another difference is that the patient for the psychotherapist-patient privilege may include a person who is examined pursuant to research studies on mental or emotional problems.

Those who seek help for some reason other than diagnosis or treatment might not be considered patients. When there are multiple reasons for engaging in psychotherapy, the courts will look at the dominant purpose of the consultation. The general rule is that if the dominant purpose for the communication is not diagnosis or treatment, then the person will not be considered a patient for purposes of the privilege.

However, the California Supreme Court has rejected the dominant purpose test in the context of therapy that is a condition of probation. The overall goal of probation is the reformation and rehabilitation of the probationer, which is a form of treatment. The therapy is a means to that end, and any confidential communications should be privileged. Nevertheless, therapy records generated for the probation-conditioned therapy may be disclosed to the extent necessary to monitor the patient's participation and progress in fulfilling the terms of probation. The rest of the records will remain privileged. Likewise, if the probationer retains an additional therapist for therapy beyond that required as a condition of probation, communications between the additional therapist and the patient are not subject to this probation disclosure requirement.

Confidential Communications Protected communications for the psychotherapist-patient privilege are nearly identical to those in the physician-patient privilege. Information gained from the psychotherapist's examination of the patient is protected, along with any diagnosis or advice given. Additionally the communication must be made in confidence, with no disclosure to any third parties as far as the patient knows, unless the disclosure is necessary for the consultation (CEC 1012). For example, disclosure to intimate family members may not destroy the confidentiality of the communications because communications by and among family members can be an important part of treatment of mental illness. Other reasonably necessary third parties may include translators and group therapy members. As with the other professional privileges, confidentiality is presumed under CEC 917(a), and that presumption is rebuttable.

Claiming the Privilege The operation of the psychotherapist-patient privilege is identical to that of the physician-patient privilege. The psychotherapist-patient privilege has two components. The patient, who is the holder, can refuse to disclose and can prevent others from disclosing protected communications. The holder can claim the privilege whether or not he is a party to the proceeding in which disclosure is sought and can authorize others to claim the privilege on his behalf (CEC 994). The psychotherapist must also claim the privilege on behalf of the holder whenever she is present and someone seeks disclosure of a privileged communication, as long as the holder still is in existence.

The holder of the privilege is determined at the time disclosure of the privileged information is sought. The holder is the patient, unless the patient has a guardian or conservator, in which case the guardian or conservator is the holder of the privilege. If the patient is dead, then the holder is the personal representative of the patient, until the distribution of the estate is final and the personal representative is discharged. Then, there is no holder in existence, and the psychotherapist would no longer be able to claim the privilege when asked to disclose the confidential communication.

In cases involving juveniles, the attorney may also serve as the minor's guardian ad litem. If disclosure of confidential communications with the juvenile's psychotherapist is sought in the attorney's presence while she is also the minor's guardian, the attorney would be the holder of the psychotherapist-patient privilege and must assert the privilege on the minor's behalf. She must also assert the attorney-client privilege if she is present when someone seeks to disclose information protected under that privilege.

Exceptions to the Psychotherapist-Patient Privilege

There are important distinctions between the exceptions for the physician-patient privilege and the psychotherapist-patient privilege. For instance, the psychotherapist-patient privilege can apply in criminal cases, whereas the physician-patient privilege does not.

Similarities to Physician-Patient Privilege

Many of the 12 exceptions to the psychotherapist-patient privilege are familiar from the physician-patient privilege. For instance, there is a crime or tort exception (CEC 1018), claiming through the same deceased client exception (CEC 1019), intention of a deceased patient over writing affecting real property (CEC 1021), the validity of such a writing (CEC 1022), breach of duty (CEC 1020), when the patient puts his mental condition at issue (CEC 1016), when the patient brings a proceeding to determine her competence (CEC 1025), and when a required report is created for disclosure to a public employee or for filing in the public record (CEC 1026). If the defendant initiates a proceeding to determine his sanity, the privilege does not apply (CEC 1023).

Court-Appointed Therapist Exception

When the psychotherapist is court-appointed, another exception applies (CEC 1017), such as when a psychotherapist is appointed to examine a defendant to help the defense attorney determine whether his client should claim insanity as a defense. In that situation, information and communications stemming from the examination are privileged. However, if the defense asserts the insanity defense, the privilege will be waived to use the information to meet the defense's preponderance burden. (See Chapter 9 for a discussion of using expert witnesses at trial.)

The exception does not apply in criminal cases in which the therapist is appointed to help the defense lawyers obtain information necessary to advise the client on whether to enter or withdraw pleas or defenses based on a mental or emotional condition, or when the examination is to determine whether a prisoner is a violent sex offender (CEC 1017). Therapists who are appointed to help a defense lawyer evaluate whether his client should claim insanity as a defense will be considered reasonably necessary third parties, and therefore the privilege will protect those communications. Once the defendant chooses to assert an insanity defense, he will have the burden to prove insanity by a preponderance of the evidence, and will need to waive the privilege as to some therapist or mental health professional to meet that burden.

In the civil context, the Sexually Violent Predators Act permits civil (not criminal) commitment to the state department of mental health, and commitment can be extended until the person is "no longer dangerous." The court must evaluate whether the person is no longer dangerous to decide whether to extend commitment; thus, an exception applies to permit courts to order disclosure of court-appointed psychotherapist reports in these civil commitment proceedings.

Reasonable Belief in Danger and Minor Crime Victim Exceptions

There are two other important exceptions to the psychotherapist-patient privilege. The first is the reasonable belief of danger exception, which applies when the therapist reasonably believes

1. that the patient is in an emotional state that would render him dangerous to himself or others, and
2. disclosure is necessary to prevent the threatened danger (CEC 1024).

If the therapist does make the disclosure, the information is no longer privileged and can be disclosed again in subsequent proceedings even if the danger no longer exists. However, once the threatened harm already has occurred, the interest in preventing harm disappears, and if no disclosure was made in advance to prevent the danger, then that information cannot be disclosed afterward under this exception.

The reasonable belief in danger exception does not require the therapist to make the disclosure. However, if harm or injury actually occurs, the therapist may face civil lawsuits for damages and even wrongful death suits, as one did in the *Tarasoff* case.[3] In that case, a patient revealed to his therapist that he wanted to kill a girl with whom he was obsessed. The therapist reported the patient's threat to campus police, who interviewed but did not detain the patient. The patient then killed the girl. The victim's family sued the therapist, and the California Supreme Court held that when a therapist determines, or should determine based on his profession's standards, that a patient poses a serious danger of violence to another, the therapist has a duty to use reasonable care to protect the intended victim.

Reasonable care may require the therapist to warn the victim or others who will warn the victim, notify police, or take any other steps reasonably necessary under the circumstances. When the therapist knows that the dangerous patient is roaming free, warning the victim may be necessary in addition to informing the police. A therapist who does not take sufficient reasonable care to protect the intended victim may be liable for breach of that duty.

A final exception is for the minor as crime victim, which applies when a therapist has reasonable cause to believe that her patient, if younger than 16, has been a crime victim and disclosure is in the best interest of the child (CEC 1027).

Figure 12.3 compares the physician and psychotherapist privileges.

Federal Rules of Evidence Compared:
No Corresponding FRE

There is no FRE corresponding to the psychotherapist-patient privilege. The definition of *psychotherapist* in the proposed FRE 504 is limited to medical doctors and licensed psychologists engaged in diagnosis or treatment for mental or emotional conditions. There is no "reasonable belief" language and no list of additional types of therapists who can activate the privilege. The exceptions under the proposed FRE are for hospitalization proceedings, examinations by order of a judge, and when the mental or emotional condition is an element of a claim or defense in litigation involving or about the patient.

---

3. Tarasoff v. Regents of the Univ. of Cal., 17 Cal. 3d 425, 551 P.2d 334 (1976).

12.3 Physician-Patient and Psychotherapist-Patient Privileges Compared

	Physician-Patient Privilege	Psychotherapist-Patient Privilege
Nature of Privilege	Dual. The holder can • refuse to disclose, and • prevent others from disclosing.	Dual. The holder can: • refuse to disclose, and • prevent others from disclosing.
Parties to the Privilege	Physician: • Person authorized to practice medicine in any state or nation, or • Someone whom the patient reasonably believes is so authorized. Patient: • Person who consults physician or is examined by one, • For the purpose of getting a diagnosis or treatment (preventative, curative, or palliative) for a physical, mental, or emotional condition.	Psychotherapist: • Person authorized to practice medicine in any state or nation, and • Who devotes substantial time to practice of psychiatry; or • Someone whom the patient reasonably believes devotes substantial time to the practice of psychiatry; • Plus many more categories in CEC 1010. Patient: • Person who consults physician or is examined by one, • For the purpose of getting a diagnosis or treatment (preventative, curative, or palliative) for a mental or emotional condition; or • Person who is examined for a research study on mental or emotional problems.
Protected Communication	• Information obtained by medical exams, • Confidential statements between physician and patient during their relationship, and • Diagnosis and advice from the doctor, • As long as not disclosed (as far as patient knows) to others to whom disclosure is not reasonably necessary for	• Information obtained by exams for mental or emotional problems, • Confidential statements between therapist and patient during their relationship, and • Diagnosis and advice from therapist, • As long as not disclosed (as far as patient knows) to others to whom disclosure

377

	Physician-Patient Privilege	**Psychotherapist-Patient Privilege**
	transmission or accomplishment of the purpose of consultation.	is not reasonably necessary for transmission or accomplishment of the purpose of consultation.
Who Can Claim?	• The holder, or • Person authorized by the holder, or • The physician, if authorized and the holder still exists, • Whether or not the patient is a party to the proceeding seeking disclosure.	• The holder, or • Person authorized by the holder, or • The psychotherapist, if authorized and the holder still exists, • Whether or not the patient is a party to the proceeding seeking disclosure.
The Holder	• The patient, or • The patient's guardian or conservator if he has one, or • For dead patients, the personal representative.	• The patient, or • The patient's guardian or conservator if he has one, or • For dead patients, the personal representative.
Exceptions	• Crime or tort • Parties claiming through deceased patient • Breach of duty arising out of the relationship • Intention of deceased patient concerning or the validity of a writing affecting property interest • Patient-litigant • Proceedings to establish competence • Required report • Criminal proceedings • Proceedings to recover damages, if good cause • Commitment or similar proceedings • Proceeding to terminate right, license, or privilege	• Crime or tort • Parties claiming through deceased patient • Breach of duty arising out of relationship • Intention of deceased patient concerning or the validity of a writing affecting property interest • Patient-litigant • Proceeding to establish competence • Required report • Court-appointed psychotherapist • Proceeding to determine sanity of criminal defendant • Reasonable belief of danger • Child under 16 victim of crime
CEC sections	990-1007	1010-1027

378

Examples

1. Kole was removed from her mother's home after her schoolteachers reported allegations that she was a victim of child abuse. Kole participated in psychotherapy sessions while in foster care. When the dependency court held a hearing to determine whether the mother could regain custody of her child, the mother called Kole's therapist to testify. The attorney appointed as guardian ad litem for Kole objected, stating that the testimony would violate the psychotherapist-patient privilege. Kole's mother responded that the attorney could not claim the privilege as to communications made prior to his appointment as Kole's guardian because he was not the holder of the privilege at the time when Kole met with the therapist. How should the court rule, and why?

2. Cami stole a car and ran over the car's owner as she drove away. Before her death penalty trial, the court appointed Dr. Shrine to assist Cami's counsel in deciding whether Cami should plead not guilty by reason of insanity. Cami and her counsel decided to forgo the insanity defense. When the jury convicted her, Cami hired another expert psychiatrist who testified in the penalty phase that at the time of the killing Cami was schizophrenic and suffering from post-traumatic stress disorder. The psychiatric expert testified that she had relied on the evaluation provided by Dr. Shrine. In rebuttal, the prosecution sought to call Dr. Shrine to testify. Cami objected that her communications with Dr. Shrine were covered by the psychotherapist-patient privilege. The prosecution responded that Cami had waived the privilege by putting her mental state at issue in the penalty phase. How should the court rule?

3. Tory served some jail time after being convicted of a sexual assault. When he was released on probation, one condition was that he attend psychotherapy sessions. When Tory committed another sexual assault, the prosecution sought discovery of his psychotherapy records. Tory objected that the records were protected by the psychotherapist-patient privilege. The prosecution responded that the privilege does not apply because Tory's dominant purpose for seeking treatment was to get probation, not to seek diagnosis or treatment of a mental issue, and therefore he was not a patient as defined in the CEC. How should the court rule, and why?

4. Angelo is a convicted sex offender who was ordered into civil commitment under the Sexually Violent Predators Act. After two years, he sought release, and the court appointed a therapist to evaluate Angelo's mental condition and likelihood of continuing to act as a sexual predator. The court-appointed therapist evaluated Angelo and determined that he was a likely reoffender. The court reviewed the therapist's report and determined that Angelo still was a danger to society and ordered

that he remain committed for another two-year term. Angelo objects that the report was protected by the psychotherapist-patient privilege under CEC 1017 and should not have been considered by the court. How should the court rule?

5. Wingo, a former LAPD officer, was participating in psychotherapy sessions with licensed therapist Stein to deal with his recurring depression after a shoot-out in which two officers were wounded. When the shooter Goldy was acquitted, Wingo's depression worsened considerably. At Stein's suggestion, Wingo checked himself into a psychiatric hospital. Stein visited Wingo in the hospital and met Wingo's father. Wingo's father told Stein that Wingo said he wanted to hurt Goldy and that Wingo still had his service revolver and ammunition at his house. Stein wrestled with the idea of reporting Wingo, but decided that because Wingo was in the hospital, he was not a danger to himself or to Goldy. The next day, Wingo checked himself out of the hospital, went home to get his weapon, killed Goldy, and then killed himself. Wingo's father and Goldy's wife each sued Stein under the *Tarasoff* case for wrongful death. Stein claimed that because the communication was from the father, the exception for reasonable belief of danger did not apply and Stein was prevented from disclosing the information. How should the court rule?

Explanations

1. The court should sustain the privilege objection. The holder of the privilege is determined at the time disclosure is sought, not at the time the communication was actually made between the therapist and patient. The appointed counsel for a juvenile in dependency court is the guardian ad litem and therefore is a proper holder of the psychotherapist-patient privilege. Thus, the privilege claim should be upheld.

2. The court should overrule the privilege objection and permit the rebuttal testimony of Dr. Shrine. Even though court-appointed experts maintain the privilege when appointed to assist the defense in criminal cases, Cami has waived that protection. When Cami called experts to testify that they relied on Dr. Shrine's confidential report, Cami waived the privilege as to the material that the expert relied on. Thus, Dr. Shrine can testify about any matter used by the other expert in reaching her conclusion.

3. The court should sustain the privilege objection and deny the motion to review Tory's psychological records. The fact that Tory was required to participate in therapy as a condition of probation does not mean that he was not trying to obtain a diagnosis or treatment of his condition. The dominant purpose analysis is irrelevant for probation-conditioned

therapy because the therapy assists with the goal of probation, which is the reformation and rehabilitation of the probationer; it thus qualifies as treatment. What matters in this situation is that Tory actually engaged in psychotherapy with a therapist, not his motive for attending the sessions. Tory qualifies as a patient, and the information will be protected by the privilege. Limited disclosure of court-ordered therapy would be permitted to monitor the patient's compliance with the probation condition, however, but not for use as evidence for a separate crime.

4. The court should overrule Angelo's privilege claim. CEC 1017 gives an exception to the privilege when the court appoints a therapist to examine the patient. Angelo is relying on a portion of CEC 1017 that provides an exception to that exception, allowing the privilege to remain intact when the therapist is appointed by the court to help the defendant's attorney present a defense based on a mental or an emotional condition. However, the exception to the exception applies only in criminal proceedings, and the commitment proceeding under the Sexually Violent Predators Act is civil. Thus, the exception to the exception does not apply, and the therapy communications are not privileged. The court properly permitted disclosure of the court-appointed therapist's report.

5. The court should consider the communication between Stein and Wingo's father as a protected communication as long as it was delivered confidentially for the purpose of assisting with Wingo's therapy. Speaking with a patient's close family often is a reasonably necessary part of therapy, and the communications by and among the family members with the therapist also can be covered by the psychotherapist-patient privilege. However, it is unclear whether Wingo was part of this conversation and whether his father's statements were as a necessary third party during a protected communication. If the privilege applies to the statement, then the exception also applies to permit disclosure of the statement if Stein had a reasonable belief that (1) Wingo was dangerous to himself or Goldy, and (2) that disclosure was necessary to prevent harm. Stein thought about it and decided that the hospitalization was sufficient to prevent the threatened harm. The remaining factual question is whether Stein's belief was reasonable under the circumstances. If not, then Stein could be liable under *Tarasoff* for failing to warn Goldy and the authorities about Wingo's threat.

Personal, Relationship, Counseling, and Other Privileges

CHAPTER 13

Evidentiary privileges in the CEC prevent certain information from being admitted as evidence in court. The three basic types of privileges are

1. confidential communications;
2. testimonial; and
3. content.

Confidential communications privileges protect information that is relayed in the course of certain relationships. Chapter 12 addresses 3 of these privileges in the context of professional relationships (attorney-client, physician-patient, and psychotherapist-patient). This chapter discusses 6 other confidential communication privileges in relationships involving spouses, victims and counselors, and clergy members.

The CEC recognizes 9 privileges that fall under the second or third categories above. *Testimonial privileges* permit a person to decline to testify in certain situations, such as when the testimony would incriminate him or when the case involves his spouse. *Content privileges* protect certain information from disclosure. These privileges exist to protect certain rights, most especially the right to privacy. Some of these privileges protect other rights, such as the right of freedom of the press and the right not to incriminate oneself.

Of the 15 privileges addressed in this chapter, 2 apply only to criminal defendants, 3 apply specifically to married people, 3 apply to various counseling relationships, and 2 apply to clergy. The remaining privileges protect the identity of informers, official information, the secrecy of one's vote, trade secrets, and newspaper sources. This chapter describes each of these additional privileges. Recall from Chapter 12 that privileges apply only in proceedings in which testimony can be compelled, such as hearings, depositions, and trials. Testimony cannot be compelled in mediations or administrative hearings unless the agency has subpoena power. The only privileges that California state courts recognize are those in the CEC or other statutes, and judges cannot create new privileges.

PRIVILEGE AGAINST SELF-INCRIMINATION

The federal and California constitutions grant several rights to criminal defendants, and the CEC has codified these rights into two evidentiary privileges:

1. Not to be called as witnesses in their own criminal cases
2. Not to testify in their own criminal cases

In addition, each person who is called as witness, whether the case is criminal or civil, has both a constitutional right and an evidentiary privilege to refuse to disclose any information that may incriminate her. The CEC recognizes these privileges to the same extent as the California and federal constitutional rights. Figure 13.1 illustrates the privileges against self-incrimination.

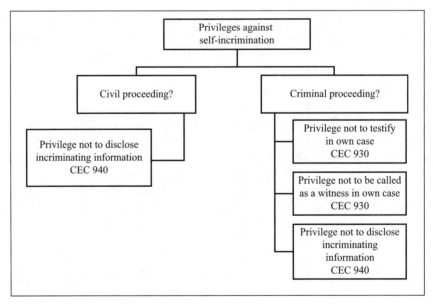

Figure 13.1. Privileges Against Self-Incrimination

CEC §930 Privilege not to be called as a witness and not to testify

To the extent that such a privilege exists under the Constitution of the United States or the State of California, a defendant in a criminal case has a privilege not to be called as a witness and not to testify.

CEC §940: Privilege against self-incrimination

To the extent that such a privilege exists under the Constitution of the United States or the State of California, a person has a privilege to refuse to disclose any matter that may tend to incriminate him.

The privilege not to be called as a witness provides substantial protection to a criminal defendant. It prevents the prosecution from listing the criminal defendant as one of its witnesses and calling him to the witness stand during trial. If the prosecution were to call the defendant to the stand, then the defendant would have to object on the grounds of privilege, asserting either his privilege not to testify or his privilege not to disclose incriminating information. If the jurors hear either of these defense objections, they may infer that the defendant is trying to hide something by refusing to testify about a particular topic. If the jurors make that inference, they may be more likely to decide the case based on this inference rather than on the evidence presented at trial. To avoid the potential prejudice that might result from requiring the defendant to claim those privileges in front of the jury, a privilege prevents the prosecution from even calling the defendant as a witness.

Scope The scope of these privileges is a matter of constitutional law and not evidence law and is covered in criminal procedure courses. Sometimes the scope of the privilege is subject to other considerations. For example, when a person is given immunity (which means that the prosecutor promises not to prosecute the person for any crimes he would reveal in his testimony), then that information is no longer incriminating and that person may be compelled to testify.

In other cases, the defendant's due process rights may require a witness to testify in a self-incriminating way. When the accused wants to impeach a prosecution witness, the courts balance the constitutional rights of the accused to confront the witness against him (under the Confrontation Clause discussed in Chapter 5) against the witness's privilege not to disclose incriminating information.

These privileges do not confer a right to withhold information about one's physical or mental characteristics when they are relevant to the issues in the case, as long as no questions seek incriminating information. For instance, in a mental competency hearing, a witness may be questioned about his mental condition for purposes of determining whether commitment is appropriate. The reasoning behind this specific exception is that self-incrimination refers to potential criminal liability. Civil commitment, while restraining a person's freedom, is not incarceration, and it is done for the purpose of treating rather than punishing the mentally ill.

Why Are There Three Privileges All Covering Similar Situations in Criminal Cases?
The main reasons are errors, oversights, and waiver of the privileges. For instance, if the prosecution errs and calls the criminal defendant to the witness stand, defense counsel still can object based on the privilege not to testify so that the defendant will not have to answer any questions and can leave the witness stand. If the defense counsel forgets to object when the witness list shows the criminal defendant, then the prosecution may think that the defense acquiesced in its request to have him testify, and therefore waived the privilege. Moreover, if the defendant chooses to testify voluntarily in his defense case (or *case in chief*, as discussed in Chapter 8), he can still assert the privilege against self-incrimination to prevent disclosure of other incriminating information. The jury may be instructed to draw no inference from the assertion of the privilege under CEC 913 (as discussed in Chapter 12).

Waiver The general waiver rules such as those discussed in Chapter 12 do not apply here because this is a testimonial rather than a protected communication privilege. The waiver of one of these privileges does not waive the others. For instance, when a defendant waives his privilege not to testify because he wishes to testify on his own behalf, he retains the privilege against self-incrimination. He can testify in response to his attorney's questions on direct examination, but still decline to answer certain prosecution questions on cross-examination if he successfully asserts the self-incrimination privilege.

However, when a defendant represents himself and either does not know about or chooses not to exercise his privilege against self-incrimination, the failure to exercise the privilege during cross-examination will act to waive the privilege. The court is not required to instruct the defendant about his privilege, but it is not prevented from giving such an instruction. Thus, where a pro se defendant fails to exercise this privilege on cross-examination, he forfeits his right against self-incrimination and cannot later appeal on the subject.

In addition, when a witness who is not the criminal defendant in the case waives the privilege against self-incrimination by testifying at a preliminary hearing, that waiver does not necessarily carry over to the trial in that matter. Thus the witness can assert the privilege at trial.

Federal Rules of Evidence Compared: No Difference

Recall from Chapter 12 that the FRE did not adopt rules for privileges. There is no proposed FRE in this category, but the practical effect is the same because the privileges are available under federal constitutional law.

Examples

1. Bobby is charged with two counts of capital murder. At trial, Bobby's brother, Jesse, testified for the prosecution. When the prosecutor asked, "What led you to the building where the murders were committed?" Jesse claimed the privilege against self-incrimination in open court. Bobby objected that this claim of privilege in open court violated the rule against commenting on claims of privilege under CEC 913. Bobby also moves to strike Jesse's entire testimony. The prosecution responded that a limiting instruction would be sufficient to address any potential prejudice. How should the court rule?

2. Marky was on trial for battery and fired his attorney after the opening statements. Marky obtained court permission to represent himself and put himself on the witness stand to give his direct testimony. The prosecution then called Marky as a witness in its rebuttal case, and Marky did not object. Marky testified that he did "throw a punch once or twice." The jury returned a verdict of guilty. Marky appealed, stating that he was not advised about his privilege against self-incrimination. The prosecution responded that Marky had waived the privilege by calling himself to the witness stand and by answering questions on cross-examination that incriminated him. How should the court rule, and why?

3. Dexter is charged with murder. During the preliminary hearing, the prosecution called Kenny as a witness, without offering Kenny any immunity from prosecution. Kenny testified that he helped Dexter to kidnap the victim and then held the victim down while Dexter killed him. After Dexter's preliminary hearing, Kenny entered into a plea deal with the prosecution and was never put on trial. At Dexter's trial, Dexter called Kenny to the witness stand, but Kenny declined to testify on the grounds of the privilege against self-incrimination. Dexter argued that Kenny had already waived that privilege by testifying in a self-incriminating way at the preliminary hearing. How should the court rule?

4. Willy is on trial for kidnapping. Dusty also was charged with the crime, but he entered into a plea agreement with the prosecutors and is not on trial. The prosecution called Dusty to testify at Willy's trial. Dusty objected. At side-bar, Dusty claimed his privilege against self-incrimination.

Willy's defense lawyer argued that Dusty should be compelled to assert the privilege objection in front of the jury so the jury will understand that Dusty made a deal with the prosecution and that is why he is not on trial as a codefendant. The prosecution argued that compelling him to assert the privilege in the presence of the jury would be improper. How should the court rule, and why?

5. Sharon sued Jill, her contractor, for breach of the contract to remodel Sharon's home. Sharon testified that Jill did only a small percent of the agreed-on work, but charged Sharon the full contract price. Jill testified in her defense case in chief that she properly performed all of her duties under the contract. On cross-examination, Sharon's counsel asked Jill, "Isn't it true that you spent most of the money on illegal drugs, rather than on building supplies?" Jill's attorney objected, claiming Jill's privilege against self-incrimination. Sharon's attorney responded that Jill had waived that privilege by testifying. How should the court rule, and why?

Explanations

1. The court should overrule the objection and provide a limiting instruction to the jury. CEC 913 prevents comments on the exercise of the privilege, which the prosecution had not yet made, and provides a mechanism for giving a jury instruction when assertions of the privileges are made in open court. There is no reason to strike all of Jesse's testimony simply because he asserted the privilege as to one question about events leading up to the killing.

2. The court should decline to overturn the verdict against Marky because he forfeited his privileges against self-incrimination and against testifying in his own case by failing to assert the privileges at the proper time. When Marky testified on his own behalf, that testimony did not amount to a waiver of his privilege against self-incrimination or his privilege not to be called by the prosecution. However, because Marky was representing himself, his failure to object when the prosecution called him as a rebuttal witness forfeited that privilege. In addition, when Marky testified in an incriminating way in response to the prosecution's questions about throwing a punch, he waived the privilege against self-incrimination as well. While Marky might have been able to make an argument for ineffective assistance of counsel if a defense attorney had failed to exercise his privilege, because he represented himself, Marky put himself at risk.

3. The court should sustain Kenny's objection. The fact that Kenny waived the privilege in the preliminary hearing does not operate as a continuing

waiver at trial. Kenny is entitled to assert the privilege against self-incrimination at trial and has properly done so. Because the prosecution did not offer him immunity, Kenny's testimony may subject him to criminal liability, and therefore the privilege applies.

4. The trial court should deny the request that Dusty claim the privilege against self-incrimination (CEC 940) while the jury is present because CEC 913 prevents the lawyers from making any comments on the exercise of a privilege in front of the jury. CEC 913 also permits the judge to instruct the jury that it shall not draw any inference about the exercise of a privilege as to *any* matter at issue in the proceeding. Thus, the defense would be prohibited from referring to Dusty's invocation of the privilege to support its argument that Dusty made a deal with the prosecution.

5. The court should sustain the privilege objection. The privilege against self-incrimination applies in both civil and criminal cases whenever the question seeks information that could subject the witness to criminal charges or penalties. Here, the question asked Jill about illegal drug purchasing, which could subject her to criminal charges. Thus, Jill has the privilege to refuse to answer that question. Jill did not waive the privilege unless her direct examination testimony incriminated her in some way. Her testimony that she properly performed her duties under the contract is not incriminating, and therefore she did not waive the privilege.

SPOUSAL TESTIMONIAL PRIVILEGES

There are two spousal testimonial privileges and one confidential communications privilege. The first is the privilege to decline to testify against one's own spouse. The second related privilege applies only when one spouse is a party to the case; it prevents the other spouse from being called as a witness by an adverse party. The third privilege protects marriage partners from disclosing confidential marital communications. The policy behind all of these spousal privileges is to protect marital harmony. However, the courts have determined that the privileges apply even when the marriage is no longer "viable" or has become "moribund." As long as the parties have not divorced and neither is deceased, the privilege may apply.

Privilege to Decline to Testify Against Your Spouse

While the first testimonial privilege gives one spouse (the *testifying spouse*) the privilege *to decline* to testify against her spouse in a legal proceeding, it does not *prevent* that spouse from testifying. The testifying spouse may testify in support of her spouse if she chooses. If she does not want to testify in favor of her spouse, she nevertheless may be called to do so. The CEC 970 privilege is not available where the testifying spouse is called to testify for, or in favor of, her spouse.

CEC §970: Privilege not to testify against spouse
Except as otherwise provided by statute, a married person has a privilege not to testify against his spouse in any proceeding.

In examining whether the first privilege applies, the first question to ask is whether the witness is currently married. The marriage must be valid and still in effect at the time that the testimony is sought. Although California does not recognize common law marriage, it does respect the validity of a marriage in another state that is valid by that state's laws.

If a valid current marriage is established, the second question is whether she is being asked to testify *against* her spouse. In answering this question, consider the subject matter of the expected testimony. Does the testimony address the words or deeds of the non-testifying spouse? If so, does it reflect well or poorly on the non-testifying spouse? These questions will help you to determine whether the testimony is against the spouse.

The testifying spouse is the holder of the privilege and thus makes her own decision about whether to testify or to claim the privilege and decline to testify. The non-testifying spouse has no control over whether the testifying spouse claims this privilege or waives the privilege. The testifying spouse may choose not to exercise the privilege and voluntarily testify against her spouse. If she does testify against her spouse, that testimony will constitute a waiver of this privilege in that litigation. If she testifies against him about financial matters, for instance, and then is asked about his criminal background she no longer will be able to claim this privilege not to testify against her spouse on those other matters and will have to answer the questions. This privilege applies in both civil and criminal proceedings.

Privilege When Your Spouse Is a Party

The second testimonial privilege applies in any case in which a married person is a party to the case. A party to the case will have his or her name in the title of the action. When one spouse is a party to the litigation (the *party spouse*), the other spouse (the *non-party spouse*) has a privilege that prevents the opposing party in a civil case, or the prosecution in a criminal case, from calling that non-party spouse as a witness without prior express consent. The only exception to the prior express consent requirement is when the opposing party in good faith did not know of the marriage when calling the non-party spouse to testify. When the spouses have the same last name and address, however, the opposing party will have notice of a likely relationship and should inquire before calling the witness to testify.

CEC §971: Privilege not to be called as a witness against spouse

Except as otherwise provided by statute, a married person whose spouse is a party to a proceeding has a privilege not to be called as a witness by an adverse party to that proceeding without the prior express consent of the spouse having the privilege under this section unless the party calling the spouse does so in good faith without knowledge of the marital relationship.

The CEC 971 privilege applies in any litigation involving a spouse as a party to the litigation, and it allows the non-party spouse to claim the privilege regardless of whether her testimony would be helpful or hurtful to the party spouse. It simply prevents an adverse party from calling the non-party spouse as a witness. This privilege is not implicated when the party spouse calls the non-party spouse to testify. The non-party spouse is the holder of the privilege.

This party spouse privilege is important because it prevents the testifying spouse from having to take the witness stand and then claim the privilege and refuse to answer any questions. If the testifying spouse were to take the stand and then claim the first testimonial privilege to decline to testify against her party spouse, counsel likely would ask the judge to give a limiting instruction to the jury to prevent them from drawing adverse inferences from the exercise of the privilege. Whether the jury would abide by the limiting instruction is debatable, and the party spouse's case may suffer as a result. This party spouse privilege arose to prevent the disturbance to marital harmony that might result.

Waiving the Spousal Testimonial Privileges

CEC 973 governs the waiver of the spousal testimonial privileges. When one spouse is a party to the litigation and the non-party spouse decides to testify in that proceeding to which her spouse is a party, then she waives both testimonial privileges. She now can be called as a witness by the adverse side and can be compelled to testify against her spouse in that proceeding.

That proceeding means that if the non-party spouse testifies at the preliminary hearing in a criminal case, her privilege not to be called by an adverse party is waived at the trial in that matter. The privilege is not waived in another, different proceeding like a later civil lawsuit.

CEC §973: Waiver of privilege

(a) Unless erroneously compelled to do so, a married person who testifies in a proceeding to which his spouse is a party, or who testifies against his spouse in any proceeding, does not have a privilege under this article in the proceeding in which such testimony is given.

(b) There is no privilege under this article in a civil proceeding brought or defended by a married person for the immediate benefits of his spouse or of himself and his spouse.

The waiver of both privileges in this case prevents the unfairness that would result if a non-party spouse testified on direct examination in favor of her party spouse and then invoked the privilege to avoid undermining that testimony on cross-examination where she might have to say something adverse to her party spouse.

When neither spouse is a party to the proceeding, then the testifying spouse may testify in favor of her spouse and still claim the privilege to decline to testify against him in that proceeding. If the testifying spouse gives any testimony that is adverse to her spouse, then she will have waived the privilege to decline to testify against her spouse in that proceeding. The waiver applies to all matters, so if she testifies against him on financial matters, she can be compelled to testify against him on criminal matters as well.

The testimony will not operate as a waiver if the testifying spouse testifies only where a judge erroneously compels the testimony or fails to sustain her privilege objection. The CEC 912 general waiver provisions do not apply here because what is protected is the privilege to avoid testifying, not any particular communication. Thus, disclosing to a third party that a spouse confessed to committing a crime would not waive the privilege to avoid testifying against the spouse.

A third opportunity for waiver arises when a married person brings or defends a civil lawsuit for the benefit of the spouse or the marriage. For example, when one spouse is injured in a car accident and sues the other driver, that lawsuit will be for the benefit of the injured spouse and also may benefit the marriage. The filing of the lawsuit then would constitute a waiver of both spousal testimonial privileges. When both spouses are sued for fraud, filing the answer to the complaint constitutes a waiver of both spousal testimonial privileges. The rationale for this form of waiver is that it would be unfair to permit the spouses to bring or defend lawsuits for the benefit of one another and then decline to testify or decline to testify adversely.

Exceptions

CEC 972 contains several types of exceptions to these two testimonial privileges. Because these privileges were codified into statutes, the courts have determined that they have no power to recognize implied exceptions, as they would under the common law. The only available exceptions are those expressly listed in the statute. The first type of exception applies in *certain types of proceedings*, the second applies to *certain types of criminal cases*, and the third type applies to *specific information*. The proceedings in which the privilege is excluded are

- a proceeding brought by or on behalf of one spouse against the other;
- a commitment proceeding based on mental or physical incapacity;
- a competency proceeding brought by or on behalf of that spouse;
- juvenile proceedings involving removing a minor from parents; and
- child, spousal, and family support proceedings.

Neither of the testimonial privileges is available in the following types of criminal cases:

- Where one spouse is charged with a crime against the other spouse, a child, a parent, a relative, or a cohabitant of either, whether committed before or during marriage
- Where one spouse is charged with a person or property crime against a third party, committed *during the course* of committing a crime against the other spouse, whether committed before or during marriage
- Where one spouse is charged with bigamy or neglect of a child or spouse

Courts have determined that the crime against the third party does not need to be related to the crime against the spouse, but need happen only at the same time. The requisite relationship between the two crimes need not be close; they need only have some temporal connection to each other.

The final exception applies to certain information in situations where there are allegations of criminal acts occurring prior to the marriage. If the testifying spouse was aware of the charges or arrest for such crimes before the marriage, then the privilege will not apply to testimony about that crime. The policy behind this exception is to avoid a proposal along the lines of "I'll marry you so you cannot testify against me."

Figure 13.2 summarizes the spousal testimonial privileges.

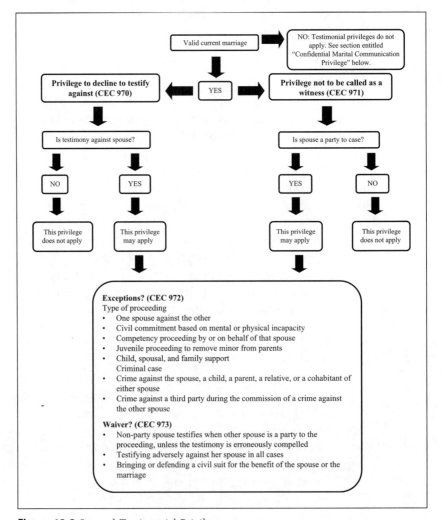

Figure 13.2 Spousal Testimonial Privileges

Federal Rules of Evidence Compared: No Corresponding FRE

Recall from Chapter 12 that the FRE did not adopt any rules on privileges, but rather defers to the common law of the federal jurisdiction. Proposed FRE 505 reflects the majority federal common law position (which is also the majority state law position) that the testimonial privilege applies only in criminal cases. It contains similar exceptions for proceedings in which the spouse is charged with a crime against the other spouse or a third party in the course of committing a crime against the spouse. Another exception exists for crimes occurring prior to the marriage and for illegal importation of aliens for immoral purposes.

The proposed FRE also states that the accused in a criminal case has the privilege to prevent his or her spouse from testifying against him in that criminal case and that the spouse is presumed to have the authority to claim the privilege on behalf of the criminal defendant. Unlike the CEC, under the proposed FRE, the criminal defendant spouse is the holder of the privilege, not the non-party spouse, and he can prevent his non-party spouse from testifying against him in a criminal proceeding. However, the U.S. Supreme Court held to the contrary, finding that the testifying spouse is the holder of the privilege in federal courts.

CONFIDENTIAL MARITAL COMMUNICATIONS PRIVILEGE

The confidential marital communication privilege is similar to the professional relationship privileges that Chapter 12 addresses. Like the professional relationship privileges, the confidential marital communication privilege protects the confidential communication that occurs between people in a protected relationship.

CEC §980 Privilege for confidential marital communications

Subject to 912 [waiver] and except as otherwise provided in this article, a spouse . . . , whether or not a party, has a privilege during the marital relationship and afterwards to refuse to disclose, and to prevent another from disclosing, a communication if he claims the privilege and the communication was made in confidence between him and the other spouse while they were husband and wife.

A Spouse Whether or Not a Party

The two parties to the communication must have been in a valid marriage *at the time of the communication*. California does not recognize common law marriage, and thus the privilege does not apply to communications between people who live together holding themselves out as spouses regardless of how long they have been together. If the parties were validly married under the laws of another state that recognizes common law marriage, then that common law marriage will be considered to be a valid marriage for purposes of asserting the privilege in a California court. The recent approval and subsequent disapproval of same-gender marriages in California has made the privilege available to those same-gender couples who were validly married in the state during the brief period that such marriages were determined to be valid, as well as to those same-gender couples who were validly married in other states during the time that they made their communications.

It does not matter whether the married person is a party to the litigation. As a practical matter, the spouse or her representative needs to be present at trial to make the objection.

Has a Privilege During the Marital Relationship and Afterward

Unlike the spousal testimonial privilege, the spouses need not be married at the time the testifying spouse seeks to assert the privilege. Thus, if the spouses have since divorced or no longer live together, the privilege still attaches to communications that were made *during the time that they were in a valid marriage*. The policy rationale is to encourage open and honest conversations between spouses. Permitting the disclosure of those frank conversations after the termination of the marriage would have a chilling effect on those frank conversations during the marriage.

To Refuse to Disclose and to Prevent Another from Disclosing

Each spouse has the dual privilege to refuse to disclose the information and to prevent another from disclosing the information in litigation.

A Communication Made in Confidence

As with the other privileges, the communication includes writings as well as conversations. Where conduct fits as a communication between spouses, such as nodding or shaking one's head, that conduct can be protected from disclosure as a confidential communication. If the conduct is not communicative, then the privilege does not apply. For instance, retrieving a weapon from the laundry hamper after seeing a spouse put it there is not a confidential marital communication and will not be protected by the privilege.

The spouses must engage in the communication under circumstances of privacy, with no third parties (even children) present. Recall from Chapter 12 that California has a presumption of confidentiality for communications made by parties in certain protected relationships. The marital relationship is included in this presumption. The presumption is rebuttable, and the opposing party can provide contrary information before the court rules on the privilege objection.

Between One Spouse and the Other Spouse While They Were Husband and Wife

The spouses must be communicating with each other. The most common situation arises when spouses are engaged in a private conversation, as long as no other people are part of that conversation. Writing notes to each other will be protected as long as the notes did not go to any third party. However, if one spouse writes a note to the other spouse and the other never receives the note, then the note was not a communication *between* the spouses, and the privilege will not prevent disclosure of the contents of the note. However, if the note was stolen or intercepted on its way to the other spouse, the thief would be considered an eavesdropper. Eavesdroppers do not destroy the privilege.

The timing issue is important because the privilege applies only to the communications made while they were spouses. Although either can assert the privilege if they are no longer married at the time of the litigation, the privilege will not cover any pre- or post-marriage communications.

Holder and Waiver

Each spouse holds the privilege, and they are referred to as *joint holders* of the privilege. Either may claim it, as can the guardian or conservator for either. When a spouse dies, no one can claim the privilege on behalf of that deceased spouse. The surviving spouse still can claim the privilege on his or her own behalf.

The general waiver rules from CEC 912 apply here because this privilege protects communications. The waiver by one spouse will not operate as a waiver of the other spouse's right to claim the privilege. If one spouse waives the privilege by disclosing a substantial portion of the marital communication to some third person, the other spouse still can prevent that third person from disclosing the confidential communication.

Exceptions

There are several exceptions. The first exception applies to communications made in whole or in part to enable or to aid anyone to commit a crime or fraud. The mere fact that the communication reveals a plan to commit a crime or fraud does not trigger the exception. The communication must be in an effort to help commit the crime or fraud.

A second exception is available only to the criminal defendant spouse. When one spouse is a criminal defendant and that criminal defendant spouse wants to introduce confidential marital communications to aid in that criminal defendant spouse's defense, an exception exists to permit him to do so. While the defendant spouse could waive the privilege, he would need the other spouse to waive it as well because the other spouse is a joint holder of the privilege. If the non-defendant spouse could claim the privilege, then she could prevent the defendant spouse from providing all of the necessary information for his defense. The rights of the criminal defendant spouse take precedence, and this exception provides that opportunity.

The final group of exceptions applies in certain types of proceedings: (1) commitment proceedings, (2) proceedings to establish competence, (3) proceedings between spouses, (4) certain criminal proceedings, and (5) juvenile court proceedings.

Figure 13.3 summarizes the material is this section on the confidential marital communication privilege.

Nature of Privilege	Dual. The holder can • refuse to disclose, and • prevent others from disclosing.
Parties to the Privilege	• Both spouses, • In a valid marriage.
Protected Communication	• Confidential statements between the spouses during their marriage, • As long as not disclosed to others.
Who Can Claim?	• The holder, or • Person authorized by the holder, • Whether or not the spouse is a party to the proceeding seeking disclosure, • Whether or not the spouses are still married.
The Holder	• Either spouse, or • A spouse's guardian or conservator if he has one. • No one may claim the privilege for a deceased spouse.

Exceptions	• In an effort to commit crime or fraud • When a criminal defendant wants to introduce confidential marital communications to aid his defense • Commitment or similar proceedings • Proceedings to establish competence • Proceedings between spouses • Certain criminal proceedings • Juvenile court proceedings
CEC Sections	980-987

Figure 13.3. Confidential Marital Communications Privilege

Federal Rules of Evidence Compared: No Corresponding FRE

There is no corresponding FRE for this privilege.

Examples

1. Ziggy was a high-functioning methamphetamine addict. He stole the drug from suspects he arrested in his day job as a police officer. Ziggy's wife Astra also was a police officer, and one day she learned about Ziggy's drug addiction and how he obtained his drugs when they were arguing about his sloppiness around the house. The internal affairs division of the police department began to suspect Ziggy of criminal behavior. During the course of the investigation, they brought Astra in for a formal interview. Astra invoked the marital privilege to avoid giving information against her spouse Ziggy. The hearing officer stated that he did not have subpoena power. Astra filed a writ with the superior court seeking a ruling on whether she can invoke the privilege. How should the court rule?

2. Suzy had been married for 23 years but had not spoken to her husband Kane for the past 17 years, ever since he killed Suzy's former boyfriend and buried his body. Suzy did not report the killing, and no one discovered the body until 15 years later. Kane was arrested and charged with murder. The prosecution called Suzy to the witness stand, and Suzy asserted the privilege not to testify against her spouse. The prosecution argued that the policy behind the privilege was to protect marital harmony, and the fact that Suzy and Kane had not spoken in 17 years meant that their marriage had no harmony left to protect. How should the court rule?

3. Shin went looking for his wife, Pei, after she left him for another man. Shin found Pei at the home of Lui, her new boyfriend. Shin attempted to

kidnap Pei, and as he dragged her away, Lui came to her rescue. Shin shot Lui in the chest, but Pei managed to escape to safety. Shin was charged with the felony murder of Lui. At Shin's criminal trial, the prosecution called Pei to the witness stand to testify about seeing Shin shoot Lui. Pei claimed the privilege not to testify against her spouse because she was afraid that Shin would try to hurt her again. The prosecution responded that the privilege did not apply because there was an exception when one spouse is charged with committing a crime against a third person in the course of committing a crime against the other spouse. How should the court rule, and why?

4. Desi was on trial for robbery, and the prosecution called his wife, Sylvia, to testify at the preliminary hearing in Desi's case. Sylvia was not represented by counsel, and no one told her that she had a privilege not to testify in a case in which her spouse was a party. After Sylvia's testimony, Desi was bound over for trial, and the prosecution called Sylvia to testify at his trial. By the time the trial date had arrived, Sylvia had talked to an attorney who had advised her of her privilege not to be called as a witness in a case in which her spouse is a party. Sylvia asserted the privilege. The prosecution objected that Sylvia had already waived the privilege and therefore the court must compel her testimony at trial. How should the court rule, and why?

5. Gato was on trial for forgery. The prosecution called Darby to the witness stand to identify Gato's handwriting on an allegedly forged document and to explain what he told her about how he would use the document. Darby claimed the privilege not to testify against her spouse, as well as the privilege to avoid disclosure of confidential marital communications. The prosecution, unaware that Darby and Gato considered themselves to be married, asked Darby to state the date of their wedding. Darby explained that they had never really gotten married because she "was not ready for that serious of a commitment," but they had lived together as husband and wife and held themselves out as husband and wife for several years while they were living in Texas. Gato's attorney argued that Texas recognizes common law marriage, and so they were and are validly married and both privileges should apply. How should the court rule, and why?

Explanations

1. The court should deny the writ and overrule Astra's privilege claim. The privileges apply only in proceedings in which testimony can be compelled. Administrative hearings are not proceedings in which testimony can be compelled unless the agency has subpoena power, which is not the case here. Therefore, the privilege is not applicable in this setting.

2. The court should sustain the privilege objection. It does not matter whether the parties have a good marriage, a viable marriage, or even whether they speak to one another or live together. As long as the parties

are legally and validly married at the time that one invokes the privilege, the privilege applies, unless an exception exists. There are no facts to indicate that an exception might apply. If the parties had gotten married after the murder of the ex-boyfriend, then the prosecution might be able to apply the exception for crimes occurring prior to the marriage. The prosecution would have to prove the circumstances for the exception by a preponderance of the evidence. If there is evidence that Kane proposed to Suzy to prevent her from testifying against him for the murder, then the exception destroys the privilege as to that crime.

3. The court should overrule the privilege claim and compel Pei to testify against her spouse. The exception for crimes committed against third parties in the attempt to commit a crime against the other spouse applies even though Shin was not charged with a crime against his spouse. As long as the harm happened in the course of committing a crime against his spouse (attempted kidnapping), the exception will apply. Courts have interpreted the phrase in *the course of* to mean simply around the same time, and therefore the exception applies to destroy the privilege.

4. The court should overrule the privilege claim and compel Sylvia to testify. Sylvia already has testified in a proceeding in which her husband is a party as a criminal defendant, and therefore she has waived the privilege. The fact that she was unaware of the existence of the privilege does not excuse her failure to claim it. The prosecution has no duty to advise a spouse about the existence of the privilege before the spouse testifies.

5. The court should apply the law of Texas to determine whether Gato and Darby are or were validly married. If they were validly married at the time of the communication about the allegedly forged document, then the confidential marital communications privilege should apply, and Darby does not have to testify about that communication. For this privilege, it does not matter whether Darby and Gato are still validly married after moving to California. However, the testimonial privilege requires that Darby and Gato be validly married at the time the testimony is sought. If their common law marriage is upheld under Texas law, then California would recognize such a marriage as valid within the state of California. In that case, the privilege not to testify against her spouse would apply, and Darby would not have to identify the handwriting. However, if the marriage is not valid or they are no longer married, then the testimonial privilege is not available. If Darby has to rely on the confidential marital communications privilege, the court would overrule her privilege claim if she invoked it to decline to testify about the identity of the handwriting. The handwriting on the document is not a "communication between the spouses" and was not confidential since it was given to someone who discovered the forgery, and therefore the privilege would not be available to her.

THE CLERGY-PENITENT PRIVILEGES

Two separate clergy-penitent privileges protect confidential communications. The first privilege is held by the *penitent* (the *confessor*) and, like the professional relationship privileges discussed in Chapter 12, is dual in nature. The penitent has the privilege to refuse to disclose and to prevent another from disclosing a penitential communication (CEC 1033).

A second separate and distinct privilege is held by the *clergy member*. Unlike the penitent, the clergy member has only the privilege to refuse to disclose a penitential communication made to him or her. The clergy member's privilege does not give the clergy member the authority to prevent another from disclosing the penitential communication. Thus, the clergy member cannot prevent the penitent from disclosing the communication.

Member of the clergy is broadly defined to include not only priests and ministers, but also a "religious practitioner or similar functionary" of a church or other religious organization (CEC 1030). In addition to meeting this definition, a clergy member must also, according to the definition of *penitential communications*, be authorized or accustomed to hear such communications under his religious practices. He must have a duty under the religion to keep the communications secret. A *penitent* is more narrowly defined because it applies only to people who make a "penitential communication" to a clergy member.

Thus, the definition of *penitential communication* becomes crucial in determining who is a penitent. A *penitential communication* is

1. made in confidence
2. without disclosure to any third persons as far as the penitent knows
3. to a clergy member
4. whose religious practices authorize or accustom him to hearing such communications, and
5. who has a duty through that religious practice to keep them secret (CEC 1032).

Despite the name, a penitential communication need not be a confession, though that was the traditional requirement and remains the most common situation in which the privilege is invoked. The communication need not be about a transgression or flawed act, nor must it request forgiveness or spiritual consolation. It is the context, not the content, that matters.

There is no allowance for disclosure of penitential communications to third parties who are "reasonably necessary to accomplish the goals" of the penitential communication. While an attorney can disclose a client's confidential information to another attorney who is working on the client's case without waiving that privilege, a clergy member cannot disclose the penitential communication to another clergy member without destroying its confidentiality.

Waiver

The general waiver rules of CEC 912 apply to the clergy-penitent privilege because it protects confidential communications. Disclosing a substantial portion of the communication or conducting the confession in a non-confidential setting waives the privilege. However, the waiver applies only to the person who acted in waiving the privilege. If the penitent discloses his confession to his coworker, the penitent will have waived his privilege and can be compelled to testify about that confession. Moreover, the penitent will not be able to object if the coworker or the clergy member is called to testify about the confession because the penitent has waived his privilege. However, if the clergy member is called to testify, he still retains his privilege to refuse to disclose the communication because he is not the one who made a disclosure. Even though the penitent has waived his privilege, the clergy member's separate privilege will not be waived by the penitent's actions.

Unlike doctors and attorneys, clergy members are not required to claim the privilege if they are present when someone seeks disclosure of a privileged communication. When the penitent does not claim his privilege through waiver, absence, death, or a simple failure to assert the privilege, the clergy member has discretion to decide whether she wants to claim her privilege or to disclose the communication. Leaving the choice with the clergy member permits consideration of the religious beliefs and tenets of her particular faith. Notably, there are no exceptions to the clergy-penitent privileges.

Figure 13.4 summarizes the material is this section on the clergy-penitent privilege.

Nature of Privilege	Clergy member: • Singular. The clergy member can refuse to disclose. Penitent: • Dual. The penitent can refuse to disclose and prevent others from disclosing.
Parties to the Privilege	Clergy member: • Person authorized as a religious practitioner or functionary of a church or religious organization, and

	• Authorized or accustomed to hear such communication under his religious practices. Penitent: • Person who makes a penitential communication to a clergy member.
Protected Communication	• Information transmitted in confidence between penitent and clergy member, • Whose religious practices authorize or accustom him to hearing, and • Who has a duty through that religious practice to keep the communications secret, as long as not disclosed (as far as penitent knows) to others.
Who Can Claim?	• The holder, or • Person authorized by the holder, or • The clergy member.
The Holder	• The penitent, or • The clergy member.
Exceptions	• None
CEC sections	1030-1034

Figure 13.4. Clergy-Penitent Privileges

Examples

1. A priest confessed to the Bishop that he had sexually assaulted a young man who worked as an altar server at evening mass. The Bishop met with the Cardinal to discuss the priest's confession and consider how to discipline the priest and how to prevent future assaults. They compelled the priest to participate in therapy and, at the completion of his course of therapy, transferred him to another parish. A year later, the priest sexually assaulted another young man, who sued the Cardinal for knowingly permitting the priest to continue to serve. At trial, the young man called the Bishop to testify, and the Bishop claimed the clergy-penitent privilege. The priest was sitting in the gallery during the trial and also asserted his privilege to prevent the Bishop from disclosing his confession to the earlier assault. How should the court rule on the privilege claims, and why? Would it make a difference if the priest knew that the Bishop would discuss the confession with the Cardinal?

2. Cardinal Roger attended a meeting with Father Bill to discuss a clergy abuse scandal and wrote a memo summarizing the outcome of the meeting. The memo noted that the attorney for the Archdiocese also attended the meeting. As they prepared for trial, the prosecution subpoenaed a

number of memos, including the one written by Cardinal Roger. The Archdiocese objected, claiming that the letter was protected by the attorney-client privilege because the attorney for the Archdiocese is also the attorney for the Cardinal and priests who are simply representatives of the Archdiocese. In addition, the Archdiocese also claimed that the meeting was a confidential communication and the memo summarizing the meeting was kept confidential and only between attorney and client. How should the court rule, and why?

3. A pastor accused of wrongdoing wrote a letter to her Bishop, explaining her side of the story and providing a list of witnesses who supported her account. When the pastor was sued, the plaintiff sought discovery of the letter. The pastor objected, claiming that the letter was protected by the clergy-penitent privilege. The plaintiff responded that the letter was not a penitential communication and therefore was subject to discovery. How should the court rule, and why?

4. Plaintiffs sued a church alleging that they were abused by a probationary clergy member at the defendant church. In discovery, the plaintiffs requested several documents, including one letter from the church's pastor to her supervisor. The pastor declared that she prepared the letter and sent it to her supervisor, who was part of a crisis management team for the church. The supervisor shared the letter with the team. Another member of that team was the church's attorney, and the pastor claimed that she intended that the attorney would see the letter, making it a confidential communication. The church objected that the letter was protected by the clergy-penitent and attorney-client privileges. The plaintiffs argued that the letter was sent to a supervisor who then forwarded the letter to the attorney, which destroyed the confidentiality of the communication. How should the court rule on the privilege claims, and why?

Explanations

1. The court should overrule the Bishop's objection and compel him to testify about the priest's confession. The Bishop waived his singular privilege when he disclosed the priest's confession to the Cardinal. Under the clergy-penitent privileges, there is no allowance for disclosure to any third parties, even reasonably necessary third parties. Therefore, that disclosure rendered the confession no longer confidential. However, the court should sustain the priest's claim of dual privilege to prevent the Bishop from testifying as long as the priest was not aware that his confession would be disclosed to the Cardinal. If the priest knew the practice was to convey such confessions to the Cardinal for rehabilitation guidance, then the privilege would not apply.

2. The court should sustain the objection because the Archdiocese has met the preponderance test for showing the existence of the attorney-client privilege. There is no evidence of waiver, nor that any exceptions apply, and therefore the privilege should be upheld.

3. The court should sustain the privilege objection in the absence of additional information. As long as the letter was transmitted confidentially and the Bishop is also a clergy member who is accustomed to receiving such information and keeping it confidential, then the letter is a penitential communication. There is no need for an actual confession. The plaintiff may argue that by providing a list of witnesses, the penitent did not intend for the communication to remain confidential because witnesses were to be contacted. However, if the court determines that the intent was to keep the letter confidential by a preponderance of the evidence, then the privilege would apply.

4. The court should overrule both privilege objections and compel disclosure of the pastor's letter to her supervisor. Even if the supervisor is a clergy member and the letter is a penitential communication, the clergy-penitent privilege will not apply because the letter was sent to the supervisor who disclosed it to others. The clergy-penitent privilege does not allow for any disclosure to anyone, whether or not the pastor knew the letter would be disclosed. The letter is also not a confidential communication for purposes of the attorney-client privilege because disclosure to the supervisor was not reasonably necessary to accomplish the purpose of the attorney-client consultation. If the pastor wanted to retain both privileges, she should have separately sent the letter to the supervisor and attorney.

OTHER LESS COMMON PRIVILEGES

Sexual Assault Victim-Counselor Privilege

Confidential communications made between a person who has experienced a sexual assault and a health care worker, a counselor, an employee, or even a volunteer can be protected by a privilege under CEC 1035. Sexual assault includes rape, sodomy, and child molestation, among other crimes. The communication must be made confidentially and disclosed only to those third parties who are reasonably necessary or present to further the goals of the consultation. This is a dual privilege that permits the holder to refuse to disclose and also to prevent others from disclosing the confidential communication.

This privilege contains two exceptions. The first applies only in criminal cases and permits the court to compel disclosure where the probative value of the communication outweighs the effect on the victim or her treatment. The second exception applies this same balancing test in any proceeding involving child abuse. The holder of the privilege is the victim, her guardian or conservator, or personal representative if the victim is deceased. The counselor who participated in the communication must claim the privilege if she is present when disclosure is sought or whenever the holder instructs her to do so. This privilege applies more broadly than the psychotherapist-patient privilege in sexual assault situations.

Domestic Violence Victim-Counselor Privilege

Domestic violence victims may claim a similar privilege for confidential communications with a person in a domestic violence victim service organization under CEC 1037. This is a dual privilege, and the two exceptions that apply to the sexual assault counselor privilege also apply to the domestic violence victim privilege. The holder of the privilege is the victim, conservator, or guardian, unless that conservator or guardian is accused of perpetrating the domestic violence against the victim. The counselor also may claim the privilege, and must claim the privilege when disclosure is sought if the holder still is in existence. This privilege applies more broadly than the psychotherapist-patient privilege in domestic violence situations.

Human Trafficking Caseworker-Victim Privilege

A victim of human trafficking has a dual privilege to refuse to disclose and prevent others from disclosing confidential communications between the victim and a human trafficking caseworker under CEC 1038. The privilege expires if there is no holder of the privilege in existence. An exception exists to compel disclosure in criminal proceedings for a crime allegedly perpetrated against that victim if the probative value outweighs the effect on the victim, the counseling relationship, or counseling services. The court can also compel disclosure if the victim is dead or is not the complaining witness in a criminal case against the perpetrator.

Official Information and Identity of Informer Privilege

A public entity has two privileges to maintain confidential information, and so this privilege is based on the *content* of the information. The first applies to official information, and the second applies to the identity of informers.

Each privilege is dual, allowing the entity to refuse to disclose and to prevent another from disclosing the information.

Official information is defined as information acquired in confidence by a public employee in the course of her work. Official information is protected when an act of Congress or a California statute prohibits public disclosure of that information or when disclosure is against the public interest.

An *informer* is defined as a person who furnishes information to a law enforcement officer or representative of an administrative agency, purporting to disclose a violation of state or federal law. The privilege protects the informer's identity when disclosure is prohibited by an act of Congress or by state law or when disclosure is against the public interest.

In determining whether disclosure is against the public interest, the courts balance whether the necessity for preserving the confidentiality of the information or identity outweighs the need for disclosure. In both cases, consent to disclosure will waive the privilege. In addition, CEC 915(b) permits disclosure of this information in the judge's chambers if that disclosure is necessary to ascertain whether the privilege should apply. If the court determines that the information is privileged, that in camera disclosure is not a waiver, and anyone present during that disclosure is prohibited from revealing the information.

Official Information in Criminal Cases

In criminal cases, the prosecution may assert the official information privilege to avoid disclosing evidence that the defendant may seek in discovery or later at trial. That information can include police personnel records (on matters such as disciplinary actions, civil rights complaints, or excessive force claims), the location of surveillance teams, and crime reports. Exercising this privilege has greater consequences when the evidence is material. Recall that *material evidence* is evidence that plays an important role in deciding the outcome of the case. The failure to admit material evidence would infringe on the criminal defendant's right to a fair trial. If the court determines that the evidence is material and the prosecution asserts the privilege nonetheless, then under CEC 1042 the court shall make an order or a finding adverse to the prosecution on any issue as to which that privileged information is material. The defendant or prosecution may request an in camera review of the official information to determine whether the privilege should apply and whether the information is material.

The disciplinary records for an officer accused of excessive force may be material if the criminal defendant is asserting self-defense to a charge of battery on a police officer. To obtain police officer records of an officer accused of misconduct against the criminal defendant, the defendant must demonstrate good cause. The defendant can show good cause by showing that the evidence is material and that he has a reasonable belief that the agency has the type of information sought.

Materiality is a higher standard than mere relevance, and asserting the privilege as to relevant evidence will not result in the adverse finding penalty. For instance, the location of a surveillance team is relevant but is not material unless there is an issue about whether the location provided an opportunity for accurate and complete surveillance. However, the assertion of the privilege will not prevent an inquiry on cross-examination about the distance and angle from which the officer made the observations.

Political Vote Privilege

People who vote in public elections by secret ballot have a privilege to refuse to disclose their votes under CEC 1050. The voter is the holder of the privilege, and this is a content privilege as well; it applies only to information about a secret ballot. The only exception applies when the person voted illegally. The privilege can be waived if the voter previously disclosed her vote.

Trade Secrets Privilege

Trade secrets are proprietary information essential to the operation or running of a business or industry. The kinds of information that can constitute trade secrets include "secret recipes," databases and customer lists, methods and actuary tables to determine customer rates, as well as computer programs, evaluation checklists, and even the formula or method of computing damages. This is a content privilege also.

When a person or company owns a trade secret, that owner has a privilege to prevent disclosure of that trade secret. The owner of the trade secret is the holder of the privilege, and the privilege may be claimed by the owner, her agent, or an employee. This is a dual privilege, giving the option to refuse to disclose and to prevent others from disclosing the privileged information. The only exception to the privilege is when the use of the privilege would conceal a fraud or otherwise be unjust.

Parties often assert the trade secret privilege at the discovery stage of litigation. When a party makes a claim, it would be improper for that party to then refuse to provide the proprietary information that would be needed to support that party's own claim. Where privileged information is at the core of a party's claim, the privilege must yield to the doctrine of fundamental fairness. In such cases, courts compel disclosure of trade secret information.

When concealing the trade secret would help to conceal a fraud, the courts will overrule privilege objections. For instance, in cases of unfair competition or illegal monopolies, it may be unjust to permit the alleged wrongdoer to withhold advertising strategy information at the discovery stage if the unfair competition cannot be proven without that information. In cases of securities fraud, permitting the securities broker to claim the privilege and refuse to disclose funding mechanisms for a hedge fund would tend to help conceal a fraud. In each of these cases, the fraud exception would apply to destroy the privilege.

The courts use a balancing test to determine whether upholding the privilege to prevent disclosure would work an injustice. The factors to consider include whether the information is available from some other source; whether the need for the information can be satisfied without disclosure to the opposing party, such as with an in camera review; or whether a more limited disclosure of information or more limited scope of disclosure can satisfy the litigants.

Newspaper Immunity Privilege

News reporters, publishers, and editors have a privilege that prevents them from being held in contempt for declining to disclose the sources, notes, and other background from their news stories. The California Constitution contains a similar privilege to that of the CEC.

This content privilege broadly protects anyone associated with the dissemination of the news, and also applies to radio and televisions reporters as well as Internet "reporters" and bloggers. Courts have found that Internet sites are analogous to print media because there are "pages" of text that the reader "opens" and "closes."

To qualify for immunity from contempt, the person must show the following:

1. She is connected to the news as a reporter, a publisher, an editor, or otherwise.
2. She obtained or prepared the information she seeks to protect in the process of gathering, receiving, or processing information to communicate to the public.
3. She did not publish or otherwise disseminate to the public the information she seeks to protect.

The third element is not absolute because prior public disclosure of a source, or some of the information the person seeks to protect, will not waive the privilege as to the other unpublished information. For instance, when a reporter names a source in the text of a newspaper article, the reporter's notes about the conversation with that source still will be protected. Courts also have declined to compel disclosure of information to confirm a named source.

In criminal cases, this newspaper privilege can be overcome by a criminal defendant's due process rights. A criminal defendant seeking disclosure has the burden to prove that upholding the privilege would deprive her of a fair trial. The court applies a balancing test that considers these factors:

1. Whether the unpublished information is confidential or sensitive such that disclosure would impact the reporter's future ability to do her job
2. Whether other circumstances demonstrate no adverse consequences to disclosure (such as when the criminal defendant is the source of the unpublished information)
3. The degree of importance of the information to the criminal defendant
4. Whether there is an alternative source for the unpublished information

If the criminal defendant fails to convince the court that due process requires disclosure, the information will remain protected.

Examples

1. Touché filed a class action case against Rodin for sending unsolicited advertisements by facsimile machine in violation of a Consumer Protection Act. Touché served discovery requests, seeking the database that Rodin used to send the faxes, so that Touché could contact all potential class members. Rodin objected that the database of customer lists was a protected trade secret and privileged from disclosure. How should the court rule, and why?

2. Farmar Insurance Company failed to file a mandatory disclosure statement with the California Department of Insurance. The disclosure statement asked for statistical information about Farmar's customers, pricing policy, and other business. Once filed, disclosure statements are available for public inspection. Farmar claimed that the statistical information was protected by the trade secret privilege. The state insurance commissioner sought to compel disclosure, arguing that Farmar provided the same information to its shareholders in an annual report. How should the court rule?

3. Hughley hired Morey to build a circuit board for its manufacturing facility. Morey subcontracted some of the work to Electric Supply Company. One day the circuit board shorted out, causing a 16-hour power outage at the facility, which meant that two shifts of workers were unable to do their jobs. Hughley sued Morey, and Morey sued Electric Supply under an indemnity agreement. After months of discovery, Hughley settled with Morey, and Morey focused on trying to recover

the settlement amount from Electric Supply. Electric Supply served discovery requests on Morey, asking how the damages amounts were calculated. Morey objected that the method of computing damages was a trade secret and declined to provide any information except for the final settlement amount. Electric Supply responded that because a crucial component of an indemnity claim is to test the reasonableness of the settlement amount, the damages calculation information is crucial to the case. How should the court rule on the objection?

4. Gary was the head football coach for a local college. After he was fired, the local newspaper ran a story about the reasons for his termination and listed several sources for the article. Gary sued the newspaper and the reporter for defamation. In discovery, Gary sought to take the deposition of the reporter to question her about the background for the story. The reporter objected, asserting the newspaper privilege. Gary responded that the reporter had waived the privilege by disclosing the names of sources in the news article. How should the court rule?

5. Lew is on trial for possession with intent to distribute rock cocaine. The primary evidence against Lew is Officer Ojos's testimony. Officer Ojos testifies that he observed Lew over the course of several weeks from a hidden location and saw Lew holding, showing, and selling rock cocaine to numerous patrons. On cross-examination, Lew's attorney asked Officer Ojos where he has hiding when he allegedly observed the alleged drug sales. The prosecution objected on the grounds of the official information privilege. Lew's attorney argued that the surveillance location was material to the case because otherwise he could not undermine the credibility of the officer. Lew's attorney also requested an in camera review of the surveillance reports, so that the court could rule on whether a penalty should attach if the prosecution asserted the privilege. What should the court do, and how should the court rule?

6. LinusXO has an Internet blog, and one day he posted some proprietary information he had obtained about the computer company, Mapple. Mapple sued LinusXO for wrongful dissemination of trade secrets on an Internet website. Mapple served a subpoena on the Internet service provider, seeking disclosure of the real name for the person with the username LinusXO. The Internet service provider objected, claiming the newspaper privilege. Mapple responded that a blogger is not a news source and a website is not a newspaper because the information is not permanent and is subject to change, and therefore the privilege does not apply. How should the court rule, and why?

7. Oscar was charged with killing his ex-girlfriend and her new husband. While in jail awaiting trial, Oscar granted an interview with Vanessa, a reporter for a local newspaper. Vanessa wrote a story about Oscar's case

and included some direct quotations and paraphrases of some of her conversation with Oscar. At Oscar's trial, the prosecution called Vanessa as a witness and asked her on direct examination to discuss her interview with the defendant. Vanessa objected on the grounds of the newspaper privilege. The prosecution responded that he was not asking about any unpublished information and merely wanted her to describe the portions of the interview that she had reported in her story. How should the judge rule? If the defense seeks to cross-examine Vanessa about the unpublished portions of the interview and she objects again, how should the court rule?

Explanations

1. The court should sustain the objection and prevent disclosure of the fax database. The customer lists can be a proprietary trade secret and, if so, will be protected from disclosure. Touché may argue that the information cannot be obtained in any other way, and therefore it would be unjust to permit Rodin to hide behind trade secret protection. The court then would balance Rodin's need for secrecy against the importance of identifying the class members, and likely will find another way to provide notice to potential class members that does not involve disclosure of the database.

2. The court should deny the privilege and compel disclosure. Statistical information about an insurance company's customers, businesses, and prices can constitute a trade secret. If the information is subject to mandatory disclosures to a state commissioner, the court may find that the mandatory disclosure may outweigh the policy behind the privilege. In this case, however, Farmar already has waived the privilege to the extent that it has disclosed the information to its shareholders. Thus, disclosure of that information is appropriate.

3. The court should sustain the privilege objection only if Morey dismisses its indemnity claim against Electric Supply. In an indemnity claim, it is important to prove the amount claimed, and Morey's failure to provide the information on the damage calculation prevents Electric Supply from determining the reasonableness of the settlement with Hughley. While the calculation method may be a trade secret, fundamental fairness requires Morey to waive the privilege if it wishes to continue with the litigation.

4. The court should sustain the privilege objection. The person asserting the privilege is a news reporter, and she obtained background information in the course of preparing her story. That background information is unpublished and meets the elements of the privilege. The fact that she

disclosed some sources to the public does not waive the privilege as to any other information. Therefore, the privilege applies to protect her from giving a deposition about the story.

5. The court should deny the motion for an in camera review to determine whether the prosecution is asserting the privilege appropriately because the mere location has not been found to be material without additional information. The assertion of the privilege does not prevent Lew's attorney from inquiring on cross-examination to test the accuracy of the surveillance by asking questions about the distance, the angle, the time of day, and other matters that will help to undermine the witness's testimony. If there was additional information to suggest that the officer was being untruthful in testimony about his surveillance report, then the court should grant the motion for in camera review of the surveillance reports and other information before ruling on whether to order the adverse finding penalty against the prosecution.

6. The court should sustain the privilege objection. The Internet provider fits the definition of a news *publisher* because it is analogous to a newspaper or other periodical publisher. The statute has been broadly interpreted to include Internet sites as analogous to print media because there are pages of text that the reader "opens" and "closes." The fact that the content is not permanently fixed does not destroy the privilege.

7. The court should overrule Vanessa's first objection because the prosecution is merely seeking information that has already been published and disseminated to the public by this reporter. The judge should instruct Vanessa to testify about the published portions of the interview. If Oscar's defense lawyer then attempted to cross-examine Vanessa about the unpublished information, then Vanessa should object and again assert the newspaper privilege. Oscar's lawyer may argue that preventing cross-examination on the unpublished information would result in an unfair trial because it is important that the jury have this information about what the reporter did not report. That argument will not be enough to meet the burden to prove that an unfair trial would result. There is an alternative source of the information available because Oscar knows what he said to the reporter even if it was not published. There are no adverse consequences from non-disclosure when the defendant already has the information he seeks. Therefore, the court should uphold the privilege as to the defense cross-examination.

Selected Sections of the California Evidence Code

CEC 240: Unavailable as a witness

(a) Except as otherwise provided in subdivision (b), "unavailable as a witness" means that the declarant is any of the following:

(1) Exempted or precluded on the ground of privilege from testifying concerning the matter to which his or her statement is relevant.

(2) Disqualified from testifying to the matter.

(3) Dead or unable to attend or to testify at the hearing because of then existing physical or mental illness or infirmity.

(4) Absent from the hearing and the court is unable to compel his or her attendance by its process.

(5) Absent from the hearing and the proponent of his or her statement has exercised reasonable diligence but has been unable to procure his or her attendance by the court's process.

(b) A declarant is not unavailable as a witness if the exemption, preclusion, disqualification, death, inability, or absence of the declarant was brought about by the procurement or wrongdoing of the proponent of his or her statement for the purpose of preventing the declarant from attending or testifying.

(c) Expert testimony which establishes that physical or mental trauma resulting from an alleged crime has caused harm to a witness of sufficient severity that the witness is physically unable to testify or is unable to testify without suffering substantial trauma may constitute a sufficient showing of unavailability pursuant to paragraph (3) of subdivision (a). As used in this section, the term "expert" means a physician and surgeon, including a psychiatrist, or any person described by subdivision (b), (c), or (e) of Section 1010.

The introduction of evidence to establish the unavailability of a witness under this subdivision shall not be deemed procurement of unavailability, in absence of proof to the contrary.

CEC 403: Determination of foundational and other preliminary facts where relevancy, personal knowledge, or authenticity is disputed

(a) The proponent of the proffered evidence has the burden of producing evidence as to the existence of the preliminary fact, and the proffered evidence is inadmissible unless the court finds that there is evidence sufficient to sustain a finding of the existence of the preliminary fact, when:

(1) The relevance of the proffered evidence depends on the existence of the preliminary fact;

(2) The preliminary fact is the personal knowledge of a witness concerning the subject matter of his testimony;

(3) The preliminary fact is the authenticity of a writing; or

(4) The proffered evidence is of a statement or other conduct of a particular person and the preliminary fact is whether that person made the statement or so conducted himself.

(b) Subject to Section 702, the court may admit conditionally the proffered evidence under this section, subject to evidence of the preliminary fact being supplied later in the course of the trial.

(c) If the court admits the proffered evidence under this section, the court:

(1) May, and on request shall, instruct the jury to determine whether the preliminary fact exists and to disregard the proffered evidence unless the jury finds that the preliminary fact does exist.

(2) Shall instruct the jury to disregard the proffered evidence if the court subsequently determines that a jury could not reasonably find that the preliminary fact exists.

CEC 405: Determination of foundational and other preliminary facts in other cases

With respect to preliminary fact determinations not governed by Section 403 or 404:

(a) When the existence of a preliminary fact is disputed, the court shall indicate which party has the burden of producing evidence and the burden of proof on the issue as implied by the rule of law under which the question arises. The court shall determine the existence or nonexistence of the preliminary fact and shall admit or exclude the proffered evidence as required by the rule of law under which the question arises.

(b) If a preliminary fact is also a fact in issue in the action:

(1) The jury shall not be informed of the court's determination as to the existence or nonexistence of the preliminary fact.

(2) If the proffered evidence is admitted, the jury shall not be instructed to disregard the evidence if its determination of the fact differs from the court's determination of the preliminary fact.

CEC 451: Matters which must be judicially noticed

Judicial notice shall be taken of the following:

(a) The decisional, constitutional, and public statutory law of this state and of the United States and the provisions of any charter described in Section 3, 4, or 5 of Article XI of the California Constitution.

(b) Any matter made a subject of judicial notice by Section 11343.6, 11344.6, or 18576 of the Government Code or by Section 1507 of Title 44 of the United States Code.

(c) Rules of professional conduct for members of the bar adopted pursuant to Section 6076 of the Business and Professions Code and rules of practice and procedure for the courts of this state adopted by the Judicial Council.

(d) Rules of pleading, practice, and procedure prescribed by the United States Supreme Court, such as the Rules of the United States Supreme Court, the Federal Rules of Civil Procedure, the Federal Rules of Criminal Procedure, the Admiralty Rules, the Rules of the Court of Claims, the Rules of the Customs Court, and the General Orders and Forms in Bankruptcy.

(e) The true signification of all English words and phrases and of all legal expressions.

(f) Facts and propositions of generalized knowledge that are so universally known that they cannot reasonably be the subject of dispute.

CEC 452: Matters which may be judicially noticed

Judicial notice may be taken of the following matters to the extent that they are not embraced within Section 451:

(a) The decisional, constitutional, and statutory law of any state of the United States and the resolutions and private acts of the Congress of the United States and of the Legislature of this state.

(b) Regulations and legislative enactments issued by or under the authority of the United States or any public entity in the United States.

(c) Official acts of the legislative, executive, and judicial departments of the United States and of any state of the United States.

(d) Records of (1) any court of this state or (2) any court of record of the United States or of any state of the United States.

(e) Rules of court of (1) any court of this state or (2) any court of record of the United States or of any state of the United States.

(f) The law of an organization of nations and of foreign nations and public entities in foreign nations.

(g) Facts and propositions that are of such common knowledge within the territorial jurisdiction of the court that they cannot reasonably be the subject of dispute.

(h) Facts and propositions that are not reasonably subject to dispute and are capable of immediate and accurate determination by resort to sources of reasonably indisputable accuracy.

CEC 453: Compulsory judicial notice upon request

The trial court shall take judicial notice of any matter specified in Section 452 if a party requests it and:

(a) Gives each adverse party sufficient notice of the request, through the pleadings or otherwise, to enable such adverse party to prepare to meet the request; and

(b) Furnishes the court with sufficient information to enable it to take judicial notice of the matter.

CEC 600: Presumption and inference defined

(a) A presumption is an assumption of fact that the law requires to be made from another fact or group of facts found or otherwise established in the action. A presumption is not evidence.

(b) An inference is a deduction of fact that may logically and reasonably be drawn from another fact or group of facts found or otherwise established in the action.

CEC 603: Presumption affecting the burden of producing evidence defined

A presumption affecting the burden of producing evidence is a presumption established to implement no public policy other than to facilitate the determination of the particular action in which the presumption is applied.

CEC 646: Res ipsa loquitur; instruction

(a) As used in this section, "defendant" includes any party against whom the res ipsa loquitur presumption operates.

(b) The judicial doctrine of res ipsa loquitur is a presumption affecting the burden of producing evidence.

(c) If the evidence, or facts otherwise established, would support a res ipsa loquitur presumption and the defendant has introduced evidence which would support a finding that he was not negligent or that any negligence on his part was not a proximate cause of the occurrence, the court may, and upon request shall, instruct the jury to the effect that:

(1) If the facts which would give rise to a res ipsa loquitur presumption are found or otherwise established, the jury may draw the inference from such facts that a proximate cause of the occurrence was some negligent conduct on the part of the defendant; and

(2) The jury shall not find that a proximate cause of the occurrence was some negligent conduct on the part of the defendant unless the jury believes, after weighing all the evidence in the case and drawing such inferences therefrom as the jury believes are warranted, that it is more probable than not that the occurrence was caused by some negligent conduct on the part of the defendant.

CEC 700: General rule as to competency

Except as otherwise provided by statute, every person, irrespective of age, is qualified to be a witness and no person is disqualified to testify to any matter.

CEC 703: Judge as witness

(a) Before the judge presiding at the trial of an action may be called to testify in that trial as a witness, he shall, in proceedings held out of the presence and hearing of the jury, inform the parties of the information he has concerning any fact or matter about which he will be called to testify.

(b) Against the objection of a party, the judge presiding at the trial of an action may not testify in that trial as a witness. Upon such objection, the judge shall declare a mistrial and order the action assigned for trial before another judge.

(c) The calling of the judge presiding at a trial to testify in that trial as a witness shall be deemed a consent to the granting of a motion for mistrial, and an objection to such calling of a judge shall be deemed a motion for mistrial.

(d) In the absence of objection by a party, the judge presiding at the trial of an action may testify in that trial as a witness.

CEC 703.5: Judges, arbitrators or mediators as witnesses; subsequent civil proceeding

No person presiding at any judicial or quasi-judicial proceeding, and no arbitrator or mediator, shall be competent to testify, in any subsequent civil proceeding, as to any statement, conduct, decision, or ruling, occurring at or in conjunction with the prior proceeding, except as to a statement or conduct that could (a) give rise to civil or criminal contempt, (b) constitute a crime, (c) be the subject of investigation by the State Bar or Commission on Judicial Performance, or (d) give rise to disqualification proceedings under paragraph (1) or (6) of subdivision (a) of Section 170.1 of the Code of Civil Procedure. However, this section does not apply to a mediator with regard to any mediation under Chapter 11 (commencing with Section 3160) of Part 2 of Division 8 of the Family Code.

CEC 704: Juror as witness

(a) Before a juror sworn and impaneled in the trial of an action may be called to testify before the jury in that trial as a witness, he shall, in proceedings conducted by the court out of the presence and hearing of the remaining jurors, inform the parties of the information he has concerning any fact or matter about which he will be called to testify.

(b) Against the objection of a party, a juror sworn and impaneled in the trial of an action may not testify before the jury in that trial as a witness. Upon such objection, the court shall declare a mistrial and order the action assigned for trial before another jury.

(c) The calling of a juror to testify before the jury as a witness shall be deemed a consent to the granting of a motion for mistrial, and an objection to such calling of a juror shall be deemed a motion for mistrial.

(d) In the absence of objection by a party, a juror sworn and impaneled in the trial of an action may be compelled to testify in that trial as a witness.

CEC 710: Oath required

Every witness before testifying shall take an oath or make an affirmation or declaration in the form provided by law, except that a child under the age of 10 or a dependent person with a substantial cognitive impairment, in the court's discretion, may be required only to promise to tell the truth.

CEC 722: Credibility of expert witness

(a) The fact of the appointment of an expert witness by the court may be revealed to the trier of fact.

(b) The compensation and expenses paid or to be paid to an expert witness by the party calling him is a proper subject of inquiry by any adverse party as relevant to the credibility of the witness and the weight of his testimony.

CEC 723: Limit on number of expert witnesses

The court may, at any time before or during the trial of an action, limit the number of expert witnesses to be called by any party.

CEC 730: Appointment of expert by court

When it appears to the court, at any time before or during the trial of an action, that expert evidence is or may be required by the court or by any party to the action, the court on its own motion or on motion of any party may appoint one or more experts to investigate, to render a report as may be ordered by the court, and to testify as an expert at the trial of the action relative to the fact or matter as to which the expert evidence is or may be required. The court may fix the compensation for these services, if any, rendered by any person appointed under this section, in addition to any service as a witness, at the amount as seems reasonable to the court.

Nothing in this section shall be construed to permit a person to perform any act for which a license is required unless the person holds the appropriate license to lawfully perform that act.

CEC 731: Payment of court-appointed expert

(a) In all criminal actions and juvenile court proceedings, the compensation fixed under Section 730 shall be a charge against the county in which such action or proceeding is pending and shall be paid out of the treasury of such county on order of the court.

(b) In any county in which the board of supervisors so provides, the compensation fixed under Section 730 for medical experts in civil actions in such county shall be a charge against and paid out of the treasury of such county on order of the court.

(c) Except as otherwise provided in this section, in all civil actions, the compensation fixed under Section 730 shall, in the first instance, be apportioned and charged to the several parties in such proportion as the court may determine and may thereafter be taxed and allowed in like manner as other costs.

CEC 732: Calling and examining court-appointed expert

Any expert appointed by the court under Section 730 may be called and examined by the court or by any party to the action. When such witness is called and examined by the court, the parties have the same right as is expressed in Section 775 to cross-examine the witness and to object to the questions asked and the evidence adduced.

CEC 733: Right to produce other expert evidence

Nothing contained in this article shall be deemed or construed to prevent any party to any action from producing other expert evidence on the same fact or matter mentioned in Section 730; but, where other expert witnesses are called by a party to the action, their fees shall be paid by the party calling them and only ordinary witness fees shall be taxed as costs in the action

---

CEC 750: Rules relating to witnesses apply to interpreters and translators

A person who serves as an interpreter or translator in any action is subject to all the rules of law relating to witnesses.

CEC 751: Oath required of interpreters and translators

(a) An interpreter shall take an oath that he or she will make a true interpretation to the witness in a language that the witness understands and that he or she will make a true interpretation of the witness' answers to questions to counsel, court, or jury, in the English language, with his or her best skill and judgment.

(b) In any proceeding in which a deaf or hard-of-hearing person is testifying under oath, the interpreter certified pursuant to subdivision (f) of Section 754 shall advise the court whenever he or she is unable to comply with his or her oath taken pursuant to subdivision (a).

(c) A translator shall take an oath that he or she will make a true translation in the English language of any writing he or she is to decipher or translate.

(d) An interpreter regularly employed by the court and certified or registered in accordance with Article 4 (commencing with Section 68560) of Chapter 2 of Title 8 of the Government Code, or a translator regularly employed by the court, may file an oath as prescribed by this section with the clerk of the court. The filed oath shall serve for all subsequent court proceedings until the appointment is revoked by the court.

CEC 752: Interpreters for witnesses

(a) When a witness is incapable of understanding the English language or is incapable of expressing himself or herself in the English language so as to be understood directly by counsel, court, and jury, an interpreter whom he or she can understand and who can understand him or her shall be sworn to interpret for him or her.

(b) The record shall identify the interpreter who may be appointed and compensated as provided in Article 2 (commencing with Section 730) of Chapter 3.

CEC 753: Translators of writings

(a) When the written characters in a writing offered in evidence are incapable of being deciphered or understood directly, a translator who can decipher the characters or understand the language shall be sworn to decipher or translate the writing.

(b) The record shall identify the translator who may be appointed and compensated as provided in Article 2 (commencing with Section 730) of Chapter 3.

CEC 754: Deaf or hearing impaired persons; interpreters; qualifications; guidelines; compensation; questioning; use of statements

(a) As used in this section, "individual who is deaf or hearing impaired" means an individual with a hearing loss so great as to prevent his or her understanding language spoken in a normal tone, but does not include an individual who is hearing impaired provided with, and able to fully participate in the proceedings through the use of, an assistive listening system or computer-aided transcription equipment provided pursuant to Section 54.8 of the Civil Code.

(b) In any civil or criminal action, including, but not limited to, any action involving a traffic or other infraction, any small claims court proceeding, any juvenile court proceeding, any family court proceeding or service, or any proceeding to determine the mental competency of a person, in any court-ordered or court-provided alternative dispute resolution, including mediation and arbitration, or any administrative hearing, where a party or witness is an individual who is deaf or hearing impaired and the individual who is deaf or hearing impaired is present and participating, the proceedings shall be interpreted in a language that the individual who is deaf or hearing impaired understands by a qualified interpreter appointed by the court or other appointing authority, or as agreed upon.

(c) For purposes of this section, "appointing authority" means a court, department, board, commission, agency, licensing or legislative body, or other body for proceedings requiring a qualified interpreter.

(d) For the purposes of this section, "interpreter" includes, but is not limited to, an oral interpreter, a sign language interpreter, or a deaf-blind interpreter, depending upon the needs of the individual who is deaf or hearing impaired.

(e) For purposes of this section, "intermediary interpreter" means an individual who is deaf or hearing impaired, or a hearing individual who is able to assist in providing an accurate interpretation between spoken English and sign language or between variants of sign language or between American Sign Language and other foreign languages by acting as an intermediary between the individual who is deaf or hearing impaired and the qualified interpreter.

(f) For purposes of this section, "qualified interpreter" means an interpreter who has been certified as competent to interpret court proceedings by a testing organization, agency, or educational institution approved by the Judicial Council as qualified to administer tests to court interpreters for individuals who are deaf or hearing impaired.

(g) In the event that the appointed interpreter is not familiar with the use of particular signs by the individual who is deaf or hearing impaired or his or her particular variant of sign language, the court or other appointing authority shall, in consultation with the individual who is deaf or hearing impaired or his or her representative, appoint an intermediary interpreter.

(h) Prior to July 1, 1992, the Judicial Council shall conduct a study to establish the guidelines pursuant to which it shall determine which testing organizations, agencies, or educational institutions will be approved to administer tests for certification of court interpreters for individuals who are deaf or hearing impaired. It is the intent of the Legislature that the study obtain the widest possible input from the public, including, but not limited to, educational institutions, the judiciary, linguists, members of the State Bar, court interpreters, members of professional interpreting organizations, and members of the deaf and hearing-impaired communities. After obtaining public comment and completing its study, the Judicial Council shall publish these guidelines. By January 1, 1997, the Judicial Council shall approve one or more entities to administer testing for court interpreters for individuals who are deaf or hearing impaired. Testing entities may include educational institutions, testing organizations, joint powers agencies, or public agencies.

Commencing July 1, 1997, court interpreters for individuals who are deaf or hearing impaired shall meet the qualifications specified in subdivision (f).

(i) Persons appointed to serve as interpreters under this section shall be paid, in addition to actual travel costs, the prevailing rate paid to persons employed by the court to provide other interpreter services unless such service is considered to be a part of the person's regular duties as an employee of the state, county, or other political subdivision of the state. Payment of the interpreter's fee shall be a charge against the county, or other political subdivision of the state, in which that action is pending. Payment of the interpreter's fee in administrative proceedings shall be a charge against the appointing board or authority.

(j) Whenever a peace officer or any other person having a law enforcement or prosecutorial function in any criminal or quasi-criminal investigation or proceeding questions or otherwise interviews an alleged victim or witness who demonstrates or alleges deafness or hearing impairment, a good faith effort to secure the services of an interpreter shall be made, without any unnecessary delay unless either the individual who is deaf or hearing impaired affirmatively indicates that he or she does not need or cannot use an interpreter, or an interpreter is not otherwise required by Title II of the Americans with Disabilities Act of 1990 (Public Law 101-336) and federal regulations adopted thereunder.

(k) No statement, written or oral, made by an individual who the court finds is deaf or hearing impaired in reply to a question of a peace officer, or any other person having a law enforcement or prosecutorial function in any criminal or quasi-criminal investigation or proceeding, may be used against that individual who is deaf or hearing impaired unless the question was accurately interpreted and the statement was made knowingly, voluntarily, and intelligently and was accurately interpreted, or the court makes special findings that either the individual could not have used an interpreter or an interpreter was not otherwise required by Title II of the Americans with Disabilities Act of 1990 (Public Law 101-336) and federal regulations adopted thereunder and that the statement was made knowingly, voluntarily, and intelligently.

(l) In obtaining services of an interpreter for purposes of subdivision (j) or (k), priority shall be given to first obtaining a qualified interpreter.

(m) Nothing in subdivision (j) or (k) shall be deemed to supersede the requirement of subdivision (b) for use of a qualified interpreter for individuals who are deaf or hearing impaired participating as parties or witnesses in a trial or hearing.

(n) In any action or proceeding in which an individual who is deaf or hearing impaired is a participant, the appointing authority shall not commence proceedings until the appointed interpreter is in full view of and spatially situated to assure proper communication with the participating individual who is deaf or hearing impaired.

(o) Each superior court shall maintain a current roster of qualified interpreters certified pursuant to subdivision (f).

CEC 754.5: Privileged statements; deaf or hearing impaired persons; use of interpreter

Whenever an otherwise valid privilege exists between an individual who is deaf or hearing impaired and another person, that privilege is not waived merely because an interpreter was used to facilitate their communication.

CEC 755: Hearings or proceedings related to domestic violence; party not proficient in English; interpreters; fees

(a) In any action or proceeding under Division 10 (commencing with Section 6200) of the Family Code, and in any action or proceeding under the Uniform Parentage Act (Part 3 (commencing with Section 7600) of Division 12 of the Family Code) or for dissolution or nullity of marriage or legal separation of the parties in which a protective order has been granted or is being sought pursuant to Section 6221 of the Family Code, in which a party does not proficiently speak or understand the English language, and that party is present, an interpreter, as provided in this section, shall be present to interpret the proceedings in a language that the party understands, and to assist communication between the party and his or her attorney. Notwithstanding this requirement, a court may issue an ex parte order pursuant to Sections 2045 and 7710 of, and Article 1 (commencing with Section 6320) of Chapter 2 of Part 4 of Division 10 of the Family Code, without the presence of an interpreter. The interpreter selected shall be certified pursuant to Article 4 (commencing with Section 68560) of Chapter 2 of Title 8 of the Government Code, unless the court in its discretion appoints an interpreter who is not certified.

(b) The fees of interpreters utilized under this section shall be paid as provided in subdivision (b) of Section 68092 of the Government Code. However, the fees of an interpreter shall be waived for a party who needs an interpreter and appears in forma pauperis pursuant to Section 68511.3 of the Government Code. The Judicial Council shall amend subdivision (i) of California Rule of Court 985 and revise its forms accordingly by July 1, 1996.

(c) In any civil action in which an interpreter is required under this section, the court shall not commence proceedings until the appointed interpreter is present and situated near the party and his or her attorney. However, this section shall not prohibit the court from doing any of the following:

(1) Issuing an order when the necessity for the order outweighs the necessity for an interpreter.

(2) Extending the duration of a previously issued temporary order if an interpreter is not readily available.

(3) Issuing a permanent order where a party who requires an interpreter fails to make appropriate arrangements for an interpreter after receiving proper notice of the hearing with information about obtaining an interpreter.

(d) This section does not prohibit the presence of any other person to assist a party.

(e) A local public entity may, and the Judicial Council shall, apply to the appropriate state agency that receives federal funds authorized pursuant to the federal Violence Against Women Act (P.L. 103-322) for these federal funds or for funds from sources other than the state to implement this section. A local public entity and the Judicial Council shall comply with the requirements of this section only to the extent that any of these funds are made available.

(f) The Judicial Council shall draft rules and modify forms necessary to implement this section, including those for the petition for a temporary restraining order and related forms, to inform both parties of their right to an interpreter pursuant to this section.

CEC 755.5: Medical examinations; parties not proficient in English language; interpreters; fees; admissibility of record

(a) During any medical examination, requested by an insurer or by the defendant, of a person who is a party to a civil action and who does not proficiently speak or understand the English language, conducted for the purpose of determining damages in a civil action, an interpreter shall be present to interpret the examination in a language that the person understands. The interpreter shall be certified pursuant to Article 8 (commencing with Section 11435.05) of Chapter 4.5 of Part 1 of Division 3 of Title 2 of the Government Code.

(b) The fees of interpreters used under subdivision (a) shall be paid by the insurer or defendant requesting the medical examination.

(c) The record of, or testimony concerning, any medical examination conducted in violation of subdivision (a) shall be inadmissible in the civil action for which it was conducted or any other civil action.

(d) This section does not prohibit the presence of any other person to assist a party.

(e) In the event that interpreters certified pursuant to Article 8 (commencing with Section 11435.05) of Chapter 4.5 of Part 1 of Division 3 of Title 2 of the Government Code cannot be present at the medical examination, upon stipulation of the parties the requester specified in subdivision (a) shall have the discretionary authority to provisionally qualify and use other interpreters.

CEC 760: Direct examination

"Direct examination" is the first examination of a witness upon a matter that is not within the scope of a previous examination of the witness.

CEC 761: Cross-examination

"Cross-examination" is the examination of a witness by a party other than the direct examiner upon a matter that is within the scope of the direct examination of the witness.

CEC 762: Redirect examination

"Redirect examination" is an examination of a witness by the direct examiner subsequent to the cross-examination of the witness.

CEC 763: Recross-examination

"Recross-examination" is an examination of a witness by a cross-examiner subsequent to a redirect examination of the witness.

CEC 764: Leading question

A "leading question" is a question that suggests to the witness the answer that the examining party desires.

CEC 770: Evidence of inconsistent statement of witness; exclusion; exceptions

Unless the interests of justice otherwise require, extrinsic evidence of a statement made by a witness that is inconsistent with any part of his testimony at the hearing shall be excluded unless:

(a) The witness was so examined while testifying as to give him an opportunity to explain or to deny the statement; or

(b) The witness has not been excused from giving further testimony in the action.

CEC 772: Order of examination

(a) The examination of a witness shall proceed in the following phases: direct examination, cross-examination, redirect examination, recross-examination, and continuing thereafter by redirect and recross-examination.

(b) Unless for good cause the court otherwise directs, each phase of the examination of a witness must be concluded before the succeeding phase begins.

(c) Subject to subdivision (d), a party may, in the discretion of the court, interrupt his cross-examination, redirect examination, or recross-examination of a witness, in order to examine the witness upon a matter not within the scope of a previous examination of the witness.

(d) If the witness is the defendant in a criminal action, the witness may not, without his consent, be examined under direct examination by another party.

CEC 773: Cross-examination

(a) A witness examined by one party may be cross-examined upon any matter within the scope of the direct examination by each other party to the action in such order as the court directs.

(b) The cross-examination of a witness by any party whose interest is not adverse to the party calling him is subject to the same rules that are applicable to the direct examination.

CEC 775: Court may call witnesses

The court, on its own motion or on the motion of any party, may call witnesses and interrogate them the same as if they had been produced by a party to the action, and the parties may object to the questions asked and the evidence adduced the same as if such witnesses were called and examined by an adverse party. Such witnesses may be cross-examined by all parties to the action in such order as the court directs.

CEC 782: Sexual offenses; evidence of sexual conduct of complaining witness; procedure for admissibility; treatment of resealed affidavits

(a) In any of the circumstances described in subdivision (c), if evidence of sexual conduct of the complaining witness is offered to attack the credibility of the complaining witness under Section 780, the following procedure shall be followed:

(1) A written motion shall be made by the defendant to the court and prosecutor stating that the defense has an offer of proof of the relevancy of evidence of the sexual conduct of the complaining witness

proposed to be presented and its relevancy in attacking the credibility of the complaining witness.

(2) The written motion shall be accompanied by an affidavit in which the offer of proof shall be stated. The affidavit shall be filed under seal and only unsealed by the court to determine if the offer of proof is sufficient to order a hearing pursuant to paragraph (3). After that determination, the affidavit shall be resealed by the court.

(3) If the court finds that the offer of proof is sufficient, the court shall order a hearing out of the presence of the jury, if any, and at the hearing allow the questioning of the complaining witness regarding the offer of proof made by the defendant.

(4) At the conclusion of the hearing, if the court finds that evidence proposed to be offered by the defendant regarding the sexual conduct of the complaining witness is relevant pursuant to Section 780, and is not inadmissible pursuant to Section 352, the court may make an order stating what evidence may be introduced by the defendant, and the nature of the questions to be permitted. The defendant may then offer evidence pursuant to the order of the court.

(5) An affidavit resealed by the court pursuant to paragraph (2) shall remain sealed, unless the defendant raises an issue on appeal or collateral review relating to the offer of proof contained in the sealed document. If the defendant raises that issue on appeal, the court shall allow the Attorney General and appellate counsel for the defendant access to the sealed affidavit. If the issue is raised on collateral review, the court shall allow the district attorney and defendant's counsel access to the sealed affidavit. The use of the information contained in the affidavit shall be limited solely to the pending proceeding.

(b) As used in this section, "complaining witness" means:

(1) The alleged victim of the crime charged, the prosecution of which is subject to this section, pursuant to paragraph (1) of subdivision (c).

(2) An alleged victim offering testimony pursuant to paragraph (2) or (3) of subdivision (c).

(c) The procedure provided by subdivision (a) shall apply in any of the following circumstances:

(1) In a prosecution under Section 261, 262, 264.1, 286, 288, 288a, 288.5, or 289 of the Penal Code, or for assault with intent to commit, attempt to commit, or conspiracy to commit any crime defined in any of those sections, except if the crime is alleged to have occurred in a local detention facility, as defined in Section 6031.4 of the Penal Code, or in the state prison, as defined in Section 4504.

(2) When an alleged victim testifies pursuant to subdivision (b) of Section 1101 as a victim of a crime listed in Section 243.4, 261,

261.5, 269, 285, 286, 288, 288a, 288.5, 289, 314, or 647.6 of the Penal Code, except if the crime is alleged to have occurred in a local detention facility, as defined in Section 6031.4 of the Penal Code, or in the state prison, as defined in Section 4504 of the Penal Code.

(3) When an alleged victim of a sexual offense testifies pursuant to Section 1108, except if the crime is alleged to have occurred in a local detention facility, as defined in Section 6031.4 of the Penal Code, or in the state prison, as defined in Section 4504 of the Penal Code.

CEC 788: Prior felony conviction

For the purpose of attacking the credibility of a witness, it may be shown by the examination of the witness or by the record of the judgment that he has been convicted of a felony unless:

(a) A pardon based on his innocence has been granted to the witness by the jurisdiction in which he was convicted.

(b) A certificate of rehabilitation and pardon has been granted to the witness under the provisions of Chapter 3.5 (commencing with Section 4852.01) of Title 6 of Part 3 of the Penal Code.

(c) The accusatory pleading against the witness has been dismissed under the provisions of Penal Code Section 1203.4, but this exception does not apply to any criminal trial where the witness is being prosecuted for a subsequent offense.

(d) The conviction was under the laws of another jurisdiction and the witness has been relieved of the penalties and disabilities arising from the conviction pursuant to a procedure substantially equivalent to that referred to in subdivision (b) or (c).

CEC 791: Prior consistent statement of witness

Evidence of a statement previously made by a witness that is consistent with his testimony at the hearing is inadmissible to support his credibility unless it is offered after:

(a) Evidence of a statement made by him that is inconsistent with any part of his testimony at the hearing has been admitted for the purpose of attacking his credibility, and the statement was made before the alleged inconsistent statement; or

(b) An express or implied charge has been made that his testimony at the hearing is recently fabricated or is influenced by bias or other improper motive, and the statement was made before the bias, motive for fabrication, or other improper motive is alleged to have arisen.

CEC 795: Testimony of hypnosis subject; admissibility; conditions

(a) The testimony of a witness is not inadmissible in a criminal proceeding by reason of the fact that the witness has previously undergone hypnosis for the purpose of recalling events that are the subject of the witness's testimony, if all of the following conditions are met:

(1) The testimony is limited to those matters that the witness recalled and related prior to the hypnosis.

(2) The substance of the prehypnotic memory was preserved in a writing, audio recording, or video recording prior to the hypnosis.

(3) The hypnosis was conducted in accordance with all of the following procedures:

(A) A written record was made prior to hypnosis documenting the subject's description of the event, and information that was provided to the hypnotist concerning the subject matter of the hypnosis.

(B) The subject gave informed consent to the hypnosis.

(C) The hypnosis session, including the pre- and post-hypnosis interviews, was video recorded for subsequent review.

(D) The hypnosis was performed by a licensed medical doctor, psychologist, licensed clinical social worker, or a licensed marriage and family therapist experienced in the use of hypnosis and independent of and not in the presence of law enforcement, the prosecution, or the defense.

(4) Prior to admission of the testimony, the court holds a hearing pursuant to Section 402 at which the proponent of the evidence proves by clear and convincing evidence that the hypnosis did not so affect the witness as to render the witness's prehypnosis recollection unreliable or to substantially impair the ability to cross-examine the witness concerning the witness's prehypnosis recollection. At the hearing, each side shall have the right to present expert testimony and to cross-examine witnesses.

(b) Nothing in this section shall be construed to limit the ability of a party to attack the credibility of a witness who has undergone hypnosis, or to limit other legal grounds to admit or exclude the testimony of that witness.

CEC 804: Opinion based on opinion or statement of another

(a) If a witness testifying as an expert testifies that his opinion is based in whole or in part upon the opinion or statement of another person, such other person may be called and examined by any adverse party as if under cross-examination concerning the opinion or statement.

(b) This section is not applicable if the person upon whose opinion or statement the expert witness has relied is (1) a party, (2) a person identified with a party within the meaning of subdivision (d) of Section 776, or (3) a witness who has testified in the action concerning the subject matter of the opinion or statement upon which the expert witness has relied.

(c) Nothing in this section makes admissible an expert opinion that is inadmissible because it is based in whole or in part on the opinion or statement of another person.

(d) An expert opinion otherwise admissible is not made inadmissible by this section because it is based on the opinion or statement of a person who is unavailable for examination pursuant to this section.

CEC 810: Application of article

(a) Except where another rule is provided by statute, this article provides special rules of evidence applicable to any action in which the value of property is to be ascertained.

(b) This article does not govern ad valorem property tax assessment or equalization proceedings.

CEC 811: Value of property

As used in this article, "value of property" means market value of any of the following:

(a) Real property or any interest therein.

(b) Real property or any interest therein and tangible personal property valued as a unit.

CEC 812: Market value; interpretation of meaning

This article is not intended to alter or change the existing substantive law, whether statutory or decisional, interpreting the meaning of "market value," whether denominated "fair market value" or otherwise.

CEC 813: Value of property; authorized opinions; view of property; admissible evidence

(a) The value of property may be shown only by the opinions of any of the following:

(1) Witnesses qualified to express such opinions.

(2) The owner or the spouse of the owner of the property or property interest being valued.

(3) An officer, regular employee, or partner designated by a corporation, partnership, or unincorporated association that is the owner of the property or property interest being valued, if the designee is knowledgeable as to the value of the property or property interest.

(b) Nothing in this section prohibits a view of the property being valued or the admission of any other admissible evidence (including but not limited to evidence as to the nature and condition of the property and, in an eminent domain proceeding, the character of the improvement proposed to be constructed by the plaintiff) for the limited purpose of enabling the court, jury, or referee to understand and weigh the testimony given under subdivision (a); and such evidence, except evidence of the character of the improvement proposed to be constructed by the plaintiff in an eminent domain proceeding, is subject to impeachment and rebuttal.

(c) For the purposes of subdivision (a), "owner of the property or property interest being valued" includes, but is not limited to, the following persons:

(1) A person entitled to possession of the property.

(2) Either party in an action or proceeding to determine the ownership of the property between the parties if the court determines that it would not be in the interest of efficient administration of justice to determine the issue of ownership prior to the admission of the opinion of the party.

CEC 814: Matter upon which opinion must be based

The opinion of a witness as to the value of property is limited to such an opinion as is based on matter perceived by or personally known to the witness or made known to the witness at or before the hearing, whether or not admissible, that is of a type that reasonably may be relied upon by an expert in forming an opinion as to the value of property, including but not limited to the matters listed in Sections 815 to 821, inclusive, unless a witness is precluded by law from using such matter as a basis for an opinion.

CEC 815: Sales of subject property

When relevant to the determination of the value of property, a witness may take into account as a basis for an opinion the price and other terms and circumstances of any sale or contract to sell and purchase which included the property or property interest being valued or any part thereof if the sale or contract was freely made in good faith within a reasonable time before or after the date of valuation, except that in an eminent domain proceeding where the sale or contract to sell and purchase includes only the property or property interest being taken or a part thereof, such sale or contract to sell and purchase may not be taken into account if it occurs after the filing of the lis pendens.

CEC 816: Comparable sales

When relevant to the determination of the value of property, a witness may take into account as a basis for his opinion the price and other terms and circumstances of any sale or contract to sell and purchase comparable property if the sale or contract was freely made in good faith within a reasonable time before or after the date of valuation. In order to be considered comparable, the sale or contract must have been made sufficiently near in time to the date of valuation, and the property sold must be located sufficiently near the property being valued, and must be sufficiently alike in respect to character, size, situation, usability, and improvements, to make it clear that the property sold and the property being valued are comparable in value and that the price realized for the property sold may fairly be considered as shedding light on the value of the property being valued.

CEC 817: Leases of subject property

(a) Subject to subdivision (b), when relevant to the determination of the value of property, a witness may take into account as a basis for an opinion the rent reserved and other terms and circumstances of any lease which included the property or property interest being valued or any part thereof which was in effect within a reasonable time before or after the date of valuation, except that in an eminent domain proceeding where the lease includes only the property or property interest being taken or a part thereof, such lease may not be taken into account in the determination of the value of property if it is entered into after the filing of the lis pendens.

(b) A witness may take into account a lease providing for a rental fixed by a percentage or other measurable portion of gross sales or gross income from a business conducted on the leased property only for the purpose of arriving at an opinion as to the reasonable net rental value attributable to the property or property interest being valued as provided in Section 819 or determining the value of a leasehold interest.

CEC 818: Comparable leases

For the purpose of determining the capitalized value of the reasonable net rental value attributable to the property or property interest being valued as provided in Section 819 or determining the value of a leasehold interest, a witness may take into account as a basis for his opinion the rent reserved and other terms and circumstances of any lease of comparable property if the lease was freely made in good faith within a reasonable time before or after the date of valuation.

CEC 819: Capitalization of income

When relevant to the determination of the value of property, a witness may take into account as a basis for his opinion the capitalized value of the reasonable net rental value attributable to the land and existing improvements thereon (as distinguished from the capitalized value of the income or profits attributable to the business conducted thereon).

CEC 820: Reproduction cost

When relevant to the determination of the value of property, a witness may take into account as a basis for his opinion the value of the property or property interest being valued as indicated by the value of the land together with the cost of replacing or reproducing the existing improvements thereon, if the improvements enhance the value of the property or property interest for its highest and best use, less whatever depreciation or obsolescence the improvements have suffered.

CEC 821: Conditions in general vicinity of subject property

When relevant to the determination of the value of property, a witness may take into account as a basis for his opinion the nature of the improvements on properties in the general vicinity of the property or property interest being valued and the character of the existing uses being made of such properties.

CEC 822: Matter upon which opinion may not be based

(a) In an eminent domain or inverse condemnation proceeding, notwithstanding the provisions of Sections 814 to 821, inclusive, the following matter is inadmissible as evidence and shall not be taken into account as a basis for an opinion as to the value of property:

(1) The price or other terms and circumstances of an acquisition of property or a property interest if the acquisition was for a public use for which the property could have been taken by eminent domain.

The price or other terms and circumstances shall not be excluded pursuant to this paragraph if the proceeding relates to the valuation of all or part of a water system as defined in Section 240 of the Public Utilities Code.

(2) The price at which an offer or option to purchase or lease the property or property interest being valued or any other property was made, or the price at which the property or interest was optioned, offered, or listed for sale or lease, except that an option, offer, or listing may be introduced by a party as an admission of another party to the proceeding; but nothing in this subdivision permits an admission to be

used as direct evidence upon any matter that may be shown only by opinion evidence under Section 813.

(3) The value of any property or property interest as assessed for taxation purposes or the amount of taxes which may be due on the property, but nothing in this subdivision prohibits the consideration of actual or estimated taxes for the purpose of determining the reasonable net rental value attributable to the property or property interest being valued.

(4) An opinion as to the value of any property or property interest other than that being valued.

(5) The influence upon the value of the property or property interest being valued of any noncompensable items of value, damage, or injury.

(6) The capitalized value of the income or rental from any property or property interest other than that being valued.

(b) In an action other than an eminent domain or inverse condemnation proceeding, the matters listed in subdivision (a) are not admissible as evidence, and may not be taken into account as a basis for an opinion as to the value of property, except to the extent permitted under the rules of law otherwise applicable.

CEC 823: Property with no relevant, comparable market

Notwithstanding any other provision of this article, the value of property for which there is no relevant, comparable market may be determined by any method of valuation that is just and equitable.

CEC 824: Nonprofit, special use property

(a) Notwithstanding any other provision of this article, a just and equitable method of determining the value of nonprofit, special use property, as defined by Section 1235.155 of the Code of Civil Procedure, for which there is no relevant, comparable market, is the cost of purchasing land and the reasonable cost of making it suitable for the conduct of the same nonprofit, special use, together with the cost of constructing similar improvements. The method for determining compensation for improvements shall be as set forth in subdivision (b).

(b) Notwithstanding any other provision of this article, a witness providing opinion testimony on the value of nonprofit, special use property, as defined by Section 1235.155 of the Code of Civil Procedure, for which there is no relevant, comparable market, shall base his or her opinion on the value of reproducing the improvements without taking into consideration any depreciation or obsolescence of the improvements.

(c) This section does not apply to actions or proceedings commenced by a public entity or public utility to acquire real property or any interest in real property for the use of water, sewer, electricity, telephone, natural gas, or flood control facilities or rights-of-way where those acquisitions neither require removal or destruction of existing improvements, nor render the property unfit for the owner's present or proposed use.

CEC 870: Opinion as to sanity

A witness may state his opinion as to the sanity of a person when:

(a) The witness is an intimate acquaintance of the person whose sanity is in question;

(b) The witness was a subscribing witness to a writing, the validity of which is in dispute, signed by the person whose sanity is in question and the opinion relates to the sanity of such person at the time the writing was signed; or

(c) The witness is qualified under Section 800 or 801 to testify in the form of an opinion.

CEC 911: Refusal to be or have another as witness, or disclose or produce any matter

Except as otherwise provided by statute:

(a) No person has a privilege to refuse to be a witness.

(b) No person has a privilege to refuse to disclose any matter or to refuse to produce any writing, object, or other thing.

(c) No person has a privilege that another shall not be a witness or shall not disclose any matter or shall not produce any writing, object, or other thing.

CEC 912: Waiver of privilege

(a) Except as otherwise provided in this section, the right of any person to claim a privilege provided by Section 954 (lawyer-client privilege), 980 (privilege for confidential marital communications), 994 (physician-patient privilege), 1014 (psychotherapist-patient privilege), 1033 (privilege of penitent), 1034 (privilege of clergyman), 1035.8 (sexual assault counselor-victim privilege), or 1037.5 (domestic violence counselor-victim privilege) is waived with respect to a communication protected by the privilege if any holder of the privilege, without coercion, has disclosed a significant part of the communication or has consented to disclosure made by anyone. Consent to disclosure is manifested by any statement or other conduct of the holder of the privilege indicating consent to the disclosure, including failure to claim the privilege in any proceeding in which the holder has the legal standing and opportunity to claim the privilege.

(b) Where two or more persons are joint holders of a privilege provided by Section 954 (lawyer-client privilege), 994 (physician-patient privilege), 1014 (psychotherapist-patient privilege), 1035.8 (sexual assault counselor-victim privilege), or 1037.5 (domestic violence counselor-victim privilege), a waiver of the right of a particular joint holder of the privilege to claim the privilege does not affect the right of another joint holder to claim the privilege. In the case of the privilege provided by Section 980 (privilege for confidential marital communications), a waiver of the right of one spouse to claim the privilege does not affect the right of the other spouse to claim the privilege.

(c) A disclosure that is itself privileged is not a waiver of any privilege.

(d) A disclosure in confidence of a communication that is protected by a privilege provided by Section 954 (lawyer-client privilege), 994 (physician-patient privilege), 1014 (psychotherapist-patient privilege), 1035.8 (sexual assault counselor-victim privilege), or 1037.5 (domestic violence counselor-victim privilege), when disclosure is reasonably necessary for the accomplishment of the purpose for which the lawyer, physician, psychotherapist, sexual assault counselor, or domestic violence counselor was consulted, is not a waiver of the privilege.

CEC 913: Comment on, and inferences from, exercise of privilege

(a) If in the instant proceeding or on a prior occasion a privilege is or was exercised not to testify with respect to any matter, or to refuse to disclose or to prevent another from disclosing any matter, neither the presiding officer nor counsel may comment thereon, no presumption shall arise because of the exercise of the privilege, and the trier of fact may not draw any inference therefrom as to the credibility of the witness or as to any matter at issue in the proceeding.

(b) The court, at the request of a party who may be adversely affected because an unfavorable inference may be drawn by the jury because a privilege has been exercised, shall instruct the jury that no presumption arises because of the exercise of the privilege and that the jury may not draw any inference therefrom as to the credibility of the witness or as to any matter at issue in the proceeding.

CEC 915: Disclosure of privileged information or attorney work product in ruling on claim of privilege

(a) Subject to subdivision (b), the presiding officer may not require disclosure of information claimed to be privileged under this division or attorney work product under subdivision (a) of Section 2018.030 of the Code of Civil Procedure in order to rule on the claim of privilege; provided, however, that in any hearing conducted pursuant to subdivision (c) of Section 1524 of the Penal Code in which a claim of privilege is made and the court determines that there is no other feasible means to rule on the validity of the claim other than to require disclosure, the court shall proceed in accordance with subdivision (b).

(b) When a court is ruling on a claim of privilege under Article 9 (commencing with Section 1040) of Chapter 4 (official information and identity of informer) or under Section 1060 (trade secret) or under subdivision (b) of Section 2018.030 of the Code of Civil Procedure (attorney work product) and is unable to do so without requiring disclosure of the information claimed to be privileged, the court may require the person from whom disclosure is sought or the person authorized to claim the privilege, or both, to disclose the information in chambers out of the presence and hearing of all persons except the person authorized to claim the privilege and any other persons as the person authorized to claim the privilege is willing to have present. If the judge determines that the information is privileged, neither the judge nor any other person may ever disclose, without the consent of a person authorized to permit disclosure, what was disclosed in the course of the proceedings in chambers.

CEC 950: Lawyer

As used in this article, "lawyer" means a person authorized, or reasonably believed by the client to be authorized, to practice law in any state or nation.

CEC 956: Exception: Crime or fraud

There is no privilege under this article if the services of the lawyer were sought or obtained to enable or aid anyone to commit or plan to commit a crime or a fraud.

CEC 956.5: Exception: Prevention of criminal act likely to result in death or substantial bodily harm

There is no privilege under this article if the lawyer reasonably believes that disclosure of any confidential communication relating to representation of a client is necessary to prevent a criminal act that the lawyer reasonably believes is likely to result in the death of, or substantial bodily harm to, an individual.

CEC 957: Exception: Parties claiming through deceased client

There is no privilege under this article as to a communication relevant to an issue between parties all of whom claim through a deceased client, regardless of whether the claims are by testate or intestate succession, non-probate transfer, or inter vivos transaction.

CEC 958: Exception: Breach of duty arising out of lawyer-client relationship

There is no privilege under this article as to a communication relevant to an issue of breach, by the lawyer or by the client, of a duty arising out of the lawyer-client relationship.

CEC 959: Exception: Lawyer as attesting witness

There is no privilege under this article as to a communication relevant to an issue concerning the intention or competence of a client executing an attested document of which the lawyer is an attesting witness, or concerning the execution or attestation of such a document.

CEC 972: Exceptions to privilege

A married person does not have a privilege under this article in:

(a) A proceeding brought by or on behalf of one spouse against the other spouse.

(b) A proceeding to commit or otherwise place his or her spouse or his or her spouse's property, or both, under the control of another because of the spouse's alleged mental or physical condition.

(c) A proceeding brought by or on behalf of a spouse to establish his or her competence.

(d) A proceeding under the Juvenile Court Law, Chapter 2 (commencing with Section 200) of Part 1 of Division 2 of the Welfare and Institutions Code.

(e) A criminal proceeding in which one spouse is charged with:

(1) A crime against the person or property of the other spouse or of a child, parent, relative, or cohabitant of either, whether committed before or during marriage.

(2) A crime against the person or property of a third person committed in the course of committing a crime against the person or property of the other spouse, whether committed before or during marriage.

(3) Bigamy.

(4) A crime defined by Section 270 or 270a of the Penal Code.

(f) A proceeding resulting from a criminal act which occurred prior to legal marriage of the spouses to each other regarding knowledge acquired prior to that marriage if prior to the legal marriage the witness spouse was aware that his or her spouse had been arrested for or had been formally charged with the crime or crimes about which the spouse is called to testify.

(g) A proceeding brought against the spouse by a former spouse so long as the property and debts of the marriage have not been adjudicated, or in order to establish, modify, or enforce a child, family or spousal support obligation arising from the marriage to the former spouse; in a proceeding brought against a spouse by the other parent in order to establish, modify, or enforce a child support obligation for a child of a nonmarital relationship of the spouse; or in a proceeding brought against a spouse by the guardian of a child of that spouse in order to establish, modify, or enforce a child support obligation of the spouse. The married person does not have a privilege under this subdivision to refuse to provide information relating to the issues of income, expenses, assets, debts, and employment of either spouse, but may assert the privilege as otherwise provided in this article if other information is requested by the former spouse, guardian, or other parent of the child.

Any person demanding the otherwise privileged information made available by this subdivision, who also has an obligation to support the child for whom an order to establish, modify, or enforce child support is sought, waives his or her marital privilege to the same extent as the spouse as provided in this subdivision.

CEC 990: Physician

As used in this article, "physician" means a person authorized, or reasonably believed by the patient to be authorized, to practice medicine in any state or nation.

CEC 994: Physician-patient privilege

Subject to Section 912 and except as otherwise provided in this article, the patient, whether or not a party, has a privilege to refuse to disclose, and to prevent another from disclosing, a confidential communication between patient and physician if the privilege is claimed by:

(a) The holder of the privilege;

(b) A person who is authorized to claim the privilege by the holder of the privilege; or

(c) The person who was the physician at the time of the confidential communication, but such person may not claim the privilege if there is no holder of the privilege in existence or if he or she is otherwise instructed by a person authorized to permit disclosure.

The relationship of a physician and patient shall exist between a medical or podiatry corporation as defined in the Medical Practice Act and the patient to whom it renders professional services, as well as between such patients and licensed physicians and surgeons employed by such corporation to render services to such patients. The word "persons" as used in this subdivision includes partnerships, corporations, limited liability companies, associations, and other groups and entities.

CEC 997: Exception: Crime or tort

There is no privilege under this article if the services of the physician were sought or obtained to enable or aid anyone to commit or plan to commit a crime or a tort or to escape detection or apprehension after the commission of a crime or a tort.

CEC 998: Criminal proceeding

There is no privilege under this article in a criminal proceeding.

CEC 1002: Intention of deceased patient concerning writing affecting property interest

There is no privilege under this article as to a communication relevant to an issue concerning the intention of a patient, now deceased, with respect to a deed of conveyance, will, or other writing, executed by the patient, purporting to affect an interest in property.

CEC 1003: Validity of writing affecting property interest

There is no privilege under this article as to a communication relevant to an issue concerning the validity of a deed of conveyance, will, or other writing, executed by a patient, now deceased, purporting to affect an interest in property.

CEC 1010: Psychotherapist

As used in this article, "psychotherapist" means a person who is, or is reasonably believed by the patient to be:

(a) A person authorized to practice medicine in any state or nation who devotes, or is reasonably believed by the patient to devote, a substantial portion of his or her time to the practice of psychiatry.

(b) A person licensed as a psychologist under Chapter 6.6 (commencing with Section 2900) of Division 2 of the Business and Professions Code.

(c) A person licensed as a clinical social worker under Article 4 (commencing with Section 4996) of Chapter 14 of Division 2 of the Business and Professions Code, when he or she is engaged in applied psychotherapy of a nonmedical nature.

(d) A person who is serving as a school psychologist and holds a credential authorizing that service issued by the state.

(e) A person licensed as a marriage and family therapist under Chapter 13 (commencing with Section 4980) of Division 2 of the Business and Professions Code.

(f) A person registered as a psychological assistant who is under the supervision of a licensed psychologist or board certified psychiatrist as required by Section 2913 of the Business and Professions Code, or a person registered as a marriage and family therapist intern who is under the supervision of a licensed marriage and family therapist, a licensed clinical social worker, a licensed psychologist, or a licensed physician certified in psychiatry, as specified in Section 4980.44 of the Business and Professions Code.

(g) A person registered as an associate clinical social worker who is under the supervision of a licensed clinical social worker, a licensed psychologist, or a board certified psychiatrist as required by Section 4996.20 or 4996.21 of the Business and Professions Code.

(h) A person exempt from the Psychology Licensing Law pursuant to subdivision (d) of Section 2909 of the Business and Professions Code who is under the supervision of a licensed psychologist or board certified psychiatrist.

(i) A psychological intern as defined in Section 2911 of the Business and Professions Code who is under the supervision of a licensed psychologist or board certified psychiatrist.

(j) A trainee, as defined in subdivision (c) of Section 4980.03 of the Business and Professions Code, who is fulfilling his or her supervised practicum required by subparagraph (B) of paragraph (1) of subdivision (d) of Section 4980.36 of, or subdivision (c) of Section 4980.37 of, the Business and Professions Code and is supervised by a licensed psychologist, board certified psychiatrist, a licensed clinical social worker, or a licensed marriage and family therapist.

(k) A person licensed as a registered nurse pursuant to Chapter 6 (commencing with Section 2700) of Division 2 of the Business and

Professions Code, who possesses a master's degree in psychiatric-mental health nursing and is listed as a psychiatric-mental health nurse by the Board of Registered Nursing.

(l) An advanced practice registered nurse who is certified as a clinical nurse specialist pursuant to Article 9 (commencing with Section 2838) of Chapter 6 of Division 2 of the Business and Professions Code and who participates in expert clinical practice in the specialty of psychiatric-mental health nursing.

(m) A person rendering mental health treatment or counseling services as authorized pursuant to Section 6924 of the Family Code.

CEC 1024: Exception: Patient dangerous to himself or others

There is no privilege under this article if the psychotherapist has reasonable cause to believe that the patient is in such mental or emotional condition as to be dangerous to himself or to the person or property of another and that disclosure of the communication is necessary to prevent the threatened danger.

CEC 1027: Exception: Child under 16 victim of crime

There is no privilege under this article if all of the following circumstances exist:

(a) The patient is a child under the age of 16.

(b) The psychotherapist has reasonable cause to believe that the patient has been the victim of a crime and that disclosure of the communication is in the best interest of the child.

CEC 1030: Member of the clergy

As used in this article, a "member of the clergy" means a priest, minister, religious practitioner, or similar functionary of a church or of a religious denomination or religious organization.

CEC 1033: Privilege of penitent

Subject to Section 912, a penitent, whether or not a party, has a privilege to refuse to disclose, and to prevent another from disclosing, a penitential communication if he or she claims the privilege.

CEC 1042: Adverse order or finding in certain cases

(a) Except where disclosure is forbidden by an act of the Congress of the United States, if a claim of privilege under this article by the state or a public entity in this state is sustained in a criminal proceeding, the presiding officer shall make such order or finding of fact adverse to the public entity bringing the proceeding as is required by law upon any issue in the proceeding to which the privileged information is material.

(b) Notwithstanding subdivision (a), where a search is made pursuant to a warrant valid on its face, the public entity bringing a criminal proceeding is not required to reveal to the defendant official information or the identity of an informer in order to establish the legality of the search or the admissibility of any evidence obtained as a result of it.

(c) Notwithstanding subdivision (a), in any preliminary hearing, criminal trial, or other criminal proceeding, any otherwise admissible evidence of information communicated to a peace officer by a confidential informant, who is not a material witness to the guilt or innocence of the accused of the offense charged, is admissible on the issue of reasonable cause to make an arrest or search without requiring that the name or identity of the informant be disclosed if the judge or magistrate is satisfied, based upon evidence produced in open court, out of the presence of the jury, that such information was received from a reliable informant and in his discretion does not require such disclosure.

(d) When, in any such criminal proceeding, a party demands disclosure of the identity of the informant on the ground the informant is a material witness on the issue of guilt, the court shall conduct a hearing at which all parties may present evidence on the issue of disclosure. Such hearing shall be conducted outside the presence of the jury, if any. During the hearing, if the privilege provided for in Section 1041 is claimed by a person authorized to do so or if a person who is authorized to claim such privilege refuses to answer any question on the ground that the answer would tend to disclose the identity of the informant, the prosecuting attorney may request that the court hold an in camera hearing. If such a request is made, the court shall hold such a hearing outside the presence of the defendant and his counsel. At the in camera hearing, the prosecution may offer evidence which would tend to disclose or which discloses the identity of the informant to aid the court in its determination whether there is a reasonable possibility that nondisclosure might deprive the defendant of a fair trial. A reporter shall be present at the in camera hearing. Any transcription of the proceedings at the in camera hearing, as well as any physical evidence presented at the hearing, shall be ordered sealed by the court, and only a court may have access to its contents. The court shall not order disclosure, nor strike the testimony of the witness who invokes the privilege, nor dismiss the criminal proceeding, if the party offering the witness refuses to disclose the identity of the informant, unless, based upon the evidence presented at the hearing held in the presence of the defendant and his counsel and the evidence presented at the in camera hearing, the court concludes that there is a reasonable possibility that nondisclosure might deprive the defendant of a fair trial.

CEC 1104: Character trait for care or skill

Except as provided in Sections 1102 and 1103, evidence of a trait of a person's character with respect to care or skill is inadmissible to prove the quality of his conduct on a specified occasion.

CEC 1119: Written or oral communications during mediation process; admissibility

Except as otherwise provided in this chapter:

(a) No evidence of anything said or any admission made for the purpose of, in the course of, or pursuant to, a mediation or a mediation consultation is admissible or subject to discovery, and disclosure of the evidence shall not be compelled, in any arbitration, administrative adjudication, civil action, or other noncriminal proceeding in which, pursuant to law, testimony can be compelled to be given.

(b) No writing, as defined in Section 250, that is prepared for the purpose of, in the course of, or pursuant to, a mediation or a mediation consultation, is admissible or subject to discovery, and disclosure of the writing shall not be compelled, in any arbitration, administrative adjudication, civil action, or other noncriminal proceeding in which, pursuant to law, testimony can be compelled to be given.

(c) All communications, negotiations, or settlement discussions by and between participants in the course of a mediation or a mediation consultation shall remain confidential.

CEC 1128: Subsequent trials; references to mediation

Any reference to a mediation during any subsequent trial is an irregularity in the proceedings of the trial for the purposes of Section 657 of the Code of Civil Procedure. Any reference to a mediation during any other subsequent noncriminal proceeding is grounds for vacating or modifying the decision in that proceeding, in whole or in part, and granting a new or further hearing on all or part of the issues, if the reference materially affected the substantial rights of the party requesting relief.

CEC 1150: Evidence to test a verdict

(a) Upon an inquiry as to the validity of a verdict, any otherwise admissible evidence may be received as to statements made, or conduct, conditions, or events occurring, either within or without the jury room, of such a character as is likely to have influenced the verdict improperly. No evidence is admissible to show the effect of such statement, conduct, condition, or event upon a juror either in influencing him to assent to or dissent from the verdict or concerning the mental processes by which it was determined.

(b) Nothing in this code affects the law relating to the competence of a juror to give evidence to impeach or support a verdict.

CEC 1152: Offers to compromise

(a) Evidence that a person has, in compromise or from humanitarian motives, furnished or offered or promised to furnish money or any other thing, act, or service to another who has sustained or will sustain or claims that he or she has sustained or will sustain loss or damage, as well as any conduct or statements made in negotiation thereof, is inadmissible to prove his or her liability for the loss or damage or any part of it.

(b) In the event that evidence of an offer to compromise is admitted in an action for breach of the covenant of good faith and fair dealing or violation of subdivision (h) of Section 790.03 of the Insurance Code, then at the request of the party against whom the evidence is admitted, or at the request of the party who made the offer to compromise that was admitted, evidence relating to any other offer or counteroffer to compromise the same or substantially the same claimed loss or damage shall also be admissible for the same purpose as the initial evidence regarding settlement. Other than as may be admitted in an action for breach of the covenant of good faith and fair dealing or violation of subdivision (h) of Section 790.03 of the Insurance Code, evidence of settlement offers shall not be admitted in a motion for a new trial, in any proceeding involving an additur or remittitur, or on appeal.

(c) This section does not affect the admissibility of evidence of any of the following:

(1) Partial satisfaction of an asserted claim or demand without questioning its validity when such evidence is offered to prove the validity of the claim.

(2) A debtor's payment or promise to pay all or a part of his or her preexisting debt when such evidence is offered to prove the creation of a new duty on his or her part or a revival of his or her preexisting duty.

CEC 1203: Cross-examination of hearsay declarant

(a) The declarant of a statement that is admitted as hearsay evidence may be called and examined by any adverse party as if under cross-examination concerning the statement.

(b) This section is not applicable if the declarant is (1) a party, (2) a person identified with a party within the meaning of subdivision (d) of Section 776, or (3) a witness who has testified in the action concerning the subject matter of the statement.

(c) This section is not applicable if the statement is one described in Article 1 (commencing with Section 1220), Article 3 (commencing with Section 1235), or Article 10 (commencing with Section 1300) of Chapter 2 of this division.

(d) A statement that is otherwise admissible as hearsay evidence is not made inadmissible by this section because the declarant who made the statement is unavailable for examination pursuant to this section.

CEC 1224: Statement of declarant whose liability or breach of duty is in issue

When the liability, obligation, or duty of a party to a civil action is based in whole or in part upon the liability, obligation or duty of the declarant, or when the claim or right asserted by a party to a civil action is barred or diminished by a breach of duty by the declarant, evidence of a statement made by the declarant is as admissible against the party as it would be if offered against the declarant in an action involving that liability, obligation, or breach of duty.

CEC 1225: Statement of declarant whose right or title is in issue

When a right, title, or interest in any property or claim asserted by a party to a civil action requires a determination that a right, title, or interest exists or existed in the declarant, evidence of a statement made by the declarant during the time the party now claims the declarant was the holder of the right, title, or interest is as admissible against the part as it would be if offered against the declarant in an action involving that right, title or interest.

CEC 1231: Prior statements of deceased declarant; hearsay exception

Evidence of a prior statement made by a declarant is not made inadmissible by the hearsay rule if the declarant is deceased and the proponent of introducing the statement establishes each of the following:

(a) The statement relates to acts or events relevant to a criminal prosecution under provisions of the California Street Terrorism Enforcement and Prevention Act (Chapter 11 (commencing with Section 186.20) of Title 7 of Part 1 of the Penal Code).

(b) A verbatim transcript, copy, or record of the statement exists. A record may include a statement preserved by means of an audio or video recording or equivalent technology.

(c) The statement relates to acts or events within the personal knowledge of the declarant.

(d) The statement was made under oath or affirmation in an affidavit; or was made at a deposition, preliminary hearing, grand jury hearing, or other proceeding in compliance with law, and was made under penalty of perjury.

(e) The declarant died from other than natural causes.

(f) The statement was made under circumstances that would indicate its trustworthiness and render the declarant's statement particularly worthy of belief. For purposes of this subdivision, circumstances relevant to the issue of trustworthiness include, but are not limited to, all of the following:

(1) Whether the statement was made in contemplation of a pending or anticipated criminal or civil matter, in which the declarant had an interest, other than as a witness.

(2) Whether the declarant had a bias or motive for fabricating the statement, and the extent of any bias or motive.

(3) Whether the statement is corroborated by evidence other than statements that are admissible only pursuant to this section.

(4) Whether the statement was a statement against the declarant's interest.

CEC 1293: Former testimony by minor child complaining witness at preliminary examination

(a) Evidence of former testimony made at a preliminary examination by a minor child who was the complaining witness is not made inadmissible by the hearsay rule if:

(1) The former testimony is offered in a proceeding to declare the minor a dependent child of the court pursuant to Section 300 of the Welfare and Institutions Code.

(2) The issues are such that a defendant in the preliminary examination in which the former testimony was given had the right and opportunity to cross-examine the minor child with an interest and motive similar to that which the parent or guardian against whom the testimony is offered has at the proceeding to declare the minor a dependent child of the court.

(b) The admissibility of former testimony under this section is subject to the same limitations and objections as though the minor child were testifying at the proceeding to declare him or her a dependent child of the court.

(c) The attorney for the parent or guardian against whom the former testimony is offered or, if none, the parent or guardian may make a motion to challenge the admissibility of the former testimony upon a showing that new substantially different issues are present in the proceeding to declare the minor a dependent child than were present in the preliminary examination.

(d) As used in this section, "complaining witness" means the alleged victim of the crime for which a preliminary examination was held.

(e) This section shall apply only to testimony made at a preliminary examination on and after January 1, 1990.

CEC 1294: Unavailable witnesses; prior inconsistent statements; preliminary hearing or prior proceeding

(a) The following evidence of prior inconsistent statements of a witness properly admitted in a preliminary hearing or trial of the same criminal matter pursuant to Section 1235 is not made inadmissible by the hearsay rule if the witness is unavailable and former testimony of the witness is admitted pursuant to Section 1291:

(1) A video recorded statement introduced at a preliminary hearing or prior proceeding concerning the same criminal matter.

(2) A transcript, containing the statements, of the preliminary hearing or prior proceeding concerning the same criminal matter.

(b) The party against whom the prior inconsistent statements are offered, at his or her option, may examine or cross-examine any person who testified at the preliminary hearing or prior proceeding as to the prior inconsistent statements of the witness.

CEC 1310: Statement concerning declarant's own family history

(a) Subject to subdivision (b), evidence of a statement by a declarant who is unavailable as a witness concerning his own birth, marriage, divorce, a parent and child relationship, relationship by blood or marriage, race, ancestry, or other similar fact of his family history is not made inadmissible by the hearsay rule, even though the declarant had no means of acquiring personal knowledge of the matter declared.

(b) Evidence of a statement is inadmissible under this section if the statement was made under circumstances such as to indicate its lack of trustworthiness.

CEC 1311: Statement concerning family history of another

(a) Subject to subdivision (b), evidence of a statement concerning the birth, marriage, divorce, death, parent and child relationship, race, ancestry, relationship by blood or marriage, or other similar fact of the family history of a person other than the declarant is not made inadmissible by the hearsay rule if the declarant is unavailable as a witness and:

(1) The declarant was related to the other by blood or marriage; or

(2) The declarant was otherwise so intimately associated with the other's family as to be likely to have had accurate information concerning the matter declared and made the statement (i) upon information received from the other or from a person related by blood or marriage to the other or (ii) upon repute in the other's family.

(b) Evidence of a statement is inadmissible under this section if the statement was made under circumstances such as to indicate its lack of trustworthiness.

CEC 1313: Reputation in family concerning family history

Evidence of reputation among members of a family is not made inadmissible by the hearsay rule if the reputation concerns the birth, marriage, divorce, death, parent and child relationship, race, ancestry, relationship by blood or marriage, or other similar fact of the family history of a member of the family by blood or marriage.

CEC 1314: Reputation in community concerning family history

Evidence of reputation in a community concerning the date or fact of birth, marriage, divorce, or death of a person resident in the community at the time of the reputation is not made inadmissible by the hearsay rule.

CEC 1320: Reputation concerning community history

Evidence of reputation in a community is not made inadmissible by the hearsay rule if the reputation concerns an event of general history of the community or of the state or nation of which the community is a part and the event was of importance to the community.

CEC 1321: Reputation concerning public interest in property

Evidence of reputation in a community is not made inadmissible by the hearsay rule if the reputation concerns the interest of the public in property in the community and the reputation arose before controversy.

CEC 1322: Reputation concerning boundary or custom affecting land

Evidence of reputation in a community is not made inadmissible by the hearsay rule if the reputation concerns boundaries of, or customs affecting, land in the community and the reputation arose before controversy.

CEC 1323: Statement concerning boundary

Evidence of a statement concerning the boundary of land is not made inadmissible by the hearsay rule if the declarant is unavailable as a witness and had sufficient knowledge of the subject, but evidence of a statement is not admissible under this section if the statement was made under circumstances such as to indicate its lack of trustworthiness.

CEC 1324: Reputation concerning character

Evidence of a person's general reputation with reference to his character or a trait of his character at a relevant time in the community in which he then resided or in a group with which he then habitually associated is not made inadmissible by the hearsay rule.

CEC 1402: Authentication of altered writings

The party producing a writing as genuine which has been altered, or appears to have been altered, after its execution, in a part material to the question in dispute, must account for the alteration or appearance thereof. He may show that the alteration was made by another, without his concurrence, or was made with the consent of the parties affected by it, or otherwise properly or innocently made, or that the alteration did not change the meaning or language of the instrument. If he does that, he may give the writing in evidence, but not otherwise.

CEC 1414: Admission of authenticity; acting upon writing as authentic

A writing may be authenticated by evidence that:
(a) The party against whom it is offered has at any time admitted its authenticity; or
(b) The writing has been acted upon as authentic by the party against whom it is offered.

CEC 1420: Authentication by evidence of reply

A writing may be authenticated by evidence that the writing was received in response to a communication sent to the person who is claimed by the proponent of the evidence to be the author of the writing.

CEC 1421: Authentication by content

A writing may be authenticated by evidence that the writing refers to or states matters that are unlikely to be known to anyone other than the person who is claimed by the proponent of the evidence to be the author of the writing.

CEC 1520: Content of writing; proof

The content of a writing may be proved by an otherwise admissible original.

CEC 1552: Printed representation of computer information or computer programs

(a) A printed representation of computer information or a computer program is presumed to be an accurate representation of the computer information or computer program that it purports to represent. This presumption is a presumption affecting the burden of producing evidence. If a party to an action introduces evidence that a printed representation of computer information or computer program is inaccurate or unreliable, the party introducing the printed representation into evidence has the burden of proving, by a preponderance of evidence, that the printed representation is an accurate representation of the existence and content of the computer information or computer program that it purports to represent.

(b) Subdivision (a) shall not apply to computer-generated official records certified in accordance with Section 452.5 or 1530.

CEC 1562: Admissibility of affidavit and copy of records

If the original records would be admissible in evidence if the custodian or other qualified witness had been present and testified to the matters stated in the affidavit, and if the requirements of Section 1271 have been met, the copy of the records is admissible in evidence. The affidavit is admissible as evidence of the matters stated therein pursuant to Section 1561 and the matters so stated are presumed true. When more than one person has knowledge of the facts, more than one affidavit may be made. The presumption established by this section is a presumption affecting the burden of producing evidence.

Table of Hearsay Exceptions with Crossover to the Federal Rules of Evidence

Requirement in CEC	Requirement in FRE	CEC	FRE	Title
Declarant Unavailable	Declarant Unavailable	1230	804(b)(3)	Declaration against interest
Declarant Unavailable	No Direct Comparison	1231	807	Prior statements of deceased declarant; hearsay exception
Declarant Dead	Declarant Unavailable	1242	804(b)(2)	Dying declarations
Declarant Unavailable	Unavailability Immaterial	1251	803(3)	Statement of declarant's previously existing mental or physical state
Declarant Unavailable	Unavailability Immaterial	1260	803(3)	Statement concerning declarant's will
Declarant Dead	Declarant Dead	1261	803(3)	Statement of decedent offered in action against his estate
Declarant Unavailable	Declarant Unavailable	1290	804(b)(1)	Former testimony
Declarant Unavailable	Declarant Unavailable	1291	804(b)(1)	Former testimony offered against party to former proceeding
Declarant Unavailable	Declarant Unavailable	1292	804(b)(1)	Former testimony offered against person not a party to former proceeding
Declarant Unavailable	Declarant Unavailable	1293	804(b)(1)	Former testimony by minor child complaining witness at preliminary examination
Declarant Unavailable	Declarant Unavailable	1294	804(b)(1)	Unavailable witnesses; prior inconsistent statements preliminary hearing or prior proceeding

Requirement in CEC	Requirement in FRE	CEC	FRE	Title
Declarant Unavailable	Declarant Unavailable	1310	804(b)(4)	Statement concerning declarant's own family history
Declarant Unavailable	Declarant Unavailable	1311	804(b)(4)	Statement concerning family history of another
Declarant Unavailable	Declarant Unavailable	1350	804(b)(6)	Unavailable declarant; hearsay rule
Declarant Unavailable	No Direct Comparison	1370	807	Threat of infliction of injury
Declarant Unavailable	No Direct Comparison	1380	807	Elder abuse
Unavailability Immaterial	Unavailability Immaterial	1220	801(d)(2)(A)	Admission of party
Unavailability Immaterial	Unavailability Immaterial	1221	801(d)(2)(B)	Adoptive admission
Unavailability Immaterial	Unavailability Immaterial	1222	801(d)(2)(C)	Authorized admission
Unavailability Immaterial	Unavailability Immaterial	1223	801(d)(2)(E)	Admission of co-conspirator
Unavailability Immaterial	Unavailability Immaterial	1224	801(d)(2)(D)	Statement of declarant whose liability or breach of duty is in issue
Unavailability Immaterial	Unavailability Immaterial	1225	801(d)(2)(D)	Statement of declarant whose right or title is in issue
Unavailability Immaterial	Unavailability Immaterial	1226	801(d)(2)(D)	Statement of minor child in parent's action for child's injury
Unavailability Immaterial	Unavailability Immaterial	1227	801(d)(2)(D)	Statement of declarant in action for his wrongful death
Unavailability Immaterial	No Direct Comparison	1228	807	Admissibility of certain out-of-court statements of minors under the age of 12; establishing elements of certain sexually oriented crimes; notice to defendant
Unavailability Immaterial	Unavailability Immaterial	1235	801(d)(1)(A)	Inconsistent statements
Unavailability Immaterial	Unavailability Immaterial	1236	801(d)(1)(B)	Prior consistent statements
Unavailability Immaterial	Unavailability Immaterial	1237	803(5)	Past recollection recorded

Table of Hearsay Exceptions

Requirement in CEC	Requirement in FRE	CEC	FRE	Title
Unavailability Immaterial	Unavailability Immaterial	1238	801(d)(1)(C)	Prior identification
Unavailability Immaterial	Unavailability Immaterial	1240	803(2)	Spontaneous statement
Unavailability Immaterial	Unavailability Immaterial	1241	803(1)	Contemporaneous statements
Unavailability Immaterial	Unavailability Immaterial	1250	803(3)	Statement of declarant's then existing mental or physical state
Unavailability Immaterial	Unavailability Immaterial	1252	803(3)	Limitation on admissibility of statement of mental or physical state
Unavailability Immaterial	Unavailability Immaterial	1253	803(4)	Statements of purposes of medical diagnosis or treatment contents of statement; child abuse or neglect; age limitations
Unavailability Immaterial	Unavailability Immaterial	1270	803(6)	A business
Unavailability Immaterial	Unavailability Immaterial	1271	803(6)	Business record
Unavailability Immaterial	Unavailability Immaterial	1272	803(7)	Absence of entry in business records
Unavailability Immaterial	Unavailability Immaterial	1280	803(8)	Record by public employee
Unavailability Immaterial	Unavailability Immaterial	1281	803(9)	Record of vital statistic
Unavailability Immaterial	Unavailability Immaterial	1282	803(8)	Finding of presumed death by authorized federal employee
Unavailability Immaterial	Unavailability Immaterial	1283	803(8)	Record by federal employee that person is missing, captured, or the like
Unavailability Immaterial	Unavailability Immaterial	1284	803(10)	Statement of absence of public record
Unavailability Immaterial	Unavailability Immaterial	1300	803(22)	Judgment of conviction of crime punishable as felony
Unavailability Immaterial	Unavailability Immaterial	1301	803(22)	Judgment against person entitled to indemnity
Unavailability Immaterial	Unavailability Immaterial	1302	803(22)	Judgment determining liability of third person

Requirement in CEC	Requirement in FRE	CEC	FRE	Title
Unavailability Immaterial	Unavailability Immaterial	1312	803(13)	Entries in family records and the like
Unavailability Immaterial	Unavailability Immaterial	1313	803(19)	Reputation in family concerning family history
Unavailability Immaterial	Unavailability Immaterial	1314	803(19)	Reputation in community concerning family history
Unavailability Immaterial	Unavailability Immaterial	1315	803(11)	Church records concerning family history
Unavailability Immaterial	Unavailability Immaterial	1316	803(12)	Marriage, baptismal and similar certificates
Unavailability Immaterial	Unavailability Immaterial	1320	803(20)	Reputation concerning community history
Unavailability Immaterial	Unavailability Immaterial	1321	803(20)	Reputation concerning public interest in property
Unavailability Immaterial	Unavailability Immaterial	1322	803(20)	Reputation concerning boundary or custom affecting land
Unavailability Immaterial	Unavailability Immaterial	1323	803(20)	Statement concerning boundary
Unavailability Immaterial	Unavailability Immaterial	1324	803(21)	Reputation concerning character
Unavailability Immaterial	Unavailability Immaterial	1330	803(14)-(15)	Recitals in writing affecting property
Unavailability Immaterial	Unavailability Immaterial	1331	803(16)	Recitals in ancient writings
Unavailability Immaterial	Unavailability Immaterial	1340	803(17)	Commercial lists and the like
Unavailability Immaterial	Unavailability Immaterial	1341	803(18)	Publications concerning facts of general notoriety and interest
Unavailability Immaterial	No Direct Comparison	1360	807	Statements describing an act or attempted act of child abuse or neglect; criminal prosecutions; requirements

Index

Admissions, 164-182
  adoptive, 167-170
    express adoption, 169-170
    implied adoption, 169-170
  authorized, 170-172
  of co-conspirators, 172-175
  of party, 164-167
  silence, 169-170
  tacit, 169-170
Animals
  animal experimentation, evidence of, in
      products liability actions, 87
  statements or assertions by, 100
Assertive conduct, 101
Attorney-client privilege, 352-367
  attesting witness, attorney as, 359-360
  bodily injury, reasonable belief to prevent,
      359
  breach of duty, attorney-client, 359
  claiming of, 357
  client, 353
  communication, defined, 355
  confidential communications, 354-356
  corporate context, 353, 355-356, 362
  disclosures, 357-358
  exceptions, 358-360
  future crime or fraud, 358
  joint clients, 360
  lawyer, requirements regarding, 352-353
  same deceased client through whom others
      are claiming money or property,
      communication with, 359
  third persons, disclosure to, 354
  waiver of, 357-358, 362
Authentication, 326-334, 341
  chain of custody, 330
  defined, 326
  handwriting comparison, 328-329
  of maps, 330
  methods of, 327-329
  of moving pictures, 330
  party admission, 329
  of photographs, 330
  presumptions for, 329
  requirement of, 326
  signature recognition, 328

witness with knowledge, 327-328
  writing, defined, 327

Balancing test
  for exclusion of relevant evidence, 14-22
Battering, expert testimony on, 290
Benevolence
  inadmissibility of expressions of, 84-85
Best Evidence Rule, 325
Beyond a reasonable doubt, 303. See also Burden
    of proof
Burden of persuasion. See Burden of proof
Burden of production, 304-307
  foundational/preliminary facts,
      determination of, 305-306
  meeting the burden, 306-307
  party who has the burden, 304
  preponderance standard, 305-306, 307
  sufficiency standard, 305, 307
Burden of proof, 301-304
  beyond a reasonable doubt, 303
  clear and convincing, 303
  inferences. See Inferences
  instructions on, 302-303
  level of proof, 302
  preponderance of the evidence, 303
  presumptions. See Presumptions
  satisfying the burden, 304
  sufficiency standard, 303-304

Character, defined, 23
Character evidence, 23-73
  admissibility of, generally, 25-26
  character when character is at issue,
      proving, 26
  criminal defendant's character, evidence of
      conduct, proving, 45-48
    other domestic violence crimes,
        admissibility of, 51-53
    other sexual offenses, admissibility of,
        48-51
  dangers of, 24
  domestic violence crimes of
      criminal defendant, 51-53
  exceptions to ban on, 44-65
  kinds of, 34-37

Character evidence (*continued*)
  opinion evidence, 34
  reputation evidence, 34-35
  sexual offenses of criminal defendant, 48-51
  specific instances evidence, 36-37
  uses of
    absence of accident, 33
    absence of mistake, 32-33
    common plan or scheme, 31-32
    conduct in conformity with that character
      on particular occasion, 27-28
    consent, 33
    identity, 30
    intent, 31
    motive, 31
    opportunity, 32
    preparation, 30-31
    to prove something other than character
      or conduct in conformity, 28-33
  victim's character, evidence of
    rape shield laws, 61
    sexual abuse, civil cases alleging, 63-65
    sexual offenses, 61-63
    specialized knowledge, 33
    use by defendant to prove
      victim's conduct, 57-59
    use by prosecution to rebut evidence
      adduced by defendant, 57-59
Circumstantial evidence
  defined, 16
  probative value of, 16-17
Clear and convincing, 303. *See also* Burden of
  proof
Clergy-penitent privilege, 402-406
  member of clergy, defined, 402
  penitent, defined, 402
  penitential communication, defined, 402
  summary, 403-404
  waiver of, 403
Common plan or scheme, proof of, 31-32
Completeness doctrine, 342-343
Conditional relevance, doctrine of, 5-7
Confidential communications
  marital. *See* Marital communications privilege
  privileges, 348, 354-356, 383
Confrontation Clause, 119, 120-125,
  128-129
  forfeiture and, 153
Confrontation rights, 120. *See also*
  Confrontation Clause
Consent, proof of, 33
Content privileges, 383, 407-411

Credibility of witnesses. *See* Witnesses
Cross-examination, 244, 253
  of expert witnesses, 277-280
Custom evidence, 38. *See also* Character
  evidence; Habit evidence

Dental records
  of in-house committee's studies, 86-87
Direct examination, 244
Domestic violence
  other domestic violence by
    criminal defendant, 51-53
  privilege, victim-counselor, 407

Emergency personnel, statements to
  testimonial nature of, determination of,
    126-127. *See also* Hearsay evidence
Erroneous admission of evidence, 8
Expert opinions, 270-290
  basis for, 272-274
  cross-examination of expert, 278-279
  general acceptance test, 281-285
  improper matter as basis for, 273
  Kelly test, 281-286
  misleading aura of infallibility, 282-283
  reasonable reliance test, 272-274,
    284-285
  scientific techniques and procedures. *See*
    Scientific techniques and procedures
  on specific issues, 289-290
  on ultimate factual issue, but not legal,
    286-288
  on value of property, 289
Expert witnesses. *See also* Witnesses
  bias of, 279
  court-appointed, 288-289
  in criminal actions, 290
  cross-examination of, 277-280
  hypothetical questions to make facts
    known to expert, 274
  inadmissible information as basis
    for opinion, 274-275
  interest in outcome of litigation, 279
  intimate partner battering,
    testimony regarding, 290
  opinions of. *See* Expert opinions
  qualification as, 276-277

Former testimony, admissibility of, 143-149
  definition of former testimony, 143
  exceptions, 144-149

non-parties to former proceeding, testimony
offered against, 146-148
party to former proceeding, testimony
offered against, 144-146

General acceptance test, 281-285
Guilty pleas
offers to plead guilty, inadmissibility of,
81-83
later withdrawn, inadmissibility of, 82-83

Habit evidence, 38-39
custom of business, 38
Hearsay evidence
admissibility of. *See also* Hearsay exceptions
options for admitting statements that may
constitute hearsay, 105-107
assertive conduct, 101
defined, 99
exceptions. *See* Hearsay exceptions
exclusion of hearsay, rationale for, 96-98
multiple levels of hearsay, 211-212
non-assertive conduct, 101
non-truth purposes for use of, 107-112
consciousness, 107
effect on listener, 108
further action required, 108-109
impeaching a witness, 111
indirect state of mind or emotion,
110-111
limitations on, 111-112
notice, 107-108
relevant knowledge, 110
subsequent conduct, 108
verbal acts under substantive law,
109-110
nonverbal conduct, 101
silence, 102
statement, defined and analyzed, 99-105
verbal statements, 100
Hearsay exceptions, 134-153, 163-231
absence of entry in record, 224-225
public records, 228
admission of party. *See* Admissions
boundary or custom affecting land,
statements about, 213
business records, 221-224
character of person in community with
whom declarant habitually associates,
statements about, 213
child abuse, statements about, 152

community history, statements concerning,
213
contemporaneous statements, 205-207
criminal cases, public employee records in,
227
deceased declarant, prior statements of, 151
declarations against interest,
134-138
for documents, 220-231
dying declarations, 138-140
elder abuse, statements about, 153
estates, declarations relating to, 142-143
family history, statements concerning,
212-213
firmly rooted exceptions, 122-123
for former testimony. *See* Former testimony
identification, statements of, 192-193
multiple levels of hearsay, 211-212
past recollection recorded, 189-191
physical harm, infliction of,
statements about, 152
previously existing state of mind, 140-141
prior consistent statements, 185-188
prior inconsistent statements, 183-185
prior statements of witnesses, 183-200
procurement or wrongdoing by proponent,
effect of, 149-150
property boundaries, statements about, 213
public employee, records by, 225-227
criminal cases, 227-228
public interest in property, statements
about, 213
refreshing recollection, 188-189
reputation, statements about, 213
spontaneous statements, 202-205
state of mind declarations, 208-211
state of mind, previously existing, 140-141
testimonial statements. *See* Testimonial
statements
then existing mental or physical state,
208-210
threats, statements of, 152
unavailability of declarant. *See* Unavailability
as witness
wills, declarations relating to, 142-143
Homicide, declarant as victim of
hearsay exception, 151-152
Hospital records
of in-house committee's studies, 86-87
Human trafficking
privilege, caseworker-victim, 407

Index

Hypnosis
  witness testimony after hypnosis, 260

Identification, statement of
  hearsay exception, 192-193
Identity, proof of, 30
Inconsistent statements
  hearsay exception, 183
Indicia of reliability, 122
Inferences, 308-309
Informer
  defined, 408
  identity of, 407-408
  privilege and, 407-408
Intent
  of actor, determination of, 101-102
  proof of, 31
Irrelevant evidence, 7-8. See also Relevant
      evidence

Judges
  as witnesses, 238-239
Judicial notice, 301, 319-324
  appropriateness of, determination regarding,
      320-321
  denial of, 321
  mandatory, 319
  permissive, 320
  universally known facts, 319
Jurors
  as witnesses, 239-240

Kidnapping of declarant
  hearsay exception, 151-152

Law enforcement reports, statements in
  testimonial nature of, determination of,
      127-128
Lay opinions, 268-270
  helpfulness to trier of fact, 270
  rationally based on witness's perception,
      269-270
Leading questions, use of, 245-246
Liability insurance, evidence of
  inadmissibility of, 83-84
Limited admissibility, doctrine of, 10, 11
Limiting instruction, 10

Marital communications privilege, 395-400
  generally, 389
  conduct that is communicative, 396

nodding, 396
  shaking head, 396
  confidence, communication
      made in, 396-397
  divorce or no longer living together,
      effect of, 396
  during marital relationship, 396
  exceptions, 398
    certain criminal proceedings, 398
    commitment proceedings, 398
    competence, proceedings to
        establish, 398
    crime or fraud exception, 398
    criminal defendant spouse, 398
    juvenile court proceedings, 398
    proceedings between spouses, 398
  holder of, 397
  preventing another from disclosing, 396
  refusing to disclose, 396
  between spouses while husband and
      wife, 397
  summary, 398-399
  third parties, presence of, 397
  timing issue, 397
  valid marriage at time of communication,
      395
  waiver of, 397
  whether or not party, 395-400
  writings, 396, 397
Mediation
  defined, 85-86
  disclosures during, protection for, 85-86
Mercy rule, 45
Motive, proof of, 31

Newspaper immunity privilege, 410-411
  contempt, qualifying for immunity from, 410
  criminal cases, 410-411
  due process rights of defendants, 410-411
Non-assertive conduct, 101
Nonverbal conduct, 101

Objections to improper evidence
  irrelevant evidence, 9
  overruled, 10
  response to, 9
  sustained, 10
Offer of proof, 9
Offers to compromise, 78-81
  humanitarian offers to compromise, 79-80
Offers to discount a claim, 79

Index

Offers to plead guilty, 81-83
Official information
  in criminal cases, 408-409
  defined, 408
  privilege for, 407-409
Opinion evidence
  on character, 34
  expert opinions. *See* Expert opinions
  lay opinions. *See* Lay opinions
Opportunity, proof of, 32
Order of proof, discretion in, 175-176

Particularized guarantees of trustworthiness, 123
Past recollection recorded
  hearsay exception, 189-191
Physician-patient privilege, 368-372, 377
  exceptions to, 369-370
  holder of, 369
  patient, defined, 368
  physician, defined, 368
  psychotherapist-patient privilege compared, 377-378
  types of communications protected, 368
Police officers, statements to
  testimonial nature of, determination of, 126-127. *See also* Hearsay evidence
Political vote privilege, 409
  waiver of, 409
Prejudicial effect of evidence
  factors for evaluation of, 17-18
  probative value vs., 14-22
  undue prejudice, 11, 17-18
Preparation, proof of, 30-31
Preponderance of the evidence, 303. *See also* Burden of proof
Presumptions, 301, 308-319
  for authentication, 329
  classification of, 310
  conclusive, 301, 309-310
  criminal cases, 313-314
  effect of presumption that establishes an element, 314
  Morgan, 313-314
  rebuttable, 301, 310-313
  Thayer, 310-312
    rebutting a Thayer presumption, 312
Privileges, 347-414
  analysis of, 348-350
  attorney-client. *See* Attorney-client privilege

clergy-penitent privileges. *See* Clergy-penitent privileges
confidential communications privileges. *See* Confidential communications privileges
content. *See* Content privileges
domestic violence victim-counselor privilege, 407
exceptions to, 349-350
human trafficking caseworker-victim privilege, 407
informer, identity of, 407-408
newspaper immunity. *See* Newspaper immunity privilege
official information, 407-409
physician-patient privilege. *See* Physician-patient privilege
political vote, refusal to disclose, 409
psychotherapist-patient privilege. *See* Psychotherapist-patient privilege
of public entity, 407-409
rules on claims of, 350-352
self-incrimination privileges, 384-389
sexual assault victim-counselor privilege, 406-407
spousal testimonial privileges. *See* Spousal testimonial privileges
testimonial. *See* Testimonial privileges
trade secrets, 409-410
waiver of, 349
Probative value of evidence
  prejudicial effect vs., 14-22
Products liability actions
  animal experimentation, evidence of, 87
Proof
  burden of. *See* Burden of proof
  discretion in order of, 175-176
Psychotherapist-patient privilege, 372-376, 377-378
  claiming the privilege, 373-374
  confidential communications, 373
  court-appointed therapist, 374-375
  danger, reasonable belief in, 375-376
  exceptions to, 374-376
  minor crime victim exception, 375-376
  parties to communications, 372-373
  physician-patient privilege compared, 377-378
  physician-patient privilege exceptions, similarities to, 374

Public entity
   privileges for, 407-409

Quality assurance committees
   records of medical and psychiatric
      studies, 87
Quality of care
   proceeding of organized committees on, 87
   records of organized committees on, 87

Rape shield laws, 61
Reasonable reliance test, 272-274, 284-285.
   See also Scientific techniques and
     procedures
Re-cross-examination, 244
Redirect examination, 244
Refreshing recollection
   hearsay exception, 188-189
Relevant evidence
   admissibility of, 11
   balancing test for exclusion of, 14-22
   character evidence exclusion rules. *See*
     Character evidence
   conditional relevance, 5-7
   credibility of witness, 5
   determination of relevance, 3-5
   policy exclusions, 75-94
   prejudicial effect, 14-15, 17-18
   probative value of, 15-17
   reasons to exclude, 10-11, 14
Religious beliefs
   of witnesses, 259
Remedial measures
   inadmissibility of subsequent
     remedial conduct, 76-78
Reputation evidence, 34-35
Right to Truth in Evidence provision
   in Proposition 8, 64, 255-256

Scientific techniques and procedures
   expert opinions on, 281-286. *See also* Expert
     opinions
   general acceptance test, 281-285
   Kelly test, 281-286
   misleading aura of infallibility, 282-283
   reasonable reliance test, 284-285
Secondary evidence
   criminal cases, 336
   duplicate, 335
   oral testimony as form of, 337-340
   presumptions for proving content, 340-341

types of, 335
   unfairness, evaluation of, 336-337
Secondary Evidence Rule, 325, 334-342
   when rule does not apply, 340
Self-incrimination privileges, 384-389
   scope of, 385-386
   waiver of, 386
Sexual assault victim-counselor privilege,
     406-407
   exceptions, 407
Sexual offenses
   other sexual offenses by criminal defendant,
     48-51
Silence
   as adoptive admission, 169-170
   as hearsay, 102
Spousal testimonial privileges, 389-395
   declining to testify against spouse, 389-390
   exceptions, 393-394
   not to be called as witness against spouse,
     390-391
   waiver of, 391-393
   when spouse is a party, 390-391
Spouses, privileges for. *See* Marital
     communications privilege; Spousal
     testimonial privileges
Subsequent remedial conduct
   inadmissibility of, 76-78
Sympathy, expressions of
   inadmissibility of, 84-85

Testimonial privileges
   generally, 383
   spousal, 389-395
Testimonial statements, 123-129
   defined, 124, 125
   emergency personnel, statements to,
     126-127
   law enforcement reports, statements in,
     127-128
   police officers, statements to, 126-127
   unavailability of declarant, 128-129
Trade secrets privilege, 409-410
Translators, use of, 237

Ultimate issue rule, 286-288
Unavailability as witness, 128-134
   absence despite reasonable efforts to get
     witness into court, 132-133
   absence when court is unable to
     compel attendance, 132

Index

constructive unavailability, 130
death, 131
disqualification, 131
fake unavailability, 130
hearsay exceptions that apply only when
    declarant is unavailable, 134-149
    homicide victim declarant, 151-152
    kidnapping victim declarant, 151-152
mental illness, 131
physical illness, 131
physical unavailability, 130
privilege, 131
procurement or wrongdoing by proponent,
    149-150
Undue prejudice, 11, 17-18. *See also* Prejudicial
    effect of evidence

Verbal statements, 100
Verdict, validity of
    evidence to test validity, 86, 239
Victim
    character, evidence of, 57-65
    domestic violence victim-
        counselor privilege, 407
    human trafficking caseworker-
        victim privilege, 407
    sexual assault victim-counselor privilege,
        406-407
    sexual history of, 61-62, 259-260
Victims' Bill of Rights, 64

Witness testimony
    attitude of witness, 251
    capacity to perceive, recollect,
        or communicate, 247-248
    character of, 247
    demeanor of witness, 247
    foundations, 233-265
    hypnotized, 260
    non-existence of facts to which
        witness testified, 251
    opinion testimony, 267-299. *See also* Lay
        opinions; Expert opinions
    prior consistent statements, 250
    prior inconsistent statements, 250-251

untruthfulness, admission of, 251
Witnesses
    attitude of, 251
    bias of, 249-250
    capacity to perceive, recollect,
        or communicate, 247-248
    character evidence about
        in civil cases, 251-255
        in criminal cases, 255-256
    competency of, 234-238
    credibility of, 5
        impeaching and supporting, 246-259
        limitations on credibility attacks,
            259-261
    cross-examination of character witness, 253
    demeanor of, 247
    dishonesty, establishing bad character for,
        252, 256
    disqualification of, 234
    examination of, 244-246
    experts. *See* Expert opinions; Expert witnesses
    good character of, 252
    honesty, character for, 248-249, 253-254,
        256
    hypnotized testimony, 260
    judges as, 238-239
    jurors as, 239-240
    leading questions in examination of,
        245-246
    motive of, 249-250
    non-existence of facts, 251
    opportunity to perceive, 248
    personal knowledge of, 236-237
    prior consistent statements, 250
    prior felony convictions, 254-255
    prior inconsistent statements, 250-251
    religious beliefs of, 259
    sexual history of victim/witness, 259-260
    sincerity of, 235
    specific instances of conduct, 254
    testimony of. *See* Witness testimony
    translators, 237
    truth-telling abilities, 235-236
    unavailability of. *See* Unavailability as witness
    veracity of, 235, 248-249